## DATE DUE

| | |
|---|---|
| 10-19-08 | |
| 10-6-14 | |
| | |
| | |
| | |
| | |
| | |
| | |
| | |
| | |
| | |
| | |
| | |
| | |
| | |
| | |
| | |
| | |

GAYLORD

PRINTED IN U.S.A

D1254123

# MODERNITY DISAVOWED

A John Hope Franklin Center Book

*Sibylle Fischer*

# Modernity Disavowed

HAITI AND THE CULTURES OF SLAVERY

IN THE AGE OF REVOLUTION

*Duke University Press   Durham & London*

2004

BARRY UNIVERSITY
MIAMI, FL 33161

© 2004 Duke University Press

All rights reserved

Printed in the United States of America

on acid-free paper

Designed by C. H. Westmoreland

Typeset in Scala with Franklin Gothic display

by Keystone Typesetting, Inc.

Library of Congress Cataloging-in-Publication

Fischer, Sibylle.

Modernity disavowed : Haiti and the cultures of slavery in

the age of revolution / by Sibylle Fischer.

p. cm.

Includes index.

ISBN 0-8223-3252-3 (cloth : alk. paper)

ISBN 0-8223-3290-6 (pbk. : alk. paper)

1. Haiti—History—Revolution, 1791–1804—Literature
and the revolution. 2. Slave insurrections. 3. Blacks—
Cuba—History. 4. Blacks—Dominican Republic—
History. 5. Literature and history. 6. Slavery in literature.

I. Title.

F1923.F57 2004

972.94′03—dc22        2003017792

F
1923
.F57
2004

FOR LIAM

# Contents

# Preface

It was no doubt one of the most extraordinary events of the Age of Revolution: the overthrow of the slaveholding regime in the French colony of Saint Domingue, the "pearl of the Antilles," by insurgent slaves and their free allies and the establishment of an independent black state in 1804. One might have expected that the Haitian Revolution would figure prominently in accounts of the revolutionary period, on a par with the revolution in France and the events that led to the foundation of the United States of America. That is not so. To this day, most accounts of the period that shaped Western modernity and placed notions of liberty and equality at the center of political thought fail to mention the only revolution that centered around the issue of racial equality.

Why did this happen? And what does it mean for the ways in which we conventionally think about Western modernity? Sometimes it takes longer to arrive at a question than to produce an answer. This project started as a study of nineteenth-century Caribbean literatures and the beginnings of national cultures. Eventually I came to feel that at the core of many literary texts and literary and cultural histories there was a certain mystery: a suspended contradiction, an unexpected flight into fantasy where one might have expected a reckoning with reality, an aesthetic judgment too harsh to be taken at face value, or a failure to deal with what we know to have been the main issues of concern. I came to think that there were more, and more complex, connections between these odd moments and the "horrors of Saint Domingue" than the cursory references to the fears of the Creole population in most literary histories suggested. To be sure, the fear of a repetition of the events in Haiti led to denials of their transcendence and the suppression of any information relating to them. But silence and fear are not beyond interrogation. Was this fear directed at the same prospects in all slaveholding areas? Moreover, is it not the case that our fears often have a greater hold over us than our positive beliefs and commitments? There is by now a large body of work on historical trauma and memory, and while I tend to be skeptical about prevailing assertions about the operations of trauma and a theoretically unreflective embrace of memory, I do believe that this work shows that the impact and significance of an event that is experienced as antagonistic or even traumatic cannot be measured by merely looking at explicit statements. Another question that can be raised as regards the actual prevalence of silence: Were there not some people for whom Haiti might have signified a promise rather than a threat? Might there not be nonelite or hybrid forms of cultural production that escaped the attempts to deny or belittle what happened in Saint Domingue?

As I tried to tackle these issues, it became clear that they could not be addressed purely from within the disciplinary traditions of literary criticism and literary history. Silences only show up against some sort of discursive background. Moreover, the Haitian Revolution was not an event in what Angel Rama called the Lettered City, and its impact cannot be grasped merely through the concepts developed by Rama and others in their work on the rise of literature in Spanish America. The vast majority of slaves were illiterate, the common language—Creole—was nonscriptural, and even the first heads of state in Haiti could do little more than sign their names. Knowledge about the events in Haiti circulated among people of color throughout the Atlantic world in the form of rumors, songs, and the like. We cannot hope to take measure of the silence, track the displacements it may have produced, or give some content to what is being silenced without relying on the rich and fascinating work done by historians of slavery, slave resistance, and the Haitian Revolution. It is against the results of painstaking archival historical work that the silences of elite discourses begin to show their significance. My debt to historical scholarship goes much beyond the many titles I discuss or cite in notes.

But standards of proof and treatment of evidence are not the same in the literary fields and the social sciences: a significant part of my evidence is of a literary and cultural sort and requires a different kind of interpretative work. In fact, without a critical methodology that is attuned to precise wording, to resonances, fantasies and imagery—the kind of methodology literary scholarship customarily employs—we would not be able to bridge the gap between the officially ordained silence and the archives that tell a very different story. Sometimes a close reading is enough to track political and ideological conflicts. Sometimes psychoanalytic argument is more helpful, as it allows us to read the products of fantasy not merely as a protective shield against the onslaught of reality but as a witness to precisely the reality that needs to be kept at bay. In either case, however, it is only through sustained hermeneutical efforts that we can reach beyond literal meaning and perhaps grasp that which is meant but not, strictly speaking, said. That we cannot make assertions with complete certainty should not, I submit, lead us to reproduce the silence that dominated all issues regarding the Haitian Revolution and its significance for Western modernity.

But the question of what, precisely, was silenced also has philosophical ramifications that led me to explore the relation—or apparent nonrelation—between the events in the Caribbean and metropolitan discourses of modernity and revolution on a more theoretical level. The question is this: if it were just the events that were ignored by metropolitan thinkers of modernity, we might consider it simply another manifestation of age-old Eurocentrism and racial prejudice—a regrettable but not surprising finding. But what if the metropolitan reaction to the events in Haiti was more specifically related to the tenets of the slave revolution and the establishment of a postslavery state? After all, it is in the Age of Revolution that many of the political concepts of Western modernity took shape or were submitted to new scrutiny. And it is not the case that the events in Haiti were strictly speaking unknown. It might turn out that it is not enough to simply insist that Haiti be included in our accounts of the Age of Revolution and that the gaps in the historical and cultural records be filled. What would be needed is a revision of the concept of modernity itself so that past struggles over what it means to be modern, who can claim it, and on what grounds can become visible again. The suppression and disavowal of revolutionary antislavery and attendant cultures in the Caribbean was, among other things, a struggle over what would count as "progress," what was meant by "liberty," and how the two should relate.

I am greatly indebted to the many friends, teachers, and colleagues who have provided encouragement, advice, and support over the years. I came to this country to study with Jean Franco. Her sharp critical insights and commitment to scholarship that does not abdicate its political responsibility have been an inspiration for me.

I owe a debt of a very different sort to Patricia Benoit. A filmmaker of Haitian descent, she made me think about the Haitian Revolution in ways that I would not have had we not begun to work on an independent documentary film on the topic. Thanks to her generosity and that of her friends in Haiti, I was able to spend some time in Haiti and to come to see the passions, hopes, and desires tied to the events of the revolution to this day. If I have been at all successful in ridding myself of narrow scholarly conventionalism and writing a book that is alive—alive to the continuing significance of the events, but also alive as a narrative—it is in large part due to the many long and often heated conversations I have had with Patricia Benoit.

A debt of a third sort is owed to Liam Murphy. There are few ideas in this book that I did not first try out in conversation with Liam, and many of them were profoundly changed by his comments. I am very lucky to have had such an insightful and patient reader for my many drafts; my intellectual debt exceeds by far the limits of what can be acknowledged by scholarly convention.

Over the years, the friendship and intellectual companionship of colleagues at Duke have been invaluable: my debt to Leslie Damasceno, Meg Greer, Julia Hell, Michele Longino, Wahneema Lubiano, Jan Radway, and Antonio Viego for their professional support and unwavering friendship goes much beyond what can be acknowledged here. Deans Karla Holloway and Bill Chafe put trust in me when I most needed it; without their support, I may not have been able to bring this book to a timely conclusion.

Leslie Damasceno, Ambrosio Fornet, Anne Garreta, Julia Hell, and Michele Longino read substantial parts of the manuscript and offered crucial advice. Drafts at various stages were also read by Walter Mignolo, Valentin Mudimbe, Toril Moi, and Fred Jameson. I have also benefited greatly from encouragement, commentary, and criticism I received at various invited lectures, workshops, and conference panels where I presented my work in progress. Special thanks go to Martin Bernal, Susan Buck-Morss, Eleni Coundoriotis, Fernando Coronil, Frigga Haug, Wolfgang Fritz Haug, Margaret Higonnet, Sylvia Molloy, Alicia Rios, and Fernando Unzueta. I am especially indebted to the two readers of the manuscript for Duke University Press, Alicia Rios and Lewis Gordon, whose suggestions and enthusiasm helped enormously in the final stages, and to Reynolds Smith, my editor at the Press.

Research in Cuba and the Dominican Republic would have been impossible without the generous help from a number of researchers and librarians: Araceli García Carranza (Biblioteca Nacional José Martí in Havana), Yolanda Vidal (Instituto de Literatura y Lingüística in Havana), and Ilonka Nacidit-Perdomo (Biblioteca Nacional in Santo Domingo, D.R.); special thanks go to Nancy Machado Lorenzo (Biblioteca Nacional José Martí), who provided friendship and assistance with all kinds of bibliographical and logistical problems in

Havana. Thanks also to Roger Arrazcaeta Delgado, Antonio Quevedo Herrero, and, especially, Ivalú Rodríguez Gil in the Gabinete de Arqueología de la Oficina del Historiador.

The research was generously supported by grants from the Duke-UNC Council for Latin American and Caribbean Studies, and faculty travel grants from Duke University. An earlier version of chapter 3 appeared in the *Journal of Latin American Cultural Studies* 7 (1998): 131–49; an earlier Spanish version of chapter 4 in *Homenaje a Roberto Fernández Retamar,* ed. Elzbieta Sklodowska and Ben A. Heller (Pittsburgh: Instituto Internacional de Literatura Iberoamericana, 2000), 299–325.

# MODERNITY DISAVOWED

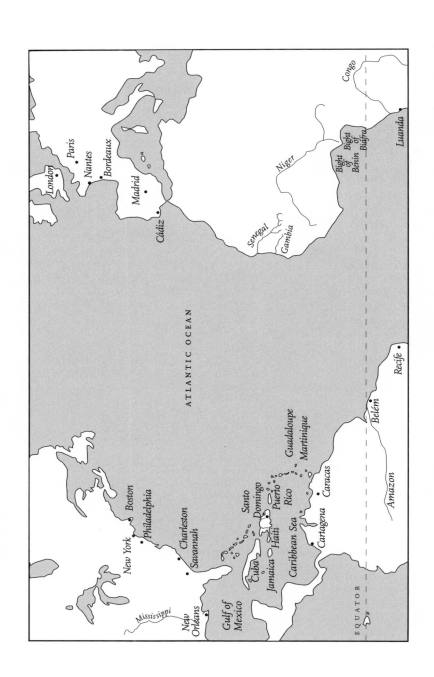

# Introduction

## TRUNCATIONS OF MODERNITY

### "The Fate of Striking Events"

This book is about a cultural and political landscape in the Age of Revolution.[1] Colonialism in the Caribbean had produced societies where brutality combined with licentiousness in ways unknown in Europe. The sugar plantations in the New World were expanding rapidly and had an apparently limitless hunger for slaves.[2] Yet it was also a time when throughout the Western Hemisphere, radical change seemed imminent. To many observers, preventing revolutions appeared a greater challenge than bringing them about.[3]

In 1804, after more than a decade of protracted battles between insurgent slaves, their free allies, and colonial armies, Jean-Jacques Dessalines had declared Saint Domingue independent from France. Under the name of Haiti, the first black state in the Americas had realized a complete reversal of imperial hierarchies and social goals: the territory's European name had been obliterated; slaves had become masters; and the process of capitalist development through the industrialization of agriculture had been severely disrupted.[4] It had become clear to slave owners and government officials in the Caribbean that unless they established tight demographic and social controls, slave insurgency might well come to threaten their states, too.[5]

In response to the colonial slaveholders' structuring of the hemisphere through slave routes and slave markets, a radically heterogeneous, transnational cultural network emerged whose political imaginary mirrored the global scope of the slave trade and whose projects and fantasies of emancipation converged, at least for a few years, around Haiti.[6] This interstitial culture cannot be grasped by the teleological narratives that conventionally dominate postindependence national literary and cultural histories. The traces and remnants of radical politics and their attendant cultural practices are scattered across languages, histories, and continents. Most of the cultural and ideological production that pertained to this hybrid formation—reports of traveling revolutionaries and radical abolitionists, trial records about the practices of insurgency among slaves and free colored populations, remnants of popular forms of cultural production, letters exchanged between colonial reformers and radicals, manuscripts that circulated between colonial territories and metropoles—did not become part of the canons of high culture and respectable political theory.[7]

This is a landscape of heterogeneous facts, practices, and ideas that to this day remain separated by disciplinary boundaries and competition between different historiographies and can often be inferred only when we interrogate the coincidental fragments that survived the process of congealment into national histories. The cultural face of the incipient struggles for local autonomy and, eventually, independence is literature. The cultural face of the transnational, hybrid culture of antislavery is much more elusive.

/Haiti and the Haitian Revolution were central to this landscape, although often only as the unspeakable, as trauma, utopia, and elusive dream. Imaginary scenarios became the real battleground. Although antislavery had achieved some of its goals by midcentury, the actual area of land cultivated by slaves had gone through a significant expansion.[8] The most important slave economies—Brazil, the United States, and Cuba—appeared to have emerged strengthened from the period of contention. Haiti had vanished from the front pages of European and North American newspapers, and even black abolitionists in the United States had ceased to hold up Haiti as the example for black liberation and achievement.[9]

But while radical antislavery was a formation that did not consolidate itself territorially beyond the confines of Haiti, it certainly did leave a deep imprint in the psyche of most of those involved in the slave trade and the plantation economy. Fantasy, paranoia, identificatory desires, and disavowal were always part of this formation.[10] There are layers of signification in the cultural records that cannot be grasped as long as we pay attention only to events and causality in the strict sense.[11] Much of this book is thus devoted to drawing a landscape around the silences and gaps that punctuate the historical and cultural records. It works from significant examples and symptomatic fragments, keeping track of what is said, and especially what is not said. It is an attempt to think about literature, culture, and politics transnationally, as forms of expression that mirrored the hemispheric scope of the slave trade; to think what might have been lost when culture and emancipatory politics were finally forced into the mold of the nation-state; and to think what might have happened if the struggle against racial subordination had carried the same prestige and received the same attention from posterity as did the struggle against colonialism and other forms of political subordination.

Of all the islands and territories of the Caribbean Sea, Cuba and Santo Domingo (later the Dominican Republic) were the ones most directly affected by the events in the former French colony. While in Santo Domingo the neighboring revolutionary black state imposed itself as an undeniable political and economic reality and produced immediate, often virulent reactions, in Cuba—the island that eventually replaced Saint Domingue as the main sugar producer in the Caribbean—Haiti was both at an infinite distance and dangerously close.

On December 15, 1802, the Matanzas newspaper *La Aurora* carried the usual assortment of news from Europe: extracts from metropolitan newspapers, transcripts of French parliamentary debates, and miscellaneous reports on European warfare and diplomacy— the stuff of official history. In the midst of this, set apart without further explanation or commentary, there is a single-sentence paragraph: "Santos Louverture (*Toussaint*) has been taken and incarcerated in the Fortress of Joux."[12] Obviously the readers of *La Aurora* were expected to be familiar with Toussaint Louverture. But if they had been relying on the contemporary Cuban press, the name would have meant nothing to them. Between 1791 and 1805, the foremost Habanese newspaper, the *Papel Periódico,* makes no mention of the revolutionary events in Saint Domingue: neither the abolition of slavery, nor the defeat of Napoleon at the hands of former slaves, nor the establishment of an independent black state in 1804. Although less than a decade later Cuba's loyalty to the Spanish Crown did not prevent detailed reports on the independence wars on the mainland, the events on the neighboring island, a mere 150 miles across the sea from the eastern town of Santiago de Cuba, were passed over in silence.

Yet this does not mean that the events were not known. As early as 1791, the Cuban governor had received letters that left no doubt about what was happening. The assembly in Saint Domingue had sent out desperate calls for help to their Cuban neighbors, complete with vivid descriptions of the atrocities: 'A hundred thousand Negroes have risen up in the Northern part: more than two hundred sugar plantations have been burned: the owners have been torn to pieces, and if some miserable woman finds herself separated from the flock, her captivity is worse than death."[13] Other letter writers concur: "Humanity has been entirely forgotten and barbarism rules, because the whites conceded to the free people of color whatever privileges they demanded, as said whites had no power to suppress the arrogance of these people. . . . they took up the tremendous work of burning all existing dwellings, killing any whites they could find . . . and thus there are no words for the atrocities that are being committed."[14]

/ In the letters and reports of white settlers, the revolution is not a political and diplomatic issue; it is a matter of body counts, rape, material destruction, and infinite bloodshed. It is barbarism and unspeakable violence, outside the realm of civilization and beyond human language. It is an excessive event, and as such, it remained for the most part confined to the margins of history: to rumors, oral histories, confidential letters, and secret trials. )

There was a consensus in the region among settlers of European descent that Haiti was not a commendable model of emancipation. In response to the revolution, a cordon sanitaire was drawn around the island to interrupt the flow of information and people.[15] The colonial authorities in Cuba prohibited the introduction of "French" slaves and even the mere mentioning of the events in Haiti. A letter from the Haitian president Jean-Pierre Boyer to John Quincy Adams, requesting the establishment of diplomatic relations, bears a handwritten note: "Not to be answered."[16] The only newly independent state in the Americas to have unequivocally abolished racial slavery (and until the 1830s, the only postslavery state in the New World),[17] Haiti was also the only one that was not invited to the Pan-American Conference in 1826. Indeed, in his draft of a position paper for the conference, Simón Bolívar, envisioning an America transitioning in an orderly fashion into a region of independent nation-states, concludes: "America would have nothing more to fear from that tremendous monster who has devoured the island of Santo Domingo, nor would she have cause to fear the numerical preponderance of the aborigines."[18]

But the silence imposed did not prevent news from traveling. In the harbors and port cities of the Caribbean, sailors, merchants, and slaves passed on the story of the successful slave uprising. The revolution set off waves of migrations that carried the story of the bloody slave rebellion from island to island. French settlers from Saint Domingue moved to Cuba's Oriente province first, then on to other islands or to Louisiana.[19] In permanent fear of Haitian incursions, Creoles from Spanish Santo Domingo continued to leave the island throughout the first few decades of the nineteenth century and settled anywhere from Venezuela to Cuba.

From 1791 onward, Cuban authorities time and again issued ordinances regarding the discussion of the events of Saint Domingue, French subjects, and Saint Domingue slaves. Diplomatic correspondence between the colonial administrators in the region and the Spanish authorities in the years between 1791 and the 1820s is replete with calls for vigilance and admonitions to maintain controls "in order to prevent the entrance . . . of any reports about what is happening in the French Islands and Empire." "Any reports that might have spread in writing, or that in general make known the disorders," are to be suppressed, and French and other foreigners are strictly forbidden from entering the territory.[20]

But it seems that these prohibitions were not enforced, or perhaps not enforceable. In early 1796, a rebellious slave was brought in front of the governor of Puerto Príncipe in Cuba. Showing clear signs of being a "French" slave, he declared "haughtily, with various expressions typical of an ignorant person puffed up with very foolish though seditious principles and ideas, that the blacks of Cap Français all were free, because they had won [*adquirido*] their liberty." The next day, all other "French" slaves were gathered in the town square to watch as he was given one hundred lashes. A sign around his neck said: "This is the fruit of the imaginary liberty of the French slaves: true freedom is found in virtue."[21]

The continued entrance of people of color was of particular concern. On August 29, 1800, the Cuban Captain General Someruelos felt it necessary to reiterate the provisions of a royal ordinance of barely a month before: "The matter requires, because of its seriousness, the utmost attention in the current circumstances; and especially since the emigration of people of color is growing excessively; I charge you with ensuring that under no circumstances more individuals of that kind are being admitted."[22]

It is possible that were we to measure the historical significance of Haiti by its causal impact on surrounding areas and its direct effect on slave insurgency in other places, it would turn out to have been minor. But as phantasma and nightmare, its ubiquity can hardly be doubted. Rumors spread throughout the Caribbean that Toussaint Louverture was planning to export the revolution. Claiming that he was directly responsible for the recent slave uprising in Jamaica, a letter to the Cuban governor said: "Appetite comes with eating, my Friend, and Toussaint, who before did not desire more than the Ysland of Santo Domingo for his rule, is now planning to successively incorporate the neighboring Ysland of Jamaica . . . then Cuba, then Puerto-Rico, and finally the whole Globe."[23] In a deeply ironic twist, it is only in a planter's paranoid fantasy that Toussaint Louverture, whose letter "from the first of the Blacks to the first of the Whites" had remained unacknowledged, becomes Napoleon's equal—both set to conquer the world.

The English captain Marcus Rainsford, who was an eyewitness to the struggles in Saint Domingue and documented his experiences in a book about Haitian independence published in England in 1805 *(A Historical Account of the Black Empire of Haiti)*, starts out with a moving reflection that deserves to be quoted at some length:

> It has frequently been the fate of striking events, and particularly those which have altered the condition of mankind, to be denied that consideration by their cotemporaries, which they obtain from the veneration of posterity. In their vortex, attention is distracted by the effects; and distant society recedes from the contemplation of objects that threaten a violation of their system, or wound a favourite prejudice. It is thus that history, with all the advantages of calm discussion, is imperfect; and philosophy enquires in vain for the unrecorded causes of astonishing transactions. . . .
>
> The rise of the Haytian empire is an event which may powerfully affect the condition of the human race; yet it is seen as an ordinary succession of triumphs and defeats, interrupted only by the horrors of new and terrible inflictions, the fury of contending elements, and destructive disease, more tremendous than all.
>
> It will scarcely be credited in another age, that philosophers heard unmoved, of the ascertainment of a brilliant fact, hitherto unknown, or confined to the vague knowledge of those whose knowledge is not admitted within the pale of historical truth. It will not be believed that enlightened Europe calmly witnessed its contrasted brilliancy with actions which, like the opaque view of night, for a sullen hour obscured the dazzling splendour.
>
> It is of ancient record, that negroes were capable of repelling their enemies, with vigour, in their own country; and a writer of modern date has assured us of the talents and virtues of these people; but it remained for the close of the eighteenth century to realize the scene, from the state of abject degeneracy:—to exhibit, a horde of negroes emancipating themselves from the vilest slavery, and at once filling the relations of society, enacting laws, and commanding armies, in the colonies of Europe.
>
> The same period has witnessed a great and polished nation, not merely

returning to the barbarism of the earliest periods, but descending to the characters of assassins and executioners; and, removing the boundaries which civilization had prescribed even to war, rendering it a wild conflict of brutes and a midnight massacre. (x–xi)[24]

But it seems that the "other age" anticipated by Rainsford has yet to arrive. In Europe, the dates and names associated with the Age of Revolution—1789, 1848, Robespierre, Napoleon, Hegel—eventually became metonymic with the history of modernity. Although the fortunes made on the colonial plantations and through the slave trade played an important part in the rise of the bourgeoisie in many European regions, the Caribbean plantation and the political upheavals in the colonies rarely make it into the canonical histories of modernity and revolution.[25] Samuel Huntington views Haiti as belonging to the category of countries that are not part of any of the world's great civilizations: "While Haiti's elite has traditionally relished its cultural ties to France, Haiti's Creole language, Voodoo religion, revolutionary slave origins, and brutal history combine to make it a lone country. . . . Haiti, 'the neighbor nobody wants,' is truly a kinless country."[26] François Furet and Mona Ozouf's voluminous *Critical Dictionary of the French Revolution,* published with some fanfare at the occasion of the bicentennial of the French Revolution and now probably one of the most widely consulted reference works on the period, has no entry for either colonialism or slavery. Of the abolitionist club Amis des Noirs, I found one mention. The revolution in Saint Domingue is not mentioned at all.[27] Even Eric Hobsbawm, whose ideological commitments certainly do not coincide with those of Huntington, Furet, or Ozouf, mentions the issue of slavery only once or twice in passing in his seminal *Age of Revolution;* of the Haitian revolutionaries, only Toussaint Louverture makes it into the narration, and then only once.[28]

But Haiti and revolutionary antislavery cause trouble for political theory as well. A particularly interesting example is Hannah Arendt's *On Revolution* of 1963.[29] Like many others before and after her, she takes the French and American Revolutions as the paradigm and fails to mention the case of Haiti (along with any other nonmetropolitan revolution). Her main argument goes as follows: Revolutions are quintessential modern events. Revolutionary politics ought to be about "the foundation of freedom," which for Arendt largely means constitutional design or, more broadly speaking, the institutional organization of the state. The French Revolution's descent into terror is due to the fact that the Jacobins gave precedence to what she calls, somewhat condescendingly, "the social question." Quoting Robespierre's exclamation "La monarchie? La république? Je ne connais que la question sociale!" [Monarchy? Republic? I know only the social question!] (56), she claims that making freedom depend on the solution of the problem of poverty allows dangerous and destructive affects—compassion or pity—to enter the stage and wreak havoc on the establishment of political freedom.[30]

Now, Arendt does not ignore the fact that those same American revolutionaries on whom she bestows such high praise for their "foundation of freedom" wrote a constitution that allowed the continuation of slavery. There were, she says, some 400,000 slaves who lived among the 1.85 million white settlers in the mid–eighteenth century, and they lived in a state of "complete destitution and misery" far worse than anything the Old World had witnessed. American revolutionaries could have reacted to this urgent "social question," but they did not.

> From this, we can only conclude that the institution of slavery carries an obscurity even blacker than the obscurity of poverty; the slave, not the poor man, was "wholly overlooked." For if Jefferson, and others to a lesser degree, were aware of the primordial crime upon which the fabric of American society rested, if they "trembled when [they] thought that God is just" (Jefferson), they did so because they were convinced of the incompatibility of the institution of slavery with the foundation of freedom, not because they were moved by pity or by a feeling of solidarity with their fellow men. And this indifference, difficult for us to understand, was not peculiar to Americans and hence must be blamed on the institution of slavery rather than on any perversion of the heart or upon the dominance of self-interest. For European witnesses in the eighteenth century, who were moved to compassion by the spectacle of European social conditions, did not react differently. . . . Slavery was no more part of the social question for Europeans than it was for Americans, so that the social question, whether genuinely absent or only hidden in darkness, was non-existent for all practical purposes, and with it, the most powerful and perhaps the most devastating passion motivating revolutionaries, the passion of compassion. (71–72)

Trying to think about slavery and revolutionary politics together (or perhaps trying to avoid just that), Arendt begins to equivocate. First she implies that *in her eyes* slavery would have qualified as a social question. Then she says that the revolutionaries considered slavery a political question. It remains unclear whether she believes that the revolutionaries made a mistake. She does not expand on her claim that the revolutionaries were "convinced of the incompatibility of the institution of slavery with the foundation of freedom." Why does Arendt, who so much prefers the *vita activa* of political engagement to the bureaucratic demands of social policy, not raise the question of whether considering slaves politically might have produced some important insight? What prevents her from thinking about slaves as potential political agents? From thinking of the politics of antislavery as part of the revolutionary spirit she studies?

Shying away from slavery as a political issue, Arendt quickly returns to the social question and then equivocates as to whether the social question was "genuinely absent" or "only hidden in darkness," thus implying that regardless of the views of the revolutionaries, slavery could be or should be a social question, after all. And why would she want to leave it open whether the social question was truly absent or simply hidden? After all, if it was truly absent—and yet slaves should have given rise to the compassion that brings out the social question—then she offers at least one story in her own voice, according to which slaves are conceptually eliminated.

What we witness here is the moment when Arendt's central distinction between the social and the political, as the very distinction that produces the "good" American Revolution and the "bad" French Revolution, self-deconstructs. This may not be altogether surprising, given that the continuation of slavery in the United States provides plenty of room for doubt about the virtues of the American Revolution. But beyond that, slavery shows that we cannot neatly separate the social from the political, and that we cannot theorize liberty without thinking about liberation and what kind of liberty ensues from what kind of liberation.[31] Revolutionary antislavery combines what in Arendt's language would be the social and the political in ways that make it intractable for her. Considering slavery as a political issue makes her recoil—a symptom of her own inability to make modern racial slavery (and its revolutionary counterpart) fit into her conceptual frame. Slavery, being neither purely political nor purely social, cannot be spoken of. Slaves vanish, first literally, through the institution that cloaks them with invisibility, and then conceptually, in the abyss between the social and the political. Revolutionary antislavery is a contradiction in terms. Haiti becomes unthinkable.

Deeply ingrained Eurocentrism, racial hierarchies that express themselves in the weight assigned to some forms of oppression over others, and a continuation of colonialist ways of assessing "what matters" are likely root causes for some of these striking omissions. There is, moreover, a long-standing tradition in the theories of capitalism, from Adam Smith and Karl Marx to Max Weber, of linking slavery and colonialism to mercantilism and backward social practices. Slavery was superseded in due time—indeed, abolished by capitalism—and thus does not really belong to the landscape of modernity and capitalism.[32] Other explanations might be found in the ways in which disciplines were formed, and power and prestige is distributed within and across them.[33] The most highly prized areas of study—such as the history of the French Revolution in France, or the study of Hegel in German philosophy—are the least likely suddenly to give up on the claim to centrality and self-containment of the subject. Interstitial kinds of scholarship—scholarship between the disciplines, between nation-states, between different cultural and political traditions—are rarely generated from within those core areas in which national ideologies reproduce themselves.

These causes combine in various ways; they reinforce each other and provide excuses. In the end, colonialism and slavery are mere disturbances on the margins of history: an anomaly, a more or less bothersome irregularity, in the march of progress and the unfolding of individual liberties. Ignoring these oppressive practices may produce certain gaps in the historiographical record, but it will not lead to any fundamental misconceptions. The history of the West can be written without them.

Now, of course, the scholarly literature on slavery and the struggles against it is by now immense. A critical historiography has emerged, too, that has shown that we cannot understand the history of the West without accounting for slavery and colonialism. But with the increased volume of scholarly production, a striking dispersion of stories has come into being. Elite abolitionism, slave resistance, Haitian independence, postcoloniality, abolitionist literature, and religious antislavery are claimed by disciplines and subdisciplines that do not always look kindly on neighboring scholarly practices. The study of abolitionism, for example, is for the most part the domain of intellectual historians, and studies in slave resistance tend to be the domain of social historians. Postcolonial studies are dominated by literary critics, while all issues concerning Haiti tend to be the domain of a very small group of specialists, often with personal links to Haiti. Different styles of argument, professional alliances, venues for publication, and so on make it increasingly difficult to see the map of the slaveholding Atlantic in its entirety, with its complex networks of communication and exchange that included Africa, Europe, and the Americas. As the study of slave resistance has become a subdiscipline in its own right and is, as a matter of course, taken up in different national histories, new lacunae of silence emerge that prevent us from perceiving the cultures that surrounded slavery and the slave trade as part of the same hemispheric cultural and economic system. There are certain ways in which things are done, certain ways in which a story is told. Linguistic difference often translates into different narrative preferences and different scholarly traditions. There is a certain solidity and continuity to the history of nations which radical antislavery does not have.

This tendency toward fragmentation has been counteracted in recent years by a new research agenda centering on the Atlantic, with Atlanticist study groups springing up in many research universities and the first faculty positions being offered for Atlantic studies. This is still a very new phenomenon, which has not yet generated a sufficient body of scholarship for us to speculate which direction this field will take, and how the difficult interdisciplinarity between historians of various stripes, literary critics, anthropologists, and others might play out.

It is my hope that the present study helps in the effort to think of a political and cultural landscape beyond the confines of disciplinary fragmentation and the categories of national language, national history, and national literature. Of course, every part of the story I am telling takes place in a specific location—La Habana, Santo Domingo, Port-au-Prince—and is thus part of a specific national history. But the story as a whole is devoid of institutional solidity. Even at the time, radical antislavery was a shadowy, discontinuous formation with a rhizomic, decentered structure. It is ephemeral, a vanishing moment overridden by the victory of nations who even when they wanted to eliminate the institution of slavery did not want to follow the model of Haiti. In fact, Haiti itself had to renounce the transnationalism of its founding ideology in order to ensure the country's survival. The rise of the nation in the nineteenth century, even where it happened against colonial rule, produced its own archives, and along the way, its own areas of deep silence.

## The Question of Modernity

As C. L. R. James observed, slaves have always wanted to be free.[34] Resistance to slavery is as old as the institution itself, and there is nothing that would make the struggle against it a modern phenomenon as such. But James also referred to the leaders of the only slave uprising in world history that led to the abolition of slavery as "black Jacobins" and argued, like Eric Williams and many others after him, that the Caribbean plantation was an intrinsically "modern system" and that the slaves led "from the very start . . . a life that was in its essence a modern life."[35] The Caribbean was never a remote area on the margins of the known world, outside modernity and beyond the reach of modernization. Far from being a remnant of traditional precapitalist practices, slavery in the Caribbean was one of the first and most brutal appearances of modernity.[36]

From the beginning, the sugar plantation was a vast machine in which uprooted and displaced people from distant regions of the African continent were meshed together and forced to enter a process later euphemistically called transculturation.[37] To be sure, internally, the plantation often reproduced old forms of subsistence economy. Slaves typically grew their own food and built their own huts but often were not able to sell their products in the marketplace. Yet the sugar plantation was also the site of the first large-scale experiment in industrial agriculture and a laboratory for the exploitation of nature and human labor.[38] The transatlantic slave trade brought about the first mass migrations driven by capitalist development and the need for a workforce, long before there was a proletariat or even a working class in Europe. The accelerated rhythms of improved agricultural technologies, the massive labor force, and the low level of skills required for the work all produced an environment that could not have been more different from a traditional subsistence economy.

Slavery and the plantation economy thus entailed a radical rationalization of labor processes, an utter disregard for traditions, and a degree of instrumentalization of human life that had never been seen in the metropolis. Would it not be surprising if the distinctively modern form of oppression and exploitation that developed in the Caribbean left no traces in people's everyday lives, their ideas of liberation, and their practices of resistance? Would it not be surprising if the radically modern living conditions did not find some expression at the superstructural level? The eminent anthropologist of the Caribbean Sidney Mintz went so far as to suggest that Caribbean social history produced "a life-style adapted to the anonymity, depersonalization, and individualization of modern life, but did so when such phenomena were by no means yet recognized for what they were."[39]

Yet it is also clear that modernity was not an ethos or a worldview that permeated society evenly, but rather a heterogeneous assemblage of strategies, effects, and forces that were brought into being by the operations of colonial power and enslavement. This is borne out by the historiographical literature on slavery, slave uprisings, and the Haitian Revolution, where we rarely find unequivocal statements such as those by Mintz. This is in part due to the fact that, in the concept of modernity, historical issues become intertwined with philosophical problems as well as thorny issues of concept formation and concept change, and partly also to the fact that the issue of modernity is adjudicated in different ways, with some scholars basing their judgments largely on socioeconomic conditions and others on ideological and cultural features. And then there are those historians and philosophers who would simply reject designations such as "the Age of Enlightenment" and "modernity" altogether as the "outmoded simplicities of period thinking"[40]—labels more concerned with present conflicts than the specificity of the past and reductive in their privileging of a few select criteria over the rich diversity of past events.

But while the question of modernity is not typically at the forefront of scholarly debate in the rapidly growing historiographical literature on slave resistance, slave uprisings, and the Haitian Revolution, there can be no doubt that on the level of motivations for scholarly projects, it continues to play an important role, and that the most controversial issues in the scholarly literature touch on precisely those features that are usually identified as indicators (or counterindicators) of modernity.

Perhaps most prominent among these issues is how to gauge the relations between the French Revolution, the Haitian events, and slave uprisings in other parts of the Atlantic. Was the Haitian Revolution an extension of the French Revolution, or was it an event in its own right, as Aimé Césaire argued?[41] How important were local developments and circumstances? What was the impact of maroon bands or vodun sects on the formation of ideologies of liberation? Were there significant African elements to the struggle? To what extent can one consider the uprisings from the late eighteenth century onward as part of the same historical or ideological formation as the French Revolution or the Spanish American wars of independence? How much did the Haitian Revolution influence slave resistance in the other slaveholding areas in the Americas?

One of the most provocative and controversial proposals comes from Eugene Genovese, who tries to construct a plot that would allow us to consider slave resistance as part of the same history of emancipation as, say, the French or the American Revolutions. He argues that there is an observable pattern in the evolution of slave resistance. It begins with "restorationist" movements in the sixteenth and seventeenth centuries that aimed merely at escaping from slavery and restoring a social structure that was roughly reminiscent of African forms of social organization (e.g., maroons). In the eighteenth century and the early nineteenth, slave resistance was drawn into the maelstrom of bourgeois-democratic revolutions and acquired a much broader, universalist political dimension. Within this story, the Haitian Revolution becomes the turning point and the moment when slave resistance becomes part of modern history. "When they [the slave uprisings] did become revolutionary and raise the banner of abolition, they did so within the context of the bourgeois-democratic revolutionary wave, with bourgeois-democratic slogans and demands and with a commitment to bourgeois property relations." The great achievement of Toussaint Louverture lies in his having claimed liberty and equality for the slaves, thereby aiming not at "secession from the dominant society but at joining it on equal terms."[42]

The great merit of Genovese's account is that it insists on linking slave resistance to world history. Slavery and the movement against it are not confined to the remote periphery of the modern world, nor is this the exclusive domain of philanthropy and religious fellow feelings.[43] Yet Genovese's account produces its own blind spots. Historians have long pointed out that it is almost impossible to separate "restorative" from "revolutionary" elements, let alone map them onto a narrative of progress and emancipation. Most slave uprisings appear to have drawn on contemporary revolutionary thought, local Creole practices, *and* African traditions. And the issue is not just whether we can distinguish quite so neatly between the two tendencies. We can agree with Genovese that the history of the modern world and the history of slavery and slave resistance cannot, and must not, be written without each other. But that does not mean that slave resistance, and the revolutionary Atlantic, can simply be subsumed under the thoroughly European concept "bourgeois," nor that we should view local syncretistic and African elements in the struggles as irrelevant remainders of a superseded past. And as far as democratic aspirations are concerned, Haiti and the Haitian Revolution just do not seem particularly good examples. Twenty years of increasingly detailed and methodologically diverse scholarship on slave resistance have produced a wealth of information. In light of that body of research, the wholesale subsumption of post-1791 uprisings under the dynamics of European revolutions seems to be a way of erasing the specific kind of struggle that took place in the Caribbean.

For strong arguments against Genovese's picture of a "modern" Haitian Revolution, we should turn to Carolyn Fick's *The Making of Haiti* of 1990.[44] From a perspective inspired by subaltern studies and "history from below," she makes an eloquent argument for the importance of popular practices in the events that led to the overthrow of slavery in Saint Domingue. She rightly insists that the absence of extensive written records about what moved slaves to act, what principles guided them, and so on does not justify a wholesale import of European revolutionary motivations for explanatory purposes. Without denying the importance of the French Revolution in the unfolding of the events, she argues, against Genovese, that "the categorization of 'modern,' if taken in an exclusive sense, would . . . tend to camouflage the dynamic nature and revolutionary role of cultural diversity" (243).

> By seeing the embodiment of the Saint Domingue revolution in the figure of Toussaint Louverture, we may interpret that revolution as part of the modern age, and rightly so. But by doing so, we also risk reducing to a level of impertinence those vital social, economic, and cultural realities of the ex-slaves whose independent relationship to the land, African in outlook, formed the foundation of their own vision of freedom, while it flew in the face of the needs of the modern state that Toussaint was trying to build. (250)

We will need to return to the tensions between the projects of the leadership and the desires of the masses of former slaves. Suffice it to say for now that Fick, in a departure from a scholarly tradition that for more than two centuries has centered around the military leaders of the revolution, focuses mostly on the formation of political and military groups, structures of authority and command, the role of maronnage, and the influence of vodun on the revolutionary ideology.[45] For her, the French Revolution is merely an important causative factor (responsible, for instance, for the breakup of the dominant class in Saint Domingue prior to 1791), and modernity is just certain concepts that may have circulated among the leaders of the revolution (or that describe those circulating ideas).

The third and final position I would like to sketch here is that of Robin Blackburn, who, like Genovese, makes the issue of modernity central to his vast canvas of the revolutionary Atlantic. Although he introduces some important nuances into the account, he continues to make a strong case for the Haitian Revolution as a modern event and for the French Revolution as the central element: "Without the emergence of 'Black Jacobins' in 1793–4, and their alliance with revolutionary France, a generalized emancipation would not have been consolidated in St. Domingue. The aspiration of the black masses for autonomy and living space required a generalising politics and programme, or what Napoleon was contemptuously to refer to as 'ideology.' "[46]

Unlike Genovese, whose account is underwritten by a relentless economic determinism, Blackburn's project is motivated by a desire to show that politics matter: that there are allies to be chosen, polemics to be sustained, concepts to be revised. Blackburn argues that ideology was the all-important tool of political discourse: slaves appropriated political discourse from Europe and turned it against the colonizers and slaveholders. The Haitian Revolution "defended the gains of the French Revolution against France itself."[47] The main goal of his study is thus "to establish to what extent anti-slavery, either in intention or result, transcended the bourgeois democratic or capitalist dynamic."[48] Blackburn, too, seems to sense that radical antislavery could not properly be conceptualized with the terms of a narrowly European Marxist narrative of the rise of the bourgeoisie and capitalist development. Indeed, his hypothesis is that radical antislavery was true to the revolutionary spirit of modern universalism in a way that the more celebrated and better-known revolutionary movements of the time were not.

While Blackburn is thus less inclined to give weight and value to cultural heterogeneity and the unevenness of modernity than Fick (and probably the majority of scholars and intellectuals from the Caribbean), his insistence that slave insurgency and elite abolitionism are part of the same revolutionary landscape is an important corrective to the current tendency in the metropolitan academy toward disciplinary fragmentation. Perhaps most importantly, Blackburn points to the possibility that among the practices, ideas, and ideologies that circulated in the revolutionary Atlantic, there may have been some that cannot be contained within the ideologies that became hegemonic in the nineteenth century.

Before ending this brief sketch of the field, I should like to note at least in passing one peculiar silence which is all the more striking, since we find it even in studies that explicitly aim at recovering a revolutionary spirit beyond the "bourgeois-democratic dynamic." It would seem that if we were looking for the seeds of radicalism in antislavery, or for emancipatory projects that remained unresolved in the nineteenth century because they were not easily subsumed under the discipline of the nation, the links between the struggle against slavery and sexual subordination would be extremely interesting. Yet in the literature on abolitionism and radical antislavery, one rarely finds more than passing mention of the fact that women were crucial actors in the metropolitan movements against slavery, especially in England and the United States;[49] that many of those women received their initiation into politics in the abolitionist movement; that the language of antislavery was taken up literally by the suffrage movement; and that the legal and political arguments against slavery provided many of the crucial arguments for the first women's movement.[50] From the horrified reactions of William Wilberforce to the sudden appearance of women in political meetings,[51] one can only conclude that, at least for some, the abolition of slavery was less of a threat to the established order than the extension of equal rights to women.

If we now turn to nineteenth-century literature, we find that in the antislavery writings of white Caribbean authors, the ideological landscape of radical antislavery and the modern qualities of the economic and social regime are as little in evidence as the local syncretistic cultures that developed around slavery and the slave trade. Most of the stories take place in the master's house, in town, with the plantation looming in the background, as the limit case of slavery, the first circle of hell where recalcitrant slaves might be sent for punishment. The narratives do not tell the story of dehumanization and ruthless quantification of life. Rather, they depict the moral degradation and psychosexual regression of slave owners whose desires are allowed to roam in the lawless space of master-slave relations. Slavery in the Caribbean is represented as a form of extremely *personal* domination, and those engaged in the slave trade are usually shown to be barbaric monsters who have never encountered the softening touch of civilization. The stark anonymity of a human being whose existence within the world of the master was reduced to the calculations of capital spent, economic output, longevity, reproductive possibilities, and replacement costs is absent from moderate abolitionism's narratives.[52]

Twentieth-century narratives about slavery tend to adopt a rather more radical perspective by extending their critique to include abolitionists. The high moral tone of "philanthropic" or "moderate" abolitionism—particularly of the British variety—is denounced as a form of false consciousness, hypocrisy, or a way of masking underlying economic and political interests. Films such as Gillo Pontecorvo's *Queimada* (Italy/France, 1968) or Humberto Solás's *Cecilia* (Cuba, 1981),[53] for instance, show that technological advances had made slavery inefficient in the British colonies: the British stood to gain a considerable competitive advantage if slavery were to be abolished in the colonies that were less advanced. The denunciation of slavery turns into a denunciation of abolitionism as a tool in the competition of empires. In the end, the abolition of slavery is nothing but the replacement of an outmoded regime of exploitation with more refined ones.[54]

No doubt, abolitionism masks as much as it exposes: for every abuse revealed there seems to be an interest concealed or an intention hidden. Yet what appears to have escaped the attention of most skeptics and critics is that moderate abolitionism also masked, consciously or unconsciously, slavery's modern character. The reasons for the refusal to recognize slavery's modernity go, I submit, much beyond strategic calculation and hypocrisy. It is a way of writing out of the picture the fact that in the shadow of the "odious commerce," a political and cultural landscape had taken shape that was every bit as progressive and contemporaneous as the cultures of the Caribbean liberal elites, but clearly gave different relative weight and meaning to the goals of progress and liberty, and was evidently not a completely European phenomenon. As we will see later, particularly in relation to the Cuban mulatto poet Plácido, one of the reasons why radical antislavery was not readily assimilable by local elites was that it did not fit into the protonational mold of other local progressive movements. Some of the most important slave uprisings intended to seize the state. But a plan by one group of the population to seize the state and liberate the slaves is not the same as Creole nationalism,[55] and in any event, it was never the intention of the white Creole populations to hand over the state to those who had been slaves. As a result, the modernity of slavery and the cultures that had developed in its shadow were routinely disavowed even by those who acknowledged and attacked the institution.

There are few exceptions to this. Particularly remarkable among them is Sergio Giral's film El otro Francisco (Cuba, 1974), which forces the viewer into a critical recognition of the melodramatic conventions of abolitionist narratives by juxtaposing them with a brutally detached representation of the base objectification of life under slavery. Another one is the nineteenth-century Brazilian novelist Machado de Assis, a mulatto writer who has often been accused of having turned a blind eye to the issue of slavery in Brazil, who offers one of the most penetrating articulations of the global scope and characteristically modern, depersonalized form of exchange that is the slave trade and the slave economy. In Memorial de Aires (1908), a novel in the form of a fictional diary, the narrator comments on the passage of the abolition law by the Brazilian parliament in 1888. He reflects on the belatedness of this step, and on its futility, and then refers to the German poet Heinrich Heine:

> Poetry will speak of it [slavery], especially in those verses by Heine in which our name is eternalized. They record how the captain of a slave ship told of having left three hundred Negroes in Rio de Janeiro, where the "House of Gonçalves Pereira" paid him a hundred ducats a piece. It is of no consequence that the poet disfigures the buyer's name and calls him Gonzalez Perreiro; it was the rhyme or his bad pronunciation that caused him to do it. Neither do we have ducats, but here it was the seller who changed in his language the money of the buyer.[56]

The different modes of exchange are linked by a distinctive inappropriateness: people are counted in pieces, Brazilian money in ducats, and words are measured in rhymes. The abstraction that makes people, words, and money exchangeable means that none of the units is able to capture the reality of the things exchanged. All units in this process of exchange and substitution—ducats, rhymes, pieces—suffer from a corruption that might invalidate or severely distort the operations. On the basis of this improper system of valuation, the true nature of the slave trade can be obscured completely: the last clause ("the seller who changed in his language the money of the buyer") is twisted so far as to efface slaves from the surface of the discourse altogether.

It is clearly no coincidence that the most brilliant writer of the Brazilian nineteenth century, a writer, moreover, who always stayed clear of abolitionism's teary rhetoric, should focus on an apparently minor aspect of the slave trade: the underlying principle of general equivalence, precisely that principle which distinguishes premodern slavery and modern racial slavery under capitalism.[57] In a radical departure from the conventions of abolitionist literature, Machado brings to the fore the fact that the slave trade has produced a global exchange and, as against this first globalization, a transnational culture of protest, in which a German Jewish writer memorializes what most Brazilians tried so hard to ignore. It is poetry that bears witness to the brutal facticity and effectiveness of a system of exchange that continues to function no matter how much words and values are distorted in the process.

In an excellent discussion of García Canclini's *Hybrid Cultures: Strategies for Entering and Leaving Modernity*,[58] the anthropologist Renato

Rosaldo points to the crucial distinction between an analytic use of the terms "traditional" and "modern" and their usage as folk or vernacular categories.[59] In the absence of an exploration of vernacular forms of speech, Rosaldo argues, the analytic usage is more likely to "reflect the social milieu and biases of metropolitan intellectuals than that of subaltern social realities" (xvi). Indices of modernity that derived from debates about slavery's capitalist nature among historians, Max Weber's theory of modernization, discussions surrounding Habermas's or, most recently, Giddens's work on modernity, would seem to pose exactly that problem.

Remembering Fick's argument about the Haitian Revolution, we may well wonder: Did the insurgent slaves in Saint Domingue or Cuba think of themselves as modern, or are we hastily assigning labels whose meaning and significance are predicated on debates in the metropolitan academy? And even if some insurgents thought of themselves as modern, does it apply to all of them? To the leadership? Or perhaps only to those European-educated mulattoes who wrote the texts we find most informative?

However, closeness to vernacular discourse is by no means a simple matter. As we have seen, some vernacular accounts of slavery in the Caribbean include vast areas of silence and tend to disguise precisely those features of the institution that were most threatening to Creole hegemony. Moreover, there simply is no single discourse and single usage of language which would qualify as vernacular in the Caribbean. Not only did slaves, free blacks, slaveholders, liberal Creoles, and international abolitionists use different languages; they also used different discourses and meant different things, even where they appeared to be using the same words—"liberty" being just the most obvious example.[60]

How should we proceed, then? If there is a legitimate usage of the vocabulary of modernity in relation to the Caribbean in the Age of Revolution, it has to be a vocabulary that allows us to think about the forms of suppression and disavowal that are so characteristic of the discourses that took shape in the cultures of slavery. The only way in which we might be able to imagine traces of alternative futures from the vantage point of the past is by staying as close as possible to the texts of the past, by interrogating them about their visions and fears, and thus uncovering in the desires, fantasies, and fictions a dimension in the past that may have vanished in subsequent struggles. Yet at the same time, we must be careful to prevent the adherence to the vernacular from blunting the critical edge of our investigation. How can we show what has been silenced if we have no account against which those silences show up?

When suppression and denial lie at the heart of an ideological landscape, there are times when we have no choice but to help ourselves to extraneous materials, rough analogies, and theoretically derived concepts. Fictional texts, in particular, are by no means direct reflections of reality and thus require particularly careful contextualizations: there is no pure vernacular in literature. The stark differences between Machado de Assis's brief text about the slave trade as a modern hemispheric business and transgression of "the order of things," and the much more common denunciations of the slave trader as barbarian, show that the only way for a critical study to proceed is by measuring what is said against what is not said. Sometimes the only way to understand what was said is by insisting on what might be veiled. No doubt, analytic theory can become a vehicle for the reproduction of hegemonic ideas of history, liberty, and progress, but so can vernacular theory.

Some of the more memorable pages of Michel-Rolph Trouillot's important *Silencing the Past* are devoted to the Haitian king Henri Christophe, the palace he built and named Sans Souci, and the sedimentations of colonial history in that name. Skeptical about the links to Frederick the Great's palace in Potsdam and European Enlightenment culture commonly asserted by non-Haitian historians, Trouillot suggests that the name might be a veiled homage to an African-born insurgent leader called Jean-Baptiste Sans Souci, who was killed by Henri Christophe for failing to submit to his leadership and the discipline of his new state. Instead of the European link—for which there appears to be no evidence—Trouillot proposes an African one. He points out that the central elements of Henri Christophe's act of naming coincide with events retained in oral history about the foundation of the empire of Dahomey, and that Christophe was likely familiar with these stories.[61] The name "Sans Souci" would thus refer us back to the Congo civil wars of the eighteenth century, which, Trouillot speculates, may well have been one of the sources for the guerrilla strategies used by the insurgent slaves. Yet it did not even occur to the Haitian elites that the military experience could be traced back to Africa: "Haitian historians (like everyone else) long assumed that victorious strategies could only come from the Europeans or the most Europeanized slaves" (67). The Haitian elites' epic renditions of the revolution may contest the silence imposed by the metropolitan historiography and politics; but they also inscribe a silence even more profound. Just as Henri Christophe's military dictatorship was built on the destruction of a more African past, Haitian historiography has not retained the memory of the knowledge and the practices that would take us back to Africa.

Clearly, for Trouillot, Sans Souci is an allegorical sentinel against attempts to subsume Haiti and the Haitian Revolution under the categories and event structure of European history. It would seem that Trouillot concurs here with Fick's admonition that labeling the Haitian Revolution "modern" threatens to erase the contributions of the black masses at the expense of a handful of leaders. What is interesting, however, is that the line that separates European from African ancestry does not coincide with the distinction between modern and traditional society. Dahomey was a highly organized empire with a strong bureaucracy whose wealth was based on the transatlantic slave trade. As Trouillot points out, Henri Christophe was known to be a great admirer of Dahomey, and his esteem for it was based on the fact that Dahomey represented the kind of highly structured, militaristic state that he intended to build in Haiti. The triangular trade and colonial commercial routes clearly produced circuits where cultural knowledge and political practices traveled back and forth across the Atlantic. Dahomey—Dahomey as it appeared to Christophe, that is—fits perfectly into an account of modernity that turns on new forms of globalization, heterogeneous cultural formation, and utopian possibilities that are rooted in precisely those features.

The real problem, it seems to me, is with accounts of modernity that claim primacy for its European face. All too often, the assumption seems to be that there are more or less "pure" cases, that the purer the cases of modernity, the more originally or authentically modern. If we read modernity from the perspective of the Caribbean colonies, the opposite view seems more plausible: that heterogeneity is a congenital condition of modernity, and that the alleged purity of European modernity is an a posteriori theorization or perhaps even part of a strategy that aims to establish European primacy. It may well be best to think of the purported homogeneity of European modernity as having been distilled out of the hybrid hemispheric phenomenon—distilled by ideological operations, forgetfulness, and active suppression of impure, hybrid elements. Familiar claims about the "unfinished project of modernity" and its utopian promise would, from this perspective, just be one of the strategies of purification.

To be sure, some of the characteristics often claimed as central to modernity cannot be found in the Caribbean. There were no great cities at the time. The diversification and autonomization of social and professional sectors that many European theorists of modernity have identified as an, if not *the,* essential feature of modernity did not really take off in the Caribbean for another hundred years, and even in the late nineteenth century it proceeded at a decidedly uneven pace, producing what Julio Ramos called "desencuentros de la modernidad"—literally, "mismeeting of modernity"—rather than modern cultures.[62] The printing press and print capitalism arrived late in most areas, as did independence. Most territories or islands did not constitute themselves as independent states until the twentieth century, and some, like Puerto Rico or the French Départements d'Outre-Mer, still have not done so.

Clearly, social and cultural development on the periphery was uneven.[63] The brutal modernity of the plantation economy and its social structure did not uniformly translate into a modern consciousness, if we employ the term in the homogenized sense developed in European theoretical discourses. Even if the transatlantic slave trade and the Caribbean plantation operated like a modernizing, rationalizing machine that kept turning in disregard of human needs and distinctions, they also gave rise to social structures that aimed to protect and defend traditions. There were the *cabildos* of slaves and free people of color, the secret societies in which religious or ethnic traditions were kept alive. Slaveholders, too, erected barriers against certain kinds of modern thought. Anything French was anathema in the slaveholding areas of the late eighteenth century and the early nineteenth, as "liberty, equality, fraternity" threatened to bring revolutionary violence into the plantation zone and recalled the "horrors of Saint-Domingue" to the ruling elites. Secularism was perceived as a threat in many places, and the Catholic Church continued to offer protection against the intrusion of modern ideas into people's living spaces. As the subtitle of García Canclini's *Hybrid Cultures* notes, modernity can be inhabited differentially—on certain occasions, for certain purposes, now and then.

From a cultural and ideological point of view, then, modernity needs to be considered under the headings of colonial heterogeneity, displacement, and discontinuity: modernity as a hypothesis, modernity affirmed and disavowed; modernity as desire, as premonition, or even as an idea that can be traced only in certain suspicions and fears. Beliefs and attributed beliefs need to be read against the grain, with an ear for improbable distortions, so that they might reveal the shadow of other futures, of projects not realized and ideas rarely remembered.[64] If we do not take into account to what extent modernity is a product of the New World, to what extent the colonial experience *shaped* modernity—in Europe and elsewhere—politically, economically,[65] and aesthetically, and to what extent modernity is a heterogeneous, internally diverse, even contradictory phenomenon that constituted and revolutionized itself in the process of transculturation, then, obviously, talk of modernity is just a reinstantiation of a Eurocentric particularism parading as universalism. Many of the readings and arguments in this book aim to provide support for this intuition: that what happened in the Caribbean in the Age of Revolution was also, among other things, a struggle over what it means to be modern, who can claim it, and on what grounds; that the suppression and disavowal of revolutionary antislavery and attendant cultures in the Caribbean was also a struggle over what would count as progress, what was meant by liberty, and how the two should relate.

In the end, this was largely a struggle between various elites. The popular masses intervened in different ways in the historical process, often in ways that elude the tools available to the literary scholar.[66] As most (though not all) of the materials I rely on are published sources, and many are literary or high cultural, certain biases and silences are inevitable. But they are not the result of the mere fact that a certain concept of modernity is used.

### Hegel and the Haitian Revolution

At the heart of Enlightenment and post-Enlightenment politics and political theory, there is a troubling contradiction. At the same time that liberty emerges as the most cherished political value, and slavery comes to signify all that is wrong with traditional forms of social organization and political rule, racial slavery—slavery as a global business, a labor regime, and a legal practice—expands to an extraordinary degree. Yet when we look at the philosophical tradition, comments about actual slaves and the slave trade are rare and rarely unequivocal.

We might have expected political writings of the revolutionary age to discreetly avoid the language of enslavement altogether. Why bring up a topic that forced so many political thinkers into double-talking excuses and evasions? After all, there are other terms that express the basic facts of oppression and exploitation. Yet Locke spoke in terms of slavery, as did Rousseau and then Wollstonecraft.[67] And so too did G. F. W. Hegel, especially in the so-called master-slave dialectic in the *Phenomenology of Spirit* of 1807, one of the most debated and celebrated pieces of philosophical writing in modern times.[68] The question, of course, is: What did these philosophers and political theorists have in mind when they used the word "slavery"? Was it a mere metaphor to them? Did it make white Europeans think of ancient Greece, even when their fortunes depended on slave labor and newspapers reported on the bloody events in the Caribbean? Were the American revolutionaries really only thinking of themselves, rather than the slaves that worked in the fields, when they railed against slavery? If so, would this not be the most perverse form of silencing—the erasure of modern racial slavery from conceptual space?[69]

The case of Hegel is particularly interesting in this respect, since one might think of the section on lordship and bondage as the moment when slaves enter history, or, more accurately, the philosophy of history. Historians of slavery and abolitionism, at any rate, seem to have read it that way: David Brion Davis, Orlando Patterson, and Robin Blackburn all offer their comments, amendments, and criticisms of Hegel's story, as does one of the foremost scholars of the postslavery Atlantic, Paul Gilroy—following the example of an earlier generation of anticolonialist activists that included Frantz Fanon and Amiri Baraka (aka LeRoi Jones). Gilroy reads Hegel as suggesting that slavery was foundational for modernity: "it [the master-slave dialectic] can be used to initiate an analysis of modernity which is abjured by Habermas because it points directly to an approach which sees the intimate association of modernity and slavery as a fundamental conceptual issue." According to Gilroy's reading, Hegel provides the terms for "a firm rebuke to the mesmeric idea of history as progress" and "an opportunity to re-periodise and reaccentuate accounts of the dialectic of Enlightenment."[70] Patterson describes one of the "major tasks" of his seminal *Slavery and Social Death* as an "empirical exploration" of the "dialectic of power in the master-slave relationship" (2), as originally proposed by Hegel. Davis goes so far as to say that the core of his celebrated *Slavery in the Age of Revolution* ought to be understood in terms of Hegel's master-slave dialectic and takes the extraordinary step of allegorizing his argument in the story of a fictional encounter between Toussaint Louverture and Napoleon, which closely follows Hegel's master-slave dialectic.[71]

It may come as a surprise, then, that among philosophers and Hegel scholars there is almost universal agreement that Hegel's text about masters and slaves has nothing to do with modern racial slavery, the Haitian Revolution, or radical abolitionism.[72]

Let me recall Hegel's account in its rough outline. There is a deadly struggle between two embodied consciousnesses of equal standing, desirous both of asserting themselves and of being recognized by the other. One consciousness is prepared to risk its life to gain recognition; the other one is not. As a result, the former becomes the lord to whose will and orders the other one—now the bondsman—has to submit. Still shaking with fear of the master, the bondsman enters a long period of service and labor. In the ensuing process, however, an inversion takes place. While the lord is tied to the world merely through consumption, enjoying the fruits of the bondsman's labor, the bondsman shapes the world in his image and recognizes himself in his work. "Through this rediscovery of himself by himself, the bondsman realizes that it is precisely in his work wherein he seemed to have only an alienated existence that he acquires a mind of his own" (119). Thus the lord stagnates and becomes dependent on the slave, and the slave develops his faculties and transforms the world.[73]

Now, what does this section refer to if it is not modern slavery? The very recent and well-documented commentary on the *Phenomenology* by Michael Forster, for instance, argues that Hegel was influenced by a 1789 work entitled *Geschichte und Zustand der Sklaverei und Leibeigenschaft in Griechenland* (The History and Condition of Slavery and Bondage in Greece) by the now largely forgotten German historian J. F. Reitemeier. Forster identifies two historical processes as the specific historical referent for the lordship and bondage sections: the decline of the "ideal culture" of fifth-century Athens and the demise of the Roman Republic from the Second Punic War onward.[74] According to Forster, Hegel, following Reitemeier, saw both of these historical periods as characterized by a "loss of political freedom by the mass of the citizenry" and a "growth in the enslavement of noncitizens."[75]

Whether or not we are persuaded by Forster's claim (he has only indirect evidence for Reitemeier's influence), it is striking that in a reading that not only admits history into our reading of the *Phenomenology* (which some commentators refuse to do) but calls for multiple historical references in a single section of Hegel's text, the possibility of a reference to contemporary slavery or perhaps of an allegorical representation of the present is not mentioned.[76]

In her article "Hegel and Haiti," Susan Buck-Morss has recently mounted a spirited attack against the canonical view on the issue of slavery in Hegel's *Phenomenology*. Her evidence is compelling indeed. The events in the French colony were reported at length in the

German and English press in the 1790s and early 1800s. We know that Hegel was a keen observer of political events, closely followed the reports about the French Revolution, and was an avid reader of the German political journal *Minerva*, which had been reporting on the Saint Domingue uprising from 1792 onward.[77] Buck-Morss concludes that "either Hegel was the blindest of all the blind philosophers of Freedom in Enlightenment Europe," even more than Locke or Rousseau, or "Hegel knew" (844).

The evidence points to the latter. He started to work on the early versions of the master-slave dialectic in 1803. He wrote the final version in 1805 and 1806, "the first year of the Haitian nation's existence" (843), and from the early drafts on continuously revised the terms in which he sees the relationship between master and slave. In a brief reading of the relevant passages in the *Phenomenology* and earlier draft versions, Buck-Morss shows that the highly abstract terms of the master-slave dialectic can be historicized in the context of legal documents such as the Code Noir, where the "thinghood" of the slave was enshrined, stressing throughout the translatability of the Hegelian terms into the terms of modern racial slavery.

So it seems that a plausible case can be made for the hypothesis that Hegel knew about Haiti, that he was possibly fascinated by the slave revolution, and that Haiti may well have inspired him to write some of his most celebrated pages. This in itself is a significant correction to the Eurocentric provincialism of most professional philosophy and an important step toward acknowledging that modern racial slavery was far more central to the making of European modernity than most are willing to admit.

Problems arise from a different direction.[78] Here is what Buck-Morss says immediately after quoting the final stage of the dialectic, when the slave has reached self-consciousness "through the transformation of material nature": "Hegel's text becomes obscure and falls silent at this point of realization. But given the historical events that provided the context for *The Phenomenology of Mind*, the inference is clear. Those who once acquiesced to slavery demonstrate their humanity when they are willing to risk death rather than remain subjugated" (848). Buck-Morss is thus inviting us as readers of the *Phenomenology* to supply the historical references we routinely supply when Hegel appears to be alluding to the French Revolution or Napoleon. And perhaps she is right. Who produces the silence in the *Phenomenology*? Is it Hegel, who rarely offered more than veiled allusions to historical events or figures; or is it rather we, who refuse even to consider the possibility of allusions to Haiti? On the other hand, we may wonder whether she is not asking us to do more than just acknowledge an allusion. After all, why does Hegel fall into "obscurity" and "silence" right at the point where the slave would have emerged victorious? From what perspective could we claim that historical actors "finish" what the commentator has left unsaid?[79]

Perhaps it does not come as a surprise that the problem in Buck-Morss's argument at this point tracks some of the most profound disagreements in the Hegel literature. The resolution of the master-slave dialectic and the question "What happens next?" have given rise to vastly different readings among commentators and Hegelians of various stripes. It is no coincidence that recently Judith Butler, whose theoretical and ideological commitments are unlikely to be the same as those of Buck-Morss, also picked up on the mysterious transition from the section on lordship and bondage to the section entitled "Freedom of Self-Consciousness: Stoicism, Skepticism, and the Unhappy Consciousness." Calling it "one of the least interrogated of Hegel's philosophical movements," Butler, too, feels compelled to fill in the sketchy transition. Unlike Buck-Morss, Butler uses the ambiguities of the transition to set the stage for an inquiry into the notion of liberation and, more specifically, the idea that the master-slave dialectic secures "a liberationist narrative for various progressive political visions." In her account, Hegel's resolution of the dialectic is "dystopic" and far closer to the Foucauldian view according to which subjects cannot, in the strict sense, be liberated from oppression, since they come into existence only as effects of just that oppression, than to any idea of revolutionary liberation.[80] In any event, what is remarkable is that both Buck-Morss and Butler need this moment "when the text falls into silence and obscurity" for their arguments, which then take them in vastly different directions.

I do not propose to adjudicate here between these various readings of the master-slave dialectic. Clearly that can only be done if we consider its role in the *Phenomenology* as a whole, the role of history and historicism in the text, along with a host of other questions. In any event, more interesting for my purposes than trying to settle the issues in Hegel scholarship is the conflict of interpretation itself. Why such profound mystery at precisely this point in the *Phenomenology*? How have commentators and philosophers interpreted Hegel's silence and obscurity at the end of the section on lordship and bondage? The issue goes to the heart of the question of how silence operates, and whether, why, and when Haiti and revolutionary antislavery vanished from the Western records.

The commentary that has had the greatest influence on the reading of Hegel's lordship and bondage section, especially outside disciplinary philosophy, is probably Alexandre Kojève's *Introduction to the Reading of Hegel,* published in 1947, but based on lectures given in Paris between 1933 and 1939.[81] In fact, it is typically this version of Hegel that keeps returning in those accounts that try to link Hegel to modern slavery.[82]

Kojève's reading is joyously practical. It stresses labor, socioeconomic oppression, and violence. There is a seductive confluence of the distant pathos of high philosophy and the vigorous bodily immediacy of a revolutionary rhetoric that is largely absent from Hegel's own account.[83] But there is also a change of emphasis that sets the text apart from other influential readings and ultimately produces a plot that may be a departure from Hegel and is certainly not explicit in the original text.[84]

Whereas Jean Hyppolite, the other great French commentator on the *Phenomenology,* opens his 1946 commentary proper by stressing the idealist roots of Hegel's thought in Fichte and Schelling, and its metaphysical and epistemological implications,[85] Kojève opens his first lecture, entitled "In place of an Introduction," by claiming "Man is Self-Consciousness. He is conscious of himself, conscious of his human reality and dignity; and it is in this that he is essentially different from animals" (3). Kojève's text thus postpones the explication of the *Phenomenology*'s long sections on consciousness' manifestations in sense certainty, perception, and understanding: what is to be an introduction to the *Phenomenology* begins with the lordship and bondage chapter. At the heart of the matter are the notions of human (as opposed to animal) reality and dignity, and the ability of being aware of these two. In other words, epistemological structures are from the beginning folded back into concerns of existential philosophy, practical philosophy, and political struggles.

While in most philosophical commentaries Hegel's dialectic is interpreted as proceeding through the slow disappearance of the master-slave dualism that stands in the way of the fully realized universality of freedom,[86] in Kojève this dualism continues to reappear as a sharp opposition that is overcome only by force. "In transforming the World . . . the Slave transforms himself, too, and thus creates the new objective conditions that permit him *to take up once more the liberating Fight for recognition*" (29; italics mine). Compare that statement with what the Canadian philosopher Charles Taylor offers as a summary of the dialectic in his study of Hegel:

The master-slave relation has thus brought about a reversal. The master's prerogative of being only a consumer leads him to stagnant self-coincidence. While the slave who is subject to the refractory existence of matter gradually turns tables, turns this resistance to account by making it the standing reflection of himself as universal consciousness. The reversal is the more complete in that he owes his transformation to his subjection; only under the discipline of service would he have undertaken the work which has raised him above his original limits.[87]

In Taylor's account, there is a gradual change as the effect of service and discipline. And even though earlier in his discussion of the master-slave dialectic he maintained that "ultimately it is mutual recognition that is the most essential" (156), recognition does not appear at the end, when the issue is the reversal of the master-slave relation. Why that should be so, he does not say. As in Hegel, there is a sudden silence here.

For Kojève, by contrast, labor does not dull or soften the opposition between masters and slaves but rather intensifies it to a point where a new struggle for recognition ensues. Clearly Kojève raises the stakes not only by dispensing with some of the more metaphysical and speculative elements in Hegel's argument but by suggesting that there will be a repeat of the life-and-death struggle with all the risk and violence that it entails. The slave is thus objectively destined to carry out the "revolutionary overcoming of the World" (29). The master, who had once risked his life in a struggle for recognition, becomes a mealymouthed reformer at best, who is bound by the strictures of a given reality. For Kojève, the future belongs to the slave.[88]

Clearly, whatever reading of Hegel we embrace, the radical freedom of the master is a dead end. The historical process is not the domain of the master. Less than a decade after the revolutions in France and Haiti, the lowly, who had been banned from the heroic stage except for comic relief, enter as protagonists in the *Phenomenology*. But now Kojève's reading brings out implications or dormant possibilities of the plot that Hegel's story of service and labor seemed to avoid. In Kojève's hands, the lordship and bondage section begins to resonate with the dramatic form historically closest to revolutionary upheaval: melodrama with its heightened emotions, its stress on the virtues of the lowly, and its distaste for mediations and rank. Compare the following account by the literary critic Peter Brooks:

The action of melodrama works toward confrontations, showdowns. Early in the play, such a confrontation will put evil in charge, so that it will seem to dictate the action for most of the rest of the play, deluding those who should know better, setting the apparent moral coordinates of society. But there has to be another showdown by the end, in which there will be a reversal. Often the showdown—particularly of that last act—involves spectacular action: combats that fill the stage, explosions, fires, floods, volcanic eruptions.[89]

Does this not read like a narratological rendition of Kojève's version of the master-slave dialectic? Of course, there is a simpleminded moralism in melodrama that has no equivalent in Kojève's story. But otherwise the similarities are striking.

Seeing how naturally the master-slave dialectic can be made to conform to melodramatic conventions, seeing also how much Kojève's version of the story appeals precisely to scholars and intellectuals who are thinking about the slaveholding Atlantic, it seems plausible that Hegel was quite aware of these latent possibilities of his story. After all, he was well informed about literary and artistic styles and wrote philosophically about them. Just fifteen years after the lifting of the rigid regulations in regard to style and social rank in French theaters, Hegel would have been aware that the most immediate result of that "liberation" had been a plethora of hugely popular melodramas, which Napoleon tried to contain again later on. No doubt Hegel would not have wanted to appear to give expression to the base revelry and rampant sentimentalism of melodrama. The magisterial tone of high philosophy, the insistence on the need for discipline, the ambiguous resolution of the lordship and bondage chapter, and the somewhat underdeveloped transition into the sections on stoicism, skepticism, and unhappy consciousness might just be a trace of this attempt to imagine a plot in which the oppressed free themselves by their own means but nevertheless do not dictate the tone ever after. Liberation without the floods and fires; liberty without the crassness of the lowly. The dualism of masters and slaves simply vanishes. From the perspective of genre, Kojève's disregard for the more metaphysical and psychological aspects of Hegel's text would appear to be neither a coincidence nor negligence,[90] but rather a natural effect of a different political and aesthetic imagination. Stark contrast and visible distinction are more important than the complex speculative interiority of a text that has been called a bildungsroman of the spirit.

Given the intractable silence and obscurity of Hegel at the moment when we might have expected closure, genre considerations may well help us to imagine what is being left out or silenced here. And that is, after all, what the question of Hegel and Haiti ultimately turns on. Our findings provide indirect but strong support for Buck-Morss's argument that "Hegel knew." But it is only from his evasiveness that we can infer what it might be that he knows. It seems that it is a traumatic knowledge, a knowledge forever caught in the structures of disavowal, outside the temporality of error and correction, beyond the reach of progress. Hegel knows and at the same time behaves as if he did not. Does he believe both—that the slaves did, and did not—carry the victory over their masters? Did he think their military victory was purely contingent, and that it behooved him, the philosopher, to produce a rational (and that is, for Hegel, "real") alternative? Or was it that he had to avert his eyes, as if in the face of a horrifying sight? What seems most plausible is that precisely *because* Hegel knew, in some sense of the word, he fell silent at the end of the master-slave dialectic.

In an astonishing convergence, both Hegel and Hannah Arendt (whose theory was explicitly anti-Hegelian) make revolutionary slaves vanish. In the case of Arendt, slaves disappear first in the disavowal attributed to European travelers and American revolutionaries, who did not "see" the slaves that labored in the fields, and then again, conceptually, in the abyss between the social and the political. In Hegel, there is a retreat into silence and obscurity at the very moment when revolutionary slaves might have appeared on the scene.

Hegel's is an ambivalent, pregnant, meaningful silence. When he picks up the narrative strands again, we are within a historical process that seems to have avoided the Haitian Revolution. Masters and slaves have vanished, probably without bloodshed, certainly without volcano eruptions and fires. Slaves have become free through service, discipline, and labor. Did they also engage in a second struggle for life and death in order to gain recognition? Was there a slave revolution in Saint Domingue? Who would know? Can it be known?

This, it strikes me, is the story of "Hegel and Haiti." It is a story of deep ambivalence, probably fascination, probably fear, and ultimately disavowal. Disavowal itself becomes productive, generating further stories, further screens that hide from view what must not be seen. Whatever happened in that dark moment, whatever got lost, or won, let us move on, move from revolutionary France to philosophical Germany; let us pick up the story where it returns to Europe, now without slaves, or, at the very least, without slavery: universal history as disavowal of slavery.

Can we recover from this the "idea of universal human history," as Buck-Morss claims? Does the "Haitian Hegel" show that we need not discard "the project of universal freedom"—that it can be rescued from the "uses that white domination has put it"? Can it be "reconstituted on a different basis"? (865). Perhaps. Buck-Morss does not say how she imagines this to work, and from her reading of Hegel, I suspect that the concept she wants to rescue is more closely tied to its European and Hegelian formulations than I think is possible. I think our revisions need to go deeper if we want to conceive human history and human freedom as one for all of us. We need to understand more fully what events and which thoughts were erased or suppressed before any of the canonical formulations of modernity came into being. There is more conflict, more resistance, more denial and fear to be accounted for before we can fully understand the role of Haiti in the *Phenomenology of Spirit* and why it is actually not fully there.

### A Counterculture of Modernity?

The debate in the background of Buck-Morss's reading of Hegel is of course one that goes far beyond issues of Hegel scholarship and the Haitian Revolution. (Although we might argue that ambivalence about modernity originates with its concept, and that means largely, with Hegel, it is probably with World War II and Nazi rule in Germany that modernity's Janus face came to be one of the most pressing theoretical questions.) How is it that modernity's dream of human emancipation turns into its opposite? How is it that the promise of freedom comes to mean a radical loss of autonomy and a ruthless instrumentalization of human life? How are modernity's utopian and dark sides linked?

One of the most passionate attempts to rescue the ebullience and utopian potential of the modern experience is Marshall Berman's widely debated *All That's Solid Melts into Air.*[91] Quoting one of Berman's more enthusiastic accounts of the modern experience as the promise of "adventure, power, joy, growth" that is shared now "by men and women all over the world," Walter Mignolo registers his surprise at the fact that the "darker side" of modernity appears to be absent from this picture. He then proceeds to point out that by extrapolating from the metropolitan experience to "men and women all over the world," Berman fails to realize that the modern experience of time and space in reality continues to be a "differential" one. Mignolo argues that modernity is by no means the same for someone who lives in a colonial or postcolonial situation as for someone who lives in a metropolis. It is, rather, "a period, in the history of the

BARRY UNIVERSITY
MIAMI, FL 33161

West, in which contact and domination between human cultures reached their peak." The study of colonial situations affords us with a "critical perspective on Western values," but also, possibly, a view on "the brighter side of a utopian future."[92]

Similar criticisms could be directed against Habermas's writings about the Enlightenment and modernity. As critics such as Edward Said, Gilroy, García Canclini, and many others have pointed out, Habermas's account of the "unfinished project of modernity" is extremely selective.[93] Of course, neither Habermas nor Berman denies modernity's record of catastrophes. The question is how we understand the relationship between this dark side and the utopian aspect; between the modernity of European expansionism, racial subordination, and genocide, and modernity as emancipation and democratization. Can we really distinguish neatly between those Western values that underwrite colonialism and slavery, and those that promote emancipation and democracy? Clearly the problem is not solved by simply adding some negative characteristics to overly flattering accounts. It may well be worth recalling Adorno's and Horkheimer's deeply pessimistic proposal in *Dialectic of Enlightenment* that modernity's emancipatory potential and its oppressive tendencies are rooted in exactly the same characteristics—the hegemony of instrumental reason and the submission of nature to a calculating rationality.

One of the most explicit and sustained efforts to address the issue of modernity and barbarism, and, specifically, modernity and slavery, has been made by Gilroy in his *Black Atlantic*. For Gilroy, the diasporic African cultures are a source for a critical revision of modernity and a reservoir for utopian ideas. As a geopolitical and geocultural configuration that came into being as a result of racial slavery, the final referent of this tradition continues to be this catastrophic experience. The transnational, hybrid cultures of the black Atlantic thus offer a unique standpoint or perspective that allows for crucial revisions to our concept of modernity. And this is not just because the historical experience of slavery operates as a corrective to any tendency to produce naively celebratory accounts. Rather, it is because the African diasporic culture is itself uniquely modern, while retaining the memory of a premodern African past. It is "a non-traditional tradition, an irreducibly modern, ex-centric, unstable, and asymmetrical cultural ensemble" (198), a "political counterculture that grew inside modernity in a distinctive relationship of antagonistic indebtedness" (191). The "ancient pre-slave past" allows the thinker of the black Atlantic "to anchor its dissident assessments of modernity's achievements" (71). Slavery and the struggle against it provide the slave with an epistemological and moral advantage—she can recognize what remains hidden from the master's view; she can see the suffering and terror that modernity brought about. Slavery shows up the brutality of a modernity driven by the rationality of profit and desire for domination.

Those who champion modernity as an unfinished project (Gilroy mentions Marshall Berman and Habermas) fail to recognize the barbarism that was part of modernity and that *as its counterpart* produced emancipatory thought. In doing so, their description of modernity becomes lopsided: modernity is seen as a reservoir for ideas of democracy and defended through the counterfactual thought rather than the oppressive practices it in fact produced.

One of the implications of Gilroy's claims is that the standoff of the 1980s between those who felt that modernity was irredeemable and needed to be superseded by new ways of articulating diversity and difference, and those who maintained that it remains unfinished, is due to an intrinsic incompleteness within both accounts of modernity. In this stalemate, the cultures of the black Atlantic offer "an opportunity to transcend the unproductive debate between a Eurocentric rationalism which banishes the slave experience from its accounts of modernity while arguing that the crises of modernity can be resolved from within," and "an equally occidental antihumanism which locates the origins of modernity's current crises in the shortcomings of the Enlightenment project" (54).

So far it would seem, then, that Gilroy's revisions are roughly what is needed to correct the silence, denial, and disavowal we found in response to slavery and, especially, the struggles against it in hegemonic theories of modernity. Much of what Gilroy describes in relation to diasporic culture in the nineteenth and twentieth centuries in Britain and the United States—the hybridity of cultural expression, the fragmented identities, the transnationalism, the coexistence of modern and premodern practices—describes well what we will see later in Cuba, Haiti, and the Dominican Republic, even though non-Anglophone areas of the black Atlantic are only nominally included in his study. Yet there is an odd silence in Gilroy's *Black Atlantic* when it comes to the events that are at the core of the history of the black Atlantic. And this, I think, is no coincidence.

The central move in Gilroy's strategy for uncovering a modern, contestatory black Atlantic is a shift from history to memory. Slavery becomes the bedrock of communal experience. It becomes a referent, that which produced and continues to reproduce a specifically modern experience of history (as loss, as catastrophe, as dispersal, as exile) but itself remains curiously inanimate.[94] Slavery, slave resistance, and radical antislavery receive only perfunctory treatment, and the African past figures exclusively as a recourse of discourse and memory. At times it thus seems that the cultures of the black Atlantic are constructed as merely reacting to a modernity that is conceived and developed elsewhere. The contestatory potential is ultimately derived from the memory of premodern traditions. It almost seems that to the extent that the black Atlantic is inside modernity, it suffers it, and to the extent that it is outside, it contests it. Events or movements such as the French Revolution, the revolution in Saint Domingue, or the struggle against slavery that played a significant role in shaping modernity in the Atlantic are barely mentioned. Instead of a substantive account of emancipatory goals (What were they? Were they achieved? Were they repressed? Forgotten?) Gilroy offers a critique of the discursive regulations that govern emancipatory accounts of the past. Ultimately, modernity thus remains the master's domain. The (former) slave is forever condemned to recoil: memory, double consciousness, critique of regulatory regimes, and so forth. The slave's relation to history is that of insertion, not that of construction. What makes the slaves' perspective different from that of the master, what provides the slaves with a privileged position, is also what takes them out of the making of history.

Gilroy wants to revise our concept of modernity, but the privileged medium in which the experiences of the black Atlantic survive is "non-representational," "non-conceptual" music, which is "not reducible to the cognitive and the ethical" (76). It is the category of the sublime that captures the experience of slavery: the unspeakable terror, the fear of death, which exceeds discursive representation (77).

From this perspective, then, it is not so surprising that Gilroy's revised account of the modern experience from the perspective of the slave—the "primal history of modernity," as he calls it, following Walter Benjamin—ends up sounding rather familiar from postmodern discourses about modernity, despite Gilroy's protestations that his is an "anti-anti-essentialist" stance (102): a critique of notions such as "universality," "fixity of meaning," and "coherence of the self." Is there really nothing in the perspective of the slave that escaped metropolitan philosophers of postmodernity? Perhaps even more importantly, can we be so confident that the modernity against which postmodern critiques are directed is essentially the same as that of the Age of Revolution?

In the end, Gilroy's "counterculture of modernity" is, I think, too closely tied to cultural phenomena that survived into the present, and too much based on the assumption of a continuous memory and history. Losses, fears, and hopes both realized and unrealized need to be accounted for concretely, not just in a general invocation of exile and dispersion. If we replace history with memory, we can no longer discern the discontinuities that are constitutive of the history of the black Atlantic and thus of Western modernity. If our conceptual alternatives are marked out by "memory" and "the unspeakable," we will find it difficult to understand how the gaps and silences in hegemonic concepts of modernity ever came into being. Instead of equating modernity with the Eurocentric regime of racial subordination and colonial exploitation that became hegemonic in the course of the nineteenth century, and then opposing that modernity with a counterculture that grows out of suffering, we need to understand the ideological, cultural, and political conflicts that led to the ascendancy of a modernity that could be claimed only by European nations (and then only by some of those). This book hopes to make a step in that direction.

The radical revision in the concept of modernity that Gilroy aspires to is urgently needed. But the way in which he articulates modernity and a counterculture of modernity does not allow for this revision. The precise content of the "counter-" in the counterculture of modernity remains obscure unless we articulate more precisely where the contestatory potential of the black Atlantic lies. Dissent in the slaveholding Atlantic was by no means confined to the non-discursive realm of music. There are, for instance, the conflicts between revolutionary antislavery and Creole movements for autonomy or independence; between moderate and radical abolitionism; and between those who felt that liberty meant securing racial equality, those who identified it with having a lot of land for themselves, and those who felt it meant keeping the state at bay. In the clashes between these conflicting emancipatory projects, we can see divergent concepts of modernity, progress, and liberty. We can observe how the issue of racial subordination (just as that of sexual subordination in other historical contexts) is relegated to the realm of the moral or of social policy and thus eventually appears to be, from the hegemonic point of view, out of reach for revolutionary action.

I propose the concept of a disavowed modernity to signal the conflictive and discontinuous nature of modernity in the Age of Revolution. "Disavowal," taken both in its everyday sense as "refusal to acknowledge," "repudiation," and "denial" *(OED)* and in its more technical meaning in psychoanalytic theory as a "refusal to recognize the reality of a traumatic perception,"[95] brings into focus the contestatory nature of human experience. Not all forms of denial or repudiation require a description in psychoanalytic terms. Only careful consideration of the cultural and historical materials—not purely theoretical or conceptual arguments—will tell us what kind of denial we are confronted with, but that is precisely what makes this notion workable for broadly historical and hermeneutical interpretation.

Like Gilroy's counterculture of modernity, it refers to an attitude or a perspective toward the past rather than the supposed characteristics of a particular moment, historical stage, or ethnic or cultural formation. But it is also a concept that only works if we remain cognizant that it is *something* that is being disavowed. As Freud explains, disavowal exists alongside recognition: "Whenever we are in a position to study them [acts of disavowal] they turn out to be half-measures, incomplete attempts at detachment from reality. The disavowal is always supplemented by an acknowledgement."[96] Unlike currently popular notions of trauma which tend to move the traumatic event into the realm of the unspeakable or unrepresentable and thus render it, in my view, quite useless for critical purposes (see chapter 6), the concept of disavowal requires us to identify what is being disavowed, by whom, and for what reason. Unlike the notion of trauma, which becomes politically inert when it cannot properly distinguish between, for instance, a traumatized slave and a traumatized slaveholder, disavowal does not foreclose the political by rushing to assign victim status to all those who find it difficult to deal with reality. It is more a strategy (although not necessarily one voluntarily chosen) than a state of mind, and it is productive in that it brings forth further stories, screens, and fantasies that hide from view what must not be seen. As the following chapters will show, the attempts to suppress certain memories of Haitian Revolution rarely produced silence.

# PART I *Cuba*

# 1

# The Deadly Hermeneutics of the Trial
# of José Antonio Aponte

In the early weeks of 1812, a rumor began to circulate among Cuban slaves and free people of color: the Spanish Cortes in Cádiz had abolished slavery, it said, and the Cuban slaveholders were cheating their slaves of their liberty. Unrest was in the air. In a letter to Salvador Muro y Salazar, Márquez of Someruelos—the Captain General of the island—someone reported having overheard a black woman announcing that "it won't be long now before the land will be ruled by Blacks, and we'll have a King."[1] Then news arrived about an assault on the sugar plantation of Peñas Altas, in the vicinity of Havana: after a brief and bloody battle, the plantation had been burned to the ground. On March 19, 1812, the authorities arrested nine conspirators. After three weeks of interrogation by a special council, the accused were sentenced to death. On the eve of the execution, Someruelos addresses himself to the Cuban people:

> There was an attempt to overturn the old and well-established submission of the serfs . . . which lacked all fact and antecedent except in the conceited and heated brain of the black José Antonio Aponte and of some others who, deceived by his clumsy and laughable calculations, wanted to quench their stupid ambition with honors and employments in the ambit of that fantastic king. It is therefore absolutely necessary that they [the slaves] be relieved of the illusion that slavery has been abolished, by telling them frankly that there is not, and never has been, such liberty. . . .
>
> In light of these facts, the public will cease to believe in the extraordinary significance and supreme transcendence that have been given to this matter, which did not exceed the knowledge of a few, without plan, coordination, help, or support of natives or foreigners. . . .
>
> What remains to be announced to this respectable public is that I have ordered the announced sentence to be executed next Thursday morning, in the usual place, and that the heads of Aponte, Lisundia, Chacón, and Barbier will be exhibited in the most public and convenient places as a warning lesson for those of their class. (217–19)

The proclamation ends with a call for calm at the time of the execution, so as to prove yet again the "enlightenment, religiosity, and understanding" at which the Cuban people had always excelled.

Someruelos is rehearsing a strategy that we will find time and again in the elite's dealings with slave rebellions and events potentially linked to Haiti. He reaffirms the hemispheric bonds of colonialism that link Cuba to Spain and denies any connections that would violate the boundaries of empire. Aponte's insurgency is presented as a unique event, the result of the megalomaniacal aspirations of one individual, with neither local nor foreign support for the uprising: the conspiracy was based on misinformation, delusions, and deception. Someruelos's proclamation betrays its secret through what it denies: by calling Aponte a "fantastic king," he conjures up the image of the Haitian king Henri Christophe, whose portrait had supposedly been in Aponte's possession. The coconspirators' attempt to "quench their stupid ambition with honors and occupations" again hints at the precedent in Haiti, where the former slaves had indeed received honors and employment by heads of state coming from their own ranks. The real specter behind Someruelos's calming and reassuring remarks to the enlightened public can be discerned only through the sequence of denials and denunciations. Haiti remains unnamed.

The political and strategic payoff of this redescription is clear. A dismissal of the political activities of the nonwhite population as delusionary fantasy would not preclude cautionary measures. But to the extent that the reality of these activities is acknowledged, their political meaning and transcendence are denied. By establishing a close link between the events of the conspiracy and the rumors about an abolitionist Spanish law, Someruelos disavows the revolutionary intent of Aponte and instead assimilates it to moderate abolitionism. This, it seems to me, is more important than his hard line on abolitionism itself: together with any possible connection with Haiti, he eliminates the third possibility, that of black agency, and of a slave revolution on the Haitian model.

Part of the extensive transcript compiled through three weeks of interrogation relates to a variety of artifacts that were reported to have been in Aponte's possession, among them portraits of Toussaint Louverture, Henri Christophe, and Dessalines. Most notable, however, was an oversized book wrapped in black oilskin that contained an eclectic array of more than sixty pictures with religious, political, and historical themes. The transcript of the interrogation about the pictures reads like a record of deadly hermeneutics: it takes us to the border point where transculturation and the fight over meaning turn into a struggle for dominance and survival, and where even the question of verisimilitude becomes a question of life or death.

## The Problem of Interpretation

The record of the Aponte trial is arguably the most powerful document we have of the imaginary of radical antislavery in the Caribbean. Like the antislavery narratives of the liberal elite, Aponte's book was, for the most part, propaganda literature.[2] It provides us with a glimpse of the forms of cultural production, the aesthetic preferences, and cultural practices that may have been associated with the struggle against slavery among those who lived in the plantation zone. It does not matter that a good number of the pictures have no obvious thematic connection to antislavery: they are testimony to forms of appropriation and resignification of cultural materials, which in turn could become the vehicle for subverting prevailing ideas of legitimate authority and articulating dissident ideas of liberation. More than any other document from the revolutionary age in the Caribbean, Aponte's transimperial, multilingual, and radically heterogeneous book is a reflection of the hemispheric scope of the slave economies as well as a testimony to the influence of revolutionary ideas coming from Haiti and France.

But like so much else that pertained to that cultural and political ambit, his work vanished. The only record we have is the transcript of the trial—not the sort of evidence to be taken at face value. And the problems go further than that. The strongly narrative character of many of the pictures described suggests that they were painted not to stand on their own but to be used in connection with oral instruction, perhaps on the model of wall paintings in Catholic churches, which always served as illustrations for the official exegetic discourse. Whereas the Creole abolitionist literature existed in a cultural sphere that was beginning to diversify and where individual works could be consumed in privacy, by simply following the rules of interpretation suggested by key terms such as *a novel* or *a cuadro costumbrista* (picture of local customs), Aponte's book is clearly more dependent on related social activities and contextual factors, which we may not be able to reconstruct.

The conflict over how to interpret the book is thus at least in part also a conflict over what sort of object it is. It is called a book, but most of the writing it contains is in Latin and English and not comprehensible for those who would contemplate the pictures. Had Aponte initiated a transnational practice of, say, revolutionary picture book making, perhaps we would now be in a better position to interpret the book. But the point of the proceedings was precisely to suppress such artifacts. So it was lost, destroyed, or stowed away in some attic and has not been seen since the time of the trial. The only remnants we have are the (interested, tainted, forced) testimonies of the accused, reflected in the transcripts of proceedings whose deadly outcome was clear from the beginning. The book's heterogeneous materials, its mixture of styles, topics, and purposes, make it almost impossible to find a historical or aesthetic term that would capture the nature of this artifact.

Further issues arise in relation to Aponte's biography. According to José Luciano Franco, Aponte was a Cuban-born cabinetmaker and artisan sculptor of Yoruba descent, who had his own workshop and occupied a position of distinction in the emerging petite bourgeoisie of free blacks and mulattoes. Like his grandfather, who had fought with the Spanish troops during the English occupation of Havana, Aponte held a military rank in the militia of free people of color. He was an active member in various religious and social organizations of African origin, the leader of his local Shangó-Tedum chapter, a member of a powerful Nigerian secret society, and a ranking member of the religious order of the Lucumí.[3] Unfortunately, Franco does not tell us in any detail where he collected this information; for the account of Aponte's activities in the Afro-Cuban religious community, Franco credits "oral history" in certain popular neighborhoods in Havana. The transcript of the proceedings, however, is completely devoid of any reference to Afro-Cuban religion.

One may wonder, then, how reliable Franco's account is, given that his gathering of oral testimony took place about 150 years after Aponte's death. But perhaps this skepticism is misplaced. The Afro-Cuban religions not only require secrecy from those inducted; they were also, throughout the nineteenth and twentieth centuries, subject to attempts to suppress them. It seems plausible that religious communities, especially if they operate in secrecy and suffer persecution, would provide an institutional frame in which memory and oral history would play a crucial role and thus be more stable and reliable than in other circumstances. If Franco's account of Aponte's role in Afro-Cuban religious and social institutions is true, it may have been Aponte's conscious decision to keep those connections out of the trial. The pictures may well have borne some similarities to contemporary Santería imagery. If so, we would also know that without information about the spatial organization of the pictures, this level of meaning will forever be beyond our reach:[4] unfortunately, the trial records give us few such indications beyond simple left and right distinctions.

But skepticism about our ability to read Aponte's book is not without its own dangers. There may of course have been some secret code or some hidden meaning in the pictures which has become lost to us through the double impact of distorted evidence and cultural discontinuity. But should we disregard the material we do have for a purely hypothetical gain or theoretical purity? Might we not, through our interpretative abstinence, end up underwriting the commission's attitude? After all, the investigators, too, assumed that Aponte's book could not be read simply as a piece of political and ideological work of the sort that anybody involved in a revolutionary struggle would produce. Interpretative humility might end up mimicking the colonial slaveholders' attempt to deny all forms of political agency and activity to the nonwhite population. Personally, I suspect that many of Aponte's pictures did not mean much more than what was obvious, and that it was the authorities' reluctance to recognize the political, ideological, and educational intent behind the pictures that prompted the prosecutors to keep asking for something else. Even if we give full weight to these cautionary considerations, they should not lead us to dismiss what we can learn about Aponte's political and educational work. The fragility of Aponte's image, its precarious status in the history of the emerging nation with traces in collective memory and criminal archives rather than official annals, is emblematic of the uncertain status of the emancipatory ideas he represents. The transcripts of Aponte's trial remain one of the most extraordinary records of the revolutionary Atlantic.

### Aponte's Book

Aponte's book appears to have been an eclectic assemblage of different media, materials, languages, and styles. The pictures range from religious to historical themes, from classical mythology to Spanish heroic history, from genre pictures to maps. There is a picture full of flames, a picture with vipers, and one that shows a broken crown and scepter that according to Aponte's testimony was given to him at the time of the French Revolution (170–71). Many of the pictures are internally syncretized and freely mix events and anecdotes from different cultures or mythologies. Picture 26, for instance, represents an encounter between the Cynic philosopher

Diogenes in his barrel and the Spanish king Rodrigo. Diogenes is shown as protected by the Egyptian goddess Isis, which explains, according to Aponte's comments on the picture, why Diogenes wins a battle of wits against the king (139–40).

The syncretism of content is mirrored by a syncretism of form: many of the pictures appear to be more like what we might call a collage than a Western-style painting. Appropriating whatever materials he could find, Aponte assembled, more than painted, the pictures. He would cut out landscapes from prints and fans, and even paste shards onto the paper (picture 1). For more complicated pictures, he relied on the assistance of a local boy who worked for a painters' shop and had a knack for drawing figures. Of course it is impossible to say what these pictures really looked like. However, it seems fairly clear that many pictures had a strong narrative character: picture 62, for instance, is described as representing the whole *Iliad* and *Odyssey*, complete with the rapture of Helena, the burning of Troy, Ulysses' travels, and the sirens (162). Given the narrative density and the enormous number of figures on some pages, I find it hard not to think of cartoon books where reductive outlining, the omission of anything that is not central to the action, and a combination of writing and drawing also allows for packed action.

One of the more incriminating pictures is described by Chacón: "There are two armies engaged in a battle, shooting, with several blacks mixed in with the one on the right: and the same on the following sheet, there are white and black soldiers; one of the black ones is on a horse, with a severed head on a pike, and another black who holds a severed head dripping with blood, the whites being here in the situation of the defeated" (113). When asked what the picture means, Chacón claims complete ignorance.

Another picture shows two ship landings, and a group of black men, some of them in secular, others in ecclesiastic, garb, among them an archbishop. Asked about the meaning of this picture, Chacón again claims ignorance but then adds that he remembers that "Cristoval Henriquez [Henri Christophe] . . . was pointing with the left hand and in the right hand [there was] a saber, with a sign at his feet which said 'Carry out what has been ordered' " (115).

One of the more puzzling moments in the trial is the discussion of an oil portrait that bears Aponte's name. In the interrogation, Chacón is asked "how he can be so sure that it is a portrait of Aponte . . . since there are no similarities between the copy and the original that would justify the designation." Chacón responds that Aponte told him so, and that he had explained that "he placed the portrait in the book so that it would be known the day of the revolution that he was an exemplary person and that it was foreseen that he would be King" (114). Now, if these pictures indeed represented Aponte, why did they not bear any resemblance to him? One possibility is that Aponte simply added his name to someone else's portrait, but that does not fit very well with the discussion of the picture during the interrogation of Aponte himself:

> The numbers twenty five and twenty six: In these the author of the book appears in a portrait, with the laurel of fidelity on his chest[,] the palm tree of victory[, and] apparently a ruler—to the left we can see the carpenter's bench where the book in question was produced . . . and infancy is represented by the figure of a child tied to a column and on the opposite page there is the face of an elderly person which means that the memory of infancy attains to old age, there are also on the bench an ink pot, a ruler, and pots of paint. (138)

Aponte denies Chacón's claim that the portrait showed him as a king after the revolution, pointing out the presence of rather unregal attributes such as a carpenter's bench and pots of paint (173).

What are we to make of a portrait that bears no similarity to the subject and that is variously interpreted as a portrait of a king and of a carpenter? Chacón's claim that it reflects Aponte's royal ambitions could be explained as an attempt to divert the blame from himself to Aponte. After all, in the end all conspirators blame each other. The council might have fed Chacón the answer, or more likely, it was obvious to him that the council was most concerned with any Haitian connection or influence, and connecting Aponte to the "Haitian" idea of a black king would have been an effective way of denouncing him. The problem with this is that it does not explain why Aponte does not simply deny that the pictures are indeed portraits of him—a more plausible defense in light of the lack of similarity between the copy and the original—and instead disputes that they show him as a Cuban king.

For these reasons, I am inclined to think that the ambiguities surrounding the pictures have deeper roots, which lead us back to the problem of the discontinuities in the cultures of radical antislavery and the fragmentation and truncation to which associated cultural practices were submitted in the early nineteenth century. It seems clear that pictures 25 and 26 did not conform to the rules of portraiture as they were known to the council. One of the great inventions of Renaissance portraiture in Europe was, arguably, a set of techniques that would allow for the skillful freezing of time. Although based on lengthy and repeated sittings, the portrait does not suggest narrative duration. Physiognomy becomes condensed, lived time. In the case of Aponte's picture, the opposite seems to be true: instead of integrating a whole life span into one quasi-fictional moment, life is divided into its phases. Instead of capturing lived time in one expressive face, the face expresses nothing, does not even establish identity. Instead of affirming a state of being, instead of condensing the past into a present moment, then, the portrait anticipates the transformation of a carpenter into a personage of special standing, possibly even a king. If the conventional Western portrait is a study in character and social status and is thus deeply invested in the established social order, Aponte's portrait is a study in becoming or transfiguration. It is a portrait, we might say, determined by the future, not the past, and therefore unconcerned with verisimilitude. The past can be submitted to a cumulative calculation: time, social standing, money, and power can be shown as having accrued in the subject, and having left their traces on the face. But no accumulation is possible from the future. Future events that would bestow power and social standing on a person cannot be shown condensed; they cannot relinquish their narrativity and can be shown only as what they are—a certain number of future events that will transform a black carpenter into a king.

Entering further into the area of speculation, we might also wonder if the dispute over whether the portrait shows Aponte as king is a reflection of the fact that the uprising envisioned by the 1812 conspirators did not aim at the establishment of any particular political regime or state form. Perhaps it simply did not matter whether the portrait showed Aponte as a king, president, elder statesman, Captain General, or simply an eminent person. As we will see in part 3, the first heads of state in postrevolutionary Haiti certainly kept changing the state form and, along with that, their titles as heads of state.[5] Clearly, this account does not answer all questions. But it does explain why the council would have been unable to recognize the picture as a portrait of Aponte, and why Aponte might have felt that it was at least plausible to claim the picture as a portrait while denying that it represented him as a king.

### Geographies of the Black Atlantic

In the transcripts of the interrogations, a political and cultural geography emerges which is strikingly different from that of later Creole writers, or metropolitan abolitionists, for that matter. Instead of the colonial bond so strongly invoked by Someruelos, Aponte's book points us to Haiti and to Africa. Abyssinia and Egypt are the background to many pictures, the Nile appears several times, and even the Nilometer is invoked once. There are African animals, and people of African descent in Roman libraries and Mediterranean battle scenes (154). As Aponte himself explained, the inspiration came, for the most part, from his readings in world history, though occasionally he also refers to oral tradition ("lo sabe por conversación" [149]) and informal channels of communication.[6]

Although Egypt and Abyssinia are named in the proceedings, Haiti's presence is more subterraneous. Clearly, the insurgents would not have voluntarily brought it up in the interrogation, and so it exists only as an allusion within the heterogeneous practices and symbolic acts that Aponte and his coconspirators developed for their political purposes. One of the conspirators adopted the pseudonym of Juan Francisco, after the Haitian general Jean François.[7] A suspected adviser to Aponte was Gil Narciso, who had fought with the Spanish against the French in Saint Domingue. An extensive investigation concerns the portraits of Haitian generals and leaders that were reported to have been in Aponte's possession. Admitting that he had at one point owned portraits of the Haitian generals, whom he refers to with their Hispanized names, Luvertú, Salinas, Juan Francisco, and Cristóbal, and describes as "French Blacks" (172), Aponte claims that he burned them when he found out that they were illegal in Cuba. He also denies that they had been sent to him from Haiti, as claimed by Chacón earlier. Rather, Aponte says, he copied two of them himself and bought the other two at the mall in the harbor of Havana at a time when these portraits were circulating everywhere. A witness's testimony is interesting here, as it speaks to the ubiquity of Haitian icons in Cuba at the time as well as to the popularity they enjoyed.

> There was a black King that Aponte had painted and he showed him [the witness] how he had done it . . . the Captain of the Militia of Blacks took the picture or portrait of said King with him, assuring him that he was called Enrique the First, King of Aiti, keeping it for something like three weeks and then returning them [sic] according to Aponte's account, who explained that many had asked him for the portrait, and that he had copied it from another one. (195)

Completely aware of the danger that any connection to the Haitian king signified, the witness claims that he went to see the portrait only to "poke fun at it."

As the proceedings are drawing to a close, an eerie incident occurs. A Spanish cadet presents himself in front of the commission with the report that a little piece of paper with a portrait of Henri Christophe had been found on the ground in the fortress of La Cabaña.[8] More witnesses are called in, and further inquiries ensue: apparently, an unnamed mulatto who was being led back to prison had dropped the folded picture on the floor. The published proceedings do not say whether the mulatto was then prosecuted, and no speculations are offered about why someone would "lose" a little folded portrait in a prison. Was it by mistake? Was this a prison communications network? Did little folded portraits circulate elsewhere? I have no answers to these questions. Perhaps one day we will be able to draw a more complete picture of the events at the time. But it will not be easy—the repression of the revolutionary Atlantic was severe, and there are few lines of tradition or continuity that would allow us to venture a hypothesis.

If we think about Aponte in the context of the Creole literary and cultural practices that were emerging in the first decades of the nineteenth century, the difference is rather striking. Unlike the costumbristas, for instance, whose reference point always was the local and picturesque, Aponte's educational and pictorial work is transatlantic and canonical in its references. His vindication of black people is based not on sheer "difference"—the emerging national discourse would appeal to that—but on high-cultural achievement. And it is in this context that Haiti and Africa appear side by side.

Given that Aponte's book needed to be persuasive, and given also his central position in Afro-Cuban life at the time, one would assume that his interest in Egypt is not entirely idiosyncratic. While in a privileged position as a literate free black man, he was most likely drawing on knowledge that was circulating in the harbor cities of the Caribbean. It seems improbable that Aponte's revolutionary geography is entirely of his own making. The interesting question that arises, then, is what explains this proximity of revolutionary Haiti, Egypt, and Africa: are they just contingently linked, or could there be genealogical connections between them? Given that both Haiti and Egypt figured prominently in early black nationalist thought in the United States, this issue has implications not just for our understanding of the Caribbean cultural context but possibly for the entire African diaspora in the Americas.[9]

The question has given rise to extended polemics, particularly in the aftermath of the publication of Martin Bernal's *Black Athena*.[10] Although this is not the place to analyze the complexities of that debate, it is worth noting that neither Bernal nor his detractors appear to have contemplated the possibility that the Caribbean plantation zone and the events of the Haitian Revolution might have been the environment where European Enlightenment ideas about Egypt were transfigured into a popular liberationist theory that would have Egypt as one of its central elements.[11]

Bernal argues that from antiquity until the late eighteenth century, Egypt was conceived as the cradle of civilization and Greece as a mere colonial outpost, a marginal culture in relation to Middle Eastern and North African cultures. Egypt exercised enormous fascination, and Freemasonry in particular—a culture very much at the center of Enlightenment cultural practices—derived its ritual aspects, names, iconography, and so on from Egyptian sources.[12] In an argument that really turns on the rise of anti-Semitism rather than the development of Afrocentric theories, Bernal shows that during the first decades of the nineteenth century, Egypt is demoted from its earlier position. Interestingly enough, he thus locates the "disappearance" of Egypt in the period in which the Aponte uprising takes place and in which, as I argue, the syncretistic transnational modernity associated with radical antislavery is suppressed along with many forms of cultural production by mulattoes and blacks. Of course, there are a number of possibilities we might consider at this point. It might be that Aponte had Masonic connections within Cuba. Since he was quite possibly involved in the anti-Spanish Masonic conspiracy of 1810, this is not altogether implausible. But it is also possible that Aponte's knowledge of Egypt and his political reinterpretation of archaeological data originated somewhere in the French cultural ambit, and that they came to him via Haiti.[13]

One of the most informative studies on Freemasonry in the French Antilles during the revolutionary period is an article by one André Combes, whose institutional affiliation is listed as "Institut d'études maçonniques (Paris)." According to Combes, by 1789 Freemasonry was well established in the Caribbean, with almost forty lodges in the French territories. Saint Domingue had the most active Masonic culture, with at least one lodge in all major towns. Whereas in the colonies these lodges were generally closed to blacks and mulattoes, it appears that at least some mulattoes were inducted while in France. Upon their return to Saint Domingue, some were allowed to enter the lodges in the capacity of apprentice or "brother servant" and were put in charge of the upkeep of the temples. Most white Masons either left the island or were killed during the civil wars; the archives were burned, and the temples were destroyed. But apparently the few white survivors continued their practice clandestinely, inducting the future Haitian general Guy Joseph Bonnet, the official Louis Dieudonné, and Toussaint Louverture. And although Freemasonry was officially prohibited during Dessalines's rule, there were four lodges in Pétion's republic. About Masonry in Henri Christophe's Kingdom of the North, Combes says that "a certain d'Obernay established a 'Maçonnerie fantaisiste de Hauts-Grades' [a fanciful Masonry of High Order]," thereby suggesting, I assume, that Masons under Henri Christophe lacked legitimacy.[14] Further links between Masonry and antislavery come from the opposite direction: Brissot, the founder of the Amis des Noirs, as well as the later abolitionist Schoelcher, were Masons, and it appears that the deputy most often chosen by the Antillean lodges to represent them in the metropolis was the Brother de Loly, a well-known antislavery activist.[15]

The question, then, is whether a link exists between Enlightenment Freemasonry and the appearance of Egypt in the imaginary of black emancipation. In *Afrotopia* Wilson Jeremiah Moses points out that Bernal's hypothesis of a Masonic link between European Enlightenment culture and Egyptocentrism in black nationalism remains largely unsubstantiated and contradicted by the fact that Egypt is strangely absent from the writings of early black Masons in the United States, who were, for the most part, clergymen who identified with the biblical Hebrews rather than the pagan Egyptians.[16] These arguments seem plausible, and Moses is certainly right to deplore the failure of both Bernal and his detractors to check their speculations against the writings of nineteenth-century black intellectuals.

However, Moses' objection to assigning a central role to Masonic culture has its own important blind spot, which comes to haunt him when he links Egyptocentrism to the socially conservative contemporary black nationalism of the Louis Farrakhan variety, with its defense of high culture and rejection of the "scatological values of gangsta rap" and "signifying monkeys" (234–35). The historical process that emerges from Moses' account is a fairly continuous development of a body of thought concerned with the vindication of achievements of people of African descent. To be sure, there are silences in this trajectory, too (as the example of Lefkowitz, among many others, illustrates), but it is ultimately a process that can be reconstructed in a recuperative narrative.

Against this picture, I submit that the trope of African Egypt may have been subjected to radical transvaluations, which in turn reflect the suppression of revolutionary antislavery in the early nineteenth century. Egyptocentrism could have entered diasporic African cultures through the connection between French revolutionary Masons and black antislavery, a connection that most likely came into being during the revolution in Saint Domingue. Under the influence of local antislavery, it would have become an ideological module that could easily become separated from specifically Masonic or hermetic practices.[17] Whether or not José Antonio Aponte was familiar with Masonic practices, it seems that in his mind, Egypt is associated with the events of the Haitian Revolution and black resistance against enslavement. Caribbean Egyptocentrism would be an outstanding example of a modern syncretism where emancipatory ideas that originated in the plantation zone and European notions of history entered into contact and congealed into a political practice of liberation, which eventually forgot (or disavowed) its own prehistory.

Like black nationalists in the United States, Haitian writers throughout the nineteenth century insisted that Egypt was the source of European civilization, that Egyptians were black Africans, and that this fact was "a major point against the doctrine of the inequality of the races."[18] Dr. Casseus, the author of the phrase just quoted, appealed in support of his views to Herodotus, who is, of course, one of the crucial sources for Bernal, as well. Now, to show that Egyptocentrism indeed entered the cultural and political imaginary of black intellectuals in the United States through the revolutionary Caribbean, further evidence from the plantation zone would be needed to bridge the gap between 1812 and the late 1820s, when the pamphlet "The Mutability of Human Affairs" (published in *Freedom's Journal*, April 6, 1827) and Robert Alexander Young's "Ethiopian Manifesto" (1829) appeared.[19] Particularly interesting would be an analysis of the interactions between biblical and revolutionary strands of thought within early black nationalism. Unfortunately, these questions exceed the scope of this book, but it would seem that any attempt to think of the black Atlantic in relation to modernity would do well to pursue these intricate processes of transvaluation and transculturation that took place in the Age of Revolution.

Not unlike negritude or other forms of twentieth-century pan-Africanism, then, Aponte celebrates Egyptian achievements and the contributions of Africans to Western culture. Yet what animates this geography is not so much Africa itself but neighboring Haiti. Whereas in the twentieth century the pan-Africanism of the negritude movement was opposed by later generations of Caribbean intellectuals, who sought to ground Antillean identity in the diasporic cultures of the Caribbean, in Aponte's book, we find traces of both views. There is a certain undeniable pan-Africanism, but the center of this pan-Africanism is located not in Africa but in the Caribbean.

The reason for this is, I think, that at the time there was still a revolutionary culture alive on both sides of the Atlantic, in which fragments of political discourse and cultural artifacts could circulate, and in which the first independent black state occupied a key position. In these informational circuits, revolutionary ideas and practices were continuously reported, commented on, appropriated, and reinterpreted. To be sure, revolutionary France was an important force in the emergence of this network and the articulation of revolutionary projects. But revolutionary antislavery itself was born in Saint Domingue rather than in Paris, and it was the events in the colony that pushed the French Assembly to finally pass the law that abolished slavery in 1794, and the revolutionary culture did not disappear when reaction took over in Paris. It is in this transnational, multilingual circuit that images of Africa and Egypt join those of kings deposed and white armies defeated.

If my hypothesis about the Caribbean transculturation of Egyptocentrism is correct, the later trajectory of this ideology in the United States could only be considered as a final bitter irony. Eventually it became a venue for debating race against the emerging forms of anthropological scientism and scientific racism, and the embattled new state of Haiti slowly lost its appeal as an example for black achievement.[20] Instead of the explicitly political and revolutionary claims of an earlier Egyptocentrism, we find a debate framed by the claims of science.[21] As the syncretistic modernity of the plantation zone, with its strong links to radical antislavery, was suppressed, even the history of transculturation of Egyptocentrism is forgotten. Having come to the Americas via revolutionary Haiti, Egypt eventually replaces Haiti as a prime example of an African civilization, now understood in the terms provided by scientistic notions of race.

### The Return of the Repressed

If we look for traces of Aponte in later years, we find very little. Cuba, like most Caribbean islands, turned inward in search for grounds of local difference. There may be a shadow of Aponte's erudite syncretism in the figure of the *negro catedrático* (Negro professor), always played in blackface, in the Teatro Bufo of the second half of the nineteenth century.[22] The play that appears to have inaugurated this genre in 1868 ends as follows:

No soy más que un catedrático,
que busca con su gramática,
Elíptica y sistemática,
La rígida clave técnica,
Política, pirotécnica,
Quirúrgica, y problemática.[23]

[I am just a "professor"
Who searches with his grammar,
Systematic and elliptical,
The rigid technical
Political, pyrotechnical,
Surgical and problematic key.]

In the sequel, also in 1868, we witness the induction of a "Congo" (meaning a black man born in Africa) whose garbled Spanish is barely intelligible, into the culture of *catedratismo*. His Cuban-born teacher excuses the slowness of his progress: "Thus far he has only studied Nebrija and Calepino and has superficially leafed through Cicero. He has only taken two courses at the lyrical university, which is why he is not shining in the plenitude of his enthusiasm." To which Congo replies: "Yo tá creyendo eso cosa matemáticamente sempiterna" [I believe this a mathematically sempiternal matter] (85–86). The jokes clearly turn on the absurdity of people of African descent appropriating erudite European culture—a process that obviously entails radical resignification, since the appropriation takes place outside those institutions that reproduce and legitimate knowledge, and it may be more than coincidence that a book entitled *Arte Nebrija* was among the books found in Aponte's possession.[24] The "lyrical university" of the "Negro professors" is the street and neighborhood, where the epistemological asceticism of European higher education would be of little use and creative grafting of exotic vocabularies becomes, judging from the play, a competitive game. It is not surprising, then, that in the third part of the play, the Congo turns into the only positive figure of the comedy when he rejects the pretensions of the Creole blacks and returns to work on the docks of Havana.

Yet despite all of this, the memory of the Aponte uprising continued to linger in popular oral traditions and in the minds of people fearful of what might happen if proper precautions were not taken. Almost a hundred years later, on the eve of the declaration of the Cuban Republic, the events of the 1812 conspiracy are called up again by Francisco Calcagno, the author of the first study of poets of color in Cuba and certainly no apologist for slavery. His historical novel *Aponte* opens with a gory depiction of the conspirator's severed head, surrounded by flies and an unbearable stench: a barbaric monster with "a soul as black as his face" and savagely sharpened crocodile teeth who had modeled himself on Dessalines and Christophe.[25] The novel's story, however, stays clear of Aponte and instead focuses on a fictional mulatto slave who joins Aponte after having been used as bait in a complicated plot of revenge that turns on class prejudice among whites. The insurgent hordes remain a threatening, dangerous force beyond the limits of the narrative. Aponte is the name of the unspeakable catastrophe that ensues if Cuban society cannot resolve the tensions between social classes.

In Calcagno's novel, Aponte, and racial warfare in general, are contained, it seems, through a narrative displacement: what seemed prior—namely, racial warfare—is shown to be posterior; what seemed to be the cause of danger is shown to be the effect. The political claims of the enslaved population and their allies exist only as epiphenomena of other conflicts. The literary fiction thus transposes a conflict that apparently cannot be addressed directly. It is Calcagno's merit to have found an articulation that lets a repressed, fearsome memory seep back into public sphere; to become knowledge again. But in doing so, he illustrates the fact that even after abolition, independence is thinkable only after the black insurgent is eliminated from the body politic. Aponte's name continues to mark the distance between conflicting ideas of emancipation.

# 2

## Civilization and Barbarism

CUBAN WALL PAINTING

If José Antonio Aponte was not just the deluded and obscure individual the Count of Someruelos made him out to be; if he was, Someruelos's disavowal notwithstanding, a member of some import in the emerging culture of free people of color who understood how to represent the stories, ideas, and images that were circulating among the people he associated with, we may wonder whether the method of instruction he chose for his educational and political work has some significance, as well. Was it merely a coincidence that he chose to produce a picture book? Was he just an inventive *bricoleur,* or was he using a cultural idiom that was of particular prestige among the people he was addressing? If the latter, what happened to that idiom and to the people who were familiar with it in the course of the nineteenth century?

In 1996 I went to Havana with these questions in mind. One can of course imagine any number of venues for the articulation and dissemination of radical ideas—the Afro-Cuban social and religious associations that José Luciano Franco mentions in connection with Aponte are as plausible as the informal circuits of communication in Caribbean harbors documented by Julius Scott.[1] But it seemed to me that one should not simply forget the fact that Aponte's ideological work expressed itself through paintings.

Historical accounts of the visual arts in Cuba usually acknowledge an early painterly tradition under the rubrics of "the primitives" or "the precursors"—a folk tradition of sorts about which we know very little.[2] Most of the artisans remained anonymous, appeared to be men of color in their majority, and worked outside the European traditions of academic and religious painting. The story that emerges from Cuban art histories thus typically posits an archaic practice which is discontinuous with later high-cultural painting and is eventually replaced by the more academic styles that were introduced in Cuba with the foundation of the Academy San Alejandro in 1818.[3]

Mindful of Aponte, the artisan, sculptor, and picture book maker, I thought that perhaps those so-called primitive painters, or at least the fact of their disappearance, could be tied to the suppression of radical antislavery and the subaltern circuits of communication in which knowledge about Haiti was passed on. If one only asked the right questions, perhaps information would turn up.

To my surprise and initial gratification, I arrived in Havana to find much more physical evidence of the primitive painters than I had expected. In the process of the restoration of Old Havana, crews were taking down recent alterations to the buildings and removing layers of paint and plaster. Mural paintings that had not been seen since the 1840s or 1850s were reappearing in many places in the old city (figs. 1 and 2). With new optimism, I turned to library collections and archives to see whether I might find some information about the artists who decorated the colonial mansions. What was their social status? How did they operate, and how were they trained? Why did such a popular custom disappear? I looked through several decades of the *Papel Periódico* (the first Cuban newspaper), the official *Diario del Gobierno de La Habana,* the printed *Actas de las Juntas Generales* of the Real Sociedad Económica de Amigos del País, and even the manuscripts of the minutes of the society's meetings. I read the archival materials about the first Cuban Academy of Drawing and Painting. I consulted with research librarians and specialists on colonial art in Havana museums. I talked to church archivists and historians at the Cathedral of Havana and the Franciscan convent in Guanabacoa. With the physical evidence that was emerging in the old city in mind, I thought that buried somewhere in the extensive collections of colonial documents there must surely be some information about the people who had produced these paintings.

What I found were plentiful polemics against the primitive painters and artisans, but very little that could be counted as positive documentation. That these painters were typically people of color was beyond doubt; further details were hard to come by. After two months of following up on any possible lead, it became clear that if there was a political story to be told, it had to be reconstructed indirectly. Between the visual evidence that is now reemerging and the textual evidence that can be gathered from nineteenth-century sources, it is possible to get a sense of what the popular paintings may have looked like. The story of the devaluation and suppression of certain "barbaric" forms of cultural production can also be documented. The moralization of questions of taste, the slightly excessive expressions of disgust, the frequent remarks about the

1. The mansion of the Marquéz de Arcos in the process of reconstruction; note the small window opened to a wall painting under the plaster (bottom left) and the note by the restorers, "Do not touch." Photo by Sibylle Fischer.

*Below*
2. Facade of a building facing the Plaza Vieja, Old Havana, with mural decorations, probably from the eighteenth century. Photo by Pedro Abascal.

undesirability of a class of artisans of color, and so on certainly suggest that more was at stake than aesthetic concerns. It is clear that the worries that transpire in the elite discourses about popular painting were not independent of the fact that most of the artisans were men of color. In the end, I found that this is the story that can be told. However, the culture that vanished—its mode of operation, its composition, its origins, its political role—remains elusive.

Like Aponte's picture book, and like Plácido's poetry, which I will discuss in the next chapter, the story of the primitive painters thus illustrates the deeply conflictive, contestatory nature of Caribbean culture in the Age of Revolution. The pronounced anxiety among white Creoles about the fact that people of color had come to dominate most forms of cultural production suggests that it was the memories of the Haitian events and related uprisings that in the end shaped Cuban culture and cultural politics. From the polemics that developed around painting, we can see that aesthetic discourse became a form of legitimization of white Creole hegemony. In some sense, the primitive painters are a creation of those who claimed to have superseded them. Conventional narratives of modernization that adopt the tripartite scheme of archaic, utilitarian, and autonomous art unwittingly obscure this fact, it seems to me, even where they acknowledge the racial implications of the marginalization of the popular painters. What came to be taught in the first academy of the arts in Cuba may look to us like merely utilitarian art. But for white Creoles at the time, the main issue was aesthetic hierarchies: they preferred drawing to painting not because it was more useful but because it was not contaminated by the primitive practices of the painters of color.[4]

## Winged Hearts, Tame Deer:
### The Vices of Popular Taste

Nineteenth-century travelers in Cuba occasionally commented on the fanciful paintings the local population used to decorate the walls and facades of their houses.[5] In 1828 the Reverend Abiel Abbot, a visitor from the United States who was hoping to cure his tuberculosis in the beneficial climate of the Caribbean, writes, bemused and perhaps a little titillated, that wherever one looked there were wall paintings of "birds, animals, snakes, men and women at work and having fun, and some things and images that, although not strictly forbidden by the law, do not represent anything in heaven or on earth or in the waters below the earth."[6] He refrained from elaborating on how something that does not represent anything in particular can still be against the spirit of the law, but fortunately other travelers' sensibilities were not quite as easily offended.

A quarter of a century later, Frederika Bremer, a feminist writer of Swedish-Finnish extraction who spent three months in Cuba in 1851, also comments on the paintings. In her letters, she praises Havana for its romantic atmosphere of ruins and decaying structures. "Next to a brilliantly painted wall," she writes, "there is a crumbling wall with faded frescos some of which have peeled off with the plaster. And nobody repairs the old wall, or touches up the old painting."[7] By midcentury, murals are associated with things of the past. Bremer, clearly more intrepid than most travelers at the time, also tells us about her discovery of paintings in the Afro-Cuban cabildos: the *gangás,* she reports, exhibit, in among Catholic pictures and devotionalia, a huge and well-executed picture of a leopard— probably, she speculates, the symbol of their nation, whereas in the cabildo of the *congos* there is a wall painting of a human face.[8]

The local elite tended to be less indulgent about the primitive painters and typically failed to see the romantic aspect of crumbling frescoes. Beginning with the first issues of the Havana newspaper *Papel Periódico* in the early 1790s, we find articles and columns that severely criticize the state of neglect of the colony and the absence of "good taste," even in urban areas. In a letter to the editor, someone complains about misspelled street signs and similar manifestations of backwardness: the "Calle de Paula" is "Calle de Paubla," the "Calle de San Isidro" "Calle de Isdro," and in this vein, there are "an infinite number of absurdities which discredit the good taste that generally rules in this country. . . . And what do we say when we observe those signs of ignorance even in the Sanctuary, where everything should be grave and majestic! Upon entering the church of the monastery of M., the first thing one notices is a picture of our Lord of the Rescue, and along with some enormous imperfections in the artistic execution, one reads a sign at the bottom which says that the picture had been touched up by some blacks; and true enough, the handwriting and the orthography shows that it was put there by them, and that they had recently arrived from Angola. It is embarrassing to repeat here the sign as it can be seen in the original. May the curious go and find it."[9] The letter ends with a call for popular education to eradicate these sorts of things.

Barely a year later, the *Papel Periódico* again publishes denunciations of the bad taste displayed in the decoration of public buildings: "In churches, where good taste, propriety, and delicacies of Architecture ought to rule, we do not see anything except the madness and infelicitous whims of an unruly imagination. Instead of noble and majestic facades that would announce the dignity of the house of the Lord, we only see monstrous bodies, members out of proportion, ridiculous moldings, overcrowded adornments, without skill, without judgement, and without expression."[10] Another article, published the following month, proclaims that "the best decoration is painting used economically, with good taste."[11] Yet all over Havana there is a craze for decorations of the facades with "piled-up adornments" and "the worst kinds of paintings" amounting to "monstrous faces" for the otherwise perfectly regular bodies of the mansions.

More than a half century later, after the capital city and public buildings have undergone extensive renovation, the annexationist Maturin M. Ballou writes:

As the visitor penetrates further into the island, he will frequently notice on the facades of the piled-up dwellings attempts to represent various birds and animals, similar to anything other than what they are meant to signify; the most surprising characteristic [of these paintings] is the garish color and the considerable size. Pigeons have the colossal appearance of ostriches, and the dogs are excessively elephantine in proportions. This strange fantasy can be observed amply in the outskirts of Havana, where attempts have been made at painting domestic scenes and characters of both sexes who are engaged in corresponding occupations. If such ridiculous things were found anywhere outside Cuba, they would be called caricatures, but here they are regarded with the utmost complacency and naively considered ornamental. For some reason, this is a very generalized passion among the lower classes and can be observed in the vicinity of Matanzas and Cárdenas, as well as further away in the interior of the island, in small hamlets.[12]

The Cuban novelist and essayist Cirilo Villaverde gives us a similar view of the practice. In his travel narrative of the late 1830s titled *Excursion to Vuelta Abajo,* he describes the moment when he and his foreign travel companion enter a little store for a light lunch.

It was something to be seen—the bad paintings [*mamarrachos*] that were daubed on the walls, especially in the living room. On the front wall to the left, there was a landscape, or an attempt at that, with various trees and a hunter in the foreground, the latter being recognizable by the rifle he was carrying, in a shooting position; also by the birds that rested on it, taking it perhaps for a branch of a tree. Facing this outlandish, bizarre painting there was a domestic scene of our peasant population, with an attempt to imitate their way of dressing. The figures—there were four of them—

seemed as if made of cardboard and were so crude that they could have been puppets. The first is, or seems to be, a pig that follows a laborer who has assumed the posture of receiving from the hands of a peasant girl—who is seen from the front—a winged heart that she presents to him on a fork; between the two characters a deer is sticking out its head, a deer that is no more fearful of people than of the grass under its feet. What would the world think of us if, as a result of a catastrophe like the one that buried Pompeii, these paintings were transmitted to posterity? All of this would not matter, nor would the wall daubing in the country inns call for our attention . . . were it not the case that, thanks to our backwardness in the arts and our poor taste, the obsession with daubing the walls of our houses is, though less intensely in the present, still very common not only in the villages, but also in our very city.[13]

Oblivious of the laws of perspective and the rules of good taste, the popular painters create their two-dimensional, cartoonlike figures by merely filling in outlines. With little concern for realism and proportion, they paint a fantastic scene of imaginary beasts and licentious behavior. Clearly, trusting deer and winged hearts on pitchforks are offensive to an aesthetics that prizes local realities for their ability to inspire awe, and artistic representations for their realistic rendition of these realities. Where a European traveler—leaning perhaps on the memory of Roman and Greek ruins—might experience the romantic sublime, local writers saw a convergence of colonial baroque and folk art in a taste that betrayed only back-wardness and barbarism. Bremer's romantic reverie encounters its mirror image in Villaverde's horror at the very thought that the paintings might be preserved by a volcanic eruption. Whereas the murals of Pompeii testify to civilization's origins, their Cuban coun-terparts prompt the nightmare of an eternal monument to primitiv-ism: underdevelopment is not the condition for future development but its eternal fetter.

But of course, Villaverde's worries were misplaced. Were it not for his own travel narrative, along with a few others, the Cuban mural tradition might have been lost entirely. Most paintings disintegrated in the humidity. Others were destroyed together with the structures that carried them or were covered under layers of plaster and paint. What might have been a topic for art historians has thus become an archaeologist's project of discovery and restoration.[14]

To complicate matters further, there is a striking discrepancy be-tween the accounts of nineteenth-century travelers and the archae-ological evidence. The latter indicates that it was the wealthy mer-chants and the richer churches and convents who requested the

3. View of the little salon with several panels of floor-to-ceiling paintings; from left to right: a harbor scene (see fig. 4), a riding scene (third panel), and a formal garden; in the foreground, a bust and a display case unrelated to the paintings (today Calle Tacón 8 in Old Havana). Photo by Pedro Abascal.

4. Detail of fig. 3: a harbor with a large vessel in the right quarter of the picture and palm trees arching over the water from the background. Photo by Pedro Abascal.

services of the painters. The number and location of the recently discovered paintings suggest that they were highly appreciated by the white Creoles. Yet Creole writers typically argued that wall paintings corresponded to the taste of the popular classes and were mostly found on the outskirts of the city and in the countryside.[15] The only written indication that the murals were in fact valued by the local elite is a record of an estimate that the well-known painter Nicolás de la Escalera (1734–1804) made of some murals in what is today the Casa de Guasamín in Old Havana, probably at a time when the house was put up for sale.[16] It appears, then, that between the late eighteenth century and the mid–nineteenth century, the taste of the Creole elite underwent considerable change, and that while the popular classes continued to appreciate fanciful decorations of their houses, the elite abandoned this custom in favor of more Europeanized styles of decoration, so that by the middle of the century, Bremer would describe wall paintings either as part of the decaying structures or as the property of specific subcultures.

This is borne out by the archaeological record. Although to my knowledge no murals of oversize birds, elephantine dogs, and men and women engaged in inappropriate activities have appeared so far, there is a fairly wide range of style in the murals that have resurfaced. One of the most intriguing sites is what the restorers humorously refer to as the "Sistine Chapel of La Habana":[17] a fairly small salon, originally probably a sitting or sewing room, on the second floor of a colonial dwelling in Old Havana, decorated on all four walls with figurative murals in pastel shades of blue and green that reach from the floor to the ceiling (fig. 3). One of the central, and best-preserved, panels depicts a natural harbor from a bird's-eye perspective familiar from old maps (fig. 4). While the bay and the surrounding hills are presented in semirelief and give a fairly good sense of the geographic features—in fact, the bay bears a striking resemblance to the shape of the harbor of Havana—other elements are added for clearly decorative purposes, most notably a couple of palm trees that arch over the bay from the background and dwarf all other features of the painting, including a vessel that seems grand in relation to the size of the bay, but minute compared to the palm trees. Other panels represent landscapes and tree-lined avenues with little cartoonlike figures, men on horseback, and similar picturesque scenes one might perhaps otherwise expect on a vase or a plate. The size and location of the room indicate that the decorative painting was unlikely to have been commissioned for the purpose of public representation of the power and wealth of the family. It was meant, it would seem, to provide comfort and amusement to the women who gathered there to perform their chores.

But this is not true for all murals. The former mansion of the preeminent theorist of the slaveholding aristocracy, Francisco Arango y Parreño,[18] contains a huge romantic landscape of European character—clearly not representing any Cuban site—that was probably the main feature of a large entry hall and stairwell. Since the building has been converted into *solares* (tenements), with little cubicles constructed on the side of a staircase facing the patio, the painting now covers the inside wall of a narrow staircase. Light fixtures and wires have been attached to the mural, and large pieces of paint have been chipped off over the years. Nevertheless it is obvious that Arango y Parreño's mural by no means represents the popular style described by Villaverde and Ballou.

Buildings that have murals at all often have several layers of them: up to twelve layers have been found in private homes, and up to twenty-three in the Convent of San Francisco de Assis. Generally speaking, the changes reflect the increasing Europeanization and standardization of taste.[19] The earliest paintings from the late eighteenth century and the early nineteenth are often boldly representational or at least integrate representational features (figs. 5 and 6); in later layers, we find more geometrical, neoclassical ornamentation. While mural decorations in living quarters tend to continue to include little vignettes, stairwells typically have ornamental repetitive patterns which in the course of a few decades develop from Pompeian-inspired patterns into imitations of marble and *azulejos* (tiles) (figs. 7, 8, and 9).[20] Instead of freehand drawing, which gave plenty of room for imaginative perspectives and proportions, the use of stencils became more and more common. This change of taste, from the fanciful barbarism of nonperspectival drawing to the ornamental symmetries of neoclassicism, tracks a decline in cost (and thus prestige value), as well: it was clearly cheaper to have local artisans repaint the wall than to put up tiles, which were a recent innovation in Cuban architecture and had to be imported, or wallpaper, which would have required frequent replacement in the humid climate.

Recovery of the tradition that fell out of favor has its own technical and methodological challenges. In the early days of the restoration of Havana, archaeologists tended to take all layers of plaster and paint off to expose the oldest one. Nowadays they usually expose only the most recent layer of wall painting, perhaps creating little "windows" that would show older layers. This way, the more recent

5. Small figurative vignette, part of painted wainscoting: putti frolicking on apples; freehand drawing, probably late eighteenth century. Photo by Pedro Abascal.

6. Small figurative vignette, part of painted wainscoting: uniformed guard with landscape in the background; freehand drawing, probably late eighteenth century. Photo by Pedro Abascal.

7. Pompeian-style wainscoting in a second-floor salon (today Calle Obispo 103, Old Havana); the break in the middle is probably due to a partition wall that at some point divided the salon into two separate rooms. Photo by Pedro Abascal.

8. Wall painting as imitation of *azulejos;* note an earlier layer (probably Pompeian style) in a window in the center of the picture (mansion of the Marquéz de Arcos). Photo by Pedro Abascal.

9. Wall painting in neoclassical style: imitation of marble (today Calle Mercaderes 111). Photo by Pedro Abascal.

layers are not destroyed for all future generations—but of course, the early period of the late eighteenth century and the early nineteenth remains even more remote and inaccessible. Other problems are of a technical nature. Most of the murals are not pure frescoes but combine fresco techniques, semifresco, and painting on finished walls. Perhaps the painters did not work fast enough to finish before the wall was dry; perhaps only a few were trained to do frescoes, which are technically more demanding than semifrescoes and wall painting. The problem is that the latter are much less durable, and exposed paintings deteriorate very quickly once they have been exposed to light by restorers.

While the reconstruction of Old Havana is proceeding, and more and more paintings are being uncovered, no specialized studies of the wall paintings have been published so far, and we still have to make do without concrete data: we have no names for these painters, no dates, no addresses of workshops—not even contracts, bills, or fee schedules. We still know very little about the mode of operation of the artisans of the primitive style: most of the paintings (certainly all the murals, but also the majority of the portraits) are anonymous; no archives of painters' guilds have been found so far, indicating, possibly, the institutional weakness of the associations that doubtless existed; those archives of churches and monasteries—which had been important employers for the painters—that survived the English occupation of Havana were lost when monastic orders were expelled from Cuba (1820) and then, after their return, often moved into new quarters.[21] And after the revolution of 1959, finally, the church itself appears to have sold off or hidden some of its archives.[22]

In the absence of further evidence, it is difficult to speak to the issue of the social role of the painters and the paintings. It is fairly clear that painting was the domain of the emerging petite bourgeoisie of color, but we do not know whether significant numbers of slaves were employed as painters. It is also important to keep in mind that "popular" is not the same as "of color." The example of the well-known mulatto portraitist Vicente Escobar is particularly interesting here. Escobar was married to a white woman and owned a couple of domestic slaves. Although his birth was registered in the books for persons of color, his death is listed in the register of whites. At the recommendation of Governor Vives, Escobar was invited to visit Spain, where he was appointed "Painter of the Royal Chamber." Indeed, he was so closely identified with the colonial power that at least one art historian has argued that this, rather than the quality of Escobar's work, was the reason that he was not appreciated by the emerging Creole bourgeoisie.[23] While this may well be true, however, we should not forget that any evaluation of the pro- or anti-Spanish stance is severely complicated by the issue of slavery. If many people of color put more trust in the Spanish Crown than in the local bourgeoisie, this has probably more to do with the attitude of local whites than the position of the Spanish Crown. One of the central institutions in the social ascent of people of color was, for instance, the Militia of Blacks and Mulattoes, in which not only Aponte but also Escobar's father had served. The militia was of course in the service of the Spanish authorities and was always eyed with suspicion by the local elite. Social status, aesthetic evaluation, and political position thus form an intricate web in which any unequivocal assessment of what counts as progressive and what as aesthetically valuable, and what is "popular" and what is not, is extremely difficult. To complicate matters further, the fears of one social class about an antagonistic class did not necessarily correspond to reality: Escobar may well have been a pro-slavery Spanish loyalist, yet he was perceived as a potentially dangerous actor in the struggle against slavery.

If this diagnosis is accurate, it would shed new light on an interesting passage in the most famous Cuban novel of the nineteenth century, Villaverde's *Cecilia Valdés*. There Villaverde places a portrait by the mulatto Escobar in the house of the (fictional) Spanish slave trader Gamboa. This might seem an unlikely convergence to contemporary readers, but I doubt that it surprised nineteenth-century Cubans. It was clearly meant to denounce Gamboa as an uneducated, aesthetically insensitive, and altogether undesirable subject. Gamboa is responsible not only for incest and murder but also for the increasing Africanization of the island and the spread of bad taste. When a Cuban twentieth-century critic claims that the novel's "sweet and spiritual" heroine, Isabel Ilincheta, would never have allowed a painting by Escobar in her parlor, but would rather have chosen a painting by Vermay, Colson, or any other of the European painters who were brought to Cuba after the creation of the Academy San Alejandro, he might be right.[24] But perhaps for reasons he did not suspect, or did not care to know.

### "The Arts Are in the Hands of the People of Color"

When the Spanish Bishop Espada arrived in Havana in 1802, he was patently horrified at the backward state of culture and education.[25] Teaching had become the domain of the nonwhite population. An inquiry commissioned by the Sociedad Económica in 1793 had come to the conclusion that there were thirty-nine locations in the city that could be described as schools: seven for boys, thirty-two for girls. Some of the teachers are given individual write-ups: "Juana Teresa Ruiz, a free mulatta, teaches ten girls Christian doctrine, reading, and the principles of sewing. The dwelling is very small and she receives two *reales* per month." "Brígida Hernández, free mulatta, has eighteen girls, whom she teaches the doctrine, reading, and sewing; three receive their education for free, the others for four *reales* for reading, and eight *reales* for sewing." By contrast, the Convent of Belén—one of the few officially sanctioned institutions for basic education in Havana—suffered from extraordinary overcrowding: two monks were in charge of a total of six hundred boys, four hundred for the one who taught the writing classes, and two hundred for the one who taught reading classes. A similar report from 1801 counted seventy-one schools in the city for more than two thousand children, many of them under the leadership of free women of color "who lack education, order, and method, to the point that they do not even know how many students they have." When in 1827 a free black woman by the name Ana del Toro applied to the colonial government to be allowed to open a school for girls of color, she was denied a permit. The records are quite explicit about the reason for the rejection: "the supreme dictates of our security and survival" prohibit it.[26]

In response, Espada, whose own teachers had included important representatives of the Spanish Enlightenment, embarked on a program of reform. He sent Bernardo O'Gavan, the son of one of Cuba's foremost families, to Spain to study. When he returned and proposed reforms in light of Pestalozzi's educational ideas, the office of the Inquisition in Cuba severely rejected them on account of their modern character (O'Gavan had imprudently appealed to Condillac and Locke in his proposal) and their projected costs. In the end, Cuban officials settled for the Lancasterian system of mutual education. It seems that Espada's reforms did not usher in a golden age for education in Cuba. In fact, according to Bachiller y Morales, 1818 marks the beginning of decadence in education—at least for free education.

Espada's aesthetic and architectural reforms had a more lasting effect. In the cathedral, he had the stone floor replaced with marble, removed the primitive altars and replaced them with altars of mahogany, threw out paintings that he considered of little artistic value, and replaced the thick baroque columns with neoclassical ones. He ordered that "altars with coarse images" be used for firewood at the hospital. An anecdote reports that Espada discovered in a local church a painting of the Last Supper, with the apostles dressed as monks and Mary present, dressed as a nun. Horrified, Espada ordered the picture destroyed. For the redecoration of the cathedral, Espada first engaged José Perovani, an Italian painter of some renown. When Perovani could not finish his work, Espada began to look for a substitute. He eventually heard that a student of the famous French painter David by the name of Jean Baptiste Vermay was living in Louisiana since his escape from France after Napoleon's fall. It was Vermay who introduced academic painting in Cuba.

There are few indications that Espada's reforms were anything other than the fairly typical actions of a man eager to implement the Enlightenment ideas that his teachers had instilled in him. Of course, one may wonder at the massive investment in architectural and artistic reform given the shortage of funds for education and other urgent issues. What interests me, however, is how Espada's "Enlightenment as style" interacts with local political issues.

In his "Memorandum about Slavery," the Cuban clergyman Félix Varela writes: "The freemen devote themselves almost exclusively to the arts, the technical as well as the liberal ones, so that one could say that for every white artist there are twenty of color. . . . some exercise their craft with considerable perfection, although they do not compare with foreign artists, because they have not had other means of instruction than their own ingenuity. . . . Effectively, since the arts have ended up in the hands of the blacks and mulattoes, they have become vile for the whites."[27] José Antonio Saco—one of the leading intellectuals in Cuba of the 1830s and 1840s—is less sanguine about the situation. In his prize-winning "Memorandum about Idleness in Cuba" of 1831, Saco includes a section entitled "The Arts Are in the Hands of the People of Color."[28] "Among the enormous evils that this [i.e., African] race has brought to our land," he begins, "is that they have alienated our white population from the arts. . . . all of them became the exclusive patrimony of the people of color, leaving for the whites the literary career and two or three others that were taken to be honorable. . . . In this deplorable situation, no white Cuban could be expected to devote himself to the arts, because the mere fact of embracing them was taken to mean that he renounced the privileges of his class" (58–59). Some progress has been made lately, Saco continues, since a few foreigners have settled in Cuba, who may "serve as an example for the Cubans," but much needs to be done to reverse this deplorable situation.

The Academy San Alejandro was notoriously underfunded. Students complained about the crowded space, the lack of air and light, and the generally unhealthy environment. Its French director, Vermay, was well aware of this and often tried to make the case for better financial support. In a speech on the occasion of public examinations of his students, later published in the Acts of the Sociedad Económica, he insists that so many professions—from architecture to anatomy and military science—depend on the ability to draw that the Ecole Polytechnique in Paris does not even admit students who have not acquired that skill. "It would be easy for me to cite the great number of professions that require drafting; its utility is too well known to be repeated here" (388).[29] Judging from the archival records pertaining to the Academy San Alejandro and the general discourse on culture, Vermay did not quite understand why Cubans employed him to teach the arts. His utility argument was not taken up. Instead we find a continuation of the arguments about the importance of "good taste" and the civilizing benefits to be derived from it.

While compiling evidence of the activities of the primitive painters, Rigol insists that their practices did not have the admirable results that we know, for instance, from Mexico.[30] "There is a well-known colonial scene: monks teach the indigenous peoples of the Americas painterly techniques," and after the extermination of the indigenous, they were replaced with blacks.[31] "Nothing could be more wrong than this scene" in the case of Cuba. The people of color "learned nothing from the monks and artists who were imported by the orders." They were taught the mechanics, but not the art, of painting. "In other words, the dark-skinned artisans . . . were basically autodidacts or they taught each other the rudimentary skills of their profession." Thus the plastic arts in Cuba are "born with the infamous mark of discrimination."[32]

The politics surrounding Cuba's first academy of fine arts, San Alejandro, in 1818 illustrate the point. None of the local painters, not even well-established portraitists such as Vicente Escobar, were given teaching positions. Let me quote from the minutes of the meeting of the Real Sociedad Patriótica of November 1817—only months before the academy opened its doors:

> The need was discussed to establish a set of rules which would guard us against the inconvenience of having to admit all kinds of students: they must all be white, the parents must be known, and they must have a good education and good behavior. Our friend Duarte took this occasion to insist on the backwardness of the arts and crafts in our country, a fact which he attributed to the abuse they have suffered at the hands of the colored population; once in the hands of the colored population, the arts and crafts were abandoned by the white population because they did not want to enter into contact with the colored population.[33]

According to the minutes, Duarte then went into a lengthy and passionate speech against black and mulatto artisans, and in favor of limiting the activities of the colored population. In the end, the gathered members agreed to have Duarte draft a memorandum with suggestions about how to persuade the white population that artistic activity "wouldn't confound them with the colored population, but rather would afford them with effective superiority."

Since the founding documents for the Academy San Alejandro are lost, it is impossible to say whether or not racial provisions were included in the original charter. However, there are indications that race was a central criterion for admission.[34] When in March 1821 a mulatto named Francisco Valdés asked to be admitted, his request was passed on to a committee.[35] In August, Valdés presented his trequest again, and this time a new committee was formed. That is the last time that Francisco Valdés's name appears in the archives of the Sociedad Económica.[36]

As Bachiller y Morales and others have pointed out, San Alejandro was founded as an academy for drawing (rather than painting) in part because "blacks and mulattoes had not exercised drawing, and therefore the corporation believed that the education would be fruitful, because the art had not fallen into the hands of those 'who could have inspired some blemish'" (89).[37] Wall painting or the advanced techniques of fresco were not included in the syllabus. Clearly, the move to withdraw prestige from the painters of color was largely successful: as early as 1865, Bachiller y Morales could write: "I remember that I once suggested that we *return* to the good old custom of facilitating for them [the population of color] the exercise of the Fine Arts and the crafts."[38] In *Poetas de color* (1878), a biographical dictionary that did not adhere to a strict distinction between artisanal culture and academic art, Calcagno claims there were no painters among black Cubans, adding that blacks had shown remarkable gifts in the other arts but had not received the education and technical skills necessary for painting. Clearly, Calcagno is writing from the vantage point of the 1870s, when the artisanal culture had been thoroughly suppressed, since in the same work he claims (probably wrongly), in the entry for the mulatto poet Plácido, that he had been a student in Escobar's workshop.[39] In the 1920s the art historian Bernardo Barros uses the occasion of his first speech as a regular member of the National Academy of Arts and Letters to reflect on the history of Cuban art. He describes the Academy San Alejandro in its early years as the "refuge of a very small group of cultivators of the arts, cradle of a weak rejuvenation—but rejuvenation it was—of good taste that goes on to destroy prejudices and to create the beginnings of a new aesthetic tendency. When Vermay dies, the arts are no longer the exclusive patrimony of the race of color."[40]

Thus in the first decades of the nineteenth century, strategies were developed with the explicit goal of reclaiming cultural production for the white population. At a time when cultural development was a general concern, when the groundwork for a Cuban literature was laid, and urban and architectural reform aimed at "civilizing" the island,[41] the arts were, it seems, the target of explicitly racial politics. San Alejandro was supposed to reconnect Cuba to the European contemporary arts, whereas the colored artisans continued to work, at least for a while, within a colonial, hybrid tradition. This, too, changed in 1844, but that will be the topic for the following chapters.

Once the suppressed tradition is brought back to light, we can see that the aesthetic standards a Villaverde developed in his travel essays are not just an appropriation of European norms but also—and this is crucial—an alternative to the preferences of popular art, which in turn is racially constructed. His reflections on perspective are an example of this dual orientation of his argument. At one point in *Excursión a Vuelta Abajo*, the travelers, who include a French painter by the name of Moreau, contemplate a spread-out village from a hilltop. Villaverde comments that the sight is of no interest to the painter: "Because the houses [are] scattered and hidden in many points by leafy groves (because every yard has its own), they do not offer a single view, but various and diverse ones, difficult to comprehend in a single landscape" (58). In the ideal "unified vision," aesthetic structures and those of urban planning, architecture, and landscaping converge and lead toward modernization and development.[42] Artistic representation—both visual and literary—is *part* of modernization, and to the extent that modernization makes the environment representable, it is part of an artistic process; it is almost as if perspective were as much a quality of the world as of its representation. And yet a full account of the multiple contexts of Villaverde's call for perspectival painting needs to include the fact that perspective serves as one of the points of distinction between the cultural production of white Creole artists and of black or mulatto artisans. The representational practices of a Villaverde and a Moreau are structurally and institutionally involved in the autonomist project of the Creole elites. This was not to be true for the tradition of the black and mulatto artisans.

Villaverde's *Excursión a Vuelta Abajo* and other elite texts concerned with the state of the arts exemplify the extreme complexity of questions regarding the political and social valence of representational practices and aesthetic arguments in colonial situations. The heightened artistic self-awareness that results from this complexity is lost when we make nineteenth-century Cuban art conform to the narrative of archaic, utilitarian, and autonomous art, each superseding the previous mode in due time. Contrary to what is commonly suggested in contemporary discussions of politics of representation that are informed by postmodernist assumptions, Villaverde's politics are not repressive by virtue of failing to recognize their own artificial, constructed nature. In fact, it is precisely the aesthetic self-consciousness, the knowledge that representation does not come naturally, that allows for new, Europeanizing representational strategies to be turned against older popular forms of cultural production. In the suppression of that tradition, racial and aesthetic criteria are confounded in a way that opens up the possibility of new beginnings for the white Creoles.

# 3

# Beyond National Culture, the Abject

## THE CASE OF PLÁCIDO

Few figures in nineteenth-century Cuba are more troubling, more ambiguous, and more resistant to interpretation than the mulatto poet Gabriel de la Concepción Valdés, better known under his pseudonym Plácido.

Plácido was executed in 1844 as the supposed leader of an antislavery conspiracy. The international antislavery movement soon adopted his case to illustrate the moral degradation of the slaveholding regime,[1] while in Cuba he became a martyr of colonial despotism and a hero of the Cuban struggle for autonomy. Plácido's work has been anthologized and reissued more frequently than that of any other nineteenth-century Cuban poet, including José María Heredia.[2] Yet Plácido's status and significance have never been uncontroversial. As a victim of Spanish colonial rule, his memory was soon invoked for the cause of Cuban independence. But as a poet, Plácido represented a colonial culture Cuban Creoles strove to overcome. As a free man of color and suspected antislavery conspirator, finally, he was an unwelcome reminder of a revolutionary project that was anathema to the Creole elite.

The violence of his death, the unresolved questions that surround his life and work, and the fact that Plácido, more than anyone else in the nineteenth century, embodied the uneasy relationship between antislavery and anticolonialism have produced what can only be called a traumatic memory. From the moment of his death to the present, the name of the poet continues to return like a memory that can be neither erased nor assimilated. Was he a gifted poet or a bard for sale? A hapless victim of colonial machinations or a precursor to the Cuban revolution of 1959? An embarrassing example of colonial dependency or a sublime hero of resistance? An accomplice of the colonial elite or a precursor to Afro-Cuban expression?

The figure of Plácido never consolidated into a single shape. The first books and collections of essays devoted to the poet oddly combine high agitation with an obstinate determination not to settle any issue, no matter how trivial, and a tendency toward compulsive repetition of a few commonplaces about his poetry.[3] This does not change after Cuban independence in 1902. As a subject of countless academic debates, theater plays, and films, Plácido has continued to produce passionate debate throughout the twentieth century. In 1944, at the centenary of Plácido's death, the government of Grau San Martín issued a two-centavo stamp with his likeness, but in 1962, when the Cuban poet Nicolás Guillén used his regular column in the newspaper *Hoy* to call for renaming the *Faro O'Donnell* in the harbor of Havana in honor of Plácido, agitation arose again. There was an outpouring of letters from readers, some of which Guillén later reprinted in his column.[4] While to the revolutionary spirit it could not but seem scandalous that the lighthouse should bear the name of the Spanish captain-general responsible for Plácido's death rather than the poet's name, it became clear once again that Plácido, more than any other nineteenth-century figure, fell into a dubious space where customary political and aesthetic judgments failed to give definitive answers.

Plácido's spectral presence continues to reflect desires that were never realized and fears that remained unspoken. The black Cuban director Sergio Giral represents him as the ferocious leader of an antislavery revolution: at the same time hero of black consciousness and nightmare that emerges from the profoundly paranoid imagination of the colonial authorities and the white Creoles (*Plácido*, 1986).[5] Even more explicit about the phantasmagoric character of Plácido's memory is Abelardo Estorino's play *La dolorosa historia del amor secreto de José Jacinto Milanés* (The painful story of José Jacinto Milanés's secret love).[6] At first glance, Plácido is only a minor character in this play, which is based on an extensive study of historical documents from the nineteenth century and offers a broad panorama of the misery of colonial Cuba. *La dolorosa historia* takes place in the shadowland of the dead and the almost dead, a Cuban Comala where the entire past has become an eternal present from which there is no escape. Unlike Giral, Estorino resurrects Plácido as the polite, humble, and generous poet that his most favorable critics in the nineteenth century portrayed. He does not appear until the last act, entitled "Delirium." At first there are only pure sounds on a dark stage: whips, drums, screams, and then "Fire!"—the scene of Plácido's death by firing squad. When the poet finally appears, it is from beyond the grave. Plácido's voice is conceived as a return. It is both minor and unique, self-effacing and haunting. More graphically dead than anyone else in the play, Plácido is also the most vivid presence.

## Plácido and the Escalera Conspiracy

Born in 1809 as the son of a Spanish dancer and a free Cuban mulatto, Gabriel de la Concepción Valdés probably inherited his last name from the same orphanage that bestowed its name on Cirilo Villaverde's fictional heroine Cecilia. Eventually his father recognized him and brought him up at his home. Plácido's identity as a free person of color was thus always clear, even though he could apparently have passed quite easily as white. His relationship with his mother remained distant and limited by the strict etiquette that regulated all social relations between whites and people of color. His formal education was short and discontinuous. As the son of a financially insecure barber, he was not able to attend school until the age of ten and always had to weigh schooling against the need to contribute to the family income. Until the last two years of his life, when he joined the staff of a newspaper in Matanzas as the editor of the literary section, he depended for his livelihood on his trade as a comb maker.

By most accounts, Plácido was an agreeable person with an excellent memory, a gift for poetic improvisation, a quick and inoffensive wit, and a strong desire to please. He achieved early literary fame peddling his poems on the streets of Havana and participating in poetry competitions. Eventually newspapers started to print his poems, and soon he was the writer of choice whenever someone wanted to honor a friend or family member, or to curry favor with people of high social station by dedicating a poem. While the intellectual elite tended to dismiss his poetic inventions as incorrect and vacuous, Plácido was frequently invited by the colonial aristocracy to make a show of his skills for after-dinner entertainment. By 1836, the local publisher Boloña was negotiating with Plácido for the publication of his first book-length collection of poems in Cuba. Those plans never came to fruition, but in 1838 and 1842, two volumes of his poetry were finally published by his mentor Sebastián Alfredo de Morales.

In 1844 Plácido was found guilty of having participated in a conspiracy of slaves and free people of color, which, according to the sentence, had the goal "to exterminate all whites, and to become masters of the Island and to claim it for themselves with the help and protection of foreign powers," that is, Haiti and England.[7] To the last moment of his life, he denied all charges. In the hagiography that developed in the course of the nineteenth century as part of the anticolonial discourse, Plácido walked up to the firing squad reciting his most famous poem, the "Plegaria a Dios" (Plea to God), in which he proclaims his innocence one last time and entrusts his soul to God. Until quite recently, the consensus among most historians and commentators was that Plácido was the innocent victim of colonial despotism, and that the so-called Escalera Conspiracy was a fabrication of the Spanish authorities. This consensus no longer exists, but the events of 1844 remain shrouded in doubt and uncertainty.

The apparent impossibility of closure in the case of Plácido is due to a certain excess in his story—an excess, I will argue, that stems from the fact that it cannot be contained in the political and aesthetic categories of a historiography and literary history that developed in the course of the nineteenth century. In some ways, what was suppressed in the early decades of the nineteenth century remains unassimilable to this day: the prevalent narratives of nineteenth-century modernization and national integration simply have no place for a figure such as Plácido. Modern national cultures on the periphery came about through the suppression of precisely those projects and practices Plácido represents. Plácido is a reminder of the time when Creole culture was in the process of gestation—a reminder that things could have developed differently. National teleologies never take kindly to this realization.

As a free man of color, Plácido belonged to a social class that was viewed with the greatest concern and suspicion by the colonial authorities.[8] The sugar boom had brought considerable wealth to the island. But as the white population considered work the domain of slaves, the economic upswing disproportionately benefited the free population of color.[9] Villaverde's *Cecilia Valdés* gives a lively account of the social activities of that segment of the population in the 1830s—an account confirmed by other observers such as the patrician José del Castillo, who remarked that among the free people of color were many with "abundant wealth who in their lifestyle, in their dress, and in their speech imitated those white gentlemen who still remained in Cuba, and among them [there was] no lack of people fond of reading serious books and even making verse."[10]

After some nine years in Cuba, Captain-General Francisco Dionisio Vives had returned to Spain in 1832 and briefed the Spanish authorities about the situation on the ground. Although he had had to break up several separatist conspiracies of white Creoles, Vives saw the main threat to colonial rule neither in the liberal elites, nor in the slaves by themselves, but in the free population of color: "The existence of free blacks and mulattoes in the middle of the enslavement of their comrades is an example that will be very prejudicial some day, if effective measures are not taken in order to prevent their [the slaves'] constant and natural tendency toward emancipation, in which case they may attempt by themselves or with outside help to prevail over the white population."[11]

No doubt, Vives's assessment influenced his successors Valdés and O'Donnell, under whose rule relations between free people of color and whites steadily declined, and rumors of slave uprisings became ubiquitous. The following letter from the British consul in Havana—the radical abolitionist David Turnbull—to Captain-General Pedro Téllez de Girón in 1840 gives a good sense of the charged atmosphere of the years leading up to 1844:

> Since the period when Your Excellency thought fit, under the influence of unwise and dangerous councils, to refuse to receive me in the rank and station to which I have been raised by the favor of my Sovereign . . . I have been daily assailed with the darkest threats of deportation and murder. . . . But your Excellency will permit me to suggest that if I am visited with deportation, the voice of the exile will be heard in every corner of Europe; that if I become the victim of assassination, while residing under the immediate protection of Your Excellency, the blood of the first Martyr which this fair island shall have given to the cause of freedom will cry out aloud for vengeance, and will serve to nourish and invigorate that glorious Tree of Liberty which first planted under the British Banner . . . is destined to spread like the Blessed Banyan until its shadow encircles the Earth throughout the whole extent of the broad Girdle of the Tropics.[12]

Eventually Turnbull was removed from his post. The policies directed against the class of free blacks and mulattoes culminated in the horrendous repression of 1844, a year that has gone down in Cuban history as the Año del Cuero (Year of the Whip), and Turnbull was convicted in absentia of having been the prime mover of the conspiracy.

Unlike most slave conspiracies, the Escalera Conspiracy was named after a method of torture: the beating of the accused tied to a ladder. Estimates of how many people of color fell victim to the repression after the trials vary wildly, from fewer than one hundred to several thousand.[13] There cannot be any doubt, however, that the free population of color was the main target of the repression, and that it lost its intellectual leadership as a result.

The white liberal elite, too, suffered severe setbacks. Accusations were brought against two of the leading intellectuals, José de la Luz y

Caballero and Domingo Del Monte. It was Plácido's testimony in particular that implicated both of them. Although it is still not entirely clear what Del Monte's role in the conspiracy was, we do know that in 1842 he had sent a letter to the U.S. diplomat Alexander Everett in which Del Monte denounced the plans for an extensive antislavery conspiracy promoted by Turnbull and supported by England. Although both Del Monte and Luz y Caballero were eventually absolved, Del Monte never returned to Cuba.[14] In correspondence with Everett, he explained that he feared that "some black man" would assassinate him as a traitor to a cause to which he had never belonged.[15] Having left the island out of fear of the colonial regime, he could not return out of fear of the population of color: a remarkable reflection of the contradictions between conflicting projects of emancipation.

In the aftermath of the trial, new legislation was enacted that ostensibly offered a compromise to Great Britain and liberal Creoles: it established severe penalties for anyone who continued to engage in the slave trade, but banned any investigation of the origins of slaves that were the property of Cubans. In effect, this put an end to the meddlesome inquiries and interference of British abolitionists in Cuba. It also meant that the trade could continue more or less undisturbed. Under the heading of property rights, the new compromise law achieved two goals, both of them detrimental to abolitionism and to the pursuit of local autonomy: it strengthened the institution of slavery in Cuba, and it ameliorated problems that had made an annexation of Cuba to the United States popular among some white Creoles before 1844.[16]

As in the case of the Aponte Conspiracy, the investigators of the Escalera Conspiracy were particularly interested in any detail that might suggest links to Haiti. In a letter to Lord Aberdeen of 1846, Turnbull relates that he had visited Haiti before taking up his post in Cuba and that he conversed with "some of the most intelligent and influential of the citizens," including President Boyer, about the "valuable assistance to the cause of freedom and humanity" Haiti might give.[17] No doubt these links were known to the colonial authorities. While no evidence has emerged to the effect that Haiti in fact supported or promised to support the uprising, the trial records do show that several witnesses claimed that the idea was to follow the example of Haiti and that the conspirators had hoped that once the uprising was in motion, Haiti would step in.

Until recently, most historians inside and outside Cuba believed that the conspiracy was a fabrication of the colonial authorities, who used it in order to tighten control over the island.[18] As the moral and political evaluation of resistance to slavery and revolutionary antislavery even in mainstream historiography has changed in the last few decades, scholars have begun to review the records. Most recent work tends to argue that there may have been a conspiracy, although perhaps not the vast, coordinated one the colonial authorities claimed to have uncovered. Paquette, for instance, concludes that there were a number of conspiracies between 1842 and 1844, which were linked perhaps only in the paranoid imagination of the slaveholders.

Plácido's role in the political events—if he ever had one—also continues to cause substantial disagreement. While throughout the nineteenth century, Plácido's innocence appeared to be unquestionable, Cué Fernández has argued recently that the poet's incessant travels in the years in question, as well as certain details of the trial record, suggest that Plácido probably was involved in some kind of conspiratorial plot. It is indicative that one of the most recent critical studies of Plácido, published by Miami International University, settles for a compromise: Plácido was indeed involved in conspiratorial activities, but he was also innocent. This view, proposed by Jorge Castellanos, holds that in the course of the preparation for the uprising, a conflict erupted between the mulattoes who wanted to abolish slavery but had no plans to kill white Cubans, and the black insurgents, who became increasingly radicalized and wanted to follow the example of the Haitian Revolution.[19] According to this picture, Plácido, who was of mixed ancestry and a deeply religious man, had a falling out with the radical black insurgents and withdrew from the conspiracy. It was on these grounds, Castellanos claims, that Plácido's "Plea to God" in the moments before his death was not a blasphemous lie. While not entirely implausible,[20] it is striking that this theory transforms Plácido into a symbol of racial harmony under the umbrella of Catholicism and equality before the law. One suspects that it owes as much to the conflicts between Cubans in exile and Cubans in Cuba after 1959 as it does to historical evidence. In Plácido's fate, and in the memory that has haunted Cuba ever since his premature death by firing squad, the tensions between different notions of liberation, between different cultural practices, and finally between different notions of what Cuba's future should be, have left an indelible imprint. Plácido continues to be a pawn in ideological battles over Cuban identity.

The politics surrounding Plácido's fate and memory would not be nearly so complicated if he had not left behind a sizable amount of poetry of questionable quality and dubious political orientation. Of course, were it not for his poems, he might be entirely forgotten today—the execution of poets by unjust rulers has always been cause for scandal in a way that deaths of ordinary people are not. But at the same time, his poetry has made any easy appropriation impossible. What are we to make of the many poems in praise of Spain and the colonial authorities? What to make of the fact that most poems are in blatant violation of the standards of taste that the liberal elite took such pains to inculcate in young writers?[21] Even his most well-meaning critics said about him that "his means of instruction were the books that fell into his hands, disjointed readings more apt to pervert his taste than to further develop it as he was taking the first youthful steps on the way to literature."[22] As a poet who in an unwitting confusion of earthly facticity with heavenly immateriality kept saying "empirical" when he meant "empyreal," who happily broke the rules of meter and rhyme, and offered his services to anyone who could afford them, he could not but be a source of acute embarrassment at a time when the project of national literature was one of the main venues for promoting national emancipation. Plácido's fate was sublime, but his poetry, for the most part, was not.

Of course, Plácido is remembered today not only as the poet of bad taste. Well-known poems like "Flor de caña" (The flower of sugarcane), "Jicotencal," "Plegaria a Dios" (Plea to God), and "Despedida a mi Madre" (Goodbye to my mother) have been celebrated and taken as a sign that Plácido would have been a fine poet had he lived under different circumstances. Although he never spoke out on the topic of slavery,[23] "The Death of Gessler," "The Judgment," and those poems devoted to European countries suffering under foreign occupation have been taken to reveal his progressive leanings. In fact, these poems may well explain why Plácido came under suspicion in the first place. In a colony where censors bristled at the mere mention of the word "liberty," Plácido's celebration of the Polish struggle for independence and his praise of the Spanish regent's measures of liberalization must have caused considerable consternation. Before turning to his political poems, however, I would like to consider some of the poems that in all likelihood were among those that greatly embarrassed the Creole elite and led to the rejection of Plácido as a poet.

The following incidental poem is probably quite typical of the kind of poetic practice Plácido represented. It came about in a game called *pie forzado* (the tied foot), in which someone was challenged to improvise a poem that would end with a verse proposed by another person. In the present example, someone suggested "besar la cruz es pecado" [to kiss the cross is sin] and added, to make things more difficult, that the poem should not contain any heresies. Plácido's response was as follows:

> Bostezó Minerva un día
> e hizo una cruz en los labios,
> y sin proferirle agravios
> le dije: — 'Minerva mía,
> yo besar desearía
> esa cruz que te has formado';
> volvióme el rostro indignado
> y me respondió ella así:
> —"¿Usted no sabe que aquí
> *besar la cruz es pecado?*"[24]

> [One day Minerva yawned
> and made a cross on her lips
> and without wanting to insult her
> I said, "My dear Minerva
> I would love to kiss that cross
> that you made"
> She turned to me indignant
> and replied like this:
> "Do you not know that here
> kissing the cross is sin?"]

Minerva, the goddess of the arts, sciences, and wisdom, flirting with a humble mulatto poet; a comb maker intruding into the realm of divine knowledge; wisdom that yawns . . . The anecdote of Roman inspiration proceeds to make a merry mess of neoclassical solemnity. Obedience of one rule—no heresy—leads to the breaking of countless others; the laws of the local game supersede those of universalizing neoclassicism.

Plácido's most favorable critics and supporters did their best to eliminate such trifles from the corpus of his poetry. Defenders of the poet took his friend Sebastián Alfredo de Morales to task for having indiscriminately included all sorts of unworthy poems in his edition and "corrected" Plácido's versions. The best service one could do to the poet, some argued, would be to collect the few good poems and burn the rest.[25] Horrego Estuch, one of Plácido's most devoted and articulate advocates in the twentieth century, goes to quite some lengths to show that although Plácido began his career as a light-hearted improviser, he eventually found his true voice as a serious poet committed to the cause of Cuban independence and should be remembered as such.[26] Yet whatever we might think about Plácido's ultimate commitments and achievements, it seems that we cannot form an accurate picture of what Plácido represented at the time just on the basis of his "best" poems. In fact, creating a Plácido corpus that vaguely conforms to high-literary expectations may in the end only reinscribe the erasures of earlier times under a more benevolent sign.

Here is another little-known poem entitled "¡Cuánta Ilustración!" (So Much Enlightenment!), which may help us to further understand his poetic practice and the reactions it produced in the intellectual elite.[27] The first stanza reads as follows:

> Amigos, silencio,
> Pasito, chitón . . .
> Vamos a la escuela
> del nuevo Platón,
> Del Diógenes nuevo,
> Del nuevo Solón.
> Digo, y que de valde,
> Con santa intención,
> En públicos diarios
> Nos da la lección,
> Con más elocuencia
> Que el gran Cicerón.
> *Caramba, ¡qué sabio!*
> *¡Cuánta ilustración!*

> [Friends, silence,
> hush, be quiet . . .
> We are going to the school of the new Plato,
> of the new Diogenes,
> The new Solomon
> I say that for free,
> And with saintly intentions
> In public papers
> He gives us lessons
> With more eloquence
> Than the great Cicero
> *Caramba, how wise!*
> *So much enlightenment!*]

Again, a slight little poem. A parade of names as eponyms of erudition and wisdom. Again the sublime symmetries of antiquity disintegrate among colloquialisms and a sudden syncopation: "caramba que sabio / cuánta ilustración." It is as if the particular had irrupted into the universal. The anecdote of the poem tells us how the lingua franca of civilization penetrates into vernacular culture: this is the story of enlightenment and progress, but the burlesque works the other way around: the vernacular penetrates the classicist imagery.

This is the context in which to read a polemic that centered around a poem titled "El poeta envilecido" (The vile poet) (1837) by the highly regarded Cuban poet and playwright José Jacinto Milanés:[28]

> Por más que su alma presuma,
> Hácele tomar la pluma
> Necesidad.
> Y en su mal nacida rima,
> La adulación se echa encima
> De la verdad.
> ¡Torpe, que a su pensamiento
> Siendo libre como el viento
> Por alto don,
> Le corta el ala, le oculta
> Y en la cárcel le sepulta
> Del corazón!
> Y ¿qué es mirar a este vate
> Ser escabel del magnate
> Cuando el festín;
> Cantar sin rubor ni seso,
> Y disputar algún hueso
> Con el mastín?

> [However much his soul presumes,
> what makes him take up the pen
> is necessity.
> And in his lowly rhyme
> adulation overcomes
> truth.
> Clumsiness—to clip the wings of his thought
> that was free like the wind
> through a high gift
> to hide it
> and bury it in the prison
> of the heart!
> And, what about a poet

who makes the high-up shine
at his banquet?
about singing without shame or brain
and arguing over a bone
with the mastiff?]

The poem does not name the "vile poet." Yet the first edition of Milanés's *Obras* contains the following stanza, which was suppressed in the second edition (1846):

Y si la suerte le hizo
De color negro o cobrizo,
¡Mísero de él!
Pues su horizonte es sombrío,
Su aire seco, su sol frío,
¡Su amor de hiel!

[And if fate gave him
black or copper color,
the poor thing!
For him the horizon is darkened
his air dry, his sun cold,
his love is of bile!]

In 1845 Domingo Del Monte had written a brief essay entitled "Two Black Poets—Plácido and Manzano," in which he favorably compared the writing of the former slave Juan Francisco Manzano (who had attended Del Monte's circle for a while) with that of Plácido. Del Monte's conclusion is unequivocal: "my aesthetic principles and my philosophy agree more with the lament torn from the heart of the oppressed, than with the clamorous concert of the poet crowned with laurels, of the vile poet [*poeta envilecido*], of Plácido."[29] At the end of his essay, Del Monte quotes the last two stanzas of Milanés's poem, thus clearly identifying Plácido as its subject.

Many years later—José Jacinto Milanés was long dead, and Spain had thoroughly lost support among Cuban Creoles—Federico Milanés came to his brother's defense (1886) and tried to refute Del Monte's identification. "El poeta envilecido" was, he argues, a veiled criticism of the "pernicious conditions" of colonial culture where "fiestas and public feasts were teeming with lampoonists and poetasters."[30] Plácido was just one of a whole class of people, and this class was a typical expression of colonial culture. Plácido himself overcame the colonial conditions on the eve of his execution "when he rose in all his grandeur, with the sublime inspiration that his misfortune imparted on him."[31] The whole nasty affair, in which color prejudice and claims of cultural legitimacy combined, is finally subsumed under the apparent inclusivism of the anticolonial struggle. Plácido's moment of transcendence came when the colonial culture from which he emerged turned against him.

Whatever the intended reference of J. J. Milanés's poem might have been, the aesthetic criteria he establishes for vileness are highly significant. At first glance, we might be tempted to think that the objections against the "poeta envilecido" are directed simply against premodern, backward aesthetic practices. The references to banquets, hunting dogs, and after-dinner entertainment suggest the utilitarian art of feudal times—a far cry from the autonomous art cherished by the eighteenth- and nineteenth-century bourgeoisie. Yet this reading does not account for the moralizing and misanthropic rhetoric that is most striking about Milanés's poem. It abounds in morally charged terms that indicate a certain instability, a queerness, or degradation rather than simply backwardness. Instead of *vil* (vile) there is *envilecido*, which adds an element of "becoming."[32] The poetry of Plácido is *mal nacida*, a term that can mean plebeian, perverse, or somehow despicable on account of a moral failure. This nature is in turn explained by the fact that it was born out of necessity—it is a poetry that does not transcend the limitations of material life, a poetry that does not project into the realm of freedom and autonomy. The verses that were suppressed in the second edition further add to this image of a poetry that remains imprisoned by corporeal life and its necessities. Bile, the symbol of resentment and spite, is the most bitter of bodily fluids; a fluid that helps to transform the source of sensual pleasure—food—into elements that can be absorbed by a digestive apparatus that obeys only the laws of nature and is oblivious to aesthetic criteria. We move from the realm of sweetness, taste, and splendor—the realm of poetry—to darkness and bitterness of the bodily cavity blindly devoted to physical survival. Plácido is thus not so much a sign of historical backwardness as a sign of a regression, a return to a more primitive state, a corruption of existing customs and practices, a source of disintegration and decomposition. He stands not for the "not yet" of the discourse of progress and development but for the loosening of civilized rules and laws, a crisis in the process of human individuation and subjectification.

Taking up an idea put forth by Julia Kristeva in *The Powers of Horror*, we might read this as a discourse of the abject. In a poststructuralist companion piece to Freud's essay on the uncanny, Kristeva seizes the experience of horror where it is a reaction to the repulsive: disgust and recoil. Like the uncanny, the abject straddles the divide between the aesthetic and the psychic, but their respective temporalities are strikingly different. In Freud's account, the uncanny is an emotional reaction to events that resonate with certain magical or animistic beliefs we no longer hold (thus the frequent association between the uncanny and mysterious repetitions). The abject, in Kristeva's account, is more problematic and resistant to closure. We encounter the abject in moments of revulsion at things we cannot incorporate or ingest—certain foods, excrement, blood, vomit, corpses. It is what the body had to expel to constitute itself as a subject. The expulsion of that which is revolting becomes the subject of primary repression; the experience of abjection in an adult is tied not to "lack of cleanliness or health" but to what "disturbs identity, system, order. What does not respect borders, positions, rules. The in-between, the ambiguous, the composite."[33] The process of this repression is thus never fully completed. The abject continues to threaten the subject from the margins, as it were: without precise location, it is at the same time memory, trace of the fragility of the subject, and dangerous future possibility.

Although Kristeva's concept of the abject originates in the analysis of the psychic development of the individual, its most striking instantiations occur in the moral and aesthetic sphere. "Abjection . . . is immoral, sinister, scheming, and shady: a terror that dissembles, a hatred that smiles, . . . a friend who stabs you" (4). The abject is "an artist who practices his art as a 'business.' Corruption is its most common, most obvious appearance. That is the socialized appearance of the abject" (16). It is on the grounds of the expulsion of the abject that the spiritual, the sublime, the incorporeal, separates itself from the dark matter of physiological functions.

As subject of the discourse of the abject, Plácido mixes what culture has happily separated. He is not a premodern poet, or a poet who by chance continued practices of an obsolete past, but the poet of regression and decomposition. Plácido's poetry is a debased representation of the classical tradition. Erudite culture becomes an inventory of disjointed phrases and names. His poetry is a ridiculous parade of nymphs, exotic geographies, and Greek philosophers. "His mind reflected everything he read, yet these reflections were always unfortunate, because he was unable to assimilate things in their entirety."[34] Within this discourse, Plácido is neither innovator nor traditionalist. He is transgressive precisely because he neither submits to the law nor overthrows it. He represents what humans are prior to successful subjectification.

The discourse of the abject derives its high emotional charge by tapping into psychic structures beyond the reach of rationalist aesthetic judgment. Neoclassical aesthetics would have told us merely that Plácido's poetry was at times incorrect. Unlike incorrection, the abject makes an arcane debate about standards of taste available for political and social fantasies: Plácido becomes the ghost that reminds us what lies beyond the boundaries that came to define Creole culture, a reminder of all that was ruled out in the cultural processes of the nineteenth century.

Plácido was not entirely unaware of the rhetoric that was ferried out by his critics. On the occasion of the premiere of the play *El Conde Alarcos* by Milanés, Plácido dedicates a poem to the writer who had denounced him, sardonically crediting the legitimate poet with all he himself supposedly lacked. It opens with "Salve á tu nombre, trovador preclaro, / de inspiración y de modestia lleno" [Salve to you, eminent troubadour, / full of inspiration and modesty], proceeds to praise the writer for being "beyond flattery," only to then compare him to Homer and Plutarch in an outrageous and practically incomprehensible list of classical titles, names, and allusions. He ends by anticipating the poet's death: Matanzas "pondrá en tu losa una inscripción que diga / *Aquí yace el autor del Conde Alarcos*" [will place on your tombstone an inscription that says / *Here lies the author of "El Conde Alarcos"*]. Surely we are supposed to hear in the Latinate style of the two opening verses allusions to "Ave Maria, gratia plena, Dominus tecum / benedicta in mulieribus et benedictus fructus ventris tui": an address in Latin, followed by praise for "the fruit," and then, instead of the "ora pro nobis . . . in hora mortis nostra," the anticipation of the author's death: "Aquí yace el autor de *El Conde Alarcos*." What flattery is greater than that which declares the addressee impervious to flattery? And assuming that Plácido was indeed as religious as the contemporaries claimed, what could be more hyperbolic than equating the purity of a writer who had launched a vicious attack against Plácido and his kind with the sublime purity of the woman who was, they say, born without sin and gave birth to the Savior?[35]

Plácido's contemporaries did not consider the possibility of irony in his poetry. For them, Plácido was like the primitive fetishist who, failing to realize that value does not reside in objects themselves but is produced through contexts and structures, attributes magical powers to the signifiers by themselves. Instead of meaning, he produces mere shiny surfaces. In an essay from 1894, one of Plácido's most venomous detractors in Cuba, Manuel Sanguily, writes: "He puffs up his cheeks . . . and with ridiculous emphasis and an air of solemnity that is very funny when it is not irritating, he lets escape swollen, ringing, nonsensical, empty words—words, words, words!—and the worst is that often he does not even know their meanings."[36] This invective responds to an earlier, comparatively moderate piece by the eminent Spanish critic Marcelino Menéndez Pelayo:

> He was really just a half-cultured man, with a good memory and lively wit, in whose mind everything he read or heard imprinted itself as if in soft wax; he aspired to improve on the beauty of the great masters, like a lackey who dons the clothes of his master. We do not know what kind of poetry the Ethiopian race would produce if it was left to its own devices, but it would certainly be very different from the mannered accomplishments, the inane fables and tasteless epigrams with which Plácido inundated the newspapers in Havana and Matanzas.[37]

Leaving aside the racist implications in the suggestion that Plácido imitates his master, we may remember here that the ideas of memory and skillful imitation were conventionally used in accounts of the cultural practices of people of color. Praise for the portraitist Escobar was typically limited to the fact that he was an excellent physiognomist who could paint portraits from memory. We may also recall that the skills Juan Francisco Manzano claimed for himself were his excellent memory and facility of recital and mimicry.

But there is more than just conventional racial prejudice in Menéndez Pelayo's criticism. Setting up a rigid dichotomy between European poetry and "Ethiopian" poetry "when left to its own devices" (which, at any rate, Menéndez Pelayo believed did not yet exist in the late nineteenth century), he objects that Plácido does not fit either identitarian category. He falls into a dubious, embarrassing in-between space that produces no Law, no Rule; a space where the "I" and "the Other" are not distinct and where the only relation available is that of a servant imitating the master. It is a space of ontological impossibility where nothing of substance or permanence can reside, where there is no Subject or where the Subject begins to disintegrate. Plácido gains recognition only in the moment when he puts on the master's clothes, thus taking on the appearance of the critic's Self. He exists only as an imitation of something he is not.

Again we see the discourse of the abject, here tied directly to the idea of the abject as a threat to the stability of the subject.

Compare the following response by the Cuban intellectual Enrique José Varona to the puzzle of Plácido's identity (1886):

> Who was Plácido? The most spontaneous poet in the whole of Spanish-American literature; a man who came from the most humble of social classes in a Spanish colony, badly educated and badly taught, and who through the effort of a surprising genius lifts himself up occasionally to the cusps of poetic inspiration, to fall down vertiginously again later; a grandiloquent and incorrect writer, a street versicler, a dinner poet of domestic festivities and sublime lyrical poet. From his lips stream, flood-like, the most sonorous verses and the most trivial phrases; his fantasy catches fire with grandiose images and goes astray in chase of futile conceptions. Rarely does he manage to leave a finished composition, and rarely does he improvise a décima that does not shine with some beauty. When he composes he seems like a man who has his pockets stuffed with pebbles and precious stones, and when he pulls his hand out, he carelessly tosses off whatever it may be, whether diamonds or rough stones.[38]

Clearly, by the time Varona is writing these lines in the 1880s, after the social and political changes that were brought about by the Ten Year War, Plácido has become a martyr, and outright contempt has given way to a more generous assessment of his poetic gifts. Still, Varona picks up on the same imagery that we saw in Milanés's poem. Plácido is a poet who, despite his natural gifts, never managed to free himself from exterior forces and continued to live in an almost infantile world. Children have their pockets full of pebbles and do not know the difference between ordinary stones and diamonds. Legitimate art is the result of selecting the materials nature offers, the result of working and polishing them. Art comes about when the subject exercises its supreme will and control (and we may here remember that for Kant, the artist is the image of God as the autonomous creator, and that the idea of artistic autonomy derives in large part from this analogy). Obviously Plácido does not fit this ideal: verses flow from his mouth, a gift from nature rather than exercise of an autonomous will. The problem is not, it seems, that Plácido wrote some good and some bad verses but that the sublime is forever imbricated with the banal. Like Milanés and Del Monte, Varona is disturbed by the carelessness with which Plácido mixes the facile and the difficult, the banal and the sublime—precisely those things that culture is supposed to separate. Plácido continues to be the poet of regression and abjection.

Throughout the nineteenth century, cultural and political discourse in Latin America centered around the notion of progress, or what in the twentieth century came to be called modernization and development. The discourse of the abject is strangely at odds with the dominant discourse. Regression cannot be overcome by progress, by simply going ahead. Unlike backwardness or primitiveness, the dangers of regression can be overcome only through a continuous process of purification and expulsion. What under the heading of "modernization" might appear as a simple antecedent, a happily forgotten past that only occasionally resurfaces in historical narratives or as the object of a nostalgic gaze, continues to threaten from the future in the rhetoric of the abject. Within the logic of modernization, the merely backward will disappear if we simply let history take its course; not so the abject, which requires constant vigilance and a firm determination not to let things get out of hand.

Obviously, the discourse of the abject was intended to contain Plácido and all that he might have represented. But we can also read it against the grain: as the recognition that Plácido and the whole cultural formation he represented was, at some point, a definite possibility for the future, and a highly undesirable one at that; not a memory of underdevelopment but an anticipation of history taking a path akin to that of Haiti perhaps, where radical antislavery had become state ideology, racial equality the core of the idea of liberty, and the likes of Plácido had become ministers and authors of constitutions.[39] Menéndez Pelayo was quite right to insist that Plácido cannot be seen as a belated medieval jongleur or troubador, as some critics had suggested, but must be assessed in the context of modern literature: Plácido is as much a product of modernity as the liberal Creoles. But while Del Monte and Luz y Caballero are representatives of hegemonic modernity in the plantation zone, Plácido's relationship to modern culture is distinctly oblique. In the discourse of the abject, we can see a trace of alternatives, of a route not taken, of unsuccessful historical projects. Even in the rhetoric of the victor can we discover what Walter Benjamin in his *Theses on the Philosophy of History* called the wreckages of the past.

Interpretive approaches that focus on the politics of the form are unlikely to be helpful here or at least would have to be radically modified. We cannot assume that artistic forms—the sonnet, the romance—bear political inscriptions the same way they do when used in high-cultural contexts. Perhaps it is true that in Europe artistic forms were submitted to slow processes of absorption and sedimentation; cultural development in the early-nineteenth-century Caribbean, by contrast, may better be understood on the model of the cut-and-paste strategy that we saw, for example, in Aponte's book. Like Aponte some thirty years earlier, Plácido appropriates themes and materials that come his way, and like Aponte, his knowledge of the European repertoire comes from fairly random sources. Instead of assimilating the classical canon under the Law—be it the aesthetic law, the prescriptive guidance of educated Creoles, or years of schooling—Plácido appeared to submit to no rule at all. Or at least no rule that was recognizable to the elites. He had developed his poetic skills outside the litero-centric circles of the elites, on the streets, in poetry competitions and games. Indeed, his incidental poetry may be understood best in the terms Mañach used to define the Cuban *choteo* (literally, taunt or tease): "A human and social attitude whose instinctive goal it is to affirm one's own identity against that of some other that declares itself to be superior or equally powerful. Every taunt in fact presupposes an authority, or at least a competition."[40]

Like all improvisers, Plácido depended on established phrases and formulas to cope with time pressure. Jazz improvisation is possible only within the boundaries marked out by memorized scales and standard motifs. In his study of oral poets, Albert Lord showed that poetic skill manifests itself not in the invention of new themes or original ways of speaking but in variations and elaborations of established themes.[41] Plácido's riffing on classical and mythical names probably needs to be understood in similar terms: as an improvisational technique and mnemotechnic aid. Creole intellectuals who perceived Plácido's poetry as transgressive and outside the aesthetic law simply failed to see that his practice followed rules that originated in the choteo, oral recital, and improvisation rather than in the manuals that circulated at the time.

Plácido's syncretistic approach to high culture can be understood in similar terms. Like the jazz musician who does not much care about where a musical phrase comes from, Plácido seizes themes and motifs from legitimate high culture and integrates them into a practice that follows its own rules. He uses the European tradition as an archive of names and allusions whose meaning reconstitutes itself in the new context. We are used to viewing the Caribbean cultural process as one of syncretization between European, African, Amerindian, and Asian traditions. What we observe here is something different: a practice that draws exclusively on European cultural history but combines these elements in a truly syncretistic fashion, according to rules generated in a new environment. They seize high culture and claim it for the purpose of entertainment. From his peripheral location, Plácido mixes precisely what nineteenth-century culture took such pains to separate: the high and the low, the popular and the academic, the amateur and the trained artist. It does not matter that Plácido, as a self-taught mulatto, most likely had no choice in this respect. What matters is that his practice takes place on precisely the same ground that the Creole elite claimed. His oeuvre resembles an oblique inversion of the classic metropolitan institution of the museum of natural history: a display of artifacts from cultures around the world, taken out of context, displayed for entertainment, instruction, and the aesthetic delectation of an admiring audience; yet at the same time a display of power and of the appropriating capacity of the collector. As in the case of Aponte and the negro catedrático, Plácido's displays of erudition are also attempts to establish his authority.

From this perspective, it seems clear that Del Monte's peculiar mixture of romantic and neoclassical prescription was not just an idiosyncratic idea of what culture in the New World should look like, but shaped in response to the syncretistic appropriation of European high culture in the plantation zone. Injecting romantic ideas of the authentic and the organic into the neoclassical repertoire would seem a promising safeguard against the "lampoonists and poetasters" who acquired cultural knowledge and prestige by imitation and ingenious rearrangement. Whereas neoclassical styles may have a certain affinity to montage and rough-cut imitation, romanticism's concern with originality and authenticity would provide a protection against any external appropriation of cultural icons as ready-made fragments. An assemblage of objets trouvés would not count as original. And against this normatively charged originality, poets like Plácido and painters like Escobar were variously praised and criticized for their memory and their imitations.

## Liberty Won Is Liberty Lost:
### Conflicting Projects of Emancipation

Whether or not nineteenth-century elite writers were conscious of the implications of their aesthetic program, the discourses of the abject are traces of fears that did not dare speak their name and that in nineteenth-century slaveholder societies were usually dealt with by other means. Plácido signifies a threat to those identitarian and cultural categories on which Creole ideas of a Cuban national culture were built. The question that remains to be answered is whether Plácido's unassimilability is merely a result of his aesthetic practices, or whether there are political aspects to his poems that would underwrite or reinforce the perceptions of the Creole elite.

For a number of reasons, the issue of politics in Plácido is not easy. His participation in the 1844 conspiracy (if there ever was a conspiracy) remains speculative. As far as his direct political statements are concerned, we have to remember that he was writing under a political and social regime that could (and eventually did) become lethal for him. Strict rules of censorship and the need to make a living, moreover, left as strong a mark on his poetic production as any political commitment might have.

Like his nonpolitical poems, Plácido's political poetry is neither radically different, independent from modern European political practice and theory, nor behind its time and subservient to outmoded models of despotic rule. Rather, it is an obliquely critical engagement with themes and commonplaces established by the hegemonic tradition with roots in the more radical notions of liberty and equality of the late eighteenth century. This did not endear him to liberal Creoles, who failed to perceive the possibility of a vision of liberation that went beyond local autonomy and independence. The Puerto Rican writer and intellectual Eugenio María de Hostos, for instance, complained in 1872 that while Cuba and Puerto Rico cursed Isabel II, Plácido sang her praises. While they pilloried Maria Cristina as a prostitute, Plácido celebrated her glories. His poetry is, in Hostos's view, "devoted to rhymed adulation."[42]

It has also been pointed out that slavery does not appear as a topic. Unlike Manzano, Plácido does not decry the suffering of slaves in his writing. It is easy enough to excuse this silence: after all, Manzano's writings were passed on through elite abolitionist channels and intended for publication in England, not in Cuba. Moreover, for Manzano, writing was a means for securing the support of liberal Creoles and thus eventually achieving his freedom from slavery. The same people who assisted Manzano in his attempt to buy himself freedom had nothing but scorn for Plácido's poetry. Ironically, the slave probably was more able to speak his mind than the free mulatto. Because he was arguably the first Cuban poet to have made a living as a writer, the need to create a space for himself in the marketplace clearly imposed severe restrictions on what Plácido could say.

To begin, we should look at some political poems that talk about issues at first sight far removed from Cuba. The following sonnet is devoted to the misfortunes of Poland (33):

A Polonia
Calma, nación heróica, tu agonía,
Y contempla olvidando tus horrores,
Que mil pueblos se hicieron opresores
Y sufrieron después la tiranía.
    Medio siglo cabal no há todavía
Que en Moscow y Marengo tus señores
Delante de los galos vencedores
Abatieron sus águilas un día.
    Si andando el tiempo con la Europa embiste
Horda inmensa de bárbaros armada
Y ves al Czar doblar la frente triste,
    Exclamarás á su enemiga aliada:
"Esas son las cadenas que me diste,
Tuyas son, te las vuelvo, estoy vengada."

[To Poland
    Heroic nation, calm your agony
and consider, forgetting your horrors,
That a thousand nations became oppressors
And later suffered tyranny.
    It is not even half a century ago
that in Moscow and Marengo your masters
in front of the victorious Gauls
lowered their eagles one day.
    If in the course of time Europe is assaulted [?]
By an immense armed horde of barbarians
And you see the Czar lowering his sad brow,
    You will cry to his inimical ally:
"These are the chains you gave me,
They are yours, I return them to you, I am avenged."]

This sonnet, along with those dedicated to Greece and to Wilhelm Tell's victory over Gessler, clearly shows Plácido engaging with one of the main themes of the Enlightenment and the Age of Revolution: the unsurpassable value of liberty, national sovereignty, the superiority of the virtuous subject to those who seize power by force. Whether or not Plácido intended this poem to be read as a veiled denunciation of Spanish colonial rule in Cuba, there is something rather striking about this poem. The lines "A thousand nations became oppressors / And then later suffered tyranny" suggest an image of history as a wheel that keeps turning and turning: "today oppressor, tomorrow oppressed" is hardly a strong endorsement for the cause of liberty as the ultimate goal of human endeavors. In fact, it is reminiscent of the skeptical conservative position that appeals to a cyclical notion of history as a reason for abandoning liberty and social justice as the aim of political action, or holds that liberty and happiness cannot be achieved by deliberate political action.

But there is an alternative interpretation. Taking into account that the cycle of the oppressed turning into oppressors is tied to the history of nations in this poem, it could be read as a way of *separating* the issue of national sovereignty from that of liberty. In this picture, national liberation may not serve the cause of liberty at all. Indeed, if we were to read "A Polonia" as an allusion to Cuba, we might conclude that once liberated, the oppressed Cubans might turn into oppressors.[43] Are we to understand that unless slavery is abolished, independence would not further the cause of liberty? Perhaps. But even if Plácido intended this conclusion—as I will show in a moment, there is additional evidence that supports this reading—it does not mean that Plácido was oblivious to oppression through colonialism and expansionism.

It cannot be a coincidence that all the poems in this group point to the history of imperialism. A sonnet devoted to Venice contains the following lines:

> Entonces fuiste como Albión guerrera
> Y como ella también conquistadora.
>
> [Back then you were, like Albion, a warrior
> and like her, too, a conqueror.]

By following the "ejemplo fatal" [the fatal example] of imperial Rome and Greece, Venice brought about its own demise and now is nothing but "ruinas entre blanca espuma" [ruins among white spray].[44] The sonnet "A Grecia" opens with the following lines:

> Como las olas de la mar sombría
> Tal es la libertad, pues por un lado
> Un pueblo cubre, y deja abandonado
> Otro pueblo á la horrenda tiranía.
>
> [Like the waves of the dark sea
> Such is liberty, as on one side
> She covers one nation, and thus exposes
> Another nation to horrendous tyranny.]

The tercets offer yet another turnabout:

Tornó á llenar su página en la historia
Y si de Navarino en las arenas
Al ver las llamas, símbolo de Gloria
   Que abrasaban las naves sarracenas
Cantó la Grecia el himno de Victoria
Pasaron á Polonia sus cadenas.

[History turns another page
And when seeing on the beaches of Navarine
The flames, symbol of glory,
   Which were burning the Saracen ships,
Greece sang its hymn of victory
Her chains passed on to Poland] (33).

As before, the cause of liberty seems tied to a wheel, part of natural history, of the infinite breaking of waves on opposing shores: liberty won for Greece is liberty lost for Poland. The immediate event Plácido is alluding to is the Greek war of independence and the defeat of the Ottoman Empire in 1827 by an alliance of the Russians, French, and British. Plácido's association of Polish and Greek liberty is by no means specious: it was indeed the czar's imperialist designs on southeastern Europe that moved Russia to support the Greek struggle, and it was czarist expansionism that led to Russian invasions of Poland.[45]

Again, we could read this as a skeptical view according to which liberty gained and liberty lost will always remain in balance, and *sub specie eternitatis* there are no net gains to be had. But there is an alternative reading. We could say that the mistake lies in the hope to attain liberty for people by liberating nations. It seems plausible that someone whose most urgent concern is slavery and the legal and social rights of people of color would be deeply skeptical about the notion of liberty that is relayed through rules of territorial autonomy or national belonging. As the example of the American Revolution would have made abundantly clear, autonomy or independence by no means implied liberty for slaves and an end to racial subordination, and the attitude of most Cuban Creoles toward the issue would have only supported this suspicion. It is thus clear that Plácido did not mean to separate the issue of liberty from that of imperialism but tried to conceptualize this relationship in such a way that liberty is not synonymous with independence and national sovereignty, and certainly does not exhaust itself in independence.

This is the context in which we should read Plácido's poems devoted to Spain. The most daring of these is "La sombra de Padilla" (The shadow of Padilla), in which the leader of the *comuneros* uprising in Toledo in 1520 appears to the Cuban poet as a ghost and tells the story of his struggle for liberty, his defeat in Villalar, and his execution, ending with a defiant *Liberté ou mort* in neoclassical garb: "Pues vale más ser presa de la parca / Que privado de un déspota Monarca" [It is better to be prisoner of the Parca / Than property of a despotic Monarch] (368). The comuneros uprising in sixteenth-century Spain in fact marks the final consolidation of absolutism and a definitive loss of municipal liberties. A less fortunate Wilhelm Tell, Padilla is invoked as the defender of popular liberties against the claims of an absolutist ruler. Once we strip away the historical disguises, it becomes obvious that "La sombra de Padilla" speaks to one of the most pressing political issues at the time: constitutionalism and constitutional restrictions on the power of the monarch. Apparently this did not escape the censors, and Plácido was briefly incarcerated on account of this poem.

But what about Plácido's poems in praise of the Spanish monarchy that still enraged Eugenio María de Hostos in the 1870s? Are they purely opportunistic attempts at flattery and thus in direct conflict with "La sombra de Padilla"? There are a few poems that contain nothing but generic adulation of the Spanish monarchs. The more interesting ones, however, are more complicated. "La Ambarina" (The Queen of Ambar) (180–81), "La profecía de Cuba a España" (Prophecy from Cuba to Spain) (373–74), and "La sombra de Mina" (The shadow of Mina) (32) combine praise with accounts of a specific political event: the Carlist War of 1834–1839.

We cannot understand Plácido's argument without briefly explaining the events in question.[46] The immediate cause of the Carlist War was a dynastic dispute. Before his death Fernando VII had reinstituted an ancient Spanish law according to which women could succeed to the throne. Since Fernando VII had two daughters by his third wife, María Cristina, this meant that his brother Carlos, who had been hoping to be the next king of Spain and had been vigorously courted by ultraconservative forces in the church and the military, had lost all hope. After the death of Fernando VII, María Cristina became the regent until her daughter Isabel would reach maturity. The Carlists took up arms.

The dynastic dispute was, of course, only the catalyst in a political conflict that refers back to the post-Napoleonic period and the emergence of Spanish liberalism. In 1812 Spanish liberals had written a constitution that was inspired by the most progressive political documents of the late eighteenth century, the French constitution of 1791 and the American Declaration of Independence. It placed strict limitations on the monarch's power through a two-chamber system of representation and general male suffrage, and on church power by abolishing the Inquisition. The document was hotly contested as being too liberal. On his return to Spain in 1814, Fernando VII refused to accept it, returned to absolute rule, and reinstated the Inquisition. However, in 1820, after a military uprising in Cádiz under the leadership of two ranking officers, Fernando VII was finally forced to accept the constitution of 1812. The constitutional government lasted only three years. During the reign of terror that followed, tens of thousands of liberals were killed, imprisoned, or driven into exile. Fernando VII assumed absolute rule again but this time refused to reinstate the Inquisition. The formation of a Carlist faction, consisting of military and church leaders in alliance with sections of the popular and artisanal classes who felt disadvantaged by the reforms brought in by liberal modernizers, can be traced back to these events.[47]

When María Cristina became queen regent in 1833, she struck an alliance with the liberals against the Carlist challenge to her daughter's right to the throne, and soon there was civil war in Spain. In 1836 she enacted a new constitution. It was greeted in Cuba with enthusiasm, as it seemed to promise an end to the despotism of years past. In 1837, however, the Cuban representatives were expelled from the Cortes. Spain had decided not to extend the constitution to the colonies: Cuba was to be ruled by special laws.

We can see that liberal Creoles would have objections against anyone extending lavish praise to the monarch. Still, choosing the Carlist War as his main topic would seem to have been a clever decision on Plácido's part, since it allowed him to be a loyalist and yet talk about liberty and despotism. "La Ambarina" (180–81), subtitled "En los días de S. M. la Reina Gobernadora" (In the days of Her Majesty the Regent Queen), is a lengthy poem of seven stanzas of eight verses each. It portrays María Cristina as the supreme benefactor of Spain and Cuba and confronts her purity and love of liberty with the betrayal of the Carlists and the devastation of war. The Inquisition is compared to an Asian tiger that devours sweet little lambs, while María Cristina is a "radiant star in the horrible stormy night." "Cúbrese el campo de alegres flores / Al divo aspecto de su deidad, / Y desde Gades hasta Pirene / Resuena el grito de Libertad" [The fields cover themselves with cheerful flowers / At the divine sight of her deity / And from Cádiz to the Pyrenee / Resounds the cry of Liberty]. After another attack on the Carlists,[48] "La Ambarina" ends with María Cristina declaring:

> ¡Viva la patria! ¡Viva el progreso!
> Decid al punto de me enterrad [?],
> Y yo os ofrezco de responderos [?]
> ¡Vivan! Y viva la Libertad.

> [Say, when you bury me
> Long live the fatherland! Long live progress!
> And I offer to respond
> May they live long! And long live Liberty!]

We do not know whether Plácido wrote this poem before or after 1837. But most likely Plácido's praise would have been more direct prior to the decision not to extend constitutional rights to Cuba. Only after the refusal, when it had become clear that constitutional rule in the metropolis did not mean constitutional rule in the plantation zone, was there a need to highlight liberalism's achievement by portraying it as opposed to the forces of reaction in Spain. If that is so, we can see that Plácido might be inviting us to read his praise of María Cristina according to the paradigm he established for the case of Poland and Greece: the wheel has turned, and the agent of liberty has become the oppressor.

This reading requires us to fill in something that is actually not there—"La Ambarina" tells only the positive part of the story of eternal return, though probably retrospectively. But obviously Plácido was even less in a position to denounce the colonial power than white Creoles, who had more economic resources and could count on a measure of protection. It would thus not be surprising at all if he had chosen to disguise his views in this manner. As in the cases of Poland and Greece, the operations of empire produce an inequality that bestows liberty on one coast while withdrawing it from the other: the forces of dark reaction, as symbolized by the Inquisition, are defeated in Spain but run wild in the colony. Since the Inquisition did not play a major role in Cuba, we must conclude that Plácido is talking about the likes of Tacón and later O'Donnell, who enforced absolute rule *ultramar*.

Now, Plácido must have been aware that after 1837 his poem would have pleased neither liberal Creoles in Cuba nor the colonial administration. Pure opportunism is simply not a plausible explanation for this poem. What lies behind it is, I think, a pointed critique of a contradiction that plagued Spanish *and* Cuban liberals: Cubans were demanding representation in the Cortes, but representation was to be limited to the white population; Spanish liberals were demanding a constitutional regime, but representation was to be limited to the residents in the Iberian Peninsula. Plácido may well have known that one of the reasons adduced in the refusal to extend the constitution to Cuba and allow Cuban representatives in the Cortes was that free people of color would have been excluded from the Cortes by the Cubans. This would have been in conflict with the provision in the Spanish constitution according to which all people born free in the empire were Spanish citizens.[49]

The solution Spain adopted—the colonies were to be ruled by special laws—obviously just displaces the contradiction. Plácido probably realized that the conflict between liberal Creoles and liberal Spaniards was just an apparent one. In fact, both sides tried to solve their problems with the same strategy: by limiting the universality of liberty along the lines of geopolitical location or color. In this respect, Plácido is the exact reverse of those historians and constitutional theorists in the United States who argue that independence was simply the logical first step and that liberty was extended in due course to the whole population, including those of African descent.

In the absence of further evidence about Plácido, this reading has to remain somewhat speculative. What seems beyond doubt, however, is that all of the poems discussed, including those that Plácido wrote in praise of the Spanish monarchy, suggest that liberty is at the core of (legitimate) sovereignty, not the other way around. When the desires of nations and empires take precedence over a commitment to liberty, the wheel turns, and history turns a page—the agents of liberation become oppressors again. In other words, sovereignty resides with the people, not with nations or states. The view that underlies Plácido's poems thus refers us straight back to the heyday of revolutionary thought in the late eighteenth century.

By 1830 it had become clear that the concepts of nationhood and national sovereignty had won the day, and concepts such as universal citizenship had been dropped from elite political discourse. From a formal point of view, Plácido's poems may seem naive, grammatically incorrect, and aesthetically flawed. The reasoning behind them, however, is as incisive as any of the lengthy dissertations of nineteenth-century elite writers and far more radical. Plácido's view points directly to conflicts at the heart of the Haitian and French Revolutions. Speaking from a peripheral social and geopolitical position, with slavery present in all its emotional and physical immediacy, Plácido produces a decidedly slanted discourse in which the unresolved tensions and promises of the revolutionary age are still visible. Underlying the ideological and cultural battles over Plácido, then, is the political and theoretical conflict between revolutionary concepts of emancipation that would have included racial equality, and an independence or autonomist movement that was increasingly grounded in exclusionary nationalism. Liberty is eventually subsumed under national sovereignty. It is this subsumption that Plácido's political poems refuse.

No wonder, then, that Eugenio María Hostos, who insisted that all forms of universalism and cosmopolitanism needed to be rooted in nationalism, found Plácido's poems thoroughly repulsive. "There are some unfortunate people in the world who, under the pretext that men's fatherland is the world, do not want to hear about their fatherland. . . . This is not the cosmopolitanism that we consider our duty."[50] Hostos's objections to Plácido may thus have deep roots in ideological conflicts of the nineteenth century. Instead of articulating these conflicts, however, Hostos helps himself to the discourse of the abject: "For a long time now have we detested the cult of forms for the sake of forms, and we will not commit the cruelty of presenting Plácido's vain literary beauties as a merit. . . . Let these poems remain in the book[s] to prove that evil [el mal] is more deformed the more it dresses up and embellishes itself. . . . The poems Plácido dedicated to the authors of colonial corruption are venomous."[51] It is the very moralization of Plácido's artistic failings that allows his political ideas to vanish from sight.

Hostos, who was not a bad man, probably never spent much time trying to read Plácido's rough-cut poems. It may never have occurred to him that underlying Plácido's apparent complacency could be a universalism that refused to subsume liberty and popular sovereignty under the nationalist project. For all I can tell, the memory of the earlier radical project of emancipation had been thoroughly suppressed by the 1870s, and Plácido's poetry had become even less legible than before, when his outrageous displays of the neoclassical inventory pushed the limits of intelligibility.

What is left of Plácido is the contradictory image of the sublime martyr of Spanish despotism and the ridiculous poet of trifle and flattery, both symbol of the heroic anticolonial struggle and embodiment of debased colonial culture. José Antonio Aponte could be executed and then publicly ridiculed as a monstrous megalomaniac whose personal ambitions led him to plot the genocide of whites;

his politics thus clearly disrupted any cultural significance he might have had. The artisanal culture of the early nineteenth century seems largely to lack direct political significance. In Plácido, politics and poetry converge—a convergence that killed Plácido but then made it impossible to eradicate the traces of a modernity disavowed. More dead than any other nineteenth-century poet, Plácido keeps returning.

# 4

# Cuban Antislavery Narratives
## and the Origins of Literary Discourse

The links between the development of a Cuban literature and fears about slaves and slavery are beyond dispute. In the 1830s, the first literary salon gathered around Domingo Del Monte, an intellectual with close ties to the Sociedad Económica and the local elite as well as to British abolitionist circles. Encouraged by Del Monte and supported by the liberal views of many of the group's members, the aspiring writers took up slavery as their topic of choice. With the exception of Gertrudis Gómez de Avellaneda's novel *Sab* (1841),[1] all early Cuban narratives that dealt with slavery originated in this context.[2] Juan Francisco Manzano, a former slave who occasionally attended the salon, composed his life story at Del Monte's request.[3] After revisions by the Creole writer Anselmo Suárez y Romero, it was sent to the British abolitionist Richard Madden for inclusion in an antislavery dossier and published in England in 1840.[4] Other texts that were written in the context of the Del Monte circle include Félix Tanco y Bosmeniel's "Petrona y Rosalía" (written in 1838, first published in 1925), the story of the slave girl Rosalía who is coerced into having sexual relations with the master's son;[5] Suárez y Romero's fictional *Francisco: El ingenio o Las delicias del campo (Las escenas pasan antes de 1838)* (Francisco: The sugar mill, or The delights of the countryside [The scenes occur before 1838])—the story of true love between the African-born Francisco and the Cuban-born mulatta Dorotea, which is destroyed by the intervention of the white master's son Ricardo, who demands that Dorotea give in to his sexual advances.[6] The early versions of Cirilo Villaverde's famous novel *Cecilia Valdés* (1882), too, were written in the context of Del Monte's circle. Although some of these texts were not published in Cuba until well into the twentieth century, the antislavery imaginary became a cornerstone of the Cuban national culture, and Villaverde's heroine Cecilia Valdés ascended to the status of a national symbol and improbable patron saint.

Thus while the origins of academic painting in Cuba in the 1820s refer us back to the free population of color and the suppression and replacement of popular forms of cultural production that had been their domain, the origins of narrative literature in Cuba are inseparable from slavery and the struggle against it. But this is not to say that the political and ideological assessment of Cuban antislavery has not been the object of considerable disagreement among historians and literary critics. Some assign fairly strong critical and subversive characteristics to the narratives. While typically admitting the ideological ambiguities in the texts in question, they insist that the positions taken by the writers were nevertheless progressive by the standards of the time. In the words of Iván Schulman, they "set a mood and undertake a morally inspired social analysis, critical of a major economic institution" in a period when slavery was still profitable.[7] In *Literary Bondage,* William Luis goes even further and claims that the antislavery novel represents what Foucault called a "counterdiscourse"—a subversive discursive formation that aims at the undoing of discourses of oppression. In Luis's narrative of Cuban literature, this tradition stretches from Manzano's *Autobiografía* to Barnet's documentary novel *Biografía de un cimarrón* (1968), César Leante's *Los guerrilleros negros* (1977), and Reinaldo Arenas's *La loma del Angel* (1987; translated as *Graveyard of the Angels).*[8]

On the opposite side are critics like Portuondo, Carbonil, and Bueno, among many others, who have called into question the position of the elite by pointing out that moderate abolitionism was far more concerned with the demographic effects of the slave trade than slavery itself and did not oppose racial subordination—indeed, may even be read as promoting new and "safer" forms thereof. Clearly, the heart-wrenching love stories and long-suffering slaves favored by the writers give us a severely distorted image of life in a slave-holding society, an image that is not borne out by the reality of endemic uprisings and numerous forms of unorganized resistance, ranging from suicide and infanticide to marronage and the notorious "laziness."[9] This lack of realism has been construed, with good reason, as a reflection of the less-than-revolutionary intention of the writers. Twentieth-century critics typically link the moderate reformist stance articulated in the antislavery narratives to the class position and strategic interests of the white elite writers and conclude that the epithet "antislavery" is largely undeserved by these narratives. Sergio Giral's film *El otro Francisco* (The other Francisco) (1974), which takes up Suárez y Romero's short novel *Francisco* and intercuts it in a Brechtian manner with a demystifying documentary commentary, is perhaps the best—and certainly the most passionate—illustration of this critique.

In a way, both positions are defensible. It is clear that severe censorship ensured that none of the narratives that depicted the brutality of slavery could be published in Cuba at the time. As the poet José Jacinto Milanés put it, "our work has to be pleasant literature and nothing more: the government will not tolerate anything else."[10] This imperative even extended to the Italian opera stage: a censor once demanded that for the Havana performance of Bellini's *I Puritani, libertà* be replaced with *lealtà* (loyalty), and a singer who refused was sentenced to time in prison.[11] However ideologically compromised and impure the position of the early Cuban writers, their texts were of a semiclandestine kind that could circulate only in manuscript form; they were passed on from hand to hand, read aloud, and discussed in the circle of friends who had gathered around Del Monte. Tanco y Bosmeniel's story "Petrona y Rosalía" was not published until 1925. *Sab*, a romantic antislavery narrative that might count as the first fully developed Cuban novel, was written and published in Spain and retained at customs to prevent it from entering the island. In the aftermath of the Escalera Conspiracy of 1844, Del Monte himself was falsely accused of having been one of the conspirators. There cannot be any doubt, then, that the activities of the Del Monte group were considered subversive and came at some personal danger and loss.

José Antonio Saco, whose fears regarding the increase in the slave population and the dominance of free blacks in the arts we have seen in previous chapters, was fully aware of this predicament: "'How imprudent you have been!' many will shout. 'How imprudent to have taken the pen to write about a topic that should always be buried in the deepest silence!' This is the accusation that is generally made against all those who dare to treat this subject."[12] Saco's reference to the officially ordained silence signals a crucial issue here. Political discourse on slavery had to contend with the fact that the slave trade had officially been banned but was tolerated by the colonial authorities (who directly benefited from it), thus creating a constellation in which the activities of the liberal Creole elites—whose main aim was to stop the trade—were always implicated in international politics and could easily be construed as acts of disloyalty against Spain. Whatever the particular aims of local antislavery forces might have been, they always took place within a horizon of potential conflicts between the claims of competing nations and empires.

But Saco's words also evoke the problem of Haiti (which, as we know, loomed large in his mind) and the strategies adopted in relation to the events on the neighboring island: complete silence and outright prohibition of mentioning the events in public. Of course, this official silence was always combined with diligent record keeping and extensive correspondence in the governmental offices. Even the most summary survey of the documents collected in the National Archive in Havana shows that the official denial was in fact shored up by a meticulous sharing of intelligence on the matter: spy reports, letter exchanges between colonial officials, and miscellaneous records of rumors about anything relating to revolutionary antislavery and particularly Haiti prove that "deepest silence" was only one side of the coin.

Finally, Saco's reference to "silence" evokes a practice that, as Orlando Patterson has argued, is constitutive for *all* forms of slavery: any kind of social recognition is withheld from the enslaved person; a slave has no existence outside the master. The mere mention of slaves would bestow a relevance they cannot have. Living in the same geographic or domestic space as slaves thus produces a serious problem for any free person. As Patterson puts it: how can a "socially dead person" nonetheless be an element of society? Can one relate to the socially dead?[13]

If this question posed a deep dilemma in slaveholding societies at any time in history, it became unanswerable in the aftermath of the Haitian Revolution. With a black state on the neighboring island—a state run by former slaves and perceived as a permanent threat—black slaves could not simply be dealt with as "socially dead." Whether or not Haiti ever actually tried to support or encourage slave uprisings on other Caribbean islands, and whether or not Cuban slaves were generally influenced by the example of Haiti, is largely irrelevant as far as the state of mind of slaveholders is concerned. The fact is that revolutionary antislavery continued to exist, and a state run by former slaves was managing to survive next door. Ever since the first horrifying reports arrived in Cuba in the early 1790s, slaves were suspected of plotting to repeat the success of Saint Domingue. The Haitian occupation of the Spanish colony of Santo Domingo from 1822 to 1844 did not help put the slaveholders' minds to rest, either.

Now, the masters' fear of the oppressed masses in itself is nothing new or even complicated. But complications arise in this case when we combine the ideology that sustained slavery—a withholding of all social recognition, a belief in the possibility of total control and submission—with the security concerns prompted by Haiti and revolutionary antislavery. How can slaves be at the same time invisible and a life threat; devoid of all agency and also potential revolutionary agents? Modernity had produced a contradiction in the plantation zone that was impossible to resolve, except through the abolition of slavery, and that was not considered an option for many decades to come.

In nineteenth-century Cuba, the reign of deepest silence needs to be understood as a profoundly contradictory state. Silence both withholds political and social agency from slaves and denies this agency. Under the regime of withholding, agency is a nonthought; under the regime of denial, it is recognized as a lingering danger that requires preventive measures. At the heart of the nineteenth-century culture of slavery, in the aftermath of the Haitian Revolution, is the act of disavowal: the slave is and is not a social being; she or he is at once submissive and a deadly threat; at once unthinking and forever plotting. Slavery in Cuba would be feasible only if both sides of the contradiction could be affirmed at the same time. It is in the epistemologically shaky position of disavowal that the contradictions of slavery after the Haitian Revolution and the foundation of the Haitian state could be contained, and it is precisely in this contradictory constellation that Cuban antislavery narrative intervenes.

One of the problems with the strategy of disavowal in response to the Haitian Revolution was that it came at a considerable political and social cost for the Creole elite: It was predicated on extremely authoritarian forms of political rule and vigilant censorship. Saco's reference to "deepest silence" by implication links slavery and colonial despotism. Undecidability may be an interestingly paradoxical psychological or epistemological (pro)position; in the realm of politics, however, the suppression of knowledge, or the pretense of certain knowledge being unavailable or unverifiable, is inseparable from the actual exercise of power. Disavowal was possible only within a political structure that ran against the autonomist interests and desire for local sovereignty of the Creole elite.

These considerations should not lead us to ignore the fact that the position held by the Creole liberals was by no means radical and did not necessarily imply any opposition to racial subordination. Neither in Cuba nor in the Spanish metropolis was there a radical association comparable to the French Amis des Noirs, and even during the brief constitutional periods (1812–1814 and 1820–1823), abolitionism did not become a central point on the agenda.[14] Elite writing against slavery or the slave trade was, as Schulman put it, "a narrative expression which looks forward from an untenable present to an unthinkable future"—the unthinkable future being a revolutionary solution to the slavery issue on the model of Haiti.[15]

Despite various international agreements against the slave trade in the first decades of the nineteenth century, slavery saw a strong recovery between 1815 and 1830. The number of slaves sold in the Americas actually increased compared to the last two decades of the eighteenth century. France had reintroduced slavery in its remaining colonies in 1802 and began to restock them with slaves. Cuba and Brazil became the leading sugar exporters in the early nineteenth century, after the demise of Saint Domingue, and along with that came a strong need to increase the labor force. Sugar production in Cuba went up from 43,000 tons in 1817 to 70,000 tons in 1827 and 162,000 tons in 1841, and the slave population increased from 199,000 to 287,000 and then 352,000 in 1841.[16] Although the treaty between Spain and England of 1817 had come into effect in 1820, the now illegal trade brought more slaves to Cuba than ever before.

However, were one to rely on official publications at the time, one might well have believed that Cuba was becoming increasingly white in those years. The more progressive sectors in Cuba that gathered in and around the Sociedad Económica and the Ayuntamiento (city hall) of Havana kept calling for the increase of the white population and devised numerous immigration schemes meant to attract immigrants from various (Catholic) parts of Europe. These plans were promoted vigorously, and in great detail, especially after the Escalera Conspiracy of 1844. It seems, however, that the only actual increase in population was that of slaves.[17]

It is quite possible that an enforcement of the ban on the slave trade would have put the moral qualms of a Del Monte to rest, and not just because racial prejudices, along with considerations of personal and class interest, were a big factor in the calculations of the sons of the Creole sacarocracy who were gathering in the Del Monte circle. At a time when the concept of progress structured the discursive fields that stretched from morality to aesthetics and the economy, slavery marked a troubling contradiction at the heart of Cuban society. If slavery was the source of rapid development, it was also the source of barbarism: the more slaves, the more development, the more barbarism. Revolutionary antislavery was but the most fearful of those barbaric futures. The following quote from a letter by the writer Tanco y Bosmeniel articulates these concerns: "What hopes [are there] . . . that our land will be better with statutes, or new town halls . . . while they are packing us in all over with blacks? What sinful civilization—what progress will there be among us if this is pure barbarism and savagery [*cafrería*], the most abominable region on earth? God would allow for these black brutes to be all transformed into tigers, bears, serpents . . . and would not leave alive anyone of the cursed Caucasian race."[18] In 1848, after years of exile and with no censor to fear, Del Monte writes against any revolutionary solution of the Cuban situation and then recommends "to end the slave trade first and then to suppress slowly slavery itself, without disturbance or violence; and finally to cleanse Cuba of the African race."[19]

While Del Monte may have been ambivalent about slaves, he certainly was not ambivalent about the need for a truly Cuban literary culture. Earlier in the 1830s, he had put considerable effort into a plan to create an academy of literature.[20] After the plan gained approval from the regent María Cristina, much back-and-forth ensued between liberal Creoles and the representatives of slaveholders' interests in the Sociedad Económica. Eventually the academy was suppressed by the Captain General Tacón. Having thus failed in a very public way once before, why would Del Monte from 1835 onward deliberately tie the fate of literature in Cuba to the most sensitive political cause, namely, slavery? It was clear that in doing so, he risked prosecution and almost certainly had to relinquish, from the start, any hope of having the texts produced under his tutelage published.

Linking literature to slavery must have held out a particular promise to Del Monte. On the one hand, it seems clear that the idea of literature was closely connected to that of progress. Literary writing and more refined aesthetic practices no doubt symbolized the overcoming of barbarism: having a specifically Cuban literature meant that civilization had taken root. Antislavery narratives, with their appeal to compassion and empathy, may have appeared particularly useful in this context. If slavery and colonial rule relied, for the most part, on domination by brute force, the antislavery texts might have held out the promise of producing readers with a more refined and subtle sensibility, subjects more susceptible to feelings of humanity and reason.[21]

There are some things literature can do that cannot easily be achieved through other genres of cultural production. The issue here is not some formalist idea of literariness. Undoubtedly all the texts in question were written with utilitarian and propagandistic purposes in mind and need to be read in relation to existing discourses and extraliterary pressures. But this does not mean that the narratives can be understood purely as more or less successful attempts at realism. It seems more plausible to think that the element of fictionality was precisely what made literature a promising venue for alleviating or resolving some of the paradoxes and tensions that characterized the political and epistemological situation in the aftermath of the Haitian Revolution.[22] Freud's concept of fantasy as an imaginary or imaginative compromise between the demands of defense and a wish or desire seems particularly promising for a reading of texts that are clearly written as a way of negotiating abolitionist ideas and the trauma of Haiti. In the element of fantasy, these texts effect certain manipulations in the belief structure of the slaveholding regime, all the while also underwriting or preserving some central elements of the ideology of slavery and of racial subordination.

The question is what these narratives do to the fears and desires surrounding slavery. In which way do they intervene in the structures of disavowal that had emerged after the Haitian Revolution? Do they in any way soften or resolve the contradictions that had emerged between the view of slaves as submissive and as lethal? As socially dead and as potential political agents? What kind of changes do they effect, and how do these changes relate to that most terrifying of all possible futures, a repetition of the Haitian events on Cuban soil? It is through the specific form of these fantasies—particularly the fantasy of the docile slave and the fantasy of incest—that we can discern traces of Haiti.

### Fantasy 1: The Submissive Slave

One of the puzzling elements in the genesis of the Cuban antislavery narrative is the role of Victor Hugo's early novel *Bug-Jargal* (1826). We know that the novel was read and discussed in Del Monte's circle and that some considered it an example for the young writers who were taking up the topic of slavery. In a letter to Del Monte (1836), Tanco y Bosmeniel writes:

> And what do you say about *Bug-Jargal*? I would love it if among us a novel was written in that kind of style. Just think about it. The blacks on the Island of Cuba are our Poetry and we do not have to think about anything else; not just the blacks by themselves, but the blacks with the whites, all mixed up, complicated, and turbulent [*revueltos*], and then develop the tableaux, the scenes, which necessarily must be infernal and diabolical; but truthful and clear. Let our Victor Hugo be born and let us learn once

and for all who we are, described with the truth of Poetry, since we know by figures [*números*], and by philosophical analysis, about the sad misery in which we live.[23]

In the symptomatic slippage between two notions of poetry, we can discern a precise articulation of the structure of disavowal: blacks are poetry in Cuba, but this poetry, once it is brought in accordance with "figures" (which I take to mean demographic studies) and "philosophical analysis," is in fact a poetry of horror.[24] Tanco y Bosmeniel does not even attempt to resolve the contradictions here. Is he thinking that a poetic (in the sense of literary or fictional) representation of the scenes would have a cathartic effect? Is he thinking that literature can be realistic where political discourse has to remain silent? The statement is clear only in one respect: that slaves are both poetic and diabolical.

The case is all the stranger, since *Bug-Jargal* is everything the Cuban antislavery novel is not. Hugo, who had written the first version of his novel in 1803 (i.e., before Haiti had even declared independence from France) and then published a revised version in 1826, seemed to have no qualms about making the plot turn on the facts of the slave uprising, while even Calcagno's 1902 *Aponte* reverts to a plot of romantic intrigue. *Bug-Jargal*, by contrast, contains plenty of graphic depiction of the events of the Haitian Revolution, told from the perspective of one of the officers in Leclerc's army, and gives ample room to derogatory descriptions of the brutality of the insurgent slaves, their barbaric rituals, and their savage thirst for blood.

The only literary text that shows some influence from Hugo and does invoke the possibility of resistance is Gertrudis Gómez de Avellaneda's *Sab*, a novel written outside Cuba. In a dramatic soul-bearing dialogue with the good-natured, intelligent, but unfortunately plain and "inexpressive," orphan Teresa, the mulatto Sab says, in pure Castillian Spanish:

Tranquilaos, Teresa, ningún peligro os amenaza; los esclavos arrastran pacientemente su cadena: acaso necesitan para romperla, oír una voz que les grite: "¡sois hombres!," pero esa voz no será la mía, podéis creerlo.[25]

[Do not worry, Teresa, no danger threatens you; the slaves drag their chains patiently: perhaps they need to hear, in order to break them, a voice that shouts: "You are men!" but that voice will not be mine, you may believe me.]

Bug-Jargal, who had joined the rebel army in Saint Domingue, is turned into Sab, who renounces insurrection. Having invoked the universalist rhetoric of revolutionary France and Haiti, Sab immediately retreats: the novel needs him to be a romantic hero, not a political agitator.[26]

Sab's beloved mistress Carlota remains unaware of his feelings for her and does not recognize them until after Sab's death. The particularism of romantic love trumps the universality of the desire for liberty. By choosing to remain, minstrel-like, "in the service of his beloved" even after he has been freed by Carlota's father, Sab is transformed from a submissive slave into a slave who chooses to submit. Doubly enslaved to his mistress Carlota—first as a legal slave and then as a lover—Sab ends up sacrificing himself to her happiness. Since as a slave and mulatto he knows that he will never be the object of his mistress's desire, he takes up the position of the intermediary through whom her desires will be realized: having won a lottery, he secretly makes this money available to Carlota, who, without a substantial inheritance, would have lost her adored suitor, the unprincipled and supremely undeserving English interloper Enrique Otway. As under the slaveholding regime, Sab, the legally free but emotionally bound mulatto, serves to fulfill the desire of the master; as under the slaveholding regime, the serf receives no immediate recognition for this. Yet quite in keeping with the Hegelian dialectic of master and slave, it is the slave who literally shapes the world around him: it is Sab who saves his masters' lives and marriage plans and thus achieves a higher form of subjectivity and moral development. By making romantic servitude a substitute for legal bondage, *Sab* enacts a fantasy in which the voluntary relinquishing of free will and liberty is recast as an act of supreme autonomy: in an act of heroic overcoming of base desires for revenge and immediate gratification, Sab asserts his superior humanity and in a sense becomes his masters' master. Even Carlota eventually comes to this realization. After her marriage to Otway has come unraveled and Sab's secret role in her life has been revealed, Carlota retreats to the site of Sab's burial and devotes herself to the upkeep of his grave.

This fantasy clearly has political implications. In *Sab*, romantic love and the voluntary servitude of a former slave open, as if for the first time, the antagonism between those of Cuban birth and of foreign birth as a romantic, moral, and thus truly justified antagonism. Devotion and self-sacrifice among those born in Cuba—white or not white—are opposed to the self-interest and manipulation of foreigners: through the transfiguration of legal into affective bondage, the submissive slave becomes the figure through which Cubans of various colors can desire and recognize each other. It is, quite literally, on the grave of the slave who renounced rebellion that this fantasy of a reconciled future Cuba takes place. From Avellaneda's *Sab* to Calcagno's *Aponte*, the possibility of Cuban autonomy and independence depends on the suppression of black insurrection and the substitution of affective, voluntary submission for submission through brute force.

However, the idyllic utopia of *Sab* should not lead us to hastily subsume all submissive slaves under the autonomist and protoindependence agenda. As a novel written by a Cuban expatriate, *Sab* displays palpable nostalgia, and the most pressing and immediate concerns seem to have been set aside in favor of a more long-term view of Cuba's future. The stories written in the 1830s on the island, with their relentless descriptions of beatings, sexual and psychological abuse, and moral depravation of the masters indicate that the immediate concerns were somewhat different and that desires for autonomy related in other ways to the opposition to slavery.

Given the fear of a repetition of the Haitian events, any hint at slaves as rebellious would have rekindled a paranoia that typically led to further repression and racial hatreds. These reactions were clearly not conducive to abolitionist designs and, in fact, often turned into arguments against white abolitionists, no matter how moderate their views. The recipients of philanthropic action needed to appear helpless and deserving. These strategic calculations were compounded by the fact that the economic and political interests of the liberal elite meant that greater autonomy from Spain was extremely desirable. While the presence of large numbers of slaves made full independence inadvisable for most Cubans, a measure of self-determination was very much part of the Creole agenda. The more dangerous the slaves appeared to be, the more dependent Cuba was on the military presence of Spain. In this sense, the suppression of the artisanal culture in the first decades of the nineteenth century, and the suppression of the slave as a political agent, are just two sides of the same coin: both strip the population of color, whether free or enslaved, of agency. The antislavery novel simply added a philanthropic element to this by offering the slave body up for white compassion. Moderate abolitionism's aim is precisely to avoid any life-and-death struggle between master and slave. This, of course, does not imply that all Creole writers thought that Cuba's future was in the hands of noble mulattoes like Sab.

Now, if we want to understand more concretely what the antislavery texts do, we need an account of how the figure of the docile slave might relate to the ideological underpinnings of a slaveholding society that had come under severe pressure through the existence of a revolutionary black state on a neighboring island. The romantically inclined submissive slave is clearly a phantasmagoric figure with little support in reality, if we imagine this support to be of a representational, realistic kind. The general paranoia, the wealth of secret communications regarding uprisings, and the nonfictional writings of a Del Monte and a Tanco y Bosmeniel show that Cubans did not fool themselves: slaves were not in fact submissive.

What do these narratives achieve by presenting the reader with the fantasy of the docile slave? Paradoxically, the docile slave was a commonplace figure not just in the antislavery narratives; it was also an essential ingredient of pro-slavery ideology. In his notorious writings about the British West Indies, Bryan Edwards, for instance, claims that if encouragement were given to those "hot-brained fanaticks and detestable incendiaries, who, under the vile pretense of philanthropy and zeal for the interests of suffering humanity, preach up rebellion and murder to the contented and orderly negroes," the same "carnage and destruction" as took place in Saint Domingue would spread through the colonial world.[27] Slaves are perfectly pliable and submissive as long as they are not manipulated by radical abolitionists. In his analysis of the differences between Saint Domingue and Cuba, the chief ideologist of the Cuban sacarocracy, Francisco Arango y Parreño (who later changed his mind and joined the abolitionist faction), insists that in Saint Domingue, the slaves were infected by the desire for freedom of the free population of color; in Cuba, where slaves were treated much better than in the French colony, there was, he claims, "a spirit of subordination and eternal and blind obedience to the Sovereign."[28] The argument is familiar enough from all slaveholding societies in the Americas and does not need to be further elaborated on: slave resistance is to be feared only when slaves are being stirred up by white agitators and the free population of color. Black slaves are by nature peaceful and meek creatures, and racial subordination is a fact of nature.

From this perspective, we might say that the image of the docile slave in the antislavery narratives is by no means unrealistic and certainly not an inappropriate and self-serving idealization. Rather, it is a fairly accurate re-presentation of the way in which the slaveholding aristocracy related to the institution. Slavoj Žižek's well-known argument that ideology is an "unconscious fantasy that structures social reality itself,"[29] rather than an illusion that could be unmasked or shown to be a form of false consciousness, may usefully be employed here: neither the common denunciation of the fantasy by critics of moderate antislavery as a romanticizing distortion that needs to be disproved, nor a defense on the grounds that the image of a submissive slave was somehow meant to unsettle pro-slavery ideology, would seem adequate. To locate the figure of the submissive slave in a debate about the "truth about slaves" would be to seriously misdiagnose the ideological operations of the narratives.

But the realization that the antislavery novels cannot be understood through the paradigm of realism or a reflection theory of ideology does not in itself answer the question of what happens when the fantasy that sustains the material practice of slavery comes to inform a literary text.[30] Where does the moment of critique come from that the writers clearly intended and that was not lost on the Spanish censors? Returning to the earlier argument about the internal contradictions of slaveholding ideology after the Haitian Revolution, I would like to suggest that by taking up the image of the docile slave from pro-slavery discourse, these narratives create an ideological trap of sorts: they underwrite an ideology that sees racial subordination as natural, but they also disrupt the dynamics of disavowal that was crucial to the continuation of slavery and the slave trade after the Haitian Revolution and to the continuation of colonial despotism.

The fantasy of the submissive slave gives expression to a belief that shores up the practice of slavery. The critical charge of these texts, however, stems from a kind of bargain between the narrator and the reader: in exchange for empathy and compassion in the face of unspeakable cruelty, the reader is offered the comforting image of a harmless, meek being that no one needs to fear—precisely one of the images that slaveholders had cherished all along, but that was rejected by most liberal Creoles in their nonfictional writings. We know from contemporary documents that grown men were shedding tears as they listened to these sentimental texts of suffering and torture: catharsis in exchange for a suspension of disbelief. The relentless representation of brute desire on the side of the masters and infinite endurance of torture and abuse on the side of the slave thus provide fantasies that promise emotional gratification—release through tears—if the reader is willing to enter the bargain.

The payoff is considerable. The stories offer a particularly protective fantasy that forecloses a knowledge that in the ideology of slavery is part of the structure of disavowal: the slave is dangerous. Reflecting the psychic structure familiar from psychoanalytic theory according to which certain repetitive fantasies serve to hide from sight a particularly disturbing event—typically the scene of castration, or what Lacan called "the lack"—the repetitive scenes of sadistic torture and meek endurance by the slave hide from view another, infinitely more horrifying sight: the murderous slave, a replay of the Haitian events. Lacan has pointed out that these kinds of protective fantasies tend to have a peculiarly immutable character. This may ultimately be what explains the strange repetitiveness in the anti-slavery narratives. They keep returning to cycles of torture, recovery, and new torture, while the perverse romance provides the semblance of a narrative arc. If a plausible narrative resolution of the excesses of torture and abuse would be either death or rebellion, these stories offer as a substitute the love story. In doing so, they provide an emotionally satisfying veil that hides from view the other, traumatic scene. What remained strangely contradictory in Tanco y Bosmeniel's letter about *Bug-Jargal*—black slaves are Cuba's poetry and the cause of its diabolical situation—is resolved in favor of the first proposition. It is on this level that Creole desire for autonomy relates to the figure of the docile slave. In exchange for tears and sympathy, the reader is allowed the fantasy of a future in which Cuba no longer needs a despotic government that legislates what can be said and what cannot be said, and what can be known and what has to remain shrouded "in deepest silence."

The stories thus offer a bargain that promises release of sorts from the instability of disavowal. But more than that, a refusal to enter the bargain—a refusal on the grounds that the submissive slave is unrealistic, for instance—would force the reader to then adopt the opposite position: slaves are in fact dangerous. This second position remains implicit and is arrived at only through logical inference. But it is the only alternative if the original bargain is rejected and sympathy is withheld. Now, of course, one might argue that a reader could simply have refused to enter the fantasy of the antislavery narratives altogether by arguing that neither are slaves treated so badly nor are they quite as docile and innocent.[31] But that is beside the point. The stark fantasies, with their clear opposition between victims and perpetrators, good and evil, pleasure and suffering, are constructed precisely to offer up as an alternative what disavowal both affirmed and denied: either slaves are submissive, in which case slavery is morally and emotionally untenable, or they are dangerous, in which case the trade should, for reasons of prudence, be stopped immediately. Any objection against the figure of the submissive slave in the antislavery texts would thus also be an objection against precisely that ideological figure that underwrites the practice and justification of slavery after the Haitian Revolution.

All antislavery narratives written by white Creoles from the 1830s onward are stories of romantic love and sexual desire. In Tanco y Bosmeniel's "Petrona y Rosalía," the master's son coerces the slave girl Rosalía into having sexual relations with him by promising to bring her mother, Petrona, from the plantation to the city, but then fails to act on his promise and does not intervene when Rosalía is savagely punished for having become pregnant. In Suárez y Romero's *Francisco,* there is a love story between the African-born Francisco and the Cuban-born mulatta Dorotea—a romance that is destroyed by the intervention of the white master's son Ricardo, who fancies Dorotea for his own amusement. With the title figure inspired by Francisco Manzano, this fantasy of the slave as a romantic lover is especially remarkable, since Manzano in his autobiography had certainly stayed clear of any romantic plot. Even Gertrudis Gómez de Avellaneda's novel *Sab,* which in many other ways does not conform to the conventions of the Cuban antislavery narratives of the 1830s, is the story of unrequited love of the mulatto Sab for his mistress Carlota.

Villaverde's treatment of the Cecilia material is particularly interesting in the present context.[32] The 1839 "primitive" version is a romance of sorts, which, at first sight, has no connection to slavery. Barely twenty-five pages long, it tells the story of a mulatta whom the narrator claims to have known in 1826 or 1827, when she was only ten years old and freely roamed the streets of Havana. As she grows up, Cecilia is seduced by a morally corrupt white man named Leocadio Gamboa. The story ends with Cecilia having vanished from sight. In the 1882 version of *Cecilia Valdés,* which does have an explicit antislavery theme, the love story becomes a drawn-out affair of several hundred pages, which ends with Cecilia giving birth to a daughter in secrecy, the male protagonist (now called Leonardo Gamboa) getting married to a white woman, and his death at the hands of a mulatto friend of Cecilia.[33]

Now, obviously, it is not at all uncommon to use the particularistic energies of desire for the telling of a much larger, political story. But on closer inspection we note that none of these narratives make proper use of the generic qualities of love stories. There is something strangely voluntaristic or arbitrary about the way they are told, which, from the standpoint of narrative coherence, could seem inept. But then again, how can there be organic development, if one of the characters can do what ever he pleases at any time? If we take the categories Aristotle develops in his *Poetics*—notions of verisimilitude, causality, reversal, and so on—as an account of classical narrative structures in the West, it would seem that under the regime of racial slavery, any story that tries to cross the boundaries between slaves and nonslaves, or even the boundaries between whites and people of color, must contend with the fact that the basic laws of narrative are disabled.

The perversity of the resulting romances shows itself, among other ways, in the frequency of incest as the effect of the often nonconsensual sexual relations between women of color and white masters.[34] This theme becomes explicit with the final version of Villaverde's *Cecilia Valdés* of 1882, where the fact that Leonardo and Cecilia have the same father becomes the central mystery of the novel. As *Cecilia Valdés* acquired the status of the Cuban national novel, incest and slavery appear to have become inseparable in the minds of Cuban authors. Already in 1891, Martín Morúa Delgado, an important mulatto writer and politician, undertook a critical rewriting of *Cecilia Valdés*. His novel *Sofía* retains the incest plot and the antislavery theme but changes the story by transforming Cecilia into a white girl who is mistakenly identified as a mulatta, robbed of her rightful inheritance, enslaved, and subsequently raped by her half brother, who is unaware of their relation.[35] In Lino Novás Calvo's *El negrero* (The slave trader) (1933), the incestuous situation is the result of the slave trader's excessive attachment to his sister.[36] In Reinaldo Arenas's *La loma del angel,* a brief comical and savage pastiche of Villaverde's *Cecilia Valdés,* finally, incest is provocatively moved to center stage: "The entire novel," Arenas proclaims in his preface, "is permeated by incessant, aptly insinuated, incestuous ramifications" (9).

Although the incest theme becomes fully developed only in the 1882 version of *Cecilia Valdés,* a closer look at early narrative texts in Cuba shows that its origins reach back into the beginnings of Cuban literature. Already in 1838, it is used to create suspense in Tanco y Bosmeniel's "Petrona y Rosalía": unbeknownst to the two protagonists, the slave girl Rosalía is a daughter of Ricardo's father. An undeveloped secondary plot then reveals that Ricardo, too, is the product of an adulterous affair, and not his father's biological son, after all. Incest avoided, by a hair's breadth. Suárez y Romero's *Francisco* does not invoke incest in the strict sense but insists that the master's son and the slave girl Dorotea, whom he forces into a sexual relationship, were *hermanos de leche* (literally, milk siblings; i.e., suckled by the same wet nurse). The son's actions are criminal not just because of his brutality but also because he is practically Dorotea's brother.

Villaverde's "Cecilia Valdés" of 1839, which most critics have considered as radically different from the 1882 novel on the grounds that the earlier text contained neither an antislavery theme nor an incest story, deserves a second look, too. The early novella in fact does contain numerous hints that there is something particularly inappropriate or transgressive about a sexual relationship between Leocadio Gamboa and Cecilia. Compare the following dialogue that takes place in the house of the Gamboa family among the children and their mother. Cecilia had been brought into the house by the young girls; there had been some bantering among the girls, and then Cecilia had taken to the street again. Suddenly one of the girls raises the question of Cecilia's strikingly familiar appearance.

> You look so much like her, you are almost indistinguishable, like two eggs. —No, it's you who looks like her. —No, not me. It's Leocadio. —Why should she look like me and not like any old person in the street? —No, it's not you. It's Papa. —Nobody less than Papa. Papa has green eyes and hers are black; Papa has blond hair, and hers is black as coal. —Girls! Like Papa . . . what a crazy idea![37]

The story leaves no room for doubt: already in 1839 Cecilia Valdés is a half-sibling of the Gamboa children. The implicit presence of incest in the early story may in fact explain an issue critics have puzzled over since the publication of the definitive version of *Cecilia Valdés* in 1882. Since most readers would guess very quickly that Cándido Gamboa is the father of both Leonardo and Cecilia, why does it take several hundred pages of cagey hints and whispered communications before the truth about their relation is finally revealed? It strikes me that incest plays such an odd role in the 1882 novel precisely because it was already the subtext of the 1839 novella. Adding vast amounts of material to the story effectively meant that the secret of Cecilia's origins had to be transformed from a mere insinuation with largely allegorical or figurative significance into a major plot line. The fact that Villaverde held onto the idea, despite the technical challenge it posed, is further evidence that the themes of incest and of slavery and racial hierarchy must have had some peculiar affinity for Cuban writers at the time. It is thus likely that it is the theme of incest that links the earlier "Cecilia Valdés" indirectly to issues of racial hierarchies and slavery.

Even Gómez de Avellaneda's *Sab*, which was written in Spain and has a very different plot from the narratives mentioned so far, suggests the possibility that the secret love the title hero, a mulatto slave, harbors for his mistress Carlota might be more familial than any of the characters would like to admit. Sab's mother never revealed to him who his father was. The novel leaves little doubt, however, that it was Carlota's uncle, which would make Carlota and Sab first cousins.

What moved Cuban writers in the 1830s to invoke various forms of endogamy, and incest as its limit case, when their immediate concern was slavery? There are no data, to my knowledge, that would support the idea that incest was a problem particular to slaveholding societies.[38] Its presence seems to be limited to highly ideological and fictional texts, and this, in turn, seems rather surprising upon reflection: in a society that practices racial slavery, cross-racial desire would presumably be linked to fears of a difference perceived as too great, as opposed to incest, which would naturally be linked to fears about excessive closeness. Why would excessive difference collapse into dangerous closeness?

Despite the oddity of the phenomenon, literary criticism has not had much to say about the issue. William Luis reads it in relation to the anthropological commonplace that the incest taboo marks the border between nature and culture.[39] Incest signifies sexual desire unbridled by societal laws and thus leads to a regression and brutalization of the human being and a breakdown of human society. In a reading of *Cecilia Valdés*, Doris Sommer interprets the incest theme in relation to racially determined power and knowledge differentials that produce fatal discontinuities: whites will not listen to blacks, and blacks are fearful of sharing their knowledge with whites. "It is secrecy that puts Leonardo at risk of incest."[40] Vera Kutzinski, who deals at length with issues of sexuality and racial anxieties, notes that "Cuban writing, from the antislavery narratives to *Cecilia Valdés* and to Morúa Delgado's *Sofía*, was obsessed with incest situations resulting from interracial rape and concubinage," but she explains the figure of incest solely as the "specter of . . . confused, and thus probably 'contaminated,' genealogies, for which women are usually held responsible."[41] They all seem to assume that the invocation of incest is a means for moral condemnation of the slaveholding society. In the most extensive treatment of incest in relation to racial anxieties to date, Werner Sollors argues that the "abolitionist-liberal trajectory"—to which all the Cuban texts undoubtedly belong—has at its foundation a "realistic hypothesis": when kinship between people of different color is denied as a matter of course, miscegenation can easily turn out to be incest.[42]

Sollors amply documents that incest and miscegenation have

been associated with each other from vastly different ideological perspectives, including a pro-slavery position. What he does not consider, however, is that, at least in the Cuban materials, the link between incest and miscegenation is itself a highly contested one. As the history of rewritings of *Cecilia Valdés* shows, someone like Morúa Delgado made an enormous effort to show that the issue of incest needs to be separated from that of miscegenation. Although Morúa Delgado does not spell out why he objected so virulently to Villaverde's apparent conflation of miscegenation and incest, it seems clear from the changes he made to the story in his own novel *Sofía* that his antagonism was somehow grounded in this feature of the story. Why so?

One of the problems with the realistic hypothesis is that in the Cuban narratives, incest does not actually appear as the most horrific of all possibilities. Neither the setups nor their resolutions are Sophoclean—incest is more often invoked as a fear, possibility, or danger than integrated into the plot and developed in tragic detail. We should remember, too, that the incest in question is not between parents and offspring but of a more distant sort, between half siblings.[43] In *Cecilia Valdés*, for instance, true horror is reserved for the depiction of the mistreatment of slaves on the plantation, whereas the birth of Cecilia's incestuously conceived daughter is very much underplayed and not accompanied by any sense of doom or catastrophe. Incest is in a sense more a structural device to create suspense than an element of the affective textures and narrative details. It has an almost phantasmagoric character in these stories: it is suggested but not quite affirmed, invoked as a possibility, almost just a mere thought, neither asserted nor denied.

Commenting on *Cecilia Valdés*, César Leante, an avid proponent of the ideal of *la Cuba mulata*, takes a further step in this direction: he seems to consider the sexual relation between Cecilia and her half brother as an allegory of race relations in Cuba, and thus as in some sense desirable.[44] Similarly, although for different reasons, Reinaldo Arenas's rewriting of *Cecilia Valdés* embraces the incest theme and indeed gives it a positive charge: real passion is the result of a search for sameness. When Cecilia's mother finally tells her the story of her true origins, thus leaving no possible doubt that her lover was her half brother, Cecilia blandly responds: "Con razón nos queríamos tanto" [That's why we loved each other so much] (135).

Arenas's intuitions are of course quite in keeping with what we know about incestuous desire. According to Freud, all desire is in its origins narcissistic, that is, a desire for sameness. There would be no need for an incest taboo if it were not unconsciously desired. In Jocasta's words, "As to your mother's marriage bed,—don't fear it. / Before this, in dreams too, as well as oracles, many a man has lain with his own mother."[45] We could also point to *Sab*, with its apparent advocacy of miscegenation,[46] as a resolution for societal antagonisms in Cuba and its idyllic account of Carlota and Sab growing up together. Sab has the most pure and unspoiled love for the girl who in all likelihood is his first cousin. Endogamy combines with the Rousseauian notion of ideal romantic love, according to which the perfect marriage is based on the growing up together of a boy and a girl "like brother and sister." Bernadin de St. Pierre's *Paul et Virginie* (1788) is the classical example of a heterosexual union being founded on a shared childhood, indeed a closeness that differs little from that of biological siblings. And it is not the case, either, that in Western culture incestuous desire has always been linked to individual or familial pathologies: within the romantic revolutionary culture of the eighteenth century, for example, sibling incest seems to have had a vaguely positive valence. As Sollors points out, in a social and political imagination that considers all humans brothers, all kinship relations would be understood as a form of endogamy or of "universal incest that is weakened, however, by being so universal."[47]

A closer look at Villaverde's 1882 novel confirms the intuition that incest occupies an ambiguous place in the narrative. The narrator seems to be torn between treating it as a horrific possibility looming on the horizon, and extending a rather more indulgent view. On the one hand, there is a familial constellation that bears striking similarities to Freud's account of Oedipal conflicts. Doña Rosa's excessive love for her son is clearly marked as somehow transgressive, and Don Cándido's inability to make his son submit to his authority is mirrored by the fact that the son is completely devoid of ethical considerations. But the affection between Leonardo and his sister Adela is treated as a rather endearing fact: if Leonardo and Adela had not been brother and sister by birth, the narrator says, "they would have loved each other as did the most celebrated lovers that the world has ever known" (171). So it is perfectly clear that Leonardo desires Cecilia precisely as a representative of his sister. The fact that Cecilia turns out to *be* his sister is simply the ultimate fulfillment of his incestuous desire—but *that* fact does not seem to worry the narrator.

The incest theme thus has two apparently contradictory faces. On the one hand, it has a weakly positive valence, as a union based on equality, shared experiences, and mutual sympathy, rooted as much in familial indulgence as in family pathologies of the sort analyzed by Freud: more closely resembling endogamy than incest properly speaking, possibly even foundational for a society based on generalized *mestizaje* and predecessor to the idea of la Cuba mulata. On the other hand, incest is invoked as the limit case of an abusive or illicit sexual relation—the sign of the moral debasement of Cuban society, sign of the most horrifying and barbaric of all possibilities.

But how can the same phenomenon be both corrosive and foundational to Cuban society, both desired and abhorred? And how can anxiety about excessive difference turn into a fantasy about excessive closeness? The peculiarities of the incest topic—its contradictory affective charge, its melodramatic and sensationalist overtones, and its suspended existence between fact and nonfact—suggest that, like the stories of submissive slaves, it is best understood as a fantasy, and that playing it out against some overriding "reality" is, once again, to miss the point altogether. Whether or not incest actually occurs (in the stories or in reality) is a secondary question compared to the issue of its overwhelming rhetorical, phantasmagoric presence. As in the case of the fantasy of the submissive slave, it is this contradictoriness itself that needs to be accounted for if we want to understand why the incest theme was so attractive for the Cuban authors and readers of antislavery texts.

What under racial slavery would be the greatest difference—namely, difference of color or race—turns into a troubling closeness. In a logically illegitimate but emotionally plausible leap, the incest fantasy seems to produce a thought of the form "If they are just like us, then . . . sexual relations are incestuous."[48] The true depth of ambivalence of Creole writers about people of African ancestry emerges as a function of the ambivalence inscribed in the very idea of incest, where horror and desire are inextricably linked.

But there is still more to the incest fantasy. Instead of recognizing an other as a subject of equal standing, these texts divert the thought process into a traumatic fantasy about the Creole self. They allow the reader to deplore the abuses of a slaveholding society while eluding the necessity of recognizing that the Other is an independently constituted subject. Again, *Cecilia Valdés* illustrates this very clearly. The infraction that constitutes the central (non)mystery stems not from Cecilia's being too different but from her being too close. Cecilia is desired not as other but as the same: a fact that is alternately treated with horror and sweet indulgence. What we find is an otherness that rather would turn into an aspect of the self than into an otherness that is recognized as such. The fantasy of incest allows the reader to avoid a constellation in which mutual recognition across the dividing lines of color and race would be the natural conclusion.

The incest story offers a scenario in which the radical alternative to the colonial slaveholding system remains veiled. The narratives forever refer us back to the horror and desire attached to the idea of incest. Incest fantasies as a form of disavowal: having chosen love stories that cross the lines of color and race and so seem to articulate the equal human status of whites, blacks, and mulattoes, the Creole writers shy away as if in the face of an unspeakable horror. As soon as human equality asserts itself, it turns into a transgressive sameness. The thought that has been avoided is one we will later encounter in the revolutionary constitution of 1805 of neighboring Haiti, which opens as follows: "In the presence of the Supreme Being, before whom all mortals are equal, and who has scattered so many kinds of different beings on the surface of the globe for the sole purpose of manifesting his glory and power through the diversity of his works; Before the whole creation, whose disowned children we have so unjustly and for so long been considered; we declare . . ." Creole writers in Cuba, by contrast, fantasize subjects whose familial and political status is scrambled in ways that make recognition almost impossible. Their status resembles more that of Antigone, who is both her father's child and his half sister, than that of Oedipus: neither the logic of kinship nor the logic of citizenship and the state accounts for their position in the colonial slaveholding society that was Cuba. The only recognition available to them is a misrecognition: as objects of incestuous desire.

# PART II

## Santo Domingo/The Dominican Republic

# 5

# Memory, Trauma, History

## Santo Domingo and Haiti I

Ayer español nací,
a la tarde fuí francés,
a la noche etíope fuí,
hoy dicen que soy inglés,
¡No sé que será de mí!

[Yesterday I was born a Spaniard,
in the afternoon I was French,
by the evening Black I was,
today they say I am English.
I don't know what will become of me!]
—Dominican popular poem

Nowhere in the Greater Caribbean did the Haitian Revolution have a more immediate impact than in Santo Domingo, and nowhere did it leave a deeper and more warped trace in the collective memory. In 1801 Toussaint Louverture occupied the Spanish colony and abolished slavery. Looking back to the scene of Toussaint's arrival, a Dominican eyewitness writes: "I remember the confusion, the terror, and the surprise with which everybody watched those regimented Blacks with their decorations and civil and military insignias, as well as the dejection of our spirits when we saw the Tricolor Flag instead of the Spanish being raised on the Fortaleza del Homenaje, thus replacing the government of Captain Joaquín García with that of the leader of the blacks, Toussaint Louverture."[1] Slavery was reintroduced the following year, when Napoleon seized the eastern part of the island of Hispaniola in his attempt to recapture the former French colony in the West. In 1805 the slaves were freed again when Dessalines invaded, but slavery was eventually reintroduced once more and continued first under French and then, after 1809, under Spanish rule.

In 1822 there was a first Dominican declaration of independence, which lasted only a few weeks, did not entail the abolition of slavery, and had very little popular support. It was followed by another Haitian invasion and twenty-two years of Haitian rule.[2] In 1844 there was a second declaration of independence. Haiti refused to recognize the Dominican Republic, and in the 1840s and 1850s there were repeated Haitian incursions across the border, which reignited Dominican fears of Haitian "imperialism." In 1861 the Dominican Republic reverted to being a Spanish territory. In 1865, after two years of popular resistance and warfare, Spain withdrew its troops and administrators, and the territory reconstituted itself as an independent republic.

The experience of repetitions and reversals must have been quite overwhelming, as even the national anthem includes a brief remembrance of it:

> Mas Quisqueya, la indómita y brava,
> siempre altiva la frente alzará;
> que si fuere mil veces esclava,
> otras tantas ser libre sabrá.

> [But the indomitable and brave Quisqueya,
> will always raise her forehead high;
> because, if she were to be slave a thousand times,
> as many times she will know how to be free.]

The repetitions that run through Dominican history in the nineteenth century serve as an implacable reminder that the homogeneous, steady time of progress and development, elusive enough on the Spanish American mainland, was simply not available in the plantation zone. Spanish Hispaniola seemed to be set on a course of eccentric loops, punctuated by violent disruptions and reversals that reproduced dependency instead of ushering in a new golden era of the modern nation-state, and left traces of traumatic memories that reasserted the power of the past at every turn. The unexpected and—for some—unassimilable event of the Haitian Revolution seemed to have thrown Dominican history off its normal course. Postcoloniality in the Dominican Republic is unlike postcoloniality anywhere else in Spanish America.

Even the simple question of the date of Dominican independence has no simple answer. Discussing the power of myths of origins in the constitution of nations and nationalism, Etienne Balibar has argued that in the history of modern nations there is never more than a single founding revolutionary event,[3] and that political divisions between Left and Right often crystallize around the interpretation of the revolution that is taken to be constitutive for the nation. Dominicans nowadays celebrate the 1844 independence as the true beginning of the Dominican nation. But from a structural point of view, we may wonder whether the choice of 1844 is not in itself already a deeply political fact rather than a fact at the foundation of all subsequent political conflict. After all, 1844 represents independence from Haiti, but the Dominican Republic's colonial history would have pointed toward independence from Spain—either 1822 or 1865—as the more significant event. If anticolonialism had been the decisive force in the constitution of the Dominican Republic, 1844 would probably not have been chosen as the date of real independence. But here, more than anywhere else in the Caribbean, the political process cannot be equated with that of decolonization.

No matter which way we look at this, it is clear that instead of a single revolutionary moment, we have multiple revolutionary moments, representing conflicting, even incompatible, emancipatory projects. The ideological and affective impact of the convulsive history of fitful starts and repetitions is compounded by the fact that a revocation of liberties is bound to be experienced with a heightened sense of injustice and unnaturalness. So it is perhaps not surprising that the historical imaginary that develops in the course of the nineteenth century has a peculiarly warped and melancholy quality. Although the Dominican Republic is not the only territory that saw independence revoked and slavery reintroduced (the latter in particular happened on several Caribbean islands), the sheer number of reversals, combined with the fact that they involved both slavery and the political status of the territory, thus affecting not merely an oppressed minority or a racially or ethnically distinct group, must have made the experience more painful, more difficult to assimilate into something that resembled a historical narrative, or even just a more or less stable experience. Although Dominican nationalism does not differ from most other forms of nationalism in its desire to present itself as the expression of an age-old communality, a Dominican identity emerged only very slowly, through the long process of reversals and changing interpellations that stretched from the 1790s to 1865.

If we looked only at Dominican texts that specifically address Haiti and the Haitian occupations, we would probably conclude that in the Dominican Republic, the complex geopolitical issues underlying the

Haitian Revolution and its aftermath were simply brushed aside. In their place, we find images of a barbarian invader. Since Haiti was always already there—on the island, in the cities, in the municipal governments—the strategies of denial and trivialization toward Haiti that Michel-Rolph Trouillot has documented in *Silencing the Past* and that we have seen at work elsewhere were not plausible responses. As Haiti remained a force to be reckoned with, the main strategy that appears to take hold is one of demonization and racist denigration.

However, this picture is far too simplistic. To be sure, the Dominican state and the forms of cultural production that gave it coherence and solidity took shape against Haiti. Yet close attention to the specific form of Dominican responses to Haiti and careful consideration of the likely impact of a historical experience of repetitions, reversals, and regressions will allow us to produce a more fine-grained picture of the impact of the Haitian Revolution. This is not the impact a positivistically inspired historiography might be looking for: it cannot be measured in figures or documented in forthright quotes. Rather, it requires all our hermeneutical skills, and like all hermeneutical work, it takes us outside the realm of what can be proved. It is an impact that needs to be tracked in the patterns of collective obsessions, in individual responses, misrepresentations, and fantasies.

Although much of this interpretative work takes place behind the back, as it were, of history in the conventional sense, it cannot be done without extensive reference to the details of Dominican economic and legal records, demography, et cetera. Both fantasies and historical facts, imaginary and actual memories, remain inert, lest we play them against a background of a different order. Perhaps it is always true that historical and political processes can only be grasped through movements between the historical, the theoretical, the psychic, and the literary levels. But in the case of a country so torn by the effects of colonialism, slavery, and the conflictive and often violent struggles against them, a country where self-determination was so hard to achieve and the idea of nationhood so elusive, it seems particularly true that a multidimensional picture of events can only be achieved by a layering operation where various registers are played off against each other. The remainder of this chapter has two aims: to set out the historical events in a way that allows us to see the interstices in which an alternative reading of the Dominican historical process can take root; and to problematize some of the more influential theoretical proposals that in recent years have become common framing devices for studies of historical trauma, memory, and suppressed events of the past.

## The Problem with Trauma

It seems rather plausible to think that the Haitian Revolution and the events of the early nineteenth century would have had a deep impact on Dominican subjectivity. With every new border conflict, every new "invasion," the memory of watching former slaves take over the municipal buildings would resurface, potentially dividing the population along racial lines by inviting conflicting identifications, and calling into question yet again the problematic interpellation of "Dominicanness."

It seems clear that the developmentalist historiography that traditionally dominates the genre of national history and national literary history (in the Dominican Republic and elsewhere) will not do. Any narrative of national redemption in which discontinuities are mere setbacks or political aberrations only further obscures the subjective element in the human dimension we call history.[4] But matters are still more complex in the case of the Dominican Republic. The extraordinary events of the slave revolution and the extraordinary resistances put up against the spread of this revolution meant that for decades Hispaniola was set on a historical path where even those events that are customarily recognized as unique, irreversible, as marking a turning point or a new era, would repeat themselves in the course of the nineteenth century. For these reasons, we need an approach that does not place subjects and their fears, fantasies, and desires on one side, and history and fact on the other, but rather is attentive to the ways in which events of the past serve as foils for the experience of the present, to the patterns of denial and remembrance that seem to inform present and past choices and expectations.[5]

In a study partly devoted to showing that psychoanalysis has valuable insights to contribute to our understanding of politics, Jacqueline Rose argues that fantasy is not "antagonistic to social reality" but rather its "precondition or psychic glue." Even if the function of fantasy were largely protective—and Rose tries to show that its function goes beyond mere protection—it typically preserves some traces of the displaced memories or the unresolved problem.[6] The following chapters are devoted to showing just that: that we can understand the political and ideological operations of the texts in question only if we recognize how they both silence *and* articulate, suppress and memorialize, disavow and assert. In the fantasies of the nineteenth-century literary texts, we can still perceive the traces of another future that existed in the imagination of those who did everything to prevent that future from becoming reality. For the purpose of critical reading, it matters little whether we find these traces expressed affirmatively, as in utopian thought, or negatively, through denials or even the dystopias of racist fantasies. Fantasies may serve to block certain memories, but they may also offer us entry points where we can explode the exclusivist projects of Creole modernity and the illusion that modernity is a unified project that slowly unfolds in the course of Western history.

If we are to avoid the either/or lenses of empiricist scholarship, psychoanalytic concepts will be indispensable. But only as long as we do not forget that what is being silenced or displaced in history is not necessarily identical with what is being displaced and silenced in individual history, and that psychoanalytic readings cannot replace a political and historical assessment of the causes and sources of trauma. We cannot dissolve history into mere historicity, and events into elements of always already distorted perceptions that are ultimately driven by the relentless demands of id and superego. As long as we remain attentive to the delicate and politically significant relationship between evasion and revelation, suppression and reinscription, silence and memory, in these texts, psychoanalytic concepts may allow us to recognize the fissures that indicate the location and outline of a disavowed past. The crucial question is not only *which* events were experienced as so excessive that they defied representation or needed to be addressed through screen memories, but why, and by whom. And we cannot answer those questions without specific reference to the geopolitical situation of the nineteenth century and to the dominant political ideologies of the day.

There is an aside in Edouard Glissant's *Discours antillais* that follows up on a discussion of the painful history of Martinique and expands on his idea of a "prophetic vision of the past" that may help us to advance our thinking about the relationship between historical experience and psychoanalysis:[7]

> Would it be ridiculous to consider our lived history as a steadily advancing neurosis? To see the slave trade as a traumatic shock, our relocation (in the new land) as a repressive phase, slavery as a period of latency, "emancipation" in 1848 as reactivation, our everyday fantasies as symptoms, and

even our horror of "returning to those things of the past" as a possible manifestation of the neurotic's fear of his past? Would it not be useful and revealing to investigate such a parallel? . . . History has its dimension of the unexplorable, at the edge of which we wander, our eyes wide open. (65–66)

Glissant takes these reflections into a discussion of "History" and "Literature," and the ways in which these were conceptualized and practiced in the metropolis so as to erase the plural histories of people on the margins of empire, but he does not expand on the psychoanalytic reading of historical experience in the Antilles. Despite its brevity, however, Glissant's suggestion opens up interesting and, for my purposes, crucial issues. Not unlike Benjamin, Glissant points to an experience of history on the margins that is qualitatively different from the experience of history in the European metropolis. Instead of a history that is experienced according to the projections of progress and emancipation, a historical experience that is made available in "hard figures" such as economic output, in educational advances, or in cultural achievements, history on the periphery is experienced as repetition—as a dimension of the unexplorable, or perhaps dimensions explorable only through a vocabulary that grasps the deep structures of psychic life.

If this reading is correct, slavery would be conceived as the limit case of an experience that characterizes much of history outside the metropolitan countries. Few people would doubt that the middle passage must have constituted a traumatic shock at the time. But for Glissant, it is not just an individual trauma; rather, it constitutes what recent psychoanalytic literature calls transgenerational trauma. Glissant thus links individual and collective experience, psychic life and historical experience. It is from this perspective that Glissant can claim that the 1848 emancipation act was the moment of reactivation of the earlier trauma: emancipation bestowed from above—the humanitarian project of most metropolitan abolitionists—is merely a reassertion of the continuing unavailability of agency. Instead of the steady time of progress, the warped, discontinuous time of the oppressed.

Glissant's remarks are far too elliptical to allow for a proper assessment of his views beyond these points. They do invite some questions, however, particularly in light of issues that have become crucial in the recent literature on trauma and history. The first and perhaps most important question is whether the psychoanalytic approach to historical experience implies an unacknowledged moral validation of those who have suffered traumatization, and if so, on what grounds this judgment is made. Surely, shock, trauma, and neurotic fantasies are not the exclusive domain of the victims of history. This question may seem naive at first, but many critics who claim to have successfully developed the relation between psychoanalysis and social history run into serious difficulties in this regard. Slavery by itself may not raise this issue, since there is no question whether or not those who were transported to the Americas as slaves were indeed victims whose histories need to be vindicated. But once we move beyond the specificity of slavery to the general question of how history is experienced, the question does require some reflection. Can the diagnosis of a traumatic shock in some sense replace critical assessments of this experience? If trauma is not the exclusive domain of the victims of history, the psychoanalytic reading would ultimately refer us back into the realm of political and historical analysis.

There are many indications that the Dominican elite experienced the arrival of Toussaint Louverture as a shock. It was something they were not prepared for, something they found incomprehensible and utterly outside any expectations they had developed in the course of their lives. Nineteenth-century Dominican literature bears the fairly clear imprint of a deeply traumatic experience that was both barred and reelaborated in later moments. However, the question is why these memories had to be blocked or reworked in the first place. Trouillot's eloquent account of the silencing of the Haitian Revolution and the unintelligibility of slave agency for slaveholders and metropolitan elites offers some compelling documentation of the ways in which a Eurocentric historiography has proved unable to understand or even perceive the events in Haiti. Trouillot's account also provides us with good reasons for discomfort with unreflective psychoanalytic readings. If we are persuaded by Trouillot's evidence, surely what we need is a critical reflection on the operations of Eurocentrism and racism in historiography and political theory, not a resigned recognition that the Haitian Revolution was simply a traumatic shock, or, as Lacanian theorists might put it, an encounter with the unsymbolizable Real and therefore naturally incomprehensible. This would be not only a politically undesirable result but also intellectually unpersuasive, since the silencing of the Haitian Revolution would in the end be nothing but an instance of a general human inability to name or directly confront the kernel of *jouissance*.

The importance of some cautionary reflections about the use of a psychoanalytic vocabulary in history becomes even clearer when we survey the enormous literature that has accrued in recent years about the event that has become the paradigmatic case of historical trauma, namely, the Holocaust.[8] Some of these studies are informed by specific psychoanalytic schools, but others operate with a less specific account of what constitutes trauma. In either case, the claim that the Holocaust is, in some deep sense, unrepresentable on account of its traumatic nature seems ubiquitous.

In her well-known essay about Paul de Man and his anti-Semitic wartime writings, Shoshana Felman, for instance, argues that de Man's failure to acknowledge or explain his writings needs to be understood as a form of testimony to the fact that no confession—indeed, no form of speech—can do justice to the catastrophe of the Holocaust. De Man's writings in literary criticism are thus construed as "a silent trace of the reality of an event whose very historicity, borne out by the author's own catastrophic experience, has occurred precisely as the event of its preclusion—the event of the impossibility—of its own witnessing." De Man thus becomes a "first-hand witness to the Holocaust's disintegration of the witness."[9] In other words, his silence bears witness to the Holocaust's unrepresentability. A lot could be said about this failure to distinguish between the silence of the victims and the silence of the collaborators, fellow travelers, and bystanders. I wonder whether Felman would extend her generosity to all those Germans who after 1945 gladly subscribed to the "Hour Zero" ideology and carried on as if nothing had happened.

More generally, it seems to me that Felman's problematic assessment stems from a failure to account for the fact that when we take psychoanalytic ways of thinking beyond the realm of the individual psyche, into the historical and political domain, we need to interpret the relationship between silence and memorialization, evasion and reinscription, itself as a politically significant relationship. Likewise, the link between trauma and unrepresentability cannot be taken to relieve us from the need to examine from a broadly speaking political and moral perspective why and by whom an event was experienced as excessive. If we use trauma in separation from other kinds of political and historical evidence, if we do not ask why some people experienced a certain event as traumatic and others did not, if we do not ask what exactly constituted the traumatic kernel of the experience, if we do not ask who felt that an event was completely unexpected and against all experiences of the past, then we run the danger of reinscribing the silences Glissant and Trouillot rightly denounced in Eurocentric historiography.

Some scholars whose work is in some ways informed by the Holocaust go even further than Felman. Cathy Caruth, for instance, argues on the basis of close readings of Freud's *Moses and Monotheism*[10] that trauma is constitutive of the possibility of history. Once we recognize the centrality of trauma, "we can begin to recognize the possibility of a history that is no longer straightforwardly referential (that is, no longer based on simple models of experience and reference)." Rethinking reference, then, aims not at "eliminating history" but at "permitting *history* to arise where *immediate understanding* may not."[11]

The basic gesture of the argument is deconstructive: if history can be shown to arise through trauma, then the structures of delay and return (or nonpresence, as some would say) that underlie trauma will in all likelihood also disrupt the greatest of all metanarratives of the West: history. Like Western metaphysics, history cannot be eliminated, only demoted in its totalizing ambitions and kept at bay in forever renewed movements of *andenken*. The name Caruth gives to these totalizing ambitions is "referentiality."[12] The question is: is this demotion of history as the greatest metanarrative of the West the same as that demanded by Glissant?

It is entirely understandable that someone whose thinking has developed in the context of the Holocaust would arrive at the profoundly Benjaminian view that history *is* catastrophe or trauma. Yet unlike Benjamin, who attributed the history-as-catastrophe view to a certain (and rather totalizing) perspective, namely, that of the Angel of History, Caruth provides a general theory to the effect that history is *born* out of the experience of catastrophe, and considers this a move against totalization. We are historical beings only because we have experienced trauma: against Freud's claim that historical trauma operates "in analogy" to individual trauma, she claims, "historical or generational trauma is in some sense presupposed by individual trauma."[13]

Sharpened to this point, Caruth's claim comes dangerously close to a tautology. We are historical beings because we have experienced historical trauma. History emerges out of the experience of the unspeakable, out of trauma, but trauma presupposes already the historical—is this not almost like saying that history emerges out of history? Or perhaps Caruth has some kind of transcendental argument in mind: to explain a certain phenomenon, we must stipulate the existence of a certain cause. However, transcendental arguments are always structural in the sense that we cannot deduce from the shape of the visible phenomenon any qualities of its transcendental condition. Individual trauma would not tell us anything about the content of historical trauma; if it did, we would be back at the analogy argument Freud used in *Moses and Monotheism*, which Caruth explicitly rejects. In the end, what "historical" means is left unexplained.

Now, one might think that the aporias of Caruth's claims stem from her reliance on deconstructive argument and particularly her identification of history as one of the West's *grands récits* with referentiality. This is not necessarily true, as my last example of a psychoanalytic approach to history will show. In *The Sublime Object of Ideology*, Žižek ends up in a very similar predicament, even though his point of departure is Lacan rather than Freud, and his philosophical allegiance is decidedly not deconstructive. Like Caruth, Žižek tries to fill in that uncertain space between the apparently purely subjective and ungeneralizable—the singular event that is experienced as excessive—and the apparent objectivity of historical events. But unlike her, Žižek is not seeking to deconstruct history as a metanarrative and then reconstitute it on the grounds of traumatic discontinuities. Transcendence of the monadism of individual psychic life is sought not through the notion of trauma itself but through the overcoming of trauma in the process of repetitions that allow for interpretation and thus make traumatic experience intelligible—a project authorized by Hegel rather than Derrida.

Žižek discusses the issue of trauma and repetition in history twice, at crucial moments in *The Sublime Object of Ideology*. The first time he takes it up it is under the heading "Repetition in History" (58–62). There the main point of the argument is to show that Hegel's account of history, particularly his notion of historical necessity, should not be interpreted as implying an implacable, objective, totalizing process. The best way to interpret Hegel is, Žižek argues, in terms of repetition: necessity is the effect of a retrospective recognition (Žižek would say misrecognition). The first time something that breaks customary expectations happens, it is experienced as contingent, accidental, and traumatic. It is an irruption of the Real that cannot be assimilated into the symbolic order. Only in the repetition can the first event be (mis)recognized as necessary. What drives this repetition is not some objective necessity but a certain guilt: the necessity that results from this is merely a symbolic one.

Žižek illustrates this thesis with the example of Caesar and the collapse of the Roman Republic. As long as Caesar was alive, people blamed him and his hunger for power for the decline of the republic. Only after Caesar had been assassinated and the Triumvirate had unwittingly paved the way for Caesarism did the event "Caesar" enter the symbolic and become the Law. Necessity is thus born out of a compulsion to repeat, the result of some debt: the murdered father is replaced with the Name-of-the-Father, what appeared contingent and traumatic becomes Law. It would seem that to put into place a new legal order, those who destroyed the old order need to be destroyed in their turn, and it would be out of guilt over the assassinated predecessors that subsequent generations repeat the original deed.[14]

The account does not lack a certain plausibility as far as the experience of historical turmoil and the ambiguities in instituting a new political regime are concerned. The problems become visible, however, when we compare it with the second passage devoted to the topic, this one entitled "Revolution as Repetition" (136–42). There Žižek returns to the notion of repetition in history through a reading of Benjamin's *Theses on the Philosophy of History*. The sections on Benjamin are quite unusual in the general context of *The Sublime Object of Ideology*. While his sections on Hegel contain not a single quote, his sections on Benjamin resonate with Benjaminian language and are supported by lengthy quotes—a somewhat surprising fact, given the centrality of Hegel for Žižek and the relatively minor role of Benjamin. The focus is for the most part on the famous phrase of the "tiger's leap into the past," which Žižek interprets in analogy to transference. In Benjamin's text, failed revolutionary attempts and ideas that fell by the wayside and did not become part of the history of the victors are appropriated and actualized in the contemporary revolution. The analogy with transference turns on the similarity of the temporal structures: the very possibility of reliving past events in extraordinary immediacy and thus cutting through the continuity of time as irreversible succession. Žižek thus tries to recast in analytic terms Benjamin's distinction between dominant history as the empty, continuous time of progress, and the discontinuous time of the history of the oppressed. Like the analytic process, revolution introduces a disruption, a moment of stasis where time is put on hold and from whence the past can be recalled as if present. The contingent, meaningless debris of history reveals its meaning only when it is seized by a revolutionary subject that forms itself in the process of revolution itself. What had remained unsymbolized in the past—like the traumatic event in Hegel—enters the historical process through a transferential reenactment in the present. History properly understood is thus neither the objective process of vulgar Marxism, nor the reified history of Rankian provenance, but one shot through with subjectivity. It is on the ground of repetition that Žižek confronts the common accusation that psychoanalysis is hostile to, or incapable of, political and historical explanation and intervention.

But why does Žižek address the issue twice? Why this need to supplement the Hegelian account of history as repetition with Benjamin, who, as Žižek himself acknowledges, would have thought himself rather un-Hegelian?[15] The question becomes even more puzzling when we realize that repetition is actually explained *differently* in relation to Hegel and to Benjamin: it was guilt that ultimately drove repetition in Hegel, yet in the reading of Benjamin, Žižek merely explains the *possibility* of a temporal structure that consists of overlapping and intersecting temporalities. There is no explanation of what drives the repetition, let alone why it would be a "compulsion."

The answer lies, I think, in that Benjamin provides Žižek with a specification, a distinction, that he could not produce otherwise. The fact that in the first section, the main example is Caesar, the collapse of the Roman Republic, and the transition to Caesarism is rather telling here: there are few historical anecdotes more loaded with connotations of authoritarianism, and few more associated with grand history as the history of the victors. If the point of the arguments around repetition really is to develop a political and historical form of psychoanalytic critique, then the inability to make a distinction between dominant history—the history of the victors—and the rubble heap of failed emancipatory projects would have seemed rather disheartening. Moving from Hegel to Benjamin, we unwittingly shift from Caesar to the toiling masses, from the Absolute Spirit to the Angel of History, from Napoleon to the Paris Commune, from history as an unfolding of reason to a history as "one single catastrophe which keeps piling wreckage upon wreckage."

The reason for Žižek's fireworks is that by closing the gap between Hegel and Benjamin, Žižek can cover up the fact that he actually derives additional, and not entirely legitimate, mileage from Benjamin. Precisely because the difference between the two is crucial for the argument, Žižek goes out of his way to show it does not exist: if it can be made to disappear, then we cannot see the gap where the political—or, more precisely, political allegiance or political affect—is generated. Žižek clearly wants to draw a distinction between wars of colonization and decolonization, or between revolution and counterrevolution, but it is Benjamin who makes this distinction for him—the notion of repetition (or trauma) itself will not do it. Even more, the same notion that disrupts the dichotomy of history and the subject—namely, repetition—also prevents him from making the distinction between the new era ushered in by Caesar and the working class as a revolutionary subject.[16]

Unlike Felman and Caruth, Žižek tries to compensate for the shortcomings of an account that disregards issues of agency and makes history *tout court* emerge out of trauma and compulsive repetition. But ultimately he runs into similar problems. Perhaps his account of grand history as built on a basic discontinuity, a misrecognition, a delay, or a repetition would allow us to undo the unwarranted opposition between subjective experience and objective history, and between politics and psychoanalysis. But Benjamin's crucial insight—an insight that returns in Glissant, namely, that history on the margins is qualitatively different from grand history, and that the traumas of the past cannot be accounted for within the outlines of grand history—remains elusive within the psychoanalytic theoretical apparatus.

As the review of some of the recent literature on historical trauma shows, the theoretical and methodological issues raised by the deployment of psychoanalytic concepts in the domain of history and politics are daunting, and we could easily lose with one hand what we gained with the other. Overextending the scope of the argument and rash claims of traumatization or unrepresentability without careful historical contextualization may end up obscuring rather than elucidating the events. In the following, we need to explore in detail not only how suppression and repetition shaped the historical process but also why certain events were not assimilable. We need to ask what exactly was being suppressed and why and by whom; we also need to ask how these suppressions and repetitions operated and what role literary and cultural production played in this process. This cannot be done if we have a purely epistemological or metaphysical account of what is traumatic. The intuition that "this story works" must not be superseded by a triumphalist "this story always applies." In other words, we need to ask according to which story or which experience something is excessive or traumatic.

### Santo Domingo and Haiti II

Because of the particular geographic and demographic situation on the island of Hispaniola, the issue of slavery could not be claimed as an issue of elite compassion or humanitarian consideration. There were relatively few slaves before 1822 in Spanish Santo Domingo—15,000 out of a population of 120,000—and the economy did not depend on large-scale plantations. The vast majority of Dominicans were free people of color. For the 1840s, the American envoy David Dixon Porter gives the following figures: a mere 5,000 are white, 60,000 are quadroons, 60,000 light-skinned mulattoes, 14,000 dark-skinned mulattoes, and 20,000 of pure African descent. This demography, combined with the presence of a revolutionary black state next door, meant that the question of the political regime could not be decided without addressing the issue of slavery. The white colonial elite fled the island in large numbers ahead of every Haitian invasion or occupation, and the few who stayed behind found it difficult to deal with former slaves in government. They would clearly have preferred any political regime to Haitian rule. The mulatto majority in the Spanish part of the island, however, was not going to support any movement for independence that was not accompanied by guarantees that slavery remain outlawed, and the neighboring revolutionary black state was certainly not prepared to tolerate a slaveholding state that might become the beachhead for metropolitan invasions of the island.

Slavery could never be discussed as a social or moral question in separation from the question of the constitution of the state. But neither did it present itself as a mostly economic concern where men who know the way of the world would grimly clench their teeth and pronounce slavery a perhaps regrettable, but nevertheless necessary, evil. Elsewhere, perhaps, slaves and former slaves themselves could be forced into silence, while slavery as an issue constituted itself as the domain where humanists and advocates of realpolitik could divide the turf between themselves. Elsewhere, perhaps, it was easy not to consider the issue of agency of slaves or former slaves, and when the issue could not be ignored, as in the context of slave uprisings, criminalization was a fairly efficient response. In Santo Domingo, the relative lack of economic importance of slavery and the proximity of the revolutionary state meant two things: first of all, that slavery and radical antislavery did not cease to be an issue of domestic and foreign politics until 1844 and lingered as a fear that could be called up to mobilize the population until 1864; and second, that people who had been slaves, or were reenslaved, or feared enslavement, were a significant political force and could by no means be contained by being "represented" by elite advocates.[17]

Creole modernity may have had an air of inevitability and necessity in Cuba and on the Spanish American mainland; it may have seemed that the only possible future, the inevitable telos of history, was the realization of models of progress and socioeconomic development taken from Europe. Santo Domingo is a remarkable exception within the ideological landscape of the nineteenth-century Caribbean. The knowledge that things could be otherwise was never suppressed completely. For that very reason, it shows that the conflicts between elite abolitionists and pro-slavery advocates marked the smaller division, though of course not for that reason insignificant, within a Creole ideology built on the assumption of unacceptability, unthinkability, or impossibility of slave agency. The more virulent antagonism was that between Creole modernity and a modernity that placed racial equality in the center of its agenda. With a state next door that originated in revolutionary antislavery and whose foundational ideology centered on racial equality, most Dominican statesmen, intellectuals, and writers were acutely aware that Creole modernity was not the only option: Haiti represented an alternative, and it needed to be avoided at all costs. At the center of the fantasies that characterize the Dominican cultural imaginary is Haiti as the nightmare of a barbarian future.

The long history of Dominican anti-Haitianism obviously involves issues that have no direct link to the events of the Haitian Revolution and its aftermath. The incendiary writings of twentieth-century figures such as José Joaquín Balaguer, Manuel Arturo Peña Batlle, M. A. Báez Machado, and their fellow travelers are not purely local responses to antagonisms that grew out of revolutionary antislavery, but would need to be considered in the geopolitical context of postcolonial authoritarianism and U.S. imperialism, as well as a history of racism that was certainly not invented in the Dominican Republic.[18] Yet these rewritings do have a local genealogy, which is all the more important because it shows the historical construction of a category of race and thus disrupts notions of racism and race as transhistorical constants.

Although the Haitian occupations were actually not preceded by wars or armed conflict,[19] the written record usually remembered them as violent and deeply traumatizing for Dominicans. In the upsurge of nationalist agitation after 1844, Haiti became increasingly demonized to a point where it was represented as a cannibalistic, witchcraft-wielding monster consumed by the desire to devour the inhabitants of the East. A collection of nineteenth-century popular poetry published during the Trujillo dictatorship includes the following example:

¡Ah! bárbaro cuadromano . . .
(a un estúpido hablador
díjole un dominicano)
—No soy bárbaro, señor.
—Pues qué eres?
—Soy haitiano.

[Ah, you four-legged barbarian . . .
(said a Dominican
to a stupid interlocutor)
Sir, I am not a barbarian.
What are you then?
I am Haitian].[20]

The troubling history of Dominican anti-Haitianism came to a head in 1937, during the Trujillo dictatorship, in the massacre of twelve thousand Haitian migrant workers.[21]

Balaguer, who was not only one of Trujillo's chief ideologues but his successor and a contender for the presidency as recently as 2000, conjures up Haiti within Malthusian fantasies. To his mind, Haitians are people who, "abandoned to their instincts and without the brakes that a relatively elevated standard of living imposes in all countries on reproduction, multiply with a speed almost comparable to that of vegetable species."[22] In the anti-Haitian imaginary, Haiti becomes the force of darkness and underdevelopment—a primitive, dangerous predator that threatens to "denationalize" Dominican civilization through weedlike proliferation on Dominican soil.

The twentieth-century vocabulary of Dominican racial identity is startling in its apparent success in erasing blackness from the self-consciousness of a nation that is evidently mulatto in its vast majority. In an act of racial alchemy, Dominican mulattoes become "Indians" and Dominican blacks "blancos de la tierra" [whites of the country]. Roosevelt's envoy Sumner Welles tells how a Dominican explained to him, the North American visitor, "Sí, soy negro, pero negro blanco" [Yes, I'm black, but a white black].[23] In Balaguer's feverish investigations into race and color in the Dominican Republic, the *guajiro* comes to be imagined as of pure European peasant stock and the bedrock of Dominican rural identity. The denial of African ancestry seems to have become so habitual that it cancels even the most obvious visual evidence: witness some of the photographic record presented in his *La isla al revés*. The vocabulary of color and race in the Dominican Republic is so far removed from any phenotypical or historical evidence, so resilient to common-sense challenges, that one suspects that some extraordinary efforts must have taken place at some point in the nineteenth century. No doubt, Haiti and the fears attached to it are crucial in this history, but just naming Haiti does not explain very much. What kind of fears attached to Haiti? And how were these fears elaborated into the fantasies that became the core of twentieth-century anti-Haitianism?

The discourses of race in the Dominican Republic are to some degree instantiations of a tradition whose origins cannot be assigned to any particular country or region, or to any particular time. Clearly, racialist and racist stereotypes did not originate in response to the Haitian Revolution. However, the tawdry familiarity of statements such as Balaguer's should not lead us to see them exclusively as expressions of perennial racism. What is most remarkable about Balaguer's discourse, and Dominican anti-Haitianism in general, what distinguishes the operations of racial denigration in the Dominican Republic from those in other parts of the Americas, is that they are, in a sense, a fantasy that seeks to block another memory of Haiti: not as the invading barbarian but as the radical reformer. In the deep shadows of the nationalist exclusivism about race and color, we can discern the outlines of a modernity disavowed.

By the time Spain ceded Santo Domingo to France in 1795, it had long lost interest in its oldest colony. Since the early seventeenth century, earthquakes, hurricanes, epidemics, and migrations to the mainland had left Santo Domingo in a general state of abandonment and stagnation. Many old buildings had fallen into disrepair. Although it covered a territory one and a half times greater than the French colony of Saint Domingue, it was sparsely populated and economically underdeveloped. Whereas the western part of the island was the center of a booming sugar industry and the first site of intensive agriculture, Spanish Santo Domingo's economy relied on extensive land use. The main exports were precious woods and hides, products that could be gathered on a casual basis in the mountainous inland regions. Wild cattle roamed on the plains of the interior, and much of the land was either owned or used collectively, or not used at all except for the occasional cutting down of mahogany trees.

When Toussaint Louverture arrived in Santo Domingo in 1801, his first measures were those of the modernizer. After proclaiming all slaves free and promulgating a constitution of patently Jacobin inspiration that outlawed all forms of bondage and racial discrimination (see chapters 11 and 13), his main efforts were directed at economic reform. Realizing that the economy was in shambles, he aimed to introduce intensive agriculture in the eastern part according to the model developed by the French in the West. Eliminating the arcane system of export taxes that fettered local development, he introduced a flat export tax rate and prohibited the exploration of new lands except for the purpose of creating new plantations. Toussaint Louverture's reforms were cut short when the French army arrived on February 25, 1802, in an ill-fated attempt to recapture the western part of the island from the insurgent blacks. With the support of Dominican landowners, the French army expelled the forces of former slaves, and slavery was reintroduced. Modernization came to a halt as French, Dominican, and Haitian forces continued to fight over the territory for the next eight years. By 1809, Spanish Santo Domingo was a devastated war zone on the verge of starvation: agriculture had come to a complete standstill, the remaining cattle had been slaughtered, and the population had decreased from 120,000 at the end of the eighteenth century to a mere 80,000.[24]

The years between the return to Spanish colonial rule in 1809 and the first declaration of independence in 1821 did not bring much relief. The effects of rebellions, a slave uprising that aimed at killing all whites, and a paralyzed colonial government combined to return Santo Domingo to a subsistence economy. Rumors of an imminent French invasion of Haiti flared up time and again and reached a fever pitch in 1820 when news spread that French ships were arriving in Martinique, from where they would sail to Spanish Santo Domingo in order to invade Haiti. Convinced that Haiti was indefensible along its remote border in the mountains of the interior and moreover that the Spanish colony would offer no resistance to a French invasion,[25] Boyer sent a number of agents across to the East to persuade the population that unification of Hispaniola was in their interest, as well. The paralyzed and parasitical colonial government had been losing support among Dominicans for a while, and the situation became increasingly unstable.

The Creole José Núñez de Cáceres decided to seize the moment and declare Santo Domingo the "Estado Independiente del Haití Español" (Independent State of Spanish Haiti) on December 1, 1821, with the idea that Santo Domingo might later join Greater Colombia. On January 11, Boyer sent a long letter to the new head of state in the East, announcing his intention of introducing "an entirely moral Revolution" while also arguing that it was not possible to have two independent states on the island. Núñez de Cáceres, well aware that the majority of the population was mulatto and might not look unkindly on unification with Haiti, wrote back that "the military chiefs and municipal leaders unanimously decided to place themselves under the protection of the laws of the Republic of Haiti."[26] On February 9, 1822, he handed over the town keys to Boyer. Boyer's first public act was to abolish slavery and to issue a promise of land distribution among the former slaves. It was land reform that would become the most contentious issue in the next decade or so.

Whereas in Haiti landed property was guaranteed through government-issued titles, in the Spanish colony landholding was not regularized.[27] Much of the land was communal or owned by several people with uncertain claims to it, and de facto land usage rather than titles constituted the basis of "ownership." Continuing the modernizing measures envisioned by Toussaint Louverture two decades earlier, Boyer put great effort in rationalizing and unifying the Dominican legal system and created a commission charged with clarifying the issue of land titles and determining which lands would be considered property of the state.[28]

When a commission determined that much of the land formerly held by the archdiocese of Santo Domingo and various church-affiliated institutions would be nationalized, tensions flared up. The church had always been strictly opposed to French secularism and was traditionally one of the most outspoken anti-Haitian factions in Santo Domingo. At the same time, opposition was growing among those Dominicans who had occupied the land abandoned by those who had fled the country. According to Dominican legal practices, a twenty-year occupation of a plot of land signified a substantial entitlement. Under the new Franco-Haitian legal system, such a claim carried no weight. In trying to address some of the inequities that appeared to follow from an abstract application of the laws, Boyer further antagonized the great landowners, who saw their properties fragmented and diminished as parcels were given out to the actual occupants of the land. The emergence of a new class of independent smallholders also meant an increasing shortage of labor for plantation owners and a significant reduction in tax income for the state. Although it had been Boyer's aim to create an export-oriented economy built on intensive agriculture, land distribution in fact meant that many former slaves in both the East and West of the island returned to subsistence farming.

In the end, Boyer's efforts at unifying the island failed. When the shortage of labor began to show itself as a problem, Boyer responded by introducing the Rural Code, which forced workers to attach themselves to a plantation, prohibited them from even leaving the property without permission, and thus, in fact, reintroduced a form of unfree labor. Although the code proved to be impossible to enforce, it, too, created much resentment. When the process of land distributions began to slow down after 1826, Boyer increasingly lost the support of the popular sectors, a problem compounded by growing tensions in the West between the medium and large mulatto landowners and the black masses. Finally, Boyer's attempt to secure Haitian independence by gaining diplomatic recognition from France led to a severe financial crisis: in exchange for recognition, France demanded astronomical reparations for properties lost or expropriated in the West in the aftermath of the revolution, and Boyer was forced to collect a special tax *(don patricio)*. Dominicans deeply resented this tax; resistance against Haiti continued to grow, first in the urban petite bourgeoisie and eventually extending to other sectors of the population, and in response, Boyer turned to authoritarian measures.[29]

Ironically, therefore, Boyer's modernizing reforms, which had aimed at creating a modern unified Haitian state on the island, in fact created conditions that were propitious for Dominican independence. Not only did he abolish slavery once and for all—without which independence was not possible, as the events of 1822 had shown. Through the land reform, a class of small landowners and peasants came into being that eventually became the popular base for the movement toward independence. The opening of commerce with the United States, France, and England and the reduction of tariffs strengthened the petite bourgeoisie. The Haitian constitutions of 1816 and 1843 established equality before the law and abolished feudal norms and privileges for the Catholic Church. Finally, Boyer established a local military force. Whereas the project of integration between Haiti and the eastern part of the island failed for a number of reasons, it was the combination of economic and structural modernization and political failures that made Dominican independence possible. In 1836 the secret society La Trinitaria, which became the seminal force in the 1844 independence, was founded.

The Haitian occupiers were quite self-conscious about their role as modernizers in the eastern provinces, as the preamble to an 1824 law relating to Santo Domingo made clear: "It is important to destroy all traces of feudalism in this part of the island in order that the inhabitants, happy under a regime of liberal principles, may lose even the memory of their former subjection."[30] With the familiar arrogance of occupying forces who see themselves as more advanced than the local people, the Haitian rulers project an image that is soon echoed by Dominicans. Far from representing the barbarian invader, Haiti occupied the place of "the authority," "the law," and "modernization."[31]

Predictably enough, the optimism of the Haitian rulers was not borne out. Here, as everywhere else, the quintessentially modern fantasy of a radical break with the past, the eradication of traditions and superstitions so as to begin anew, with a blank slate, turned out to be an impossibility. If to the Dominican elites and the clergy, Haiti came to represent Jacobin egalitarianism, secularism, modern property laws, and industrial agriculture, these civilizatory advances did not sit well with the structures of traditional authority and privilege that had developed under Spanish colonial rule. Far from forgetting the past, the Dominican Republic became, in the words of a contemporary Dominican critic, "sick with memory." It is for these reasons that in Dominican literature we find the clearest, if most hallucinatory, trace of the suppression and subsumption of the cultures of radical antislavery in the Caribbean.

In light of these extraordinarily complicated and charged events, it is not surprising that the Dominican literary and cultural record is convoluted, contradictory, and extremely difficult to read. In the literary domain, especially in the texts that came to form the core of national literature, the fears and traumas that had attached themselves to Haiti are largely displaced. After the early patriotic (and largely anti-Haitian) poetry, we find rumination over the "catastrophes" of the past—the decline of Spanish culture in Santo Domingo, the genocide of the indigenous population—while the issue of slavery never even registers in the cultural imaginary. This suppression of the memory of slavery and antislavery gets off the ground only by means of a wholesale invention of a rather implausible past. Against all evidence to the contrary, Spain and the Indians come to be considered the ancestors of the mulatto nation through fantasies that variously, and in disregard of their mutual exclusivity, imagined Dominicans to be the heirs of Spanish Golden Age Catholicism and American indigenous cultures. Eventually, Hispanism and indigenism became the two prevalent cultural ideologies.[32]

Today, three of the four museums on the Plaza de la Cultura in the Dominican capital assign a central place to the indigenous cultures of the past. Although the exhibitions consist for the most part of dioramas, reconstructions, blown-up maps, and photographs of objects that are either in private collections or in museums in Europe or the United States, the Museo del Hombre Dominicano (Museum of the Dominican People), the Museum of Natural History, and the Museum of History and Geography all give privileged space to an

10. The *Faro de Colón* in Santo Domingo. Photo by Liam Murphy.

indigenous prehistory that has become infinitely remote through the effects of the genocide of the conquest, and the operations of neo-colonial plundering. Clearly, indigenism reproduces itself through the educational and cultural institutions of the state, whereas Hispanism seems embodied materially in the buildings and the ruins and is as such essential to the facade Santo Domingo presents to the tourist. The attraction of newly restored colonial palaces is clearly enhanced by a gastronomic culture dominated by Spanish-style *mesones*, the hotels decked out in imitations of austere dark wood furniture of Renaissance Spain, the monuments to Columbus, and the reprints of Velázquez paintings in public buildings.

Returning to the nineteenth century, it is striking that Dominican literature—whether of indigenist or Hispanist orientation—develops in compulsive replays of a limited number of traumatic scenes of murder and betrayal. The texts are haunted by death, rape, and people returning from the dead. Melancholia hovers over these early writings, which are infinitely fascinated by violence, sacrifice, and repetition of violence. Far from embracing literary writing as a new practice, as new territory to be charted by the enterprising spirits of progress and civilization, most Dominican texts are weighed down by an unfathomable depth of memory and melancholia. Whereas on the neighboring island of Cuba, young writers put their ambitions and inspirations at the service of moral betterment and future progress, Dominican writers seemed to be caught in a time warp where somehow the gaze kept returning to the original scenes of discovery, conquest, and colonization. There are poems about the colonial ruins, about decay and destruction, about dying Indians and the villainous mercenaries of the Spanish Crown, and, more than anything, nostalgic celebrations of the noble indigenous race. A fairly limited cast of indigenous characters—Anacaona, Caonabo, Enriquillo, and a few others—keep reappearing. There are ghosts, prophecies, echoes, and mysterious repetitions—the whole arsenal of fantastic literature that is almost entirely absent from nineteenth-century literature in the rest of Spanish America. The obsession with Christopher Columbus's remains that reached a fever pitch in the early twentieth century and returned as recently as 1992, on the occasion of the quincentennial celebrations and the inauguration of the notorious Faro de Colón (Columbus's Beacon) (see fig. 10), is foreshadowed in those strange texts of the nineteenth century, where Columbus appears, Christlike, to Dominicans in distress.

How do we read these eccentric, haunted texts? At first sight it seems that Dominican writing is the result of simple evasions from a present that was perhaps too shocking, too unexpected, too painful to be dealt with directly by those who had access to writing. Averting their eyes at the humiliating sight of having former slaves set the agenda for progress and development, Dominican writers for the most part turned to an imaginary colonial past and romanticized indigenous cultures for inspiration. But perhaps their silence vis-à-vis radical antislavery and revolutionary Haiti is only apparent. Perhaps there are ways of making these texts speak. Rather than reading them as mere evasions, could we not read them as fantasies with a specific relation to the underlying traumatic events? We know that in the case of the psychic life of the individual, truly traumatic events usually prompt a response more elaborate and complex than mere trivialization. May this not also be true in the case of historical traumas?

# 6

## Guilt and Betrayal in Santo Domingo

By far the best-known Dominican narrative of the nineteenth century is Manuel Galván's indigenist novel *Enriquillo* (1882), the story of an insurgent chieftain at the time of the conquest. The novel moved José Martí to ecstatic praise, and in the 1950s it was translated into English by Robert Graves as part of a UNESCO-sponsored "collection of representative works" from Latin America.[1] Contemporary readers are usually more sensitive to the racist implications of a literary tradition that devotes itself to the celebration of indigenous cultures of a distant past in a country where the vast majority of the population is of mixed African and European ancestry.[2]

No doubt, Dominican ethnic and historical reality is distorted in the indigenist imaginary. For the Dominican elite, the images of coppery Indians offered a pedigree of color that was vastly preferable to that of the Africanness of the Haitian neighbor. But we would hardly have to concern ourselves in detail with these texts if their role in Dominican history was merely that of a fairly obvious, politically and socially regressive misrepresentation. However, Dominican indigenismo performed a complex set of operations that were crucial in the constitution of a Dominican national interpellation. The fantasy of the Indian that comes to occupy such a central place is only the result, the final outcome, of a much more profound renegotiation of the emotional attachments and historical memories of the people who lived in the uncertainly constituted, triply claimed territory of eastern Hispaniola. In the plot structures that emerged in these renegotiations, we can discern, as if against backlight, traces of an experience that had to be repressed from collective memory.

If we want to understand how indigenismo developed as a historical fantasy and a new ground for a Dominican interpellation, we are well advised to look beyond the canonical *Enriquillo*. At the time that Galván was writing, the literary *indigenista* movement was already fully formed, had developed its set of favored characters, along with canonical themes and plots, and constituted itself as "the first truly

Dominican national literature."[3] By 1870, the name "Haiti," which was first adopted by Dessalines at the moment of declaring independence from France in 1804 and was taken up by the leaders of the first Dominican independence when they renamed Santo Domingo the Estado Independiente del Haíti Español (Independent State of the Spanish Haiti), began to be replaced by the supposedly Taino name "Quisqueya" as the favored epithet for the Spanish part of the island. While *Enriquillo* fits comfortably into the mold of Spanish American historical novels, it is in the less restrained, smaller genres—in poems, stories, and short novels—that we find the materials that indicate how the fantasy of indigenismo might have functioned in the emerging cultural imaginary and how it related to the traumas of the first half of the nineteenth century.

The most obvious question regarding Dominican indigenismo is why, and how, it is possible that in a country where the vast majority of people are mulattoes and where the indigenous population was killed in the early years of colonization, indigenism could become the dominant ideology. There are no traces of a popular belief that Dominicans somehow descend from the indigenous inhabitants.[4] Indigenism was an invention of the intellectual elite—those who created Dominican literature, monuments, and museums—and from the beginning it was accompanied by the recognition that the Indians were killed in the early years of the conquest. Unlike twentieth-century indigenismo in Peru or Mexico, the Dominican variety was, from the beginning, a historical fantasy that takes us back to the time of the conquest. Instead of the ethnographic details and a cast of characters based on sociologically determined types of later indigenist texts, we find highly romanticized images of individual chieftains and prominent personages in neoclassical garb. If indigenism worked as an interpellation, it was not because people believed that they descended from these regal native warriors but because it somehow addressed deep-seated experiences and unresolved problems related to the historical experience on the island of Hispaniola. The second question concerns the paradoxical relation between indigenismo and *hispanismo*. How were Dominicans to subscribe at the same time to an indigenist ideology that sought to vindicate the victims of the genocide of the conquest, and a Hispanist attitude that celebrated those who were responsible for the genocide? No doubt, both indigenism and Hispanism were ideological weapons against Haitian pretensions of relatedness and brotherhood, but how can one be reconciled with the other? The third issue concerns the apparent absence of Haiti in indigenism. Was Haiti simply erased from the national imaginary, or did it leave an imprint, a trace, in the indigenist fantasy?

## Indigenism as Atonement

One of the earliest texts to include an indigenous protagonist is *La fantasma de Higüey* (The phantom of Higüey), by Javier Francisco Angulo y Guridi, which was published in 1857 and is occasionally referred to as the first Dominican novel.[5] As the title suggests, it is a ghost story—a story that explains how Spanish Santo Domingo came to be a haunted place. The events of the main plot take place in 1656 and are presented as part of oral tradition through a narrative frame that is set in 1853. By the end of the story, all the main characters are either dead or mad, but the ghost will ensure that the events will never truly be over and that the story will continue to be told. *The Phantom of Higüey* produces a past that keeps returning.

When the story begins, the protagonists are sailing from Santo Domingo to Puerto Rico. There is Don Ricardo, the director of mines in Santo Domingo, already quite advanced of age; his beautiful daughter Isabela, a virgin; Tuizla, an indigenous prince, as beautiful as a "Greek god" and very much in love with Isabela, who is promised to him; Cayetano, a Spanish monk, who, it turns out later, is no monk at all; and the pilot of the boat. Catastrophe ensues when Morgan, an English pirate, approaches out of the night, accompanied by the moans and sighs of the ghosts of his many victims who haunt his hunting grounds. He captures the boat and threatens to kill everybody except Isabela, who he intends to "reserve for himself": "—Friends!—Let us not forget the pact: the loot for you, the women for me, the men for the guns, and the boat for the Ocean" (26). Tuizla saves everybody by offering his father's treasures to Morgan in exchange for sparing their lives. As they approach land, the events take a turn for the worse. In the end, the true force of evil is not Morgan but the fake monk who despite his age and ugliness is determined to win Isabela for himself and thus plots to get Tuizla out of the way. Once on land, Morgan's daughter Lidia—a beautiful, willful amazon, offspring of one of Morgan's rapes and a base counterimage to the virginal Isabela—enters the scene. Lidia immediately falls in love with Tuizla. Due to the devious machinations of the monk, Lidia unwittingly kills Tuizla. The pilot witnesses the crime and kills the monk. Isabela goes mad with grief, and Lidia is transformed into the "Phantom of Higüey."

The intrigue of the story turns on the idea of sacred pacts between

Indians and Europeans and their subsequent violation. First there is the promise of marriage between Tuizla and Isabela, a sacred pact that is violated through the intrigues of a corrupt Spaniard. Then there is a second pact, through which the Indian Tuizla saves the Europeans' lives and which in fact cancels out Morgan's evil pact with his fellow pirates as to the division of the booty. Having been insulted by Cayetano as a "slave," Tuizla gives a moving speech in which he reminds his audience that Cayetano owes him his life, that he, Tuizla, stays with Don Ricardo and Isabela out of his free will (70), and that he is united with Isabela through the sacred pact of betrothal. These pacts are violated through the intrusion of base desires: it is because two of the protagonists—Lidia and the fake monk—are driven by sexual desire rather than sacred love that Tuizla is killed. Tragedy is thus personalized and ensues from a moral conflict rather than on structural grounds—the problem is not colonialism but transgressive behavior. The story clearly wants us to recognize the sharp divide between the sacred and the secular, between spiritual aspirations and the base desires for sex and money, between the realm of redemption and the realm of damnation, between the New World as a utopia and as the dystopic space beyond law and morality. What better way of bringing it into focus than through the figure of a fake monk? Evil masquerading as good is not only worse than evil by itself; it also suggests that good and evil are matters not of shades and degrees but of absolute difference.

*La fantasma de Higüey* already displays what eventually became one of the most characteristic features of Dominican indigenismo. On the one hand, there are Columbus and his descendants, Las Casas, and their allies, who represent the utopian ideal of creating a new Garden of Eden in peaceful harmony between the indigenous population and the newly arrived Spanish; on the other hand, there are the bad Spanish, who came in search for gold and power, and who kill the Indians in the process. This strategy is perhaps most developed in the best-known text of Dominican indigenismo, J. J. Pérez's collection of poems *Fantasías indígenas* (1877).[6] The first poem opens with a religious scene: the Indians are chanting to the "echo of the sacred tambour" in front of the altar of their Zemí (a note explains that this is the statue of an idol that mediated between humans and divinity for the Indians) and ends with the vow of vengeance by the chieftain, who already knows that the Spanish conquerors are arriving. The second poem introduces Columbus as an "immortal genius." Prevented from sleeping by "sweet insomnia," the admiral looks dreamily into the mist, where the ghostly play of shadows and lights announces to him the world he had dreamed.

> ¡Noche de sombras, de perenne anhelo,
> en que cada celaje que fulgura
> —débil reflejo de la luz del cielo—
> el nuevo mundo que soñó le augura!

> [Night of shadows, of eternal yearning,
> in which every skylight that flashes
> —weak reflection of heavenly light—
> the new world he dreamt up foreshines to him.]

When land is sighted, Columbus's thoughts turn to God:

> ¡Mundo de amor, risueño paraíso,
> verde oasis de luz en mi desierto
> yo te bendigo, porque en tí Dios quiso
> brindarme al fin de salvación el puerto!

> [World of love, smiling paradise,
> Green oasis of light in my desert
> I bless you, because in you God intended
> to grant me finally a safe harbor.]

Although the first poem shows the New World before the arrival of Columbus, it now reappears as the materialization of Columbus's fantasy. Before Columbus's appearance in the New World, the indigenous chieftain is given to savage fantasies of revenge. The real Eden lies in the misty future, as *La Pinta* approaches the Caribbean beaches. And this real Eden—one that is destroyed almost the moment it comes into existence—is that of Christian Indians:

> Sencilla y candorosa
> la grey de Maguá, en calma
> escucha esa doctrina
> de paz y esperanza. (35)

> [Simple and innocent
> the flock of Maguá calmly
> listens to this creed
> of peace and hope.]

Idolatry is overcome when the Indians convert to Christian mono-theism and transfer their pious respect from the idols to the Christian god. Both Columbus and the Indians are shown to live in a religious world of goodwill and respect, in close communion with God. Things deteriorate when depraved Spaniards, driven by greed and lust, intrude into this bucolic scenario. A Spaniard seduces an Indian woman by persuading her that her new Christian faith requires her to leave her husband and be a mistress to him, and war breaks out. Where love and respect had ruled, sex brings about ruin. The utopia of a new Garden of Eden gives way to the degradations of conquest and genocide.

We can now see why Pérez ordered his poems in a way that may seem illogical at first sight.[7] The first poem shows Indians already aware of the arrival of Columbus and planning resistance, and the second poem turns to Columbus on his ship, approaching the Caribbean coast, given to fantasies about the "smiling paradise" that awaits him ashore. But that is precisely the point. The indigenous cultures claimed by Pérez and most other Dominican indigenist writers do not in fact precede the arrival of Columbus. The poem ends with six stanzas that quote the chieftain describing his acts of vengeance: he will kill the intruders, burn them, eat them, decorate his home with their blond hair, and use their skulls to drink their blood. This bloodthirsty vision is, to my knowledge, unique in Dominican indigenist literature and contrasts strangely with the images of peaceful, amorous Indians that dominate the remainder of the poems. Before the encounter, Indians are, at best, noble cannibals. The Indians of Dominican indigenismo emerge out of Columbus's dream and Las Casas's teachings and thus mark the precise point where the sacred pact takes place, which in turn becomes the ground for a Dominican interpellation that is both Hispanist and indigenist. Indigenism *is* the celebration of the Indians of Columbus's dream.

The apparent paradox of Dominican indigenismo and hispanismo thus turns out to be no paradox at all. The two ideologies are connected at the very root in the idea of a doomed sacred pact between the Spanish and the Indians that failed in the early days of the conquest. The failure of this pact produces remainders of various kinds: a promise not kept, a guilt, an energy not absorbed into the historical process, a traumatic event not containable in ordinary narration . . . something in excess of the pure facticity of the historical process: an unfinished project or an unfulfilled future. Casting themselves as Indians, Dominicans draw on this energy and fashion an Indian future out of a Hispanist past.

## Indigenism as Natural History

Perhaps the most intricate and allegorically saturated elaboration of these themes is a short and very little known text by Alejandro Llenas entitled "La boca del indio" (The mouth of the Indian).[8] Written in 1902, it takes up one of the standard themes of indigenismo and the subject of arguably the most famous nineteenth-century Dominican painting, Desangles's *Caonabo in Prison*. Set at the time of the conquest, "La boca del indio" tells the story of the young indigenous warrior Maniatibel and the capture of the chieftain Caonabo. In the course of a battle, Ojeda, a Spanish captain, is about to kill Maniatibel. Columbus intervenes and orders Ojeda to spare Maniatibel. Ojeda takes care of Maniatibel until his wounds have healed. Before he returns to the mountains, Maniatibel offers blood brotherhood to his Spanish savior. Then, one day, Maniatibel observes from a distance Ojeda and a couple of Spaniards riding into the mountains. Knowing that his blood brother would be killed if he alerted the Indians, Maniatibel keeps quiet. When Ojeda returns, he carries Caonabo tied to his horse. Realizing that without their valiant leader the Indians are doomed, and that he is responsible for the catastrophe that will ensue, Maniatibel goes mad with grief and regret and leaps off a cliff. The story ends as follows: "His body disappeared forever in the abyss of the waters. But his spirit continues to haunt the slopes of the ravine, condemned to repeat always, always, every cry launched from the edge. . . . It is not the echo that repeats those noises, those voices: No! It is the mouth of the Indian."

The simplicity of the (probably invented) legend should not deceive us: as a phenomenon whose identity is constituted in a motion of repetition and temporal delay, echoes raise theoretically difficult questions. The theme and tone of "La boca del indio" are largely in keeping with the indigenist tradition that was well established at the time, but the image of the echo is unusual, as it provides more abstract links between the familiar indigenist theme and the issue of identity, temporality, and thus ultimately the experience of history in the Dominican Republic. Again there is a doomed pact of friendship between Indians and Spanish, a ghostly presence from beyond death, and the transformation of landscape and geography into a reminder of Santo Domingo's bloody history.[9] Physically the Indians have disappeared, but in spirit they are still there. Because of a guilt that cannot be canceled, the past continues to haunt the present. In "La boca del indio," however, this shared guilt becomes the basis for a new solidarity: the unresolved antagonism between Indians and Spaniards at the time of the conquest is in a sense overcome in the moment when the Indian speaks in the voice of the Dominican and the Dominican hears his (everything indicates that these stories are all "stories between men") words being returned by the Indian. Rather than a dialogue, the story envisions the limit case of a mimetic relation: echoes partake in the necessity of natural history.

Whereas early indigenism in Haiti was based on the idea of an imaginary political alliance against the slaveholders and colonizers, and thus on a conscious choice (the descendants of slaves avenged the crimes committed against the Indians and thus "inherited" the territory),[10] in the eastern part of the island, the "Indianness" of Dominicans is a matter not of the will but of tragic fate. Moreover, it is cast not as a pact against the Spanish but as the fulfillment of a pact between the Spanish and the Indians. If we look more closely at the role of the Spanish in this identitarian fantasy, we can see that their role is not at all that of the antagonist.

From psychoanalytic and philosophical theorizing of the issue, we know that human identity has to pass through some Other who provides accreditation of some sort in order to establish itself: oneness, identity, is at the end of a process, not at the beginning.[11] A Lacanian reading of the story would suggest that what is at stake is a deadly conflict that involves the protagonist's imaginary identification and symbolic identification, or ideal ego and ego ideal.

At the beginning of the story, the Indian's self-image, or imaginary identification, is clearly that of a good warrior. This self-image becomes a symbolic identification when accredited by the chieftain Caonabo: it is in his eyes that Maniatibel wants to appear as the good warrior. When Maniatibel incurs a debt with Ojeda—he owes him his life—he can maintain his imaginary identification only by installing Ojeda in the position of the Other: only if Ojeda's mercy is based on his respect for Maniatibel as a good warrior can Maniatibel's self-image survive the encounter. The act of offering blood brotherhood is a succinct expression of the new bond that now unites Maniatibel and Ojeda. This, however, entails the betrayal of Caonabo: Maniatibel has incorporated into his own identity Caonabo's greatest enemy. It is only logical, then, that he would choose to die when he is forced to choose between Ojeda and Caonabo. That he is condemned to become "an echo" could not be more explicit in this respect: he can no longer exist as an embodied subject, but he can also not erase himself completely; he exists in the purely symbolic realm of language, law, and guilt—the sphere of the Lacanian symbolic—but is forever forced to speak "in another language." It is from this position that his voice becomes available to Dominicans as a pure, disembodied symbol, a free-floating signifier that can be appropriated by any Dominican in his or her own identitarian fantasy.

The crucial element in Dominican indigenismo is thus not that Dominicans choose to identify with the aboriginal population but that they respond to the mandate "Be Indian!" Being Indian is authorized not by any belief or physiognomic or cultural evidence held by the Dominicans but by Spanish desire. Being Indian means to fulfill the desire of the Other of symbolic identification. It is irrelevant that Dominicans are not Indians and do not even look like Indians: symbolic identification does not rely on mimesis or a single trait but relies on the operations of an abstract principle—it is the realm of what Lacan called the Law or the Name-of-the-Father. Indigenismo thus allows for a distinctively Dominican interpellation while also strengthening the role of Spain in the Dominican cultural imaginary. In this sense, indigenismo is a form of Hispanism—most certainly not a rejection of Spain, as some literary critics have argued (see chapter 8).

To further dissect the psychological and political complexities, it may help to return briefly to a text that bears striking similarities to Llenas's story, namely, Freud's reflections on race and nation in *Moses and Monotheism*. Originally entitled *The Man Moses: A Historical Novel*, Freud's essay is a hybrid text that combines psychoanalytic argument with historical speculation and, probably, fabulation.[12] Freud's claims are notorious. Contrary to the account of the Hebrew Bible, there were two Moses figures. The first Moses was an Egyptian, who was eventually killed by his Jewish followers. Monotheism, too, was not at the origins of Jewish ethnic identity but developed as an Egyptian religion, as a kind of ideological correlate of Egypt's new status as a world empire, and was given to the Jews by Moses. Having murdered the original Moses, the Jews abandoned their new monotheistic religion for quite some time. Eventually a new leader appears, however, and assumes the role of the first Moses. Eventually, too, the beliefs rashly abandoned at the time of the original murder inadvertently begin to surface again. Jewish history thus really only begins as a repetition. It begins with a traumatic event that people responded to by forgetting or, rather, repressing. In keeping with the characteristic patterns of repetition that we know from Freud's work on the genesis of neuroses, the Jews thus constitute themselves as a people around a traumatic experience.

Published in 1939, *Moses and Monotheism* was received with considerable hostility. Freud had intended the essay to be a study of anti-Semitism and had himself had misgivings about the timing of publication. The fractured, highly problematic account of Jewish identity he offered was hardly likely to encourage Jews who were fleeing Nazi persecution. In Freud's account of Jewish identity, Jews are a people that constitutes itself extraterritorially—outside the (physical and imaginary) borders of a nation-state, but also outside any specifiable territory. Jews originated "elsewhere," around a repressed event of the past—their identity has a phantasmagoric element that lends them, in the eyes of Gentiles, a haunting, ghostlike quality. The same quality that stirs up anti-Semitic fears thus also explains the extraordinary resilience of Jewish identity. Jacqueline Rose interprets *Moses and Monotheism* as Freud's refusal to fully underwrite the Zionist project of a Jewish homeland in Palestine. According to her reading, the incompleteness of the essay, its hybrid qualities, and its insistence on the extraterritorial origins of the Jews all bear witness to the fact that Freud was trying to think belonging and identity outside the dangerously exclusive and deceptively stable categories of the nation-state.[13]

In Llenas's story, Dominicans, like the Jews in Freud's "historical novel," originate elsewhere: in this case, in Spain. As in the case of Moses, the tragic guilt that accrued in the capture and death of Caonabo (and ultimately the death of the entire indigenous population) is converted into the basis of a new interpellation, which hails through an echo. Speaking as Dominicans, they have their voice returned as Indians. Instead of the ordinary interpretation of the echo—a single voice split only through temporal delay, or the return of the voice of the self to its origin—Llenas hears a duality, a fractured identity. The returning voice is not that of the self but that of the Indian. In the echo, as in Freud's story of Moses, the original crime is both indelibly inscribed and suppressed, and the self can constitute itself only in relation to this suppressed event of the past. By responding to the mandate "Be Indian," Dominicans constitute themselves through the atonement of a past guilt.

That is the new past of Dominican indigenism—a past that is both haunting and the grounds for future reconciliation and redemption. Clearly, Dominicans do not have to believe that they are descendants of the aboriginal population for this fantasy to work. The reenactment of the structure of repetition through the figure of the echo leads to a new, open-ended nationalist interpellation. In the returning echo, the speech of the descendants of the conquerors repeats the events of the conquest: both sides are caught in a situation where they are forced to recognize the other forever. Both are caught in structures of repetition. Like Freud, Llenas produces the image of a deeply split, problematic identity that nevertheless provides a relatively stable ground. The haunted quality of the Dominican historical experience itself is turned into the base for permanence.

Now, unlike Freud, Llenas links the story of an identity constituted through guilt to a specific territory. In fact, few features of a merely physical nature constitute a tighter, more immediate link between the human subject and the ground it inhabits than an echo. In the echo, the soil speaks in a human voice—Dominican natural history, human history, and present time become one, as it were, in the duality of the echo. The recognition of a deeply traumatic nationhood, the recognition that the origins of this nationhood are in some sense beyond our grasp, that there are fissures and irreducible differences, thus does not preclude a return to the categories of the nation-state and nationalism. Only those who underwrite and assume the guilt that accrued when the original sacred pact between Indians and Spaniards failed due to the intrusion of secular desires can lay claim to Dominican nationhood. And it is only the Dominican soil that reflects the voice of the Dominican subject. As we will see later, there are other ways of imagining relations with the indigenous population. In Haiti, where the early constitutions retained notions of transnational political alliances and citizenship as the central categories, nineteenth-century indigenism appears to have been based on political alliance and vengeance. Llenas, while casting Dominican national history in terms of plot elements strikingly similar to those in Freud's *Moses and Monotheism,* in the end underwrites precisely those categories of unquestionable belonging and self-identity that Freud appears to be questioning.

The image of the echo thus brilliantly translates the historical experience in the oldest Spanish colony into a political mandate. On the one hand, it seems to show that even a past that keeps returning can form the basis for collective cohesion and futurity, and that the specific content of the past event does not determine future events. Even death and destruction can be transfigured so that they become the element in which revitalization and rebirth occur and thus show how even a historical experience as traumatic as that of Santo Domingo can become the basis for renewal and ultimately "progress."

*Guilt and Betrayal in Santo Domingo* 165

In this respect, it may not be a coincidence that Llenas chooses the term *grito* (cry or scream) in the resolution of the story. As a form of speech that invokes suffering, it is a reminder that it is in the experience of pain that the voices of the Indian and the Dominican become a fragile and internally fractured unity. As a reconfiguration of an idea of futurity and progress, the image of the echo shows that being Dominican "now!" is never entirely rooted in the past. It becomes an inference from an ever renewed future that generates a present—a structure that can be filled with new meaning every time a Dominican cries out.

Still, a certain ambiguity remains. No matter how much progress there is, it cannot overtake an echo. The voice of the Indian—the voice of the past—always returns from the future. The ultimate dream of the ideology of progress—the cutting loose from the burdens of the past—eludes us if we think of our present in terms of an echo. The image retains a melancholy recognition that we cannot be done with history. In the cry, the suffering is still alive. Because of the temporality of the echo, the death of Maniatibel can never be integrated and contained in a narrative properly speaking: no matter what might have caused the cry—no matter what it says—it is always the Indian's voice that comes back to us. The traumatic event resists closure and can be captured only symbolically, for a fleeting moment, in an echo that continues to haunt and disrupt everyday life. The success of literature in the elaboration of an indigenist national imaginary is due, in no small part, to literature's ability to sustain this ambivalence: the mournful acceptance of an indelible past crime which means that the past is always already the future, and the hopeful idea that the guilt of the past can be transfigured into a mandate from the future.

## Haiti Disavowed

The question that remains to be addressed, then, is how these difficult and fraught identitarian constructions relate to Haiti. Do they retain any specific elements of the experiences relating to Haiti, or do they simply function as a substitute? Do they block the memory of the early nineteenth century, or do they preserve some traces of that experience? Let me recapitulate briefly the essential characteristics of the Spain of the indigenist fantasy. There are the "good Spaniards," whose goal it is to convert the Indians to Christianity and to establish a Garden of Eden in the New World, and the "bad Spaniards," who are driven by secular desires. The pious dreams of the former fail because of the intrusion of the latter. The genocide of the conquest thus produces a remainder—something in excess of the historical events, a desire not consumed in reality. This remainder, which is expressed symbolically in the echoes and ghosts that haunt Dominican literature, is precisely what allows Dominican writers to wrench a future out of a traumatic past. It is also the basis on which Spain can become the authorizing figure in the Dominican imaginary—through the Spanish intervention in the history of Hispaniola, a mandate issues that transforms Spain into the Other of symbolic identification for Dominicans. Dominican writers seize the genocide of the indigenous population precisely to construe a past that would guarantee a Hispanist future.

On closer inspection, it thus turns out that the Spain of the indigenist fantasy is molded precisely so that it would fill the role of Haiti. Within the pattern of repetition of liberation and recolonization, abolition and reintroduction of slavery, Haiti and Spain were structurally on the same plane, as Santo Domingo variously declared independence from one or the other. If Haiti was the driving force behind the repetitions and reversals that haunt Santo Domingo, indigenismo retrojects them to the time of the conquest. Moreover, as we have seen in the previous chapter, in the first half of the nineteenth century, the ideas of future, progress, and modernity had become associated with the secular egalitarianism of the black Jacobins, and Haiti was perceived as the secular modernizer who destroyed Golden Age traditions in the East. Where Haiti kept returning in reality, as an invader and occupying force, Spain now returns spiritually, as it were. Indigenismo thus captures the experience of a traumatic past, of a past that constitutes itself in repetitions and shifting collective identities, but makes this experience a result of the conquest, the genocide of the indigenous population, and first colonization. True, Santo Domingo is haunted, but not by the Haitians. Casting themselves as the objects of desire of Spaniards such as Columbus and Las Casas becomes a structural equivalent of, and alternative to, the desire of the Haitians, who desecrate the temples and whose secular and perverse tastes require the Dominicans to give up their traditions and beliefs (see chapter 7). Secularism itself is transformed from being an attribute of the Haitian invaders into the irreligiosity of the Spanish conquerors. The experience that is captured and contained in the plots which transform guilt and betrayal into the foundation of a national interpellation is precisely that which is unmentionable and yet central: the experience of the Haitian occupations, the experience of having been modernized by those who were meant to be slaves.

Indigenismo thus performs an operation much more profound than the nominal transformation of mulattoes into Indians: by proposing a crime and subsequent guilt as an explanation of the traumatic character of historical experience in Hispaniola, indigenismo offers a narrative that captures the affective kernel of historical experience in the Dominican Republic while displacing and suppressing any reference to revolutionary antislavery and a peripheral modernity within the core of the Dominican imaginary. To be sure, the memory of these events cannot be read off the surface of the texts. Still, through a careful reading of the literary record, we can discern the traces of the neighboring revolutionary black state: an image not of a backward, impoverished country stuck in a barbaric past but of an enlightened, modern country that represents a different notion of progress and emancipation. Indigenismo seizes the experience of historical repetition and, by forcing it into a plot of a guilt that cannot be canceled, in fact manages to generate a Dominican interpellation that circumvents all references to the troubling neighbor.

# 7

# What Do the Haitians Want?

If the symbolic identification with Spain generates a positive mandate of the form "Be Indian," the relation to Haiti as "the other Other" in Dominican history is governed by a range of collective fantasies of a very different sort. Dominican literature by and large avoids the topic of Haiti altogether, opting instead for the complementary ideologies of indigenism and Hispanism, which aim at foreclosing precisely the space where Haiti could emerge in any kind of identificatory relation. Within a psychoanalytic logic, it is not at all surprising, then, that when Haiti does appear, it is in troubling fantasies about Haitian desire. Just as Dominicans cast themselves as the object of Spanish desire through the indigenist fantasy, so the fantasies about Haiti imagine Dominicans as the object of an Other's desire. The difference is that Haitian desire does not translate into a positive interpellation and does not generate a mandate. The persistence with which the question "What do the Haitians want?" is being raised in those texts lends support to Žižek's suggestion that the problem of the (always obscure, impenetrable) desire of the Other, Lacan's "che vuoi?," erupts in its "purest form" in racist ideologies.[1]

In the occasional stories and anecdotes that remember the entry of the Haitian troops and the occupations, the desire of the Haitians becomes essentially transgressive. The gap left by the incomprehensibility of the desire of the Other is filled, in its most extreme form, with the fantasy that Haitian desire is necrophiliac: they want Dominican virgins, and they want them dead. Instead of translating into a positive mandate, Haitian desire is scrambled to a point where it becomes utterly unanswerable. Only dead Dominicans could respond to it.

Historians differ in their assessment of popular sentiment in the face of the Haitian "invasions," but it is generally agreed that neither in 1801 nor in 1822 was there an anti-Haitian groundswell. In a letter to a clergyman who had fled Santo Domingo ahead of the arrival of

Toussaint Louverture, a Dominican woman writes: "On January 3 the insurgent Toussaint entered our city, and the only thing that was missing was receiving him under a canopy, since as far as I know we would not have done more to receive our monarch."[2] Franklin Franco Pichardo insists that the unification of Haiti and Santo Domingo in 1822 happened "without a single shot being fired, because it was based on the support of the majority of the inhabitants, with the exception of a small colonial aristocracy of whites and certain clergymen."[3] The takeover was carefully negotiated on both sides; a treaty had been drawn up, and the independent government of Núñez de Cáceres peacefully handed over the keys of the city. There had been little sympathy for an independence that had failed to commit to the abolition of slavery, and apparently the new Haitian government was greeted with some enthusiasm by the mulatto population. Even José Joaquín Balaguer, who is an unlikely suspect for secret pro-Haitian feelings, was forced to admit that there was notable popular support for Boyer at the time of the occupation in 1822 and that even some of the influential families in the northern part of the island were quite happy to live under Haitian rule.[4]

On the face of it, Haiti's goals during the first half of the nineteenth century were fairly clear: above anything else, Haiti wanted to prevent slavery from being reintroduced in the territory. The invasions of 1804 and 1822 were both motivated in part by the fear that metropolitan forces might use the Spanish part of the island as a base for an invasion of Haiti; only by occupying the Spanish part of the island could they prevent this from happening. Second, Haiti wanted to keep slavery out of the Spanish part of the island, as there was a certain amount of popular pressure in Haiti to liberate the blacks and mulattoes in Santo Domingo. And third, there were economic and political benefits to be had: more land was needed for distribution among the soldiers of the revolutionary wars, and Boyer's power depended to a significant degree on his ability to make good the promise to compensate the officials of the revolutionary war by giving them land.

However, nineteenth-century cultural and political discourse in Spanish Hispaniola rarely recognizes these motives. As the century unfolds, anti-Haitian writings seem to be driven by increasingly bizarre fantasies about the unfathomable perversity of Haitian desire. In the early nineteenth century, we can still find some texts that recognize the radical political nature of the Haitian project. By the end of the nineteenth century, radical antislavery has dropped out of the picture. Haitian desire has become identified with deviant sexuality, the desecration of everything holy, and superstitious dreams of absolute control (the zombie).

The following account of the arrival of Toussaint Louverture's army in Santo Domingo comes from a letter written by a Dominican who stayed behind to a compatriot in Cuban exile:

> During his [Toussaint's] rule we were vexed in all kinds of ways and made equal to our own slaves in the military and in all public acts. In a dance that was given to celebrate the great entry of Moyse, before the arrival of the French Armada, I was given the great distinction by the master of ceremonies of being asked to dance with a slave woman of my house, who was one of the principal ladies of the dance because she was pretty, and she had no other title or price to claim her freedom than the entry of the Blacks in this country. . . . We remained in this state, tolerating an equality that was accompanied everywhere by ignominy and cruel threats, since the black officers were already rushing to establish relations with the most distinguished young ladies of the country, compromising at every step the honor of their families.[5]

The appearance of revolutionary slaves is perceived not as reality but as carnival—a temporary reversal of hierarchies contained in the form of the social ritual of a dance; a mock revolution easily dismissed as playacting to which the demoted slave owner can submit with a wry smile. When the game turns into reality—when the dance turns into courtship—it dawns on the writer that he was witnessing not just a momentary transgression but the advent of a new social order. Bemusement gives way to a feeling of shame and humiliation.

The letter writer is by no means the first one to consider equality a mere mask, a disguise of true reality. Here is how a poem from the 1790s put it:

> ¡Oh! ¡Qué terrible maldad!
> Que mi noble jerarquía
> vuelve el francés a porfía,
> a una infame igualdad! . . .

> [Oh! What terrible wickedness!
> My noble rank
> is provocatively turned by the Frenchman
> into infamous equality!][6]

In the more expansive letter quoted earlier, "equality" seems to be considered a fiction of sorts, which then sets the scene for the subsequent events. In other words, it is the device that allows for a suspension of disbelief. The transgression that results in the writer's feelings of humiliation stems from the fact that some acts or events resist the "as if" of fiction. One can dance with one's former slave "as if . . . ," but one cannot have sexual relations "as if" they were sexual. Unable or unwilling to consider equality a real political agenda, the letter writer insists on continuing to treat racial equality as a staging device. Real sex in imaginary scenarios—in the fantasy of the letter writer, politics is refigured as pornography. Former slaves enter the historical stage as actors: the Haitian Revolution is experienced either as a theatrical trick—a breaking through the fourth wall—or as a violation of the laws of shame and human decency. As former slaves enter the political realm, history loses its smooth appearance of naturalness and comes to be related in terms of hypothetical scenarios and fantasies.

The strangeness of the letter writer's efforts to frame, quite literally, the experience of seeing former slaves dressed up in the revolutionary tricorne and running public affairs anticipates the scenes of profanation and rape that will become more common in the anti-Haitian nationalism of the later nineteenth century. Unlike later texts, however, this attempt at framing and fictionalizing the events retains the traces of the political: the claim to equality is rendered as a staging device, but it is not yet suppressed entirely. Thus framed, the letter quite literally performs the transformation of counter-revolutionary ideology into racism. Most importantly, it shows that the slaveholder apparently cannot articulate the idea of racial equality except through this kind of transformative frame.

A "Diálogo cantado entre un guajiro y un Papá bocó haitiano en un fandango en Dajabón" (Fandango dialogue sung by a Dominican peasant and a Haitian witch doctor in Dajabón) by the popular poet Juan Antonio Alix,[7] which apparently became part of folklore and was reprinted in newspapers throughout the later part of the nineteenth century, is particularly instructive. The Haitian's part is written in a mixture of Spanish and Creole. After polite introductions between the Dominican peasant and the Haitian *papá bocó* and exchanges of pleasantries such as "Yo tengo un codei de tierra, / una gata y una perra / a deposesión de uté" [I have a piece of land, a cat and a dog, at your disposition] and "Compad, contenta ta yo, / E alegra de vu coné" [Compadre, I'm pleased and happy to have met you], the dialogue disintegrates into a battle of wills in which the Haitian witch doctor wants the Dominican to come home with him to eat at his house (as becomes clear later, among the offerings are always little children); and then, most importantly, "Tu tien qui bailá vodú" [You have to dance vodun], and the Dominican refuses, "Yo si no bailo judú" [For my part I don't dance vodun] (267–69). The battle goes on and on, and in the end the Dominican stabs the Haitian to rid himself of the impertinent suggestion that he, the good Christian, should submit to Haitian vodun drums.

While a classic example of a nationalism driven by fears of Haiti, the text unwittingly also documents that the antagonism between the Dominican Republic and Haiti may not have come as naturally as some of the racist ideologues of the twentieth century have pretended. The minutiae of the battle between the guajiro and the Haitian peasant certainly bear witness to some hostility, but they also illustrate that the island was indeed growing together linguistically and culturally. I suspect that few people outside Hispaniola would understand the Creole-Spanish patois in which the story is written. Moreover, the competition itself works only because the Haitian and the Dominican are relying on the same superstitions in their attempts to establish control over the other. Radical otherness obviously had to be created before it could operate as part of Dominican nationalist ideology.

José Bonilla y España's story "La profecía" (The prophecy) is one of the relatively few texts in an educated literary register that directly speak to the Haitian invasion.[8] Invoking the image of Santo Domingo as the former "Athens of the New World," it tells the story of two Haitian soldiers and a Frenchman who choose the ruins of an old colonial monastery for a drinking orgy.[9] As their spirits rise, one of them calls for the monks to come out of their graves to join them. Disproving the secular hubris of the soldiers, a monk does appear, denounces their blasphemies, and prophesies the expulsion of the Haitians. The story ends with a statement that anticipates the 1844 independence.

The text shares a number of motifs with nineteenth-century Hispanist and indigenist texts: a ghost, a prophecy, Dominican nationhood as constituted by mystical anticipation through a past that returns from the future. Unlike José Joaquín Pérez and most other writers, however, Bonilla is explicit in that it is the Haitians (and, to a lesser degree, the French) who intrude in the venerable spaces of Dominican history and desecrate them with their profanities. Instead of displacing the conflicts surrounding Haiti into the era of the conquest, as did the literarily more ambitious practitioners of Dominican indigenismo, Bonilla y España tells it as he sees it: Dominican nationhood needs to be constructed against Haitian secularism.

In the 1890s the story was rewritten by César Nicolás Penson for inclusion in his *Cosas Añejas,* a collection of popular and not-so-popular traditions that was likely inspired by Ricardo Palma's *Tradiciones peruanas.* Under the new title "Profanación!" Penson stresses the links between Haiti and France by having the men sing the Marseillaise as they are walking along, by sprinkling the dialogue with French expressions, and describing the Haitians as "Neo-Republicans of the West."[10] The point of the story becomes even clearer when Penson ends without any prophecy of Dominican independence: it is a denunciation of Haitian secularism and Francophilia, not an attempt to derive Dominican nationhood from the rejection of Haiti. The political issues of slavery and racial equality have disappeared; instead we are offered a picture in which the revolutionary ideology is reduced to a mere collection of French words and songs and a desire to desecrate all that is venerable and holy. The answer to the question of Haitian desire does not—should not—require a reference to Dominican nationhood. Independence is achieved precisely by not responding to any demand made by the Haitians.

One of the more virulent and in many ways bizarre motifs of nineteenth-century Dominican culture is that of the "Virgins of Galindo." In 1822 the dismembered bodies of three girls were found in a well. Soon three Dominicans were captured and sentenced to prison and hard labor for the crime. In 1860 one of the most active Dominican intellectuals of the nineteenth century, Félix María Del Monte, used the story for a "historical legend" in verse titled *Las vírgenes de Galindo o la Invasión de los haitianos sobre la parte española de la isla de Santo Domingo, el 9 de febrero de 1822* [The virgins of Galindo, or The invasion of the Haitians in the Spanish part of the island of Santo Domingo, February 9, 1822].[11] In 1884 Alejandro Bonilla, one of the foremost Dominican painters at the time who frequently took up popular themes from Dominican writers, chose the virgins of Galindo as the topic for an oil painting.[12] In 1891 Penson includes a prose version of Del Monte's story in his *Cosas añejas.* In all these versions, the perpetrators of the crime are Haitians.[13]

Del Monte's text starts as an epic poem, with an account of colonial splendor, and ends with the misery of Haitian rule. Andrés Andújar, a widower who is approaching old age, lives with his three daughters and a deaf-mute slave and her son in a remote mountainous area upstream from Santo Domingo. It is the time of the ephemeral independence and the subsequent invasion of the Haitians. A young man approaches Andújar and asks for his oldest daughter's hand. When she learns that her suitor, fearing the imminent arrival of the Haitians, is about to leave for Spain, she decides that she cannot leave her old father behind. A little while later, the father is away from the house, and it is getting dark. Suddenly the family dog's barking is heard in the distance. Strange sounds abound. Then three Haitians appear. They announce that they have killed the father and proceed to beat and kill the girls. Then they rape the dead bodies, cut off their limbs, and throw them into a well. A few days later the crime is discovered by a hunter, a Frenchman who had settled in Santo Domingo after escaping from the massacres of the Haitian Revolution, who by chance notices the smell of the rotting bodies.

Penson's rewriting of the story in 1891 introduces some remarkable changes. While Del Monte's "historical legend" has all the terseness of a Spanish romance with its focus on plot and dialogue, Penson uses the descriptive possibilities of prose to allow the reader to enter the realm of fantasy and psychological motivation. Obviously aware of the literary shortcomings of the earlier text, Penson feels compelled to set the girls up as more than just chance victims. But how does he do it? He makes them desirable. The story now begins in the city of Santo Domingo, where the three girls are being educated under the benevolent guidance of an elderly lady, and the oldest girl is experiencing first love. One day, Andújar, now portrayed as a brutish and egotistical man, shows up and takes the three girls out into the wilderness with him. This sets off the chain of disasters. Two Haitian soldiers and several unnamed Dominican accessories are shown in their barracks plotting the crime in advance. One day they follow Andújar on his way back to his farm. From there, the plot is the same as that of Del Monte, but the account becomes increasingly rich in obscene detail. The night of the crime is full of foreboding and expectation. With a book called *The Voice of Nature* at her side, the oldest girl has succumbed to daydreaming.

Agueda, who felt the inner voices of her passion talking to her, was the one who was most alert. With her head of disheveled hair draped over a fine, transparent hand, the elbow on the rough table, as the house was without any embellishments, the gossamer shirt open—the heat had made her shed all other garments—so that her neck and her well-turned arms and the curved and smooth bosom were left naked, she appeared like a Venus whose shape was gracefully outlined under the soft linen that allowed it to shine through; in this night of immolation of the innocent victims, what was she reflecting about? She herself did not know. Her abandon was languid and romantic. (319)

Focusing mostly on the adolescent Agueda, Penson takes her clothes off. Innocent like de Sade's Justine, and like Justine infinitely inviting violation precisely for that reason, Agueda is both dreamy and supremely alert; she knows and she is completely innocent. As the night progresses and the father has still not returned from the city, the narrator describes Agueda again:

> There was an interesting expressiveness in the young woman's attitude at this moment. Her eyes were flashing and inquisitive, the nostrils open and her lips unfurled and a little pale like a pomegranate that has fallen from a tree and split open, her throbbing breasts which without bandages revealed themselves in almost sculptural nudity, while the light of the candle was reflected fully in her rounded, angelical, and extremely beautiful face. (320)

The murder scene is not short on detail either: there are "rough hairy hands on their angelical mouths," ripped dresses, and exposed breasts. The abuse of the dead bodies is described like this: "God! Horror of horrors! Their throbbing bodies . . . but how can I say this? . . . they served as fodder for the lubricity of those monsters. At least that is what people say" (326).

The story moves from natural instinct to criminal desire, from scopophilia to sadism. It begins by offering the reader a furtive look at young women who believe themselves unobserved inside their home. Paradoxically, but in keeping with scopophilic logic, the women's belief that they are by themselves does not mean that they exist just for themselves. On the contrary, every aspect of their physical and psychic appearance shows them as objects of male sexual desire. They do not move, they do not speak, they are unselfconscious to such a degree that they do not even have distinct thoughts. Their whole existence is contained in being sexually desirable. As they unwittingly endure the knowing gaze trained on them without them being aware of it, they are also awaiting the final "immolation" through "hairy hands." In Del Monte's version, the story is entirely driven by male action, with no attempts made to motivate or explain the events. Penson fills the gap with descriptions that make female passivity a theme of the narration, thus turning the story into a source of scopophilic pleasure. The girls are caught in a state of suspended animation, displayed solely for the purpose of the gaze. Agueda has abandoned her reading and drifted into the realm of the inner voice. *The Voice of Nature*—first introduced as a book title—transubstantiates into a voice that does not even need language (thus Agueda does not "know" what the inner voice is telling her). Clearly, the gaze has made her slip from the realm of the symbolic into the realm that the logic of the patriarchy conventionally assigns to women: the imaginary.

The climax of the scopophilic fantasy, which is disowned by the narrator in the final "at least this is what people say," is followed by a crisis of the writer: "The plume falls from my hand, unable to continue to lubricate in light of such atrocities. Look at the tigers, their nauseating appetite and their thirst for blood satiated, as they wallow in the innocence of the poor girls, already cold with death; look at them, as they consummate their wicked deed" (326). A pen that is dropped as it is unable to make its mark on the white page, lubrications that will not come forth, the admission of impotence—the sexual connotations of this passage could hardly be more obvious. "The Virgins of Galindo" is not just a pornographic crime story; it is also a story about a crisis of Dominican virility. The fulfillment of the perverse desire of the Haitians is also, it seems, the act of castrating the Dominican male. Looking at the sublime passivity of Agueda in Penson's description from this perspective, we see that she is an emblematic representation of lack, in other words, of that which reassures the male, to whose gaze she is offered, that he does not "lack." The arousal produced through the pornographic descriptions of the girl could thus be seen as aiming at precisely this: producing the proof of Dominican masculinity. To the extent that Agueda is what Laura Mulvey in her discussion of scopophilia called a "bearer, not maker, of meaning,"[14] she is the ground on which Dominican masculinity is constituted. It is thus crucial that up to the moment of the murder, the reader is made complicit in the stalking of the girls. Clearly, "The Virgins of Galindo" resolves the question of Haitian desire on the grounds of gender.[15]

From this perspective it is clear why the Haitians abuse the bodies of the girls *after* killing them: they do not desire the way Dominican men desire; they do not respond to the "voice of nature." Haitian desire is figured as the ultimate perversion of sexual aims, namely, necrophilia. Freud, who was not usually squeamish about forms of perversion, rarely mentions necrophilia. One of the few exceptions is a 1917 lecture that closely follows the argument of the *Three Essays on the Theory of Sexuality*. There he offers a hierarchy of perversions that begins with "homosexuals or inverts," then mentions various kinds of fetishists, and those who derive pleasure from the body's excretory functions. The list culminates in those who "require the whole object indeed, but make quite definite demands of it—strange or horrible—even that it must have become a defenseless corpse, and who, using criminal violence, make it into one so that they may enjoy it. But enough of this kind of horror!"[16]

What does this mean for the desire of the Haitians? Clearly, the charge of necrophilia against the Haitians takes us to the limit of human desire—a desire that can only be satisfied by the ultimate act of dehumanization, by transforming the living human body into an inanimate object. It is a desire that is not only unnatural but post-human in that it is satisfied only after humanity has vanished. While the patriarchal logic of scopophilia set up the girls for a desire whose "natural" aim is human reproduction, the necrophilic desire is satisfied through the opposite: the killing of a human body, reducing the living body to its mere materiality. The answer to the question "What do the Haitians want?" is thus both concrete—"dead bodies"—and humanly incomprehensible. Necrophilia provides the most definite closure: it puts an end to history, reproduction, life—once the desire is satisfied, nothing can come from it. It can only repeat itself in never-ending murderous sprees.

If we now read this fantasy in the context of historical experience in the Dominican Republic and specifically the experience of Haitian occupations, we can see how "The Virgins of Galindo" engages the issue of a problematic Dominican interpellation. In the necrophilic fantasy, Dominicans are indeed the object of Haitian desire, but it is a desire that absolutely resists any translation into a positive mandate, as the only possible mandate is "Be dead" or "Let yourself be killed!"

Instead of an alternative to Creole modernity and a different future, Haiti offers only the end of history. The perfectly common fact of sexual desire across distinctions of color and race is fantasized here as a desire for the nonhuman or posthuman. If sexual desire marks the outline of equal humanness, Haitian desire is construed as a desire across the most significant boundary of all—that between animate and inanimate. Any connection between the desires of the Haitians and the project of radical antislavery has been cut off. Indeed, Penson's story makes this quite clear by insisting that the family's maid had been a slave who decided to stay with her owners after the Haitians abolished slavery. Emancipation has no role in this play of desires.

This suppression of the political becomes possible by shifting the problem from one of race and racial politics to one of gender.

The putative restitution of Dominican masculinity only gets off the ground through the immobilization and silencing of Dominican women. The young girls become a means through which Dominican masculinity is articulated. The narrator's inability to describe the actual necrophilic act, his admitted impotence in light of Haitian bestiality, must thus be read as a displaced reaction to the possibility of a Haitian interpellation. The story refigures the Dominican elite's experience of disempowerment during Haitian rule as the result of an abuse of Dominican women. The narrator's inability to capture the events within the logic of the symbolic is an effect not of failing masculinity—of having lost the battle against the Haitians—but of the literally unspeakable nature of the act. The historical experience of Haitian domination is thus completely removed from the realm of politics and struggles for power into a realm of perverse sexual desires. If Dominican men were disempowered by former slaves from Haiti, this disempowerment is the result not of any direct confrontation between them but of a conflict over whose law can be imposed on Dominican women. So whereas there is an (impossible) interpellation from the Haitian Other toward Dominican women, Dominican men enter the picture only indirectly, as the representatives of a human law, opposed to the inhuman, incomprehensible laws that issue from Haitian desire.

The pornographic fantasy that was discernible only as a form of staging in the letter of 1801 about the Haitian officials who had started courting the daughters of Dominicans, and was contained in the breaks between stanzas in Del Monte's epic drama, thus culminates in Penson's version of "The Virgins of Galindo." Once we recognize the symmetries between the Hispanist interpellation that called for Dominicans to "be Indian" and the fantasies that displace any attempt to articulate a Haitian interpellation, we can see that what is at work here is much more than just the operations of age-old stereotyping on the basis of racial difference. What is at stake is the affective charge of historical experience: criollo hegemony in the mulatto nation could be achieved only if the memories of the Haitian modernizers were radically altered and reinterpreted, and the realization that things could have gone otherwise be blocked forever.

# 8

# Fictions of Literary History

According to a recent bibliographical study, in the whole of the nineteenth century only seven novels, twenty-six books of poems, three books of stories, one play, and one book of essays were published in the Dominican Republic. Only four of these were by women.[1] Many of the early texts were written and published outside the territory, and what was published inside Dominican territory often appeared in minuscule editions, in newspapers, or as collectible leaflets. No doubt, literary writing and publishing took root very slowly in the eastern part of Hispaniola.

From the beginning, the printing press was linked to the French part of the island. The first printer was a Frenchman listed under the name of Andrés Josef Blocquerst, and the first newspaper was an organ of the French government, most likely bilingual, which circulated between 1807 and 1809 under the name of *Boletín de Santo Domingo*. In his history of the Dominican printing press, Rodríguez Demorizi comments that this publication was largely military in character and thus "probably not important for the development of national culture."[2] Characteristically, the first Spanish text to be printed in Santo Domingo was a little religious pamphlet with the title "Novena para implorar la protección de María Santísima, por medio de su imagen de Altagracia" (Novena to implore the protection of Holy Mary through her image of Altagracia). In 1801, the statutes of the university Santo Tomás were printed, as was the agreement, written in French, between the Spanish governor Joaquín García and Toussaint Louverture, according to which the eastern part of the island passed over into French possession in fulfillment of the Treaty of Basle. Despite the French withdrawal in 1809, publishing in Spanish did not pick up again until almost a decade later. For a few months during the time of the ephemeral independence, two newspapers started to appear, with the last known issue published July 26, 1821.[3] During the Haitian period (1822–1843), publishing and printing appear to have been almost entirely limited to official business. It is not until independence in 1844 that the usual spread of newspapers begin to appear.

Cultural life during Haitian rule is difficult to assess. There can be little doubt that the culture of the colonial elite was severely disrupted by the Haitian occupation. The university closed its doors in 1823. Newspapers disappeared again. Censorship ensured that nothing but the most flattering comments about the rulers could be published. It is of course possible that the prolonged presence of Haitians in the Dominican territory meant that hybrid popular practices developed, but most poetry was circulated in manuscript form, and the work of improvisers like Justiniano García, a "slightly disturbed beggar" popularly called Utiano, remained for the most part oral. Although there appears to have been some pro-Haitian writing by members of the Dominican elite who chose to stay on the island, these texts became an embarrassment for later Dominican critics, and little is known about them. It seems clear that Haitian modernization focused on the economic and legal sphere rather than cultural development.

We can only speculate about what forms the commemorations of the French abolitionist Abbé Grégoire took when in 1831 Boyer ordered funeral masses for him all over the island.[4] Were they acts of state, imposed by an occupying force on Dominicans to whom the international abolitionist movement meant nothing? An occasion for popular festivities and poetry improvisations? Did those blacks and mulattoes who had welcomed the Haitians in 1822 contribute to the celebrations? The Dominican literary historian Max Henríquez Ureña laments that many of the popular songs and poems of the time were lost and quotes some rather interesting popular pamphlets which could be read as indicating that a Haitian-Dominican culture was emerging.[5] One of the examples of "Afro-Dominican" poetry Rodríguez Demorizi quotes is the following ditty:

> Dios se lo pague
> a papa Boyé,
> que nos dió gratis
> la liberté.

> [God bless
> Papa Boyer
> who gave us for free
> our liberty.][6]

Many of the verses quoted as Afro-Dominican poetry are in reality Haitian-Dominican, and the grace of these little rhymes lies in the fact that they mix Spanish and French and certain corruptions of the Spanish that are typical for French or Creole speakers. But the conflicts surrounding revolutionary antislavery in the early nineteenth century were intense, the fears extravagant, and little documentation survived those pressures. To the extent that a literary archive came into being (and it is worth remembering that it was under Trujillo that many, if not most, of the anthologies of nineteenth-century Dominican literature were assembled), it documents the formation of the nation against its Western Other, Haiti.

Cultural history in the Dominican Republic is thus full of silences and uncharted areas, and it is doubtful that these blank spots can ever be filled in. In fact, these gaps eventually became foundational for the discourses of Dominican history and literature, which constituted themselves around those blank spots—through the invention of a past that never was, as in indigenismo and hispanismo, and through plottings of literary and cultural history that excise any traces of a Haitian modernization.

### Ruins and the Elusiveness of Progress

In most areas of Spanish America, nineteenth-century writers firmly allied themselves with the project of progress and nation building. The literature they produced was an extroverted, critical, even hectoring literature that delved into national realities in search of themes and topics, written by men (and very few women) who did not mind getting their hands dirty—a highly ideological literature often in the service of a specific political program or party, produced by writers who had been presidents or would have preferred to be presidents. Romanticism may have been the dominant mood, but it was a romanticism shot through with the realist's appreciation of social reality, history, and the quickening pace of progress.

In the case of Santo Domingo, the presence of a black revolutionary state significantly shifted the ground on which cultural production took place. On an affective level, Dominican literature does not, for the most part, display the same optimism and interest in the new national realities. Dominican writers and intellectuals such as Manuel Galván, the author of *Enriquillo*, were also active participants in public life, but their interventions have a very different quality to them. It seems that the quintessential nineteenth-century ide-

ologies of national independence and progress through modernization were supremely difficult to achieve in the Dominican Republic.
Eventually, here too, progress and development became what Laclau
and Mouffe, following Lacan, called a "point de capiton"—the ruling
concept that quilts the discursive field. But this could be achieved
only indirectly, through lengthy detours into the Dominican past
and delicate manipulation of the emotional state of Dominicans.
The texts that resulted from this process bear witness to the political
and affective resistances that had to be overcome before progress
and futurity could assume their quilting function. As Dominicans
reconstituted the concept of progress on Europeanist grounds, literary activity and scholarship were seen not so much as emerging out
of the nineteenth-century processes of modernization but as a return of a past, a rekindling of a colonial spirit that had died during
the revolutionary period and was revived only after Dominican independence in 1844.

The leading intellectual figures are for the most part poets rather
than novelists or essayists, and the literary field constitutes itself
around poems, epic dramas, and brief stories. Melancholia and
mournful reverie about Santo Domingo's past characterizes most of
the texts. Nineteenth-century Dominican writers reinvent Santo Domingo as a center of erudition and pious contemplation, a New
World Athens or Alexandria that through some unnamed catastrophe fell into ruins. These celebrations of past grandeur never mention Haiti or slavery or revolutionary antislavery or the brutal civil
wars of the Haitian Revolution that severely affected the Spanish
part of the island. Santo Domingo, with its colonial palaces, its monasteries in ruins, and the oldest cathedral in the New World, appears
a lonely outpost of European culture, the site of a doomed attempt to
create a new Garden of Eden in the Americas—a Spanish island
unmoored.

In a prologue that bestows high praise on one of the first fictional
works of any length published in the Dominican Republic, the historical drama *Iguainona* by Javier Angulo Guridi (1881), José Joaquín Pérez tries to signal which path a future Dominican literature should take. Expressing his dismay at the sight of the "pallid
imitations" of foreign models that dominate the literary scene, he
argues that Dominican writers should draw on the painful history of
the territory for inspiration. In this respect, he resembles Spanish American writers and intellectuals like Altamirano in Mexico,
Domingo Del Monte in Cuba, and many others. A closer look at his

argument, however, shows that his vision of the national past and his exhortation to turn to local topics takes a particular and significant shape:

> That past is there with the immobile solemnity of its terrifying secrets, waiting for the vivifying breath of thought to bring back to life its ashes. . . . We must evoke the shadows that sleep in the night of forgetfulness, and illuminate them with the splendors of a new life. There is a whole world of poetry, of love, of heroism, of liberty, of martyrdom, under this immense shroud.[7]

National history is not just a topic waiting to be seized by a talented young writer, not just a set of dramatic themes and events that need to be developed in fiction. It is a petrified past that exists only in the material remnants. It is a past that has become a mystery. Was it forgotten? Suppressed? Destroyed? Pérez does not say. Dominican landscapes and archaeology become the sign of a history that is waiting to be resurrected by writers who can breath life into the ruins and solve the mysteries. Clearly, *this* is the charge for literature: not the production of Galdosian *episodios nacionales,* not the creation of national allegories, but the reanimation of a history that has become remote, inaccessible, and emotionally inert. Literature, with its ability to influence affect and reach levels of the psyche that remain beyond the grasp of most other forms of discourse, has to create a new future out of a past that is hidden under an "immense shroud."

Now, we must recall here that much of Dominican literature before the 1860s was actually not concerned with a remote, forgotten past at all. It was, rather, a combative, hateful, and nationalistic literature whose topic was Haiti and the Dominican struggles against it. Pérez's call to bring a long forgotten past back to life is thus also, and very importantly, an attempt to think about his country without compulsive antagonism against Haiti. Allegories of the struggle for liberty might well have referred writers back to 1801, 1822, and, just possibly, the issue of slavery. The past that lies hidden under an immense shroud is of a different order, far removed from those events of the more recent past.

Eventually a poetic practice established itself that cultivated a vague sense of sadness and loss. The poems describe a world that seems to dissolve in a foggy distance, a world available only to the poetic reflection, through memory and remembrance. In her dedicatory poem for José Joaquín Pérez's *Fantasías indígenas* (1877), Salomé

Ureña de Henríquez begins by invoking "Quejas del alma, vagos rumores / lejanas brumas, rayos de luz" [Moans of the soul, vague rumors / faraway mist, rays of light].[8] The world vanishes, and the subject retreats into the inner space of the self—the space of fantasy and diffuse imagery, where self-affectation takes the place of sensory perception. While the sense of sadness and melancholia is overwhelming, it is not always clear what is being mourned: sometimes, as in the indigenist literature, it seems to be the disappearance of the indigenous people who once populated the island; sometimes, the Spanish culture that flourished and fell into decay; at times qualities that neoclassical taste with a certain romantic inflection found particularly desirable: innocence or virginity or sacredness (all attributes whose negation would invoke, of course, the secular Haitians with their perverse desires).

In a famous passage in "Mourning and Melancholia," Freud writes: "The distinguishing features of melancholia are profoundly painful dejection, cessation of interest in the outside world, loss of the capacity to love, inhibition of all activity, and a lowering of the self-regarding feelings to a degree that finds utterance in self-reproaches and self-revilings, and culminates in delusional expectation of punishment."[9] For the subject that mourns, the world has become empty; for the melancholy subject, it is the self that appears worthless and empty. Melancholia is a narcissistic crisis in which the loss of a love object is internalized and leads to self-hatred and violence against the self. Although Freud is merely speaking about the detrimental effects of melancholia on the individual, we can easily see that as a collective sentiment, melancholia would thwart the politically desirable belief in the possibility of progress and a bright future. Clearly, the melancholy sentiment that is so characteristic of Dominican nineteenth-century poetry needs to be understood as a deeply political phenomenon.

There is a much-anthologized poem called "Ruinas" (Ruins), by Salomé Ureña de Henríquez, that may help us to unravel the fictions that were inaugurated in literature and became foundational in Dominican nationalism of later years.[10] As an instance of hispanismo, "Ruinas" is also an example of a new past. Written by one of the foremost Dominican poets, it was extremely influential. Like Del Monte's epic poem about the Virgins of Galindo, "Ruinas" served as an inspiration for one of the better-known paintings by Alejandro Bonilla and thus proliferated in the national imagination as an iconic representation of the Dominican present.

| Memorias venerandas de otros días, | Venerable memories of other times, |
| soberbios monumentos, | grand monuments, |
| del pasado esplendor reliquias frías, | cold relics of past splendor |
| donde el arte vertió sus fantasías, | into which art poured its fantasies |
| donde el alma expresó sus | in which the soul expressed its |
| pensamientos; | thoughts; |

| Al veros ¡ay! con rapidez que pasma | When I see you, oh, with stunning |
| por la angustiada mente | speed |
| que sueña con la gloria y se | runs through the anguished mind, |
| entusiasma, | which dreams of glory and enthuses, |
| discurre como alígero fantasma | like a winged ghost |
| la bella historia de otra edad | the beautiful history of another |
| luciente. | relucent age. |

| ¡Oh Quisqueya! Las ciencias | Oh Quisqueya! The gathered sciences |
| agrupadas | raised you on their shoulders |
| te alzaron en sus hombros | in front of the astounded looks of the |
| del mundo a las atónitas miradas; | world; |
| y hoy nos cuenta tus glorias | and today your forgotten glories are |
| olvidadas | told |
| la brisa que solloza en tus | by the breeze that sobs in your |
| escombros. | rubble. |

| Ayer, cuando las artes florecientes | Yesterday, when the flourishing arts |
| su imperio aquí fijaron, | erected their empire here |
| y creaciones tuvistes eminentes, | and eminent creations were yours |
| fuiste pasmo y asombro de las | you were the astonishment and |
| gentes, | amazement of the nations |
| y la Atenas moderna te llamaron. | and they called you a modern Athens. |
| . . . . . | . . . . . |

| Vinieron años de amarguras tantas, | Years came of so much bitterness |
| de tanta servidumbre, | so much servitude |
| que hoy esa historia al recordar te | that today you are frightened when |
| espantas, | you recall that history |
| porque inerme, de un dueño ante | defenseless, [ . . . ?][11] |
| las plantas, | the crowd saw you humiliated. |
| humillada te vió la muchedumbre. | |

| Y las artes entonces, inactivas, | And then the arts, inactive, |
| murieron en tu suelo, | died on your soil |
| se abatieron tus cúpulas altivas, | your haughty cupolas were demolished |
| y las ciencias tendieron, fugitivas, | and the sciences extended, as fugitives, |
| a otras regiones, con dolor, su | to other regions, with pain, their |
| vuelo. | flight. |

| | |
|---|---|
| ¡Oh mi Antilla infeliz que el alma adora! | Oh, unhappy island that my heart adores! |
| Doquiera la vista | Wherever the eager eye |
| ávida gira en tu entusiasmo ahora, | draws on your enthusiasm now, |
| una ruina denuncia acusadora | a ruin denounces accusingly |
| las muertas glorias de tu genio artista. | the dead glories of the artistic genius. |
| | |
| ¡Patria desventurada! ¿Qué anatema cayó sobre tu frente? | Unhappy fatherland! What adversity came over your forehead? |
| Levanta ya de tu indolencia extrema: | Lift yourself up from your extreme indolence: |
| la hora sonó de redención suprema | the hour of supreme redemption has come |
| y ¡ay, si desmayas en la lid presente! | and ay, if you swoon in the present combat! |
| | |
| Pero vano temor: ya decidida | But what an unnecessary fear: decidedly already |
| hacia el futuro avanzas; | you advance toward the future; |
| ya del sueño despiertas a la vida, | already from dreams you awake to life, |
| y a la gloria te vas engrandecida | and toward glory you take leave in greatness |
| en alas de risueñas esperanzas. | on the wings of smiling hopes. |
| | |
| Lucha, insiste, tus títulos reclama: | Struggle, insist, claim your titles: |
| que el fuego de tu zona | that the fire of your zone |
| preste a tu genio su potente llama, | may lend to your genius its potent flame, |
| vuelve a ceñirte la triunfal corona. | place the triumphal crown back on your head. |
| | |
| Que mientras sueño para tí una palma, | Because, while I dream up a palm tree for you |
| y al porvenir caminas, | and you walk toward the future, |
| no más se oprimirá de angustia el alma | the soul will no longer be oppressed by anxiety |
| cuando contemple en la callada calma | when it contemplates in the quiet calm |
| la majestad solemne de tus ruinas. | the solemn majesty of your ruins. |

"Ruinas" is a poem about a subject that has retreated into itself in the face of a hostile, fragmented, deadened world. Whereas the opening words, "Memorias venerandas" [venerable memories/memorials], are marked by an ambiguity between *memoria* as a physical object, a monument that reminds us of events of the past, and *memoria* as a phenomenon of the mind, the following verses delicately move us away from the world of material remnants. The second stanza opens with an unambiguous reference to the mind and its torments: "when I see you, ay!" At the end of the second stanza, we are most definitely in the realm of interiority: "the beautiful history [or story] of another relucent age / roams like a winged ghost." Moving from the outside world to the interiority of memory and fantasy, the poem eventually establishes the opposition between the realm of fantasies and thoughts, where things retain their venerable aura, and an outside world which offers nothing but "reliquias frías" [cold relics] and "escombros" [rubble].

As to the question why the territory has fallen into disrepair, the poem remains somewhat vague: although "so many bitter years, / years of so much servitude" is most likely a veiled reference to the years of French and Haitian rule, since Spanish colonialism is an integral part of past glories, the poem does not elaborate or name any specific events or agents of destruction. The glories of the past are lost to the world—they have been internalized and become qualities of the melancholy subject.

This picture entails, of course, a wholesale reinvention of the past. Dorvo Soulastre, a French traveler in the eastern territory whose reports to the government were visions of endless future possibilities of profit and wealth, if only the French chose to finally act on the Treaty of Basle and take possession of the former Spanish colony, praises the beauty and fertility of the land but has nothing but scorn for the population and the general state of development. To Soulastre's mind, Spanish Santo Domingo was suffering from its inhabitants' acute lack of application, their indulgent attitude toward racial mixture, and a severe shortage of slave labor. Even the inhabitants of the capital were proving to be indifferent to anything other than satisfying their basic needs; they were superstitious, given to primitive idolatry in their reverence for rather too sensual depictions of the Virgin Mary, and violently anti-Semitic.[12] Instead of taking charge of his possessions and making the most of them, the Dominican man gives way to his "innate indolence": "his wife works while he sleeps." This is life at its most primitive: "A miserable shack with a hammock suspended from the corner posts; a small piece of land for the cultivation of vegetables and tobacco; some rags instead of clothes are enough to make the inhabitants of these lands happy; there is no ambition that would transcend mere physical needs."

Pedro F. Bonó's account in his 1881 "Notes on the Dominican Working Classes" would have been equally devastating for those who wanted to take pride in their past: those who did not continue on their way to the Spanish American mainland but stayed behind on La Española "created nothing useful or worth of mention."[13] Spanish legal practices and in particular property laws had already fallen behind the times and encouraged a life of lazy stupor: "The landowners or lords led a superstitious, lazy, and beastly life in the abandoned and barren Dominican cities." The sharecroppers and overseers were even more beastly, "brutalized by their inequality in front of the law, their social position and their education," so that they contented themselves with eating some fried *tasajo* or unsavory stews. To Bonó, who although not driven by anti-Haitian passions was not free of racial prejudice, the Dominican lifestyle was "Caffer or Hottentot life."[14] The only positive trait he finds in the Spanish colonial practice is that the proverbial indolence of the criollo meant that the slaves became indispensable members of the household and thus were not brutalized as in the French colony.

Santo Domingo was never a latter-day Athens, and the ruins that are characteristic of the capital city have nothing to do with the years of French and Haitian rule. The sixteenth-century convents and churches that had fallen into disrepair were even at the time of their construction more representative of medieval architecture than classical grandeur and do not display the splendor of colonial architecture in Mexico. But arguments about the historical accuracy of poetry are pointless unless we can link misrepresentations to a specific tension that is being relieved or a specific contradiction that is solved through the fiction. From the conclusion of "Ruinas," we know that the problem is how to produce an idea of progress and futurity in the Dominican Republic. The poem moves from a melancholy reverie about the past to the confident assertion "you walk into the future." It thus bears witness to the difficulties of producing the concept which was the ruling idea of the day and like all such central ideological concepts taken as self-evident in most places.

The solution that "Ruinas" enacts consists of two steps. The first part of the poem consists of an elaborate diagnosis of melancholia as the Dominican malady. As we have seen earlier, there may indeed have been reasons why the Dominican elite might have felt melancholy: because of the experience of disempowerment, the degradations at the hands of former slaves, the apparent aimlessness of the political process, the continuing threats of Africanization, the problematic and unresolved nature of a Dominican interpellation, and so forth. All of these effects could have been experienced as a profound loss and ultimately as a crisis of the subject. But whether or not the diagnosis of melancholia relates to a Dominican reality, the main point is that it identifies a *loss* as that which lies at the center of Dominican nationhood, and then assigns one specific cause to this loss: the decline of a latter-day Athens and the disappearance of a

European high culture. Melancholia is explained through "ruins." A political and affective crisis unique to the colonies and slaveholding areas, unique, too, to the postrevolutionary age, thus becomes a crisis entirely contained in a Eurocentric imaginary. Haiti and revolutionary antislavery no longer exist. The colonial period becomes the object of desire.

This sets the scene for the therapeutic process. Having identified melancholia as the ailment that afflicts Dominicans, the poem lists all the losses of the past and thus offers, in keeping with Freud's notion of *Trauerarbeit* (labor of mourning), external objects that may be mourned.[15] Performing the gestures of melancholy despondency of withdrawal into interiority, the poem then moves to locate the loss in the external world and to accept it. In keeping with the logic of Hispanism and indigenism, the loss is transformed into a collective experience around which Dominicans can rally and constitute themselves as a people with a future. Paradoxically, it is only by virtue of having become ruins, only because they have been registered as a loss, that they could be libidinally cathected. But that was precisely the point. "Ruins" offers a fantasy through which the Dominican reader can learn how to relate to local reality.

Read as a symbol, the ruins are no longer a hostile, dead environment that compels the subject to withdraw into the inner space; instead of reacting to their actual physical existence and appearance—their pastness, their deadness—Dominicans are invited to react to what they might mean. In themselves, they may give us cause for grief, but as symbols or signs they are cause for pride: by the end of the poem, the ruins are being admired in their "solemn majesty." Dominican history is transformed so that it no longer bears the imprint of a marginality that resulted from unresolved conflicts and emancipatory projects that were never able to impose themselves as hegemonic—that had, indeed, become the definition of marginality: at the end of the poem, the Dominican Republic rejoins the Spanish American mainstream where "progress" had been the key word for almost a century.

The problem that "Ruinas" tries to solve is, of course, a problem for the Creole elite. It was to them that the years of Haitian occupation meant "years of servitude"—liberated slaves likely felt otherwise. Although all references to Haiti and to the history of radical antislavery have vanished, we can still discern, in the particular way in which the subject constructs its lost object of desire, an affective constellation that originates in the warped history of Hispaniola after 1791. In the tortuous detours and digressions that are needed to produce the concept of progress and a sense of futurity, we can see the outline of a past in which progress and future were synonymous with the revolutionary black state. "Ruinas" transforms the Dominican Republic from a new state of obscure origins in radical anti-slavery and popular ambivalence toward European colonizers into a state that traces its origins to European elite culture: a modern Athens.

## Problems of Literary History

The silences and blank spots generated through the poetic practices of the nineteenth century do not simply disappear later on, nor are they limited to fictional and poetic discourses. To be sure, if the ideological work of nineteenth-century intellectuals was at all successful, it meant that the origins of the commonplaces and favored strategies of Dominican historical and literary discourses would have become unknown to later writers. But even if twentieth-century intellectuals were no longer aware of the conflicts at the root of Dominican nationhood, even if the problem of Haiti had been absorbed into the developmentalist language of economists and social scientists, or alternatively, assumed the generic ahistorical language of racism, the basic operations of displacement are still in place.

A remarkable example is Max Henríquez Ureña's *Panorama histórico*. As the grandson of the writer Nicolás Ureña de Mendoza, son of Salomé Ureña, and brother of the literary critic Pedro Henríquez Ureña, Max Henríquez Ureña belonged to one of the foremost intellectual families in the Dominican Republic. His writings exude familiarity with many of the cultural figures he is writing about and a deep knowledge of Dominican traumas and mythologies. As one of the leading historians of Dominican literature and a scholar of incalculable influence over subsequent generations of critics, he offers a plot for the emergence of literary culture in the Dominican Republic that illustrates well where the problems lie.

Although written in the 1940s—the heyday of anti-Haitianism in the aftermath of the 1937 massacre—his account is not marred by the blatant racism we find in the writings of Peña Batlle, Balaguer, and others at the time. In the sober manner of the impeccable scholar, Henríquez Ureña tells us that Santo Domingo, far from being the Athens of the New World, had never been the home of flourishing arts. For the colonial period, he mentions some popular romances, *coplas,* and political satires that survived in the oral tradition and were eventually collected by nineteenth-century writers and scholars,[16] but in the absence of a printing press, most of these popular songs and plays are now lost. For the period between 1801 and 1844, he offers a plot that turns on waves of emigrations, the first wave taking place after Toussaint Louverture's invasion of 1801 and Dessalines's forays in 1805. The Haitian takeover of 1822 is discussed in a chapter entitled "The Haitian Period: New Emigrations," which claims that cultural activity stopped almost completely, but briefly mentions pro-Haitian poetry and an emerging patois of Spanish-French-Creole. There is a brief chapter dedicated to the ephemeral independence of 1822, followed by a chapter entitled "Folklore," which returns to the early colonial days of the sixteenth century. The remainder of the century is divided into the period of patriotic literature from 1844 to 1861 with a clear anti-Haitian bent and little literary value, and the period of indigenismo which according to Henríquez Ureña begins with the War of Restoration, that is, when Spain emerges as the new enemy. National literary history proper thus starts with independence in 1844, but the first real literary movement in the Dominican Republic is indigenismo.

The advantages of Henríquez Ureña's plot are clear: a truly Dominican literature emerges precisely when the loops and repetitions of emancipation and recolonization have come to an end. The history of literature and the nation have been brought into congruence. By the same token, literary history becomes the medium through which the possibility of alternative paths or other possible futures is foreclosed.

It is against the many virtues of Henríquez Ureña's carefully researched and documented account that we need to consider two strange blind spots. The first one is a plain omission: Henríquez Ureña fails to mention what was probably the first, but almost certainly the first significant, Dominican novel. The second one is an act of disavowal: Henríquez Ureña denies, against all evidence, the existence of indigenismo before 1861. Together these two blind spots constitute a highly significant trace of what needed to be suppressed from the cultural imaginary to normalize Dominican history and to erase the struggles around conflicting notions of emancipation and modernity.

In 1851 Pedro Francisco Bonó wrote *El montero,* subtitled "novela de costumbres" (novel of customs). It was published in Paris (1856), in the *Correo de Ultramar,* a Spanish-language magazine that circulated widely in the Dominican Republic.[17] Since first novels tend to occupy a special place in postcolonial societies, and *El montero* is by no means a particularly inept first novel, what explains this startling omission? Extraterritorial publication cannot be the explanation, since that did not prevent Henríquez Ureña from listing and discussing many other works by Dominican emigrants to Cuba and elsewhere—remember that he specifically allows for literature of emigration. One might point to the fact that the novel was not really known, since it had not been reedited in the nineteenth century. Yet this argument cuts the other way, as well. What was it about Bonó's perfectly conventional novel that has prevented it from being reprinted and prompted scholars to ignore it? The monumental *Antología de la literatura dominicana* of 1944 ("Colección Trujillo") does not mention it. Moya Pons's 1997 bibliography of Dominican literature does not include it. Only the Dominican writer and sociologist José Alcántara Almánzar lists *El montero* in his recent *Dos Siglos de literatura dominicana* and indeed calls it the first significant novel in the Dominican Republic.[18]

The second puzzle concerns Henríquez Ureña's account of indigenismo. He is adamant that it did not exist before the War of Restoration, even though he has to acknowledge that there were in fact several earlier texts that dealt with indigenous themes: there are poems by Javier Angulo Guridi (e.g., "Maguana" in 1840, or "La cuita" in 1842); Javier Angulo Guridi's *La fantasma de Higüey* has an Indian protagonist and clearly shares crucial features with later indigenist texts; and one of the first longer narrative texts, written by Javier Angulo Guridi's brother Alejandro and published in 1843, is entitled *Los amores de los indios.* We might also point out that already in the eighteenth century, Sánchez Valverde had chosen the term "indo-hispano" to describe the ethnicity of those born in Santo Domingo in opposition to those who descended partially or entirely from Africans;[19] Núñez de Cáceres's decision to rename the Spanish colony "Spanish Haiti" in 1822 also indicates a much earlier interest in former indigenous cultures. Finally, we may wonder whether Henríquez Ureña does not misinterpret statistical evidence when he identifies the increase in indigenist production after 1864 with the beginning of a truly Dominican literature. Would it not be more plausible to see the increase in indigenist writing as a result merely of a greater publishing volume in general?[20]

But Henríquez Ureña is unyielding on the issue, going so far as to cut off a path of further inquiry in the future: "it would be useless to search for a memory or even an allusion to the indigenous traditions in Hispaniola prior to the annexation." This is clearly false. But even if it were not: Given the scant records and the extreme difficulties in locating early Dominican texts, given also Henríquez Ureña's staunch commitment to careful historical documentation, it seems rather surprising that he would instruct future researchers to eschew further archival work.[21] Why does it matter so much to him?

There is a second claim regarding indigenismo which provides the key to the puzzle. Henríquez Ureña insists that indigenismo's political orientation was unequivocally anti-Spanish. I have argued earlier that, on the contrary, indigenism and Hispanism need to be read as complementary ideologies, and that indigenism in fact produced narratives that offered Spain a crucial position in the collective psyche: that of the Other whose accreditation we seek. But even if one remained skeptical about the psychoanalytic reading I proposed earlier, Henríquez Ureña's ideological assessment of indigenism is highly dubious. After all, Manuel Galván, the author of the quintessential indigenista novel, was an avid proponent of annexation of the Dominican Republic by Spain and wrote his *Enriquillo* in exile, after the expulsion of the Spanish. What is gained by linking indigenismo to the War of Restoration and thus to anti-Spanish sentiment?

I believe that the two blind spots in Henríquez Ureña's account are not unrelated. One of the reasons why Bonó's *El montero* has received little attention may be Bonó's unusual politics. When he wrote the novel, he was an avid proponent of Millian liberalism, and later in his life he adopted positions quite close to those of the French utopian socialists. Neither position was within the Dominican mainstream. It is not surprising that as a result *El montero* is much closer to novels such as *Facundo, Cecilia Valdés,* or *María* than to Dominican literary practices.[22] In most places where *costumbrismo* thrived, from France and Spain to Cuba and Peru, the ideology was fairly clear: to capture the quaint as the about-to-disappear essence of the national or local being. As in the better-known Spanish American tradition, a popular character—here the *montero*—is desired as the bedrock of national character and, at the same time, symbolizes all that which needs to be overcome. The affective ambivalence is ultimately resolved through a straightforward time structure: something in the past is being desired and through that very desire incorporated and assimilated into a new future being. This, we might say, fits the narrative of modernization perfectly.

But costumbrismo never took root in the Dominican Republic, and this is not because it was unknown. Salomé Ureña's father, Nicolás Ureña de Mendoza, composed, under the influence of the Cuban writer Domingo Del Monte, some romances and décimas about the guajiro while in exile in Saint Thomas, and Rodríguez Demorizi credits him for introducing the style in the Dominican

Republic. However, not even Nicolás Ureña's daughter took up the new style and instead composed neoclassical patriotic verses and indigenist poems. Costumbrismo is, it seems, the writing style of the urban writer who seeks solace and regeneration in the countryside. Like all celebrations of the rural and quaint, it works best when we are more or less comfortable with the past and confident about the future. But this was not the case in the Dominican Republic in the second half of the nineteenth century. If national history is marked by repetitions; if it is experienced time and again through the reactualization of some past trauma; if, finally, progress itself needs to be reconfigured before it can be affirmed as the future of the nation, one might fear that past differences can suddenly become future differences—instead of being the bedrock of identity, it becomes the threat of division. If we assume that Dominican elite writers, like writers all over Latin America, felt the desire and responsibility to promote progress and a sense of national identity, the most difficult problem they had to face was how to produce narratives that would erase the memory of a Haitian modernization in Hispaniola and allow for a future in which the experiences of modernization and national identity were no longer at odds. Modernity in the Dominican Republic had to invent a genealogy for itself that would not lead back to the revolutionary age and to projects of racial equality and emancipation. Instead of costumbrismo, we thus find a literature devoted to producing a future out of reinvented past.

Bonó did not underwrite this ideological project. Although his later political and economic writings are not entirely free of anti-Haitian rhetoric, they show that he recognized Haiti's role as a reformer in Dominican history. Far from painting the Haitian occupation of twenty years as a descent into barbarism and bestiality, he claims that they introduced Dominicans to liberty and represented a step forward as far as human rights were concerned.[23] Instead of encouraging the fantasies of a millennial antagonism between Dominicans and Haitians, he argues that Boyer indeed had the chance to unify the two peoples on the island but failed to adopt the appropriate measures. This does not mean that he thought Haiti held the solution for Dominican social and political problems. Casting Haiti's founding ideology as an (excusable) "racial exclusivism," Bonó proposes as an alternative for the Dominican Republic "cosmopolitanism," by which he means racial mixture and a cultural reorientation toward Europe. As we will see later, this amounts to an undoing of what was, from an ideological point of view, one of the most revolutionary acts of the Haitian leaders: the adoption of a universalist rhetoric in which the formerly subordinate element—black—comes to be used nominalistically as the universal. While his advocacy of a racial and cultural *mulatismo* (against Haitian politics of blackness) is far less troubling than the anti-Haitian patriotic literature or the Hispanist and indigenist fantasies, it clearly bears the imprint of a Eurocentric vision of the future in which the idea of progress and modernity in the Dominican Republic is severed from its Haitian roots and placed back under European tutelage.

This brings us to the question of why Henríquez Ureña is so adamant that indigenismo only comes into being with the War of Restoration. Like the issue of costumbrismo, this refers us back to the experience of history in the Dominican Republic. By setting the patriotic (i.e., explicitly anti-Haitian) literature of the 1840s and 1850s apart from indigenismo, Henríquez Ureña produces a straightforward linearity (but pays for it by having the facts contradict his claim). One style is superseded by the next. As against the compulsive repetitions, the returns of ghosts and replays of traumatic scenes that so much characterize Dominican literature on the thematic level, Henríquez Ureña's literary history is a succession of literary practices that reflect radically different political moments and increasing autonomy. This is not only more in keeping with the desires and expectations of an ideology of progress; it is also more desirable from the perspective of a more liberal political outlook, as indigenismo signifies a definitive overcoming of rabid anti-Haitianism. It reproduces a nationalist picture in which "the nation" (whose existence is always presupposed) precedes all other political and social configurations: the history of Dominican literature is being told as the history of a series of struggles against foreign antagonists—first Spain, then Haiti, then Spain again. The nation becomes the subject of history rather than that which comes into being through these struggles. Finally, Henríquez Ureña's account demotes the importance of Haiti for the history of the Dominican Republic—Dominican nationalism does not need to be ethnically grounded. As he reconstitutes Dominican literature on extraterritorial grounds, he avoids producing yet another exculpatory defense of racial violence and nationalist phobias against Haitians. Yet he also erases the last traces of a memory that Haiti was, within the Dominican imaginary, the Jacobin reformer and modernizer.

Ultimately, it seems clear that projections of linearity cannot grasp the peculiar forms of cultural production in the Dominican Republic. Haiti obviously cannot be extricated from Dominican history without producing some bizarre blind spots. A literary anecdote can serve as a final illustration of the effects of such manipulations. In 1877 José Joaquín Pérez brought out his *Fantasías indígenas*, the first book of poems to be published in the Dominican Republic. The first poem is entitled "Igi aya bongbe (Primero muerto que esclavo)" (Better dead than a slave) and tells the story of Bohechío, an indigenous chieftain who hears about the arrival of a strange people on his shores and declares war, vowing that he would rather die than become a slave. In a note to the title, Pérez explains that "igi aya bongbe" is the only surviving fragment of a war song of an indigenous tribe. However, already in 1922, the Dominican critic Tejera pointed out that "igi aya bongbe" is most likely derived from an African language, and then traces the slogan back to the Haitian Revolution—after all, most early constitutions of Haiti are headed by the slogan "Liberté ou mort." Against its own intentions, the poem reinscribes what its author, and later critics like Henríquez Ureña, take such pains to deny. It is a return of the repressed in which the attempt to produce Dominican history as indigenous history unwittingly leads to a remembrance of the struggle against racial slavery that led to the creation of Haiti. Far from being a mere coincidence, Pérez's involuntary memorialization of the modern struggles against racial slavery is testimony to the impossibility of repressing the Haitian past and the impossibility of purging Dominican culture from its African ancestry.

# PART III

## Saint Domingue/Haiti

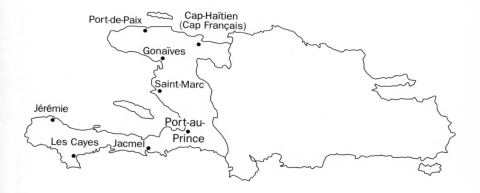

# 9

# Literature and the Theater of Revolution

In 1801 Toussaint Louverture promulgated a constitution that banned slavery, bestowed legislative authority on the Assembly in Saint Domingue, and professed eternal allegiance to the French Empire. France reacted by sending troops. Two years later, when the genocidal war under the military leadership of Napoleon's son-in-law Leclerc had finally collapsed, the generals of Saint Domingue formally declared independence from France on January 1, 1804. The only successful slave revolution in world history had come to a conclusion. Having rejected a mild-mannered first draft for the declaration of independence, Dessalines charged his secretary Boisrond Tonnerre, a French-educated mulatto, to write a new version, that would be in keeping with a pronouncement Boisrond Tonnerre himself had made on the eve of independence. His statement is notorious: "To prepare the independence act, we need the skin of a white man for parchment, his skull for a desk, his blood for ink, and a bayonet for a pen. The French name still 'grieves' [*lugubre*] our lands."[1] In a declaration which self-consciously appropriates the cannibalistic imagery the metropolis had created for describing non-European "savages," Boisrond Tonnerre depicts a rupture much more radical than a mere declaration of independence. It is a break that involves a whole set of new equivalences between (white) body parts and raw materials, writing and warfare, spirit and body, slave and master. The independence envisioned here is not merely an issue of sovereignty, even less of nationhood. If slavery deprived people of color of their personhood and humanity, the declaration of Haitian independence reduces the slaveholders to an assemblage of exploitable body parts: bones, blood, skin. However, this act of revenge is not unmediated. Under the colonial slaveholding regime, writing was a domain largely prohibited to the slave. The declaration of independence is thus also an act of wresting away writing from the former master. It is in this act of writing one's own name—Haiti—that the former master is reduced to a bag of body parts, not in the act of direct revenge. Haiti's name is thus both: written with the blood of the master and a completely new script, a different form of writing. No wonder, then, that the sentence following the cannibalistic imagery of the first one employs the neologism *lugubrer* (which I tried to render by giving "to grieve" an active sense) to capture the effect of the French on Haitian territory. If writing arrived as a colonial skill, it needs to be done with the colonialists' blood. If the French language arrived with slavery, it needs to be forced to say what it would not: "The French name still 'grieves' our lands."

By 1810, the newly founded state, second in the Americas only to the United States, had dissolved. There were four separate political entities on the island of Hispaniola now: in the South, a republic under the leadership of Toussaint Louverture's former rival, the mulatto Rigaud, who had recently returned from exile in France; in the West, a republic with the mulatto Pétion at its head; in the North, a black state—after 1811 a monarchy—with Henri Christophe at its head; and in the East, the Spanish colony Santo Domingo, which was incorporated into the Haitian state in 1822.

It would appear that the struggle against slavery and the foundation of a state proved to be two different matters. Rigaud's republic was short-lived and did not survive his death in 1812, but the northern kingdom continued to exist until 1820, when Christophe, weakened by his failing health and faced with increasing popular resistance, committed suicide, and the territory was incorporated in the republic, now under the leadership of Pétion's confidant and successor Boyer. Two years later, Boyer invades Spanish Santo Domingo and unifies the island which then becomes, in a political rhetoric clearly borrowed from France, "one and indivisible." In 1825, after lengthy negotiations, France finally recognizes Haitian independence in exchange for reparations for the loss of French property during the revolution, thus signaling the return of Haiti—or, perhaps more accurately, the return of Haitian elites—into the orbit of French culture. It is not until 1844 that Spanish Santo Domingo, taking advantage of the Haitian agitation against Boyer, declares independence from Haiti and the two nations enter into a period of uneasy neighborliness.

Boyer is eventually deposed, and in the decades that follow, Haiti suffers from increased instability and agitation, which leads to a reassertion of black political power against the mulatto faction that had dominated since Henri Christophe's demise, culminating in Soulouque's empire (1849–1859). The social divisions become increasingly bitter in these years, but also more intractable as they appear to reproduce distinctions of color despite the fact that the political discourse rarely uses racialized language, and racial discrimination remains explicitly outlawed by the constitution. Boyer had staffed his government almost exclusively from the ranks of mulattoes and thereby invited the resentment of the black elite, who accused him of neglecting the interests of the poor (mostly, but not exclusively) black peasants. To avoid a repetition of the events that led to the removal of Boyer from power, the descendants of the old *affranchis* begin to choose black figureheads who, the assumption was, could easily be controlled by the more educated mulatto elite (the so-called *doublure* system). As the experience under Soulouque showed, however, this was by no means guaranteed: although illiterate and ostensibly unsuitable for the job as president of the republic, Soulouque proved to be quite the opposite of a pliable puppet. He quickly seized the state, reestablished the empire with himself at the head as Faustin I, purged the country of many of the "kingmakers," and held onto power for twelve years. Unsurprisingly, the next three presidents were French-educated mulattoes again.

The social and racial split of the country eventually led to the foundation of the Liberal Party, largely representing mulatto interests, and the National Party, ostensibly the representative of the black population. These conflicts only became worse in the early twentieth century: after a quick succession of governments and increased social agitation, the United States seized the opportunity and invaded Haiti in 1915, installing a puppet regime largely drawn from the ranks of the mulattoes. The occupation forces did not withdraw until 1934. It was in the resistance against the U.S. occupiers in what is sometimes referred to as "the Second War of Independence" that the political and cultural discourse of indigenism emerged. Price-Mars's trenchant critique of Haitian elites and their "Bovarysme collectif,"[2] his call for recognition for the African base of Haitian national culture, and his voluminous studies of Haitian peasant culture changed political discourse forever and provided the foundations for new, socially and culturally engaged forms of cultural production.

The events of the late nineteenth century and the early twentieth show the catastrophic depth and intractability of antagonisms produced by French colonialism and slavery. If colonial society was the result of modern hubris—the criminal dream of an off-limits zone, on the other side of the ocean, devoted only to the maximization of economic output, without any human or moral constraints—

it quickly turned into a nightmare for France; and even after the French withdrawal, the antagonisms kept haunting Haitian society. Whichever way we might theorize the social divisions in nineteenth-century Haiti, whichever way we might weigh racial divisions vis-à-vis class divisions and contingently formed alliances—and there is little consensus among social scientists about this—it is clear that the fault lines of the conflicts that continued to shake Haiti throughout the nineteenth century and the early twentieth originated in the colonial regime and the caste system introduced to shore up the slaveholding regime.

## Writing after the Revolution

The most urgent task for the postrevolutionary government was the reconstruction of the devastated country. Resources were scarce, and fostering the production of a national literature would have seemed a luxury of little social and political benefit. Only a small elite was literate and spoke French, and those who spoke only the national language, Creole, remained excluded from writing altogether.[3] Around 1900 bilingual poetry began to appear, most notably Oswald Durand's "Choucoune," one of the first Haitian works to achieve international recognition. While earlier novels like Jacques Romain's *Gouverneurs de la rosée* (1944) integrate structures and characters from Haitian folktales, the first novel in Haitian Creole did not appear until 1975, when Franck Étienne published *Dézafi*, closely followed by Michel-Rolph Trouillot's history of Haiti titled *Ti difé boulé sou istoua Ayiti* (1977).

But of course, writing in Creole is not an achievement of the 1970s, nor is it necessarily linked to a progressive political agenda. The first poetic text written in Creole dates back to 1750, when Duvivier de la Mahautière, a councillor at the court in Port-au-Prince and thus a member of the class of slaveholders, quoted the popular song "Lizet kité laplenn." The Jacobin commissioner Sonthonax wrote in Creole when he decided to proclaim slavery abolished in the North. And Napoleon had his letter to Toussaint written in Creole: like French, Creole too was first used in writing by slaveholders and whites.[4]

Apart from these exceptional moments when colonialists and slaveholders used the local language to communicate with their subjects, however, writing was done in French. Literacy remained elusive in Haiti except for the urban elites. To be sure, Haiti was not the only new state in which literature was an elite endeavor. The same is clearly true for Spanish America. But when access to the republic of letters is obstructed not just through writing but through the language employed (and with that, the cultural practices that live in language), then the role of literature is necessarily limited. Moreover, literacy rates did not change much in the course of the nineteenth century. The retrospective appropriation and canonization of earlier literary texts by a growing reading public that Doris Sommer describes for Spanish America, where the foundational novels eventually become the medium for fantasies of how the fractured populations after the wars of independence actually come to be interpellated by denominations such as "Peruvians" or "Argentineans," was thus not possible, either.[5]

In one of the best-documented histories of Haitian literature, Hénock Trouillot, a trenchant critic of mulatto hegemony,[6] goes so far as to argue that "Haitian literature is, with some rare and noble exceptions, a literature developed in favor of a small, rapacious, anti-progressive, anti-popular elite." To this he opposes the writings of intellectuals such as Julien Raymond, Boisrond Tonnerre, Vastey, Prévost, Chanlatte, Madiou, Ardouin, Saint-Rémy, Anténor Firmin, Louis-Joseph Janvier, and Jean Price-Mars and his school—intellectuals who for the most part did not produce works of fiction but devoted themselves to writing declarations of state, constitutions, history, and anthropology. Taking their writings (rather than the narrative fictions produced by the "anti-progressive elite") as his basis, Trouillot claims that "our literary history is characterized in effect by its defense of the African race or of African origins."[7] Trouillot's somewhat Manichaean picture cannot be understood without taking into account the long-standing ideological battles between a black and a mulatto elite. A survey of the works rejected by Trouillot on the grounds that they merely serve the interests of the elites shows that many of those also pronounce themselves to be a defense of the "African race." Indeed, if there was any kind of consensus among the increasingly hostile factions in Haitian political culture in the nineteenth century, it was precisely this—that Haiti was the defender of "the African race." That this meant different things for different people is another matter.

Before the assassination of Dessalines in 1806, writers mostly devoted themselves to celebrating the feats of independence and of the revolutionary leaders. They played, for the most part, the role of journalists who publicize the events of the recent past and popularize the political battles that followed after independence.[8] In 1818, the first newspapers appear, and in these newspapers, patriotic poems and later longer narrative texts, like Ignace Nau's novellas, the first of which was titled "Un épisode de la révolution" (An episode of the revolution). The first Haitian novel, *Stella*, appears in 1859, in Paris. A posthumous work by a young writer who had died of consumption, *Stella* tells the vagaries of the revolts and the war of independence through the story of a young female slave and her children and was clearly intended to be read as an allegory of the union between blacks and mulattoes.[9] Until 1901 there are few other novels: there is Demesvar Delorme's *Francesca* (1872), which takes place in fifteenth-century Italy, and his *Le damné* (1877), set in Switzerland. There is Louis-Joseph Janvier's *Une chercheuse* (1884), which is set in France and Egypt and tells the story of exotic white people, and finally Amédée Brun's *Deux amours* (1895), which returns to Saint Domingue and the war of independence.[10]

Poetry, first of neoclassical and later romantic inspiration, did not fare much better than the genre of the novel. "Marivaudages," by Damoclès Vieux, for instance, alludes to the popular eighteenth-century playwright Marivaux and shows the poet as he imagines himself in the clothes of the Ancien Regime, as a marquis at the court at Versailles. Unsurprisingly, it was this poem that the Haitian writer Jacques Stephen Alexis used to illustrate his notion of "parrot poetry" practiced before 1915. As Maximilien Laroche points out, the underlying problem remains that the writers continue to be isolated and enclosed within themselves, with no chance of being read or understood by the vast majority of their compatriots. As a result, the affect that dominates in these poems is one of lugubrious depression, as manifested in Etzer Vilaire's (1872–1951) well-known poem "Les dix hommes noirs" (The ten black men), which evokes a sort of apocalypse in the course of which ten young men, none older than thirty, all dressed in black, meet in a manor house to tell each other their life stories. After the end of this, nine decide to kill themselves, and the tenth goes mad.[11]

## Postrevolutionary Theater

While most Haitian critics agree about the relative unimportance of poetry and novels in the nineteenth century, some disagreement arises when it comes to theater. While Laroche extends his assessment of Haitian literary production prior to 1915 to theatrical productions, arguing that Haitian theater did not mobilize more than a very small part of the population until 1950 and that it is characterized by an acute poverty of topics, others paint a different picture.

Cornevin claims that although the country was ravaged and the theaters themselves had been destroyed during revolution, theatrical life never subsided, and plays were performed in private houses or in large halls. Less is known about Pétion's republic and its capital Port-au-Prince, but Henri Christophe appears to have been an active sponsor of theatrical events in the North. Tragedies such as Voltaire's *La vie de César* were performed, often by actors who had received a French education. Brutus, for instance, was played by the well-known mulatto actor Lys, who had gone into exile with Rigaud.[12] In Les Cayes, a comedy in three acts by the title of *L'Haitien expatrié* was performed in 1804. According to Fouchard, this was the first theatrical piece published in Haiti. In Port-au-Prince there were theatrical performances almost every night, apparently mostly melodramas that celebrated the events of the independence. Whereas Laroche insists that the split between Creole and French made it impossible for theatrical performances to reach an audience beyond the small circle of those who received an education anyway, Hénock Trouillot claims that theater was not just a spectacle: at a time when the only system of public education consisted of a few Lancasterian schools of mutual education, theatrical performances served a clear pedagogical and ideological purpose.[13] This presupposes that people were able to understand the plays performed at the time, but Trouillot does not say how he imagines this to have worked. Perhaps the plays were written in French but performed in Creole? Or performed in a modified version of French more easily understandable to Creole speakers? Or supplemented by mime and musical acts that made the spoken words less central?

Like most forms of cultural production, postrevolutionary theater clearly had roots in colonial culture. By 1765, Cap Français, Les Cayes, Petit Goave, Jacmel, and Jérémie all had buildings reserved for theatrical performances, and though mulattoes, and later blacks too, were usually only admitted to the back of the theaters and seated separately, they were not excluded from the audience. In *Le théâtre à Saint-Domingue* Jean Fouchard reconstructs the story of Lise and Minette, two young mulatto women who became the stars of dramatic culture in the last years of the colony and most likely perished in the violence of the revolution.[14] Although his *Artistes et repertoire des scènes de Saint-Domingue* names only two or three mulatto actors, Fouchard points out that there are still boxes of uncataloged archival materials that could produce a very different picture and are likely to confirm what travelers and colonists said about the racially mixed theatrical culture in Saint Domingue.[15] Although generally dismissive about the theater in the colony, Moreau de Saint-Méry, for instance, commented with admiration on a four-hundred-seat theater that had been opened in 1786 by a mulatto woman and theater aficionado in Léogâne, who hired as the director the mulatto Labbé, a sergeant in the militia. For unknown reasons, Labbé puts it up for sale in 1788.[16] The reports of other travelers and colonists confirm that people of color and blacks played a fairly active role in colonial theatrical life and that acting was not the preserve of whites, either. The French lawyer Alfred de Laujon gives the following description of a performance:

> The actors made me laugh very heartily. There was a mistress of high-yellow [jaune] complexion, the lover was white, and some blacks played the roles of courtiers. . . . Particularly when the choir appeared I could barely contain myself. I saw in the ensemble a mixture of colors of so many different nuances that the eye got lost. Along with that I saw several voices that took me by surprise and I did not think that the piece was badly represented.[17]

Theater appears to have been one arena where blacks, whites, and mulattoes mixed with relative ease and where the laws governing theatrical performances in France were relaxed long before the "liberation of theaters" in the metropolis. Set pieces like "Creole dances" or "Negro dances" were often added to embellish the action, prompting Moreau de Saint-Méry to complain that "in provincial cities, tragedy and comedy are confounded." In Le Cap, he continues, they even share "a common temple and common disciples, and it is not unusual to see Melpomene take on the tone of a comic muse." Far from putting off audiences, these confusions appear to have been rather what drew them into the theater: "What is most singular is the eagerness, I nearly said the furor, of Creoles to see tragedies, whose grotesque character repels persons of taste."[18]

Peter Brooks has tied the decline of the traditional genres of *comédie* and *tragédie* to the "liquidation of the traditional Sacred and its representative institutions" and the "dissolution of an organic and hierarchically cohesive society," a dissolution that culminates in the French Revolution. In response to "a world where the traditional imperatives of truth and ethics have been violently thrown into question," the new genre of melodrama emerges as a mode for recovering an essential moral code in the "post-sacred world," a violently emotional drama that aspired to reveal the basic ethical and psychic truth.[19]

Read in light of Brooks's claims, the descriptions Moreau de Saint-

Méry and others have given of the irreverent, racially and stylistically mixed nature of theater in Saint Domingue may indicate more than just a slight amateurishness on the part of the performers. We may wonder, for example, whether the specific social formations that came into being during the colonial period may not have had something to do with the character of theater in Saint Domingue. If French society before the Revolution of 1789 could be considered as lacking organicity and coherence, what would one have to say about a society consisting of 85 percent slaves, half of whom had been born in Africa? A society constantly under the threat of slave uprisings, divided by rigid caste lines, ruled from a metropolitan center on the other side of the Atlantic, deprived even of the buffer of a strong local Creole class that would mediate between the interests of the colonial administration and local needs and aspirations? Would it not be rather surprising if theatrical practices in Saint Domingue adhered to standards that reflected societal and religious hierarchies of premodern times? Would it not be surprising, too, if performers developed a good grasp of "the Sacred" of social and religious hierarchies?

The social and economic order of Saint Domingue was barely 150 years old when the revolution that led to the foundation of Haiti erupted. If I am right to think that the economic and demographic structure should be seen as perhaps the first modern attempt at creating a society ruled strictly by instrumental reason, with no attempt made to justify it through "age-old tradition" or "the way we have always been," or by the missionary zeal that characterized Spanish colonization, at least on the ideological level, then this must have had an impact on incipient forms of cultural production. Institutional factors would have contributed to this. In France, the regulations of theaters according to genres and social standing presumably survived to the end of the eighteenth century because of the longevity of institutions such as the Comédie Française—institutions that serve as material embodiments of power and societal relays for its diffusion. In the absence of those venerable buildings that manifested traditional hierarchies—in the absence too of subsidiary educational structures that would produce individuals with stakes in these institutions—these regulations simply crumbled and left performers free to respond to social circumstance and the demands of the Creole audience. It is precisely because of the intrinsically modern character of the Caribbean slave societies that C. L. R. James and Sidney Mintz write about that submission to traditional rules would have seemed out of place.

As far as we can tell from the historical record, a bastardized, transculturated type of performance developed in which the original genres of comedy and tragedy mixed so as to "repel the person of taste"; not an organic sublation or transfiguration of the original distinction but a mixture of styles reminiscent of Bakhtin's account of carnival, where, for a brief moment, the peasant speaks the language of the king, and the sacred and sublime turn into burlesque. Or in Moreau de Saint-Méry's words, Melpomene speaks in the voice of the comic muse. Like the mulatto poet Plácido in Cuba, performers in Saint Domingue too appear to have taken up the classical erudite repertoire and "spoken it in their own voice." As in the case of Plácido, their renditions were received with popular acclaim, but scorn from those who took pride in their knowledge of European standards of taste.

A theatrical genre of particular interest for my purposes is that of the pantomime, a popular predecessor of the melodrama. If textual records are difficult to find for the whole colonial and postrevolutionary period, accounts of this extremely popular genre are even more rare. Yet we do have a few records regarding one play in particular, which if read carefully can be quite illuminating as to the cultural and political process at the time.

In 1787 a play entitled *L'Héroïne Américaine* by Louis-François Ribié was performed twice. Ribié was a French *variété* actor who later assumed the dramatically more effective first name of César, partook in the storming of the Bastille (Fouchard calls him "one of the heroes of the Bastille"), and in the late 1790s became the successor of Nicolet and one of the leading theater impresarios in Paris. It is unclear whether Ribié drew on local actors and actresses or brought the whole ensemble, the Troupe des Comédiens de Paris, with him from France. The only information we have about the play comes from a notice written by the playwright himself in defense of his piece against the accusation that *The American Heroine* was not a new play but simply a reissued version of a play by the title of *American Hero,* a pantomime that his troop had already performed three times in Saint Domingue.[20] Against this denunciation, Ribié claims that *The American Heroine* was "absolutely new" and in fact based on Abbé Raynal's *Histoire philosophique et politique des établissemens et du commerce des Européens dans les deux Indes:* it "followed as closely as possible this historical subject" and "made changes only when necessary to the theatrical action."[21] Dayan rightly points out that this notice does not explain whether the play dealt with Raynal's attack on slavery or with his account of the discovery of the New World and the destruction the Spanish and Portuguese brought to indigenous cultures. While that is certainly true, we can neverthe-less make some inferences on the basis of the little data we do have.

First, we should not forget that the genocide of the Native Ameri-cans and the enslavement of Africans were, almost from the time of Las Casas, considered as closely related problems, and that very early the insurgent slaves in Saint Domingue identified with the largely extinct indigenous population—hence the name of Haiti. It is thus unlikely that the play based on Abbé Raynal's work would have been perceived as entirely separate from the issues raised by slavery, even if the topic was the discovery rather than slavery.

Second, there is the explosive constellation of playwright and source. Ribié was a French boulevard actor and libertine (thus asso-ciated with the popular theaters in Paris, which became one of the main stages of political agitation during the Revolution) who only two years after putting together the play in Saint Domingue took part in the events of 1789. While he appears to have stayed clear of the highly politicized theater during the early 1790s, his biography shows that he certainly had a taste for provocation and did not mind occasional run-ins with the police. Add to this the source he is claim-ing for his new play: a text written by France's leading abolitionist in the prerevolutionary period, a work that went through fifty-five edi-tions in five languages between 1770 and 1820 and was well known in Saint Domingue.[22] In one of the more memorable, if probably apocryphal, scenes in C. L. R. James's *Black Jacobins*, we see Tous-saint Louverture read in Abbé Raynal's work of an "impending storm" and ponder over the ominous pronouncement that "the negroes only want a chief, sufficiently courageous to lead them to vengeance and slaughter. Where is this great man to be found . . . ? Where is this new Spartacus . . . ?"[23] It is highly unlikely that these words were put onstage, but they do give a sense of the potentially explosive materials Ribié could have alluded to. Even though it is not clear whether Louverture actually read Raynal's work, it was widely known in the colony, and it is thus doubtful that Ribié could have avoided these associations even if he had chosen the most innocent parts of Abbé Raynal's *Histoire*.[24]

The third point concerns the genre of pantomime. Before the lifting of the regulations of French theaters in 1791, official stages like the Comédie Française had what amounted to a monopoly of the word. Minor theaters were only allowed to put on acrobatic acts, vaudeville shows, and, very importantly, pantomimes. As the term suggests, pantomimes were originally performed without words, relying instead on highly theatrical use of nonverbal devices and clues. There was, for instance, the tableau: in a moment of crisis, the actor would freeze in the middle of a bodily movement or a gesture, in a quasi-sculptural display of heightened emotion and ecstasy. Other devices included musical accompaniment: every gesture and sentiment was translated into a musical phrase which bestowed meaning and continuity to the action as it developed. In the late eighteenth century, then, a hybrid genre called *pantomime dialoguée* (pantomime with dialogue) came into being: like its predecessor, the scripted pantomime excelled through rich decorations, a great number of tableaux, and the quick succession of highly dramatic events. The difference was that the musical phrases were now translated into words.[25]

Ribié does not say that his *Héroïne Américaine* is a pantomime, but surely if *The American Hero* and *The American Heroine* had belonged to completely different genres, confusions about the differences between the two plays would not have arisen, or alternatively Ribié might have pointed out that the plays could not be identical by virtue of their belonging to different genres. It is also somewhat implausible that a "higher" genre would have been called a "travesty" if the original was the lowly genre of pantomime. But even assuming that *L'Héroïne Américaine* was or resembled a pantomime, we still do not know whether it was a pure pantomime or a pantomime dialoguée, and, if the latter, whether it used French or some version of Creole. From what we do know—namely, the preference of colonial audiences for hybridity and nonverbal spectacle—however, we can be reasonably sure that these new plays would have helped themselves freely to musical, pantomimic, and choreographic elements. Dialogue, verbal purity, enunciation, and all the elements that made the classical French tradition unwieldy for Creole performers, inaccessible to the Creole-speaking audience, and thus politically ineffective, could be neutralized through a high degree of dramatization, elaborate staging, music, and the like.

These issues concerning genre become particularly important when we take into account that one of the very few other new plays that were performed in Saint Domingue during the revolution was entitled *Héros Africain*. It was performed in Le Cap in 1797, while Toussaint Louverture was governor-general. This, too, was a pantomime, set not in America but in Congo. As in the case of *Héros Américain* and *L'Héroïne Américaine,* we do not have any descriptions of the play, let alone a script, so we can only speculate about the character of what may have been the "first reinvention of Africa by black rebels."[26] But given the limited number of new plays that were performed in the war-torn colony, and given that we know that there had been *two* plays by Ribié with a similar title and that these plays had been the object of a dispute, they probably lingered in public memory. It is thus unlikely that the similarity in the titles was a mere coincidence. More plausibly, *Héros Africain* self-consciously echoes the French *Héroïne Américaine* and *Héros Américain* and in so doing relocates the play from America to Africa. It is not only a first imaginary "return to Africa" but a gesture that shifts the focus of cultural exchange from the routes used by the colonizers to the routes used by the slave traders—from Europe's America to America's Africa, from the contestation of European colonialism to a prefiguration of an American pan-Africanism. And unlike a correctly performed comedy or tragedy in French, the pantomimes about the American and African heroes would have been accessible to a popular audience.

We could thus read the Ribié plays of 1787 and the anonymous *Héros Africain* of 1797 as cultural emblems of a revolutionary Atlantic in which the distinctions between popular and high-cultural practices break down and the Euro-American genealogy of the "American hero" is answered by an Afro-American genealogy. It is, we might say, an internally contestatory syncretism of American, African, and European themes that cannot be reduced to a politically indifferent heterogeneity. We are dealing here, as the Cuban anthropologist Fernando Ortiz might have said, with early forms of a transculturated Caribbean theater. But it is transculturation not as the effect of an inexorable, subjectless process of cultural and economic development. Rather, it is a self-conscious and politically charged riposte that appropriates a genre while also commenting on its own origins: Afro-Caribbean syncretism not as the bittersweet ground of Caribbean nationhood but as a contestatory cultural formation in the hemispheric struggle for emancipation.

As in the case of other materials that might document this syncretistic culture in which geopolitics and power differentials are inscribed, here too the original texts are lost. Only if we read between the lines, only if we bring into play the politics of genre and language, and the unspoken implications of a mere theme, a mere name, might we be able to get a sense of this hybrid transatlantic radicalism that engaged European revolutionary culture, the cultures of Africa, and those of the New World and in the process created a popular spectacle that became part of the rumor machine that was the Caribbean Sea in those years of upheaval and revolution.

# 10

# "General Liberty, or The Planters in Paris"

One of the few texts that document revolutionary culture in colonial Saint Domingue that did survive, albeit in a single copy in the Bibliothèque Nationale in Paris,[1] is also, as Cornevin indicates, the first known piece of political theater in Saint Domingue. The catalog lists the play as follows: *"La Liberté Générale, ou Les Colons à Paris.* Comédie en un acte et en prose; par le citoyen B\*\*\*. Représentée pour la première fois sur le Théâtre du Cap-Français, le 23 Thermidor, 1'an quatrième de la République, jour anniversaire du 10 Août (Cap-Français: chez P. Roux, imprimeur de la Commission. N.d.)" (General Liberty, or The Planters in Paris. Comedy in one act and in prose; by the citizen B\*\*\*. Performed for the first time in the theater of Le Cap Français, 23 Thermidor, the fourth year of the Republic, anniversary of August 10). Apparently requested by Sonthonax, who was one of the three French commissioners at the time, the play was written by a "citizen B.," whose identity has remained unknown, and was performed in a private home in Cap Français.

At first glance, *La Liberté Générale* is a fairly conventional piece of political theater of the sort that abounded in Paris during the heyday of the Revolution. It certainly does not suggest the operations of colonial transculturation in the way the pantomimes about American and African heroes do. The play's interest lies in the way it reworks the ideological conflicts at the time. If we restore the full political and historical context to *La Liberté Générale,* yet another genealogical story emerges that explains why even some of the more hegemonic metropolitan expressions of the culture of revolutionary antislavery have been lost for us. The intricate ideological battles that are acted out in this play become visible only if we have some understanding of the conflicts surrounding the issues of colonial slavery during the French Revolution, so some digression into the history and historiography of the Revolution will be required here.

*La Liberté Générale* marks one of the few cultural events of modern radicalism in the Caribbean plantation zone for which we have more than just a title or a trial record. Clearly, it represents the more European face of revolutionary universalist politics. Because it *is* the more European face, this play, unlike *Héros Africain* or Aponte's book of paintings, was published and survived in the European archives. But survival is one thing, historical impact another. The play itself has, to my knowledge, never been mentioned, let alone interpreted, except in brief notes on Haitian literary history. Although this does not necessarily mean that it had no influence on early Haitian cultural practices and sensibility (some of the real-life figures represented in the play became important intellectuals after independence), early Haitian theater is largely undocumented.

But the obscurity of *La Liberté Générale* cannot be reduced to its uniqueness or the lack of materials that would allow scholars to assess its significance. Astonishing as it may seem, the events that are represented in the play—the intrigues of colonists and slaveholders in Paris and the passage of the law abolishing slavery on February 4, 1794—have received little attention in the historiography of the French Revolution. If one were to believe standard accounts, neither slavery nor the colonial question had any impact on the events in Europe. Some recent scholarship has argued forcefully that this was not quite so,[2] but the new interpretations of the French Revolution that emanate from the bastions of higher learning in France continue to ignore the issue to this day. Apart from a Eurocentric bias against considering issues of colonialism and slavery relevant to the high history of the metropolis, there are, I will argue, specific political concerns at work here, which led to a silencing of the battles represented in *La Liberté Générale*. We will see, here again, how certain kinds of ideological and political battles have been ignored, denied, or falsely subsumed under the headings of other battles by metropolitan historiography. *La Liberté Générale* is another fragment from a revolutionary Atlantic that was suppressed in the first decades of the nineteenth century and written out of history in the following decades.

The play itself was requested by the French commissioner Sonthonax in 1796 for the celebration of the anniversary of the storming of the Tuileries and the overthrow of the monarchy on August 10, 1792. The events represented, however, do not mention what was to be commemorated, namely, the French Republic. Rather, they are a barely fictionalized account of the events leading up to the passing of the law banning slavery on February 4, 1794.

At the time of the festivities, August 1796, Sonthonax is on his second mission to Saint Domingue. Brissot, the founder of the Amis des Noirs and a close friend of Sonthonax, is dead. Robespierre is dead. The Jacobin Club to which Sonthonax had belonged has been disbanded. The Thermidorian Constitution of 5 fructidor (August 22) has just been approved, and the Rights of Man and Citizen are now called, in an anti-universalist turn, the Rights of Man in Society. The Directory in France did not appear to have any plans to reintroduce slavery in the colonies, but the moderate bourgeoisie had taken control of the revolutionary process, and it was unclear how far to the right they might move. Written and performed in 1796, *La Liberté Générale* is thus a play of the past—a tragicomedy that remembers two of the climactic moments of a revolution that has already come to an end, or, perhaps more correctly, a revolution whose next act might feature the "return of the planters."

The planters certainly felt that the tide might be turning and were actively plotting to reconstitute the old slaveholding regime. It appears that Sonthonax, aware of the developments in France and fearful that France might send troops to Saint Domingue once a peace agreement with England had been negotiated, may have had plans for independence. Only a year after the performance of *La Liberté Générale,* representatives of planter interests in France accused Sonthonax of being "covered with the blood of whites" and demanded that he be put on trial.[3] Fearing that Sonthonax might be used as a pretext for a French invasion, Toussaint, in a startling volte-face, ordered Sonthonax, who had been his close ally and friend, to leave Saint Domingue and return to France, while also sending a letter to the Directory in which he claimed that Sonthonax had planned to massacre the whites and make Saint Domingue independent.[4]

We are thus dealing with a crucial moment when it had become doubtful that the politics of the French Republic and those of radical antislavery were still in agreement, and questions were arising whether Saint Domingue could keep slavery from returning while still under colonial rule. The issue of slavery and the issue of independence had finally shown themselves dangerously linked, although not in the simple way they are sometimes presented. Whereas planters in Paris were arguing for local autonomy under French suzerainty, Toussaint tried to dispel any suspicion of proindependence moves by casting doubt on Sonthonax's motives and goals. Depending on the assessment of the political situation in France, autonomy or independence might have seemed desirable to either the planters or the radical abolitionists (under the condition that the island be purged of remaining former slaveholders).

It seems obvious then that Sonthonax's commissioning of *La Lib-*

*erté Générale* would have fulfilled several purposes. Proposing a close link between the French Republic and abolition would presumably have functioned as a justification of his presence as a representative of the French Republic in Saint Domingue; it would also have functioned as a defense against those who were suggesting that he was promoting the independence of the colony. And finally, it worked simply as a denunciation of his mortal enemies, the representatives of the planters in Paris.

## Paris: 1792/1794/1796

Set in a seedy Paris boardinghouse, *La Liberté Générale* puts on the stage fictional characters drawn from the classical repertoire of French comedy—Madame Revêche, the *bavarde* (gossipy woman), the spoiled aristocrat Madame de Minaudière,[5] an adulteress, and her lover, the ridiculously fat Monsieur L'Incroyable, who cannot pronounce the French *r*. These fictional characters are joined by Larcheveques-Thibaut, Page, Bruley, and Verneuil, who were the real-life representatives of the colonists in Paris and are cast in roles of arch-villains here.[6] In addition to these white personages, there are Théodore, a man of color and neighbor of Madame Revêche, and Télémaque, a black Creole who speaks what Fouchard describes as "planter Creole," both of them fictional.

The story is the process of enlightenment of Madame Revêche. Although a fervent defender of the Republic, she has never heard of the "colons de Saint-Domingue" and firmly believes that the men who have been gathering in her house are honorable patriots. Prompted by the colonists' valet, she hides in a cabinet to find out what the mysterious men negotiate behind closed doors. And what she hears is shocking indeed: through various nefarious schemes and fraudulent petitions, they are intriguing to prevent the abolition law from being approved, all the while also preparing a legislative project for Saint Domingue that would inscribe the continuation of slavery by establishing special laws for the colony. The tragicomic climax of the play occurs when Bruley begins to read from a legislative project that he and his coconspirators plan to present (the play quotes literally from a plan that was proposed to the Comité de Salut Public in 1793 and signed by Page and Bruley):

> Bruley: Disposition première (il lit): *'Traiter avec une égalité parfaite, tous les citoyens, sans distinction de couleur.'* (mouvement de surprise de la part des auditeurs) que ceci, Messieurs, ne vous étonne pas: . . . vous sentez

d'ailleurs qu'il y a bien des manières d'expliquer ce mot, *égalité parfaite,* et les articles suivans vont vous donner le mot d'énigme. (Il continue de lire) *'Entretenir des espions parmi les révoltés; connaitre les blancs qui les dirigent, et mettre indistinctement leurs têtes à prix.'*

L'Incroyable: *Indistinctement!* . . . voilà déjà un mode d'égalité que je t— ouve fort—aisonnable, ma pa—ole d'honneur! (32)

[Bruley: First provision (he reads): *'To treat with perfect equality all citizens, without distinction of color.'* (Motions of surprise in his audience) This, gentlemen, must not astonish you: . . . you will soon find out that there are many ways in which to interpret that word, *perfect equality,* and the following articles will give you the clue. (He continues to read) *'To maintain spies among the rebels; to find out who the whites are that lead them, and to place without distinction a price on their heads.'*

L'Incroyable: *'Without distinction!* . . . There is a kind of equality that I find highly—easonable, my wo—d of hono—!"][7]

After a brief digression in which Thibaut explains that the uprising in Saint Domingue is spreading not because of the courage of the blacks but because of their "violent and brutal instinct," Bruley continues in his reading of the plan:

"Cela n'arrivera plus, . . . j'ai trouvé à tout cela un remède infaillible; écoutez . . . (il lit): *'Corrompre, assessiner, égorger, empoisonner les chefs de la révolte!"* (33)

[That will not happen again, I have found an infallible remedy to all of that; listen . . . (he reads): *To bribe, assassinate, butcher, poison the leaders of the rebellion!*]

After a few more exchanges of ideas for means by which the revolutionary slaves should be exterminated, Bruley concludes:

Ainsi, Messieurs, vous voilà tous d'accord sur la rédaction de l'article: *'Corrompre, assessiner, égorger, empoisonner!*

Madame Minaudière: Je voudrait qu'il fût ajouté à cette phrase, ainsi qu'à l'une des précédentes, tous les chefs *indistinctement.*

L'Incroyable (ricanant): Comment donc, et vous aussi, Madame, d'esp—it d'égalité! C'est cha—mant ma pa—ole, cha—mant! (34)

[So, gentlemen, we are all in agreement about the writing of the article: *To bribe, assassinate, butcher, poison the leaders of the rebellion!*

Madame Minaudière: I would like to add to that phrase, just like to the preceding one, all the leaders *without distinction.*

L'Incroyable (chuckling): How about that, you too, Madame, the spi—it of equality! That's cha—ming, my wo—d, cha—ming!]

At this point, when the notion of equality is being denigrated by being applied to indistinct murder, Madame Revêche, miraculously transfigured from a misogynist stereotype of the "woman who talks too much" into a skillful defender of republican principles, has had enough and steps out of the cabinet to take the men to task. In the following scene, the valet returns from the street, bringing with him the news of the passage of the law abolishing slavery. The final event is the arrival of the leader Verneuil at the boardinghouse in the company of Télémaque: it turns out that a mob had attacked Verneuil and that he in fact owes his life to Télémaque, who then joins the conversation, and, when asked whether he was happy to be finally free, declares:

> Oh! Moi libre déjà depuis bien longtemps: mais moi pas content, parce que frères à nous autres être encore dans l'esclavage . . . aujourd'hui moi bien heureux, et avoir pleuré de joie . . . et puis bonheur aussi bien grand . . . père à nous, celui-là qui premier avait dit à nous autres que nous tous libres, plus être accusé, plus tourmenté par monde méchant, pisque Convention avé fait comme yo, et dit, comme yo, que vlé que nous tous gagné la liberté. (50–51)
>
> [Oh! Me free for a long time: but me not content, because our brothers still slaves . . . today me quite happy and cried for joy . . . and then such great happiness . . . our father, he who first said that we all are free, not accused no more, not tortured no more by an evil world, cause Convention has done like him, and spoken like him who wanted that we all gain freedom.]

In this happy moment, the valet Dubois reveals himself to be an agent of the Republic and tries to arrest the planters, who nevertheless manage to escape, leaving behind the reconciled group of Madame Revêche, Télémaque, and Dubois.

The play thus captures the dramatic events that led to the passage of the abolition law by the French Convention on February 4, 1794. It is full of quotations from the pamphlets and laws that were actually debated at the time in France. In keeping with the overwhelming evidence that issues concerning the slave revolution in Saint Domingue have been treated as unworthy of attention, this session, in which a black, a mulatto, and a white representative addressed the Convention, has remained one of the least studied moments of the revolutionary process in France.[8] It is thus not only because of the specific nature of the arguments presented but also because of the silencing to which they were subjected in the course of the nineteenth century that they deserve special attention here.

Another interesting aspect of the play concerns certain parallels with the arguments presented by the deputy Louis Dufay from Saint Domingue in the National Assembly in Paris on the eve of February 4. The representatives of the planters had tried to prevent the deputies from Saint Domingue from addressing the Convention by having them arrested. Freed after four days in prison, Louis Dufay appears in front of the Convention. Gauthier's reading of Dufay's speech, which can only be summarized here, arrives at the conclusion that Dufay does not in fact plead for the abolition of slavery: slavery is *already* abolished thanks to the insurrection and Sonthonax's decree of August 29, 1793. Rather, she argues, Dufay proposes a "new social contract" between France and the former colony on the basis of the equality of its people, to the effect that republican France would commit itself to assisting in the defense of this new state of liberty against planters and against foreign powers, particularly the English and the Spanish.[9] Gauthier uses this reading to support her claim that until Thermidor there was a revolutionary political culture in France that considered individual liberty and popular sovereignty as continuous, and as overriding any claims of national interest and national sovereignty. Drawing on Balibar's argument that far from constituting an unresolved contradiction, liberty and equality are mutually dependent on each other *(egaliberté)*, and that any sacrifice of equality immediately translates into restrictions on liberty claims, she wants to disrupt the notion that there is some necessity to the transformation of "French liberty" into imperialist warfare. Whatever we might think of the details for her argument,[10] her reading of Dufay's intervention is borne out by the roles of Théodore and Télémaque in *La Liberté Générale,* and particularly by the fact that Télémaque insists on natural rights, the importance of the uprising, and the fact that he was actually free long before the act of the French Convention.

Another example of the presence of French debates in the play is the issue of semantic perversion. Robespierre and Saint Just were known to be extremely concerned about how "purity" is possible if words are constantly twisted by opponents and the same terms can be used by revolutionaries and the counterrevolution. In *La Liberté Générale* Thibaut is presented saying things like

> J'avais soumis cette proposition à votre *philantropie* et à votre *prudence.* Je dis d'abord votre philantropie: et en effet, le bien de l'humanité toute entière n'exige-t-il pas que des hommes qui, les premiers, ont osé porter la main sur le régime *bienfaisant* et *paternel* des Colonies . . . disparaissent au plutôt de la surface de la terre?[11]
> [I submit this proposition to your *philanthropy* and your *prudence.* I say, especially, your philanthropy: and in effect the welfare of all of humanity, does it not require that those men who were the first to lift their hands against the *benevolent* and *paternal* government of the Colonies . . . disappear from the surface of the earth the sooner the better?]

Time and again, the humor of the comedy turns on the colonists' cynical appropriation of revolutionary principles—liberty, dignity, humanity—for their murderous project. Indeed, the turning point of the whole play is the moment when M. L'Incroyable cheers the new meaning of equality as "equal treatment for the blacks and whites who are leaders of the uprising" and thus makes Madame Revêche come out of hiding.

But there is an even more significant inscription in this play, which also turns on one of the crucial political and ideological conflicts at the time. The core of the problem is encapsulated in the simple fact that the play celebrates the French Republic by commemorating the passage of the abolition law. On the face of it, this seems to be a facile assimilation of French republicanism to principles of universal human rights. To pretend that one can celebrate one by celebrating the other would be a serious obfuscation of the fractured political scene. The truth is that France was severely divided on the issue of slavery, and it is not clear how important the issue of slavery was in the midst of the turmoils of the Revolution. The Amis des Noirs played a minor political role, not comparable, for example, to that of Sharp and Wilberforce in England; and the revolutionary masses were concerned with other problems, especially after France had gone to war with Austria and Prussia.[12] Robespierre's attitude toward slavery has been much disputed among political theorists and intellectual historians, and even if it was true that he despised slavery, it is not certain that he was committed enough to abolition to be willing to pay the political and economic price.

But the problem is more complicated than that. The abolition law was passed by the Jacobin Convention, after the purge of the Girondins. However, the champions of abolition had been the Girondins, who had been in government before the overthrow of the monarchy and did not survive the catastrophic war of 1792 to 1793. In fact, the accusations launched against the Girondins by the Jacobins included those of "warmongering" and "royalism." By linking the cause of antislavery to that of republicanism, La Liberté Générale produces a coalition which did not in fact exist. Despite the wealth of actual historical materials used in the play, it is, we might say, counterfactual history, or to put it less strongly, it is a revindication of the Girondin faction as being natural allies of the Republic and an implicit rejection of the Jacobin accusation of "royalism." The crucial figure behind La Liberté Générale may well be Brissot, and the play may have been intended as a postmortem recuperation of Brissot's project. In fact, I am inclined to think that "Citoyen B." is not just a random pseudonym for an author who wanted to remain anonymous but a name chosen as a veiled homage to Brissot, founder of the Amis des Noirs, arch-enemy of Robespierre, good friend of Sonthonax, and beheaded in 1793.

### The Disappearance of Brissot

As a leading figure of the Girondins, Jacques-Pierre Brissot de Warville did not live to see slavery abolished. A flamboyant journalist and one of Robespierre's main adversaries in the Assembly, Brissot was a committed abolitionist,[13] and one of the few who had gone so far as to write in support of the armed rebellion in Saint Domingue. He was also one of those who advocated war as the best strategy against the counterrevolutionary forces who had found refuge in the conservative monarchies that surrounded revolutionary France. The historiography on the Girondin faction (at the time mostly called Brissotin) is surprisingly sketchy, and to this day historians disagree about who even belonged to it. No consensus has been reached whether a particular political and ideological outlook can be identified as particularly "Girondin." Most commonly, they are described as the representatives of the merchant bourgeoisie and the rich harbor cities on the Atlantic coast. Often identified with the agitation that led to France's first, disastrous, revolutionary war, their ranks also included the members of the radical clergy. It is not my purpose to enter into the debate over the specifics of Girondin politics; nor do I intend to mount a defense of the Girondin. Rather, I should like to give an account of the heterogeneous forces that led to the erasure of issues concerning slavery and colonialism from the standard accounts of the French Revolution. It is in this context that Brissot and his faction are of interest.

I have already commented on the fact that Furet and Ozouf's *Critical Dictionary of the French Revolution* does not mention the Haitian Revolution and has no entries for colonialism, slavery, or any of the antislavery activists. When it comes to the Girondins, Ozouf's entry mentions that the members of the inner circle of that faction were all "connected to Brissot through the issue of black emancipation" (353).[14] But when Ozouf later discusses possible elements of a Girondin ideology, neither slavery nor colonialism is even mentioned as a possible point of convergence. Why?

We could argue that antislavery and the Haitian Revolution have become victims of a revisionism that turns on restoring the contingencies of the historical process to what is perceived by some as the overly plotted standard narratives of the French Revolution.[15] As issues prone to produce arguments about principles and rights, neither slavery nor colonialism is promising for a project that tries to delink ideological blocs from actual events. But we could also look at it the other way around: perhaps Ozouf's deflationist view of the Girondins is a (conscious or unconscious) strategy that allows her not to address the issues of slavery and colonialism, or at least not place slavery at the center of one of the crucial conflicts of the French Revolution.

Before considering two recent alternative proposals to this view, it is worth pointing out that from a political perspective decidedly different from that of Ozouf, we come across a similar phenomenon. In his monumental study of antislavery between 1776 and 1848, Blackburn comments on Brissot a number of times, usually linking Brissot's stance on slavery to his "new forward policy which would take France to war in Europe and would reassert metropolitan authority in the Antilles."[16] Never mind that Brissot had written pamphlets like "Réflexions sur l'admission aux États généraux des députés de Saint-Domingue" (Reflections about the admission of deputies from Saint Domingue to the General Estates) where he advocates a strong autonomy for the possessions *outre-mer* and says, among other things: "It is impossible that in the whirlwind that sweeps everything toward liberty, the substantial colonies alone remain attached to bodies that are two thousand leagues away from them, and that they should consent to be governed by those." This proposition raises for Brissot the problem of slavery, since immediate autonomy would have given all the power to the planters.[17] Unsurprisingly, Brissot could not figure out a solution that would have guaranteed both abolition of slavery and autonomy, and he appears to have contradicted himself at various points. Whatever his insights or failings may have been, however, it is somewhat surprising that Blackburn presents Brissot's view on slavery as unequivocally linked to French colonialism, while also diminishing his import for the slavery question as a whole. At one point we even read the following:

> Paradoxically by the time the Convention decreed the abolition of colonial slavery in 1794 the *Amis des Noirs* no longer functioned and most of its members no longer played a role. It is almost as if enlightened abolitionism was as much part of the old order as the *exclusif* and the *acquis de Guinée*. Only once this whole superstructure was in ruins could slave emancipation be adopted in the metropolis.[18]

No mention here of the fact that one of the leading proponents of abolition, Brissot, did not play a role because he had found his end on the guillotine. No mention either of the fact that the Amis des Noirs and their Girondin supporters had been involved in a publicity war with the representatives of the planters, who, out of hatred of Brissot, had thrown their support behind Robespierre (with whom they shared nothing, of course, except hatred of Brissot), and that the demise of the Girondins has to be counted at least in part as a victory for the planters.

For some reason, Brissot appears to be an extremely uncomfortable figure in the story. Whatever Blackburn might have in mind in this somewhat obscure paragraph—the vague "as if" clearly signals an element of speculation and hesitance here—the upshot seems to be that slavery is a premodern phenomenon that vanishes only when feudalism has dissolved. Although this suggestion is quite inconsistent with the overall argument Blackburn pursues in *The Overthrow of Colonial Slavery,* the issue of the Girondins appears to push him to retreat to an economic determinism that is otherwise absent from the book. For the Girondins, antislavery was by and large a strategic matter in the attempt to expand and consolidate the French Empire. In other words, Blackburn locates in the Girondin faction a universalism of liberty that turns into imperialism—an argument we are familiar with from those who, unlike Blackburn, want to discard the whole project of an emancipatory modernity as an imperialism in disguise. Instead of confronting the underlying problem of how to resolve the potential contradictions between a universalist ideal of individual liberty, popular sovereignty, and national sovereignty head-on, Blackburn seems to run away from the problem by giving a one-sided account of the Girondin position in which antislavery becomes a mere posture.

There are thus two intersecting issues here: one concerns the political evaluation of the Girondin position; the other signals the troubling theoretical problem of how to weigh claims of individual liberty and claims of sovereignty.[19] The only two treatments devoted to these issues I have been able to find are two works I have already mentioned, Bénot's *La révolution française et la fin des colonies* and Gauthier's *Triomphe et mort du droit naturel en révolution 1789–1795–1802.* Bénot provides ample material that should force us to reconsider the dismissal of the Girondin faction, and Brissot particularly, as a bunch of conspiratorial warmongers. Interestingly, his reevaluation of the Girondins occurs within a larger project that aims at showing the extent to which colonial politics and slavery shaped the debates during the French Revolution. His book thus ends with a review of the ways in which the insurrection in Saint Domingue was erased from historiographic discourse.

Gauthier's evaluation is almost the exact opposite of Bénot's: while Bénot shows Robespierre as disinclined to intervene in the issue of colonialism and slavery, Gauthier shows him as opposing wars of conquest, standing against Brissot, and grounding his international politics on the notion of fraternity, as a concept that establishes free association as the only ground for action in the international arena. What is most interesting about her study in the present context is that she faces squarely the difficulties French revolutionaries had in weighing claims of individual liberty (antislavery) and claims of local sovereignty. The process she reconstructs is one in which the revolutionary concept of natural rights (1789 to 1793) gives way, in the aftermath of Thermidor, to a notion of rights that is subordinated to the claims of national sovereignty and national interest. The view Bénot attributes to Brissot, Gauthier attributes to Robespierre. It is not my aim here to settle the disagreements between Bénot and Gauthier. What is interesting is that despite their considerable disagreements, both Bénot and Gauthier place the issues of slavery and colonialism squarely in the center of the debates in France. Both insist that in the course of the Revolution, a theory of natural rights is articulated whose aims cannot be reduced to imperialist scheming. And finally, and perhaps most importantly, both show that the theories and practices that developed for a brief moment in the course of that revolution, and in response to the events in the colonies, did not survive the rise of nationalism and the nation-state in the nineteenth century.

Returning now to *La Liberté Générale,* we can see more clearly how this play inserts itself in the debates at the time. Written and performed when the metropolis had taken a turn away from natural rights, the play certainly wanted to remind local people of both the evil machinations of the planters and the progressive acts of the French Republic. Since the Republic had abandoned radical politics by the time the play was performed, the connection Citoyen B. establishes between the Republic and abolition could be read two ways: as an attempt to reassure Paris that Saint Domingue harbored no plans for independence, or as a veiled threat that if the Republic changed its politics concerning slavery, this allegiance might come to an end. After all, the play is remarkably void of republican rhetoric of any other kind, and the constellation suggests that the Republic merits celebration to the precise extent that it abolished slavery. But most importantly, *La Liberté Générale* places in the center of revolutionary history the issue of slavery and the colonial question. The focus on the intrigues of the planters Page and Brulley, who had proclaimed their allegiance to the Republic and had joined Robespierre in his attacks on Brissot, is by no means merely a comic device, or just an act of preventive defense by Sonthonax. By focusing on Page and Bruley on the eve of abolition, and particularly by drawing all its humor from the fake Jacobinism of these men, the play recalls that what the planters did was exploit the conflict between Robespierre and Brissot.

Whatever conclusions we might arrive at regarding Brissot and his faction, something is lost when we allow them to vanish into the background: we lose sight of the possibility that antislavery and the revolution that led to the creation of Haiti might have been a crucial element in the political struggles during the French Revolution. And we lose sight of the fact that some of the central theoretical conflicts about popular and national sovereignty, and competing notions of liberty, came to a head in the debates over Saint Domingue. What emerges here, in truly genealogical fashion, are the multiple and heterogeneous reasons why historiography so rarely contemplates this possibility.

Needless to say, uncovering the centrality of slavery and colonialism in France by no means implies assigning a minor role to the actions of the slaves themselves. On the contrary, it shows to what extent the political actions of the enslaved populations in the colonies had an impact on metropolitan politics and how undesirable that fact was for metropolitan elites and their chroniclers. If the strange, and strangely contingent, "alliance" between revolutionary slaves and French Girondins—many of them belonging to the *haute bourgeoisie* and the radical clergy—has been written out of history, the reason may well be that this alliance does not quite fit the grand narratives that became dominant in the course of the nineteenth century. It sits badly with Jacobin historiography, but it fits even less well within the increasingly nationalistic historical discourse of the nineteenth century. The truncation of an emerging transnational and syncretistic modernity we have observed in the nineteenth-century Caribbean around the phenomenon of Haiti thus has an unexpected counterpart in the silences of the historiography of the metropolis. The irreducible social heterogeneity and transnationalism of the cultures of antislavery were no more convenient in the European metropolis than they were in the plantation zone.

# 11

# Foundational Fictions

POSTREVOLUTIONARY CONSTITUTIONS I

No documents dating back to the early days of independence in Haiti speak more eloquently to the extraordinary nature of the events that had just come to a conclusion than the early constitutions. Slavery had been abolished in the uprisings of the early 1790s, a fact recognized by Sonthonax's proclamation of 1793 and confirmed by the passage of the abolition law by the French Assembly on February 4, 1794.[1] In 1801 Toussaint Louverture had issued a constitution that banned slavery, gave legislative sovereignty to the Assembly of Saint Domingue, and appointed him governor for life but stopped short of declaring independence. Dessalines's constitution of 1805, the first constitution after independence, declares Haiti an empire with Dessalines at its head. After Dessalines's assassination in 1806, a new constitution is issued which adopts a republican form of government. Objecting to the powerful Senate provided for in the 1806 constitution, Henri Christophe secedes and issues his own constitution in 1807, setting up an all-powerful presidency and appointing himself president for life. In 1811 Christophe issues a second constitution that adopts a monarchical state form. In 1816 Pétion publishes a constitution that clarifies and modifies many problems of the 1806 version and becomes the reference point for constitutional change for most of the nineteenth century.

No documents articulate more clearly the revolutionary nature of the new state, the radically syncretistic modernity of its ideological origins, and the extraordinary challenges the new state was facing in a world where slaveholding was the rule and where colonialist designs were just beginning to extend into Africa and Asia. At a time when eighteenth-century racial taxonomies were beginning to mutate into racist biology and scientific racism, the Haitian constitutions take the opposite direction and infuse distinctions of skin color with political meaning. In doing so, they enter into a difficult realm where universalist ideas of the equality of the races and identity-based claims of past injustices and future redemption need to be negotiated.

One might have expected these documents to be well known in contemporary debates about and against race. But nothing could be further from the truth. The only collection of the early constitutions is Louis-Joseph Janvier's 1886 *Les constitutions d'Haïti,* an edition hard to find in most research libraries in the United States.[2] Janvier's commentary, moreover, is strongly partisan and directed against mulatto hegemony. The only complete translation ever to be published,[3] to my knowledge, is that of Luis Mariñas Otero, under the auspices of Manuel Fraga Iribarne, Generalísimo Francisco Franco's minister of information, in the Spain of 1968. Mariñas Otero's commentary begins with a quote from, who else, the Dominican Peña Batlle to the effect that the Haitian Revolution was the "catastrophic" result of a "primeval" societal situation.[4]

The Haitian constitutions are arguably some of the most instructive and fascinating texts written during the early years of independence. The problem is that they did not correspond to the legal and political reality. Elaborating on a point Haitian intellectuals have been making since the nineteenth century, Fédéric Marcelin pokes fun at the contradictions between the legal codes and political practices and characterizes the situation as the "comic clash between dream and reality."[5] The idea, standard among liberal theorists of constitutionalism, that constitutions are binding foundational documents that impose effective constraints on the exercise of power by the state, may not be very compelling at the best of times, and conflicts between the text and reality are not all that surprising. But the problems raised by the Haitian constitutions run even deeper than that. Given that these constitutions were written collectively, in committees that would have included men trained in France and illiterate former slaves, we should expect them to reflect tensions and conflicting desires. Within the constitutional texts themselves, for instance, there are strong tensions between the ringing declarations of individual liberty (equality in front of the law, inviolability of the home, equal access to all occupations, etc.) and an equally strong paternalism that imposes severe restrictions on individuals and gives the state the right to deploy individuals according to economic necessity.

Any attempt at interpretation would need to begin from the puzzles that arise from these multiple tensions. Marcelin's opposition between dream and reality offers a clue here that may get us beyond mere denunciation of the illusory character of these documents. Just as we do not dismiss a dream as a misrepresentation of reality but rather read it for insights about how someone experienced that reality, we should not discard these constitutional texts as irrelevant chimeras of elite ideology, but rather read them as fantasies of statehood or foundational fictions (to appropriate Doris Sommer's coinage) that need to be scrutinized with careful attention to tone and implication. That they are ideological conceits does not mean they were not constitutive of reality. Whether a constitutional ban on any form of discrimination on the basis of skin color was ever enforced, could have been enforced, or was even meant to be enforced does not impinge on the question of what political and social desires are articulated in these texts. Viewed from this perspective, the early Haitian constitutions function more like declarations of independence than legal codes; they are expressions of aspirations and desires that went beyond any given political and social reality. In so doing, they bring into sharp relief conflicts that were customarily brushed aside, denied, or belittled in European post-Enlightenment thought.

## Sovereignty, Race, and the Problem of Universalism

Toussaint Louverture's constitution of 1801 enshrines freedom from slavery but stops short of claiming sovereignty for the people of Saint Domingue. Article 1 states that Saint Domingue "forms part of the French Empire, but is subject to particular laws." How exactly French sovereignty would be exercised, however, remained unclear, since Article 19 explicitly stated that no laws were valid in the territory that had not been approved by the Assembly of Saint Domingue. There were no provisions explaining what France's authority actually amounted to. This ambiguity escaped neither the French government nor other Europeans. The two Englishmen to whom we owe some of the more detailed testimonies of life during and after the revolution, W. W. Harvey and Marcus Rainsford, for instance, dated independence to 1801, and this probably not just because of the rivalry between England and France.

The terms in which Toussaint's constitution connects abolition and (French) sovereignty are in themselves worthy of comment: "Art. 3—There can be no slaves in the territory; servitude is forever abolished. Here, all men are born, live, and die, free and French." Not only are liberty from slavery and continuing French sovereignty provided for in the same article; in a striking parallel construction, "free" and "French" are posited as if inseparably linked attributes of all inhabitants. While "are born" and "live" are important specifications at a time when many abolitionists were advocating halfhearted measures such as various forms of "apprenticeship" (which de facto meant that descendants of slaves would be slaves up to a certain age), the reference to death seems to be largely rhetorical. Linking the notions of being free and French to the life cycle adds an affective element to the legal provision. But it is also possible that the invocation of death was meant to reaffirm that abolition would not in the future lead to demands for independence. Death always refers to some unknown future moment; all possible futures are contained in the carefully crafted climax: "(free and) French."

The continuing debt to the regime instituted by the French expresses itself indirectly in other provisions, as well. The plantation system is put under special protection of the state, Catholicism is declared the state religion, marriage is both civil and religious, and divorce is prohibited. Unlike Dessalines's and Christophe's constitutions of later years, Toussaint's has fairly detailed provisions dealing with the organization of the state apparatus. There are sections devoted to the issues of legislative authority, the organizational structure of the government, the court system, and municipal government, alongside an array of provisions that one might have expected to find in the legislation rather than the constitution. Article 70, for instance, provides that inventors of rural machinery will be compensated by the government—perhaps a reflection of Toussaint having heard about the invention of the plow and having expressed a strong desire to develop something of that sort in Saint Domingue. Overall, it seems that Toussaint Louverture's 1801 constitution is designed to guarantee some continuity with the French colonial past while also developing a language that would make the return of slavery impossible.

On January 1, 1804, Dessalines declared independence. Like the Jacobins in France who expressed their desire to break with the oppression of the past by adopting a new calendar, Haiti too restarts the year count: Toussaint Louverture's colonial constitution of 1801 had been dated "Year IX"; Dessalines's constitution would be dated "1805, Year Two of Independence." Apparently there had been no immediate desire to settle for any particular form of state or government. The Haitian Declaration of Independence simply broke all ties with France and bestowed absolute legislative and executive power on Dessalines, the "protecteur de la liberté." The generals who signed the proclamation swore "blind obedience" to the new head of state, whose rather modest title was "Gouverneur Général."

In the summer of 1804, however, rumor has it that Napoleon is about to be crowned emperor. Dessalines decides that to maintain equality of status with France, Haiti too must become an empire. The connection between Dessalines's ascension to the imperial throne and that of his nemesis Napoleon appears to have escaped European observers who marvel at the absurdity of "an uneducated, barbarous, though indeed successful negro, having authority over negroes as ignorant and as uncivilized as himself, and possessing but a part of a comparatively small Island, claiming the title of Emperor!"[6] On October 6, 1804, the official ceremony takes place in Cap Haïtien. Dessalines, who could only sign his name, charges his secretaries with the drafting of a constitution, which is promulgated on May 20, 1805. The Preamble immediately takes up the issue of racial equality:

> In the presence of the Supreme Being, before whom all mortals are equal, and who has scattered so many kinds of different beings over the surface of the globe for the sole purpose of manifesting his glory and might through the diversity of his works;
> Before the whole creation, whose disowned children we have so unjustly and for so long been considered;
> We declare that the terms of the present Constitution are the free, spontaneous, and determined expression of our hearts and of the general will of our fellow citizens.

In rhetoric clearly shaped by that of Enlightenment thought, as well as the French Revolution, the new imperial constitution appeals to the Supreme Being as the source of that strand of the text that establishes racial equality, and, in the social contract tradition, to free and voluntary association for that strand which leads to the formation of a new state.

What is most interesting in these opening statements is the complicated and dialectical fashion in which universalism and particularism are framed. Two sentences of the brief Preamble address the issue, and both perform a double movement: they assert a principle of universal equality and then in the same gesture affirm human diversity and difference. The first sentence states that all humans are equal, and that diversity serves the greater glory of the Supreme Being. The second sentence rejects as unjust the racial exclusivism that has led to treating Africans as "disowned children," thereby appealing implicitly to equality; at the same time, it introduces a historical consideration that becomes the basis for an identitarian reflection which would set Haitians (and any descendants of enslaved people) apart from others: it is on the very basis of having experienced a certain injustice that Haiti as a state is created. The Preamble thus sketches a conceptual frame in which equality and difference, universalism and identity-based or historical claims, show themselves as intimately linked and indeed inseparable. Universalism and particularism continuously refer back to each other— racial equality cannot be achieved without particularistic claims, and particularism is ultimately justified by a claim of universal racial equality.

This peculiar structure becomes even more visible when we consider the provisions that deal with issues of skin color in the body of the constitution:

> Art. 12—No white person, of whatever nationality, may set foot on this territory in the role of master or proprietor nor in the future acquire any property here.
>
> Art. 13—The preceding article shall not have any effect on white women who have been naturalized by the government nor on their present or future children. Included in the present provision are also the Germans and Poles naturalized by the Government.
>
> Art. 14—All distinctions of color will by necessity disappear among the children of one and the same family, where the Head of State is the father; Haitians will henceforth be known by the generic denomination of blacks.[7]

To grasp the complex relationship between universalism and particularism, we have to consider the logical structure of these articles. But before discussing some of the details—and possible contradictions—within them, we should pause for a moment to think about the implications of Dessalines's act of renaming. In an extraordinarily bold move, Dessalines's constitution seizes the language of the colonizer and submits it to radical resignification. All hierarchies based on people's skin color are abolished, and all Haitians are to be referred to by the generic term "black." From the taxonomic lunacy of a colony that had more than one hundred different terms to refer to different degrees of racial mixture and color, we have moved to a generic denomination: black. Article 13 moreover implies that white women, Germans, and Poles can become Haitians by an act of government,[8] which means that they too would count as black.[9] Just as the French revolutionaries renamed the signposts of traditional Western culture, from the months of the year to the main churches in Paris and even God, who becomes the Supreme Being, so revolutionaries in the former French colony rename the territory by restoring the Arawak name and, even more remarkably, by renaming skin color.

Disrupting any biologistic or racialist expectations, they make "black" a mere implication of being Haitian and thus a political rather than a biological category. In both cases, liberation from oppression is imagined through a complete break with the inherited past. Of course, burning down buildings also marks rupture, but unlike material structures, words cannot be destroyed and then rebuilt. Meaning cannot in fact be destroyed or changed by fiat. New meaning and old meaning will coexist for a long time; signifiers have a long memory. The very act of calling all Haitians black, regardless of their phenotype, would for a long time be recognized as a radical break from the entrenched practice of distinguishing, at the very least, between mulattoes, blacks, and whites. It is a form of violent rupture that is not consummated in the singular act of destruction. Instead, in the repetition of speech, the memory of a struggle remains alive, as well as a hope for a different future.

Through the act of renaming, the constitution of 1805 thus performs one of the most troubling paradoxes of modern universalist politics—the paradox that the universal is typically derived through a generalization of one of the particulars. Calling all Haitians, regardless of skin color, black is a gesture like calling all people, regardless of their sex, women: it both asserts egalitarian and universalist intuitions and puts them to a test by using the previously subordinated term of the opposition as the universal term.

In his work on the Haitian constitutions, Claude Moïse comments only briefly on Article 14, concluding that this is a "juridical fiction" which "bears witness to the importance that, at least in the eyes of Dessalines, attached to the color question in Haitian society."[10] Undoubtedly, it is true that Article 14 reflects Dessalines's awareness of the importance of the color question. But calling the provision a "juridical fiction" does not quite capture its essence. The comparison with an obvious example of a juridical fiction may help to tease out its peculiarity. When a corporation is called a "juridical person," it means that it is a person for the purposes of the law. It does not mean that henceforth we should include corporations among our family members or think that the corporation has subjectivity. Its "personhood" affects only its mode of operation in the legal realm. In Dessalines's constitution, however, the attribute "black" plays no legal role at all. Article 14 could have stopped after the phrase "necessarily disappear" without changing the meaning. The constitution could also have picked up on the argumentative strand from the Preamble that turns on racial equality, without tinkering with the meaning of "black." But it doesn't. The reason, I think, is that the goal is not to legislate away (or disguise) in the law the racial divisions that continued to be operative, or to clarify a possible ambiguity. Calling all Haitians "black" is clearly a political act, or what legal scholars would call "expressive lawmaking."

Returning to more legal issues concerning Articles 12 through 14, one might wonder whether they are not in some sense inconsistent. Article 12 states that no white, "whatever his or her nationality," is allowed to own property or be a master in Haiti. Article 13 states that this does not include certain naturalized whites; Article 14, that all Haitians are black. Articles 12 and 13 do not raise any questions on their own. Problems arise, however, when we add Article 14: if all Haitians are black, then Article 13 is redundant, since it affects naturalized whites, who by the definition of Article 14 are also black.

It seems clear, then, that we cannot read these articles in a synoptic fashion. As long as we read them in sequence, however, we do not have a problem understanding what they mean. In the process of clarification and political argument that presumably accompanied the drafting of the constitution, a process of redefinition of terms must have taken place which is reflected in a textual structure that has more a narrative than a legal logic. Whereas legal statutes ordinarily have an atemporal logic, that is, they aspire to backward and forward consistency, in narratives we cannot invert the order of the telling without affecting the meaning of the told, and a first reading may produce a meaning very different from a second reading. Reading Articles 12 through 14, we see how the Haitian revolutionaries started with the inherited meaning of a racialized vocabulary and proceeded by increasingly changing its meaning and valorization.

Like the terms of the Preamble, Articles 12 to 14 reflect a tension between a universalism of racial equality and particularistic claims that are based on group identity and a history of oppression. The idea that all Haitians are black seems to run counter to identity-based claims in that it erases difference; that all whites are excluded from ownership in Haiti, on the other hand, clearly enacts a legal distinction based on skin color, at least for non-Haitians.

Although it eventually became the basis for resistance against neocolonial politics, in its origins Article 12 was meant, it seems, as a political restriction on Article 6, which declares property to be sacred.[11] It is common to see Article 12 as grounded in racial exclusivism (a term popular among anti-Haitian ideologues in the Dominican Republic, for instance). This is unwarranted, however, when we take into account that slavery had not been abolished anywhere in the plantation zone and that neither France nor the United States nor the Vatican had extended diplomatic recognition to Haiti at the time of the promulgation of the constitution. Article 12 was an entirely appropriate measure and indeed required by prudence. As far as France was concerned, Haiti was simply a wayward colony. Banning whites from being masters or owning property in Haiti was motivated by the well-justified fear that the former French owners of plantations in Haiti might return, backed by the French military, and claim their property. Injecting a political meaning into the language of color is thus not just a rhetorical move but a strategy with a clear political aim.

Dessalines's attempt to rid the country of its inheritance of racial distinctions and hierarchies based on skin color did not succeed. Dessalines and his secretaries were producing the very modern fantasy of the omnipotence of the word. Eventually these juridical fictions were dropped under the onslaught of a reality that was a far cry from having abandoned racial distinctions. Later constitutions abandoned Article 14 (although Articles 12 and 13 appear in some form or other until the constitution of 1918). When Louis Pierrot, a black general, came to power in 1845, relations between mulattoes and blacks had become so tense that a "race relations act" was passed, according to which anyone who "indulged in idle talk about color likely to spread dissension among Haitians and provoke citizens one against another" would be arrested and tried.[12] Throughout the nineteenth century, the conflicts between mulattoes and blacks kept returning and indeed shaping Haitian politics. However, one may well wonder whether the ambiguity of the term *blan* in contemporary Creole and its oscillation between "foreigner" and "white" may not be a trace of the revolutionary practice of giving political meaning to formerly racialist terms.[13] This thesis could be supported, for instance, by the fact that the 1868 constitution replaced the term *blanc* in Dessalines's Article 12 with *étranger*. At the least it would seem that with Haiti's extraordinary political struggle against racial subordination, a terminology based on skin color and supported by racialist beliefs is infused with enough political meaning that the terms begin to oscillate between an individual's political status as a citizen of this or that state, and their racial meaning. Yet at the same time, a conceptual frame is proposed that contains the terminology of color and race within the imagery of a family—a conceptualization of citizenship that refers us to rather more traditional, patriarchal notions of statehood. What is remarkable, then, is that it is specifically the rethinking of racial categories in relation to politics that produces a truly radical redrawing of the conceptual map. It is an illustration of how differently political theory might have developed had thinking about liberty, equality, and fraternity been focused on issues of race and color rather than, say, class or the nation.

## Truncations of Transnationalism

Now, our reading of the operations of universal and particularistic claims in the constitution would remain somewhat formal if we did not point out that the same provisions that I have interpreted abstractly so far also have a concrete application. This application relates to the international character of antislavery. Consider, for example, the final signatory paragraph to the 1805 constitution: "We commend it [the constitution] to our descendants and, in homage to the friends of liberty and the philanthropists in all countries, as a sign of the divine goodness, which, as a result of his immortal decrees, has provided us with an occasion to break our irons and to constitute ourselves as a free, civilized and independent people." It is surely significant that the signatories of the first independent constitution would feel compelled to invoke the world stage—the "friends of liberty" and "philanthropists"—for their act of signing the first Haitian constitution. As a matter of historical fact, the newly independent state never took any decisive action to extend the benefits of the abolitionist constitution to other territories, and only Rigaud and Pétion gave some support to the cause of antislavery elsewhere. Yet this does not mean that the gesture of the signatories was purely rhetorical. As I will show in the following, the provisions governing issues of racial equality discussed in the previous section are connected, through the provisions regulating citizenship, to the transnational aspects of the emancipatory project of revolutionary antislavery. Just as the universalism of racial equality is played off against the particularism of a historically shaped identity, so the transnationalism of antislavery eventually has to confront the strictures against transnational politics imposed by the colonial powers at the time.

The resulting truncations of the ideological project that led to the foundation of Haiti had, I suspect, an enormous effect on the way in which nation and state developed in postrevolutionary Haiti, as realpolitik placed a taboo on precisely the desire that drove the slaves and people of color in Saint Domingue to overthrow the slaveholding regime. One may well be opposed to a particular political regime *sur place* but have no objections to its continuation elsewhere. But one cannot create a state on the grounds of universal racial equality and remain indifferent to the continuation of racial slavery elsewhere. This becomes clear when we take into account the development of some of the pertinent provisions in the later constitutions. It is in light of the historical development of the constitutional texts that we can discern what political or social concerns might have been behind some of the original provisions.

The constitution of 1805 states in some detail the restrictions placed on whites and their right to own property in Haiti. That seems natural enough in a new state that needs to overcome a social structure built on racial hierarchies and where property claims by whites could easily reopen the debate about slavery. But if we wonder what the general rules governing citizenship are, we find nothing. Are the children of Haitians given automatic citizenship, or do they need to be born in Haiti? What about nonwhite immigrants to Haiti? Article 1 simply states that "the people who live on the island formerly known as Saint Domingue convene to organize themselves in a free, sovereign and independent State." The only specification in relation to citizenship we find is a list of offenses that lead to the loss of citizenship.[14]

The republican constitution of 1806 drops the provision that declares all citizens to be black but gives precise and narrow criteria according to which whites can acquire citizenship: those who are part of the military, those who perform civil services, and "those already admitted to the Republic at the time of the promulgation of the present Constitution" (Article 28). This last clause probably refers again to white women married to Haitian men, Germans, and Poles. Like the constitution of 1805, it does not specify criteria of citizenship in general or rules for the naturalization of nonwhites.

What we do find in all the early constitutions, however, are clauses to the effect that Haiti will abstain from interfering in other territories' affairs. In Dessalines's 1805 constitution, we find such a clause in Article 36, which is included among the provisions that deal with the government of the new state; in the constitution of 1806, the provision has moved into a place of extreme prominence, second only to the provision that bans slavery. Under the heading of "General Dispositions," Article 2 says, "The Republic of Haiti will abstain from engaging in any wars of conquest, and never disturb the peace and internal regime of foreign islands."[15] Christophe's first constitution (1807) is particularly explicit. Under Title I, "Of the Status of Citizens," it says:

> Art. 1—Every person who resides in the territory of Haiti is free by law.
> Art. 2—Slavery is forever abolished in Haiti.

Under Title IX, "Of the Guarantees for Neighboring Colonies":

> Art. 36—The Government of Haiti declares to the powers that have colonies in its vicinity its unshakable resolve never to disturb the regime by which they are governed.
> Art. 37—The Haitian people will not make any conquests outside their island and will limit themselves to the preservation of their territory.

Pétion's constitution of 1816 contains a similar provision (Article 5), prominently featured under the heading of "General Dispositions," shortly after the provisions banning slavery. For the first time, we also find a provision that regulates the status of nonwhites who take up residence in Haiti. Title III, "The Political Status of Citizens," for the most part comprises provisions that specify when Haitians would lose their rights as citizens. However, the first article of the title reads as follows:

> Art. 44—All Africans and Indians, and those of their blood, born in the colonies or in foreign countries, who come to reside in the Republic will be recognized as Haitians, but will not enjoy the right of citizenship until after one year of residence.

The same constitution offers an expanded version of the provision that regulates citizenship for whites: those whites who were admitted to the Republic before the promulgation of the constitution of December 27, 1806, qualify for citizenship; "no others, in the future after the promulgation of the present revision, are entitled to the same right, nor can they be employed, enjoy the right of citizenship, or acquire property in the Republic" (Article 39). With this provision, Haiti's regulations on citizenship for whites have reached their most restrictive level, while the vagueness of regulations for non-whites has given way to a provision that explicitly gives the right of residence to anyone with African or Native American blood.

Considered from the perspective of the 1816 constitution, then, it seems very plausible to think that the silence on citizenship for nonwhites in the early constitutions is due to the fact that those who wrote the constitutions thought it obvious that those who had been subjected to racial slavery and genocide by white colonizers elsewhere could take up residence in Haiti. If we take Dessalines's attempt to resignify racial terminology seriously, as I think we should, it is only logical that he would not want to identify those who could take up such a right of residence in racial terms. Article 1 of Christophe's 1807 constitution ("Every person who resides in the territory of Haiti is free by law," as distinct from Article 2, "Slavery is abolished forever in Haiti") could be interpreted in the same light. Although, logically speaking, "All Haitians are black" cannot be inverted to read "All blacks are Haitians," the determinate vagueness about citizenship requirements for nonwhites suggests that the inversion was not very far from what the framers of the constitution had in mind. However, in a discursive practice that makes the term *blanc* oscillate between a reference to color and to oppressor (and by 1868 interprets it as "foreigner," thus implicitly reaffirming the clause long dropped from the constitutional text that all Haitians are black), doubts may have arisen about the possibility of identifying in advance all the kinds of people who might be enslaved under the regiment of the "blancs." At any rate, classifying them according to race or skin color would only reinscribe an ideology that needed to be overcome.

What is most striking, however, is that as the racial component of the "asylum provisions" becomes more explicit, so are the provisions that declare that Haiti will not engage in wars of conquest and will not interfere in the internal affairs of other colonies.[17] The most obvious issue would have been neighboring Santo Domingo, which had been invaded by Toussaint Louverture and Dessalines on the grounds that slavery continued to be practiced and that the territory might serve as a beachhead for an invasion of Haiti. But the issue goes much beyond Santo Domingo. First of all, there were the fears of the slaveholders in the plantation zone from Louisiana to Bahia that Haiti might instigate and support uprisings. Ever since the early days of the revolution, rumors of Haitian ships and Haitian soldiers, and of Toussaint planning to conquer other islands, had terrified the elites in the Caribbean. Indeed, Bolívar's stay in Haiti and Pétion's military and material assistance in exchange for a promise that slavery would be abolished in liberated territories (a promise Bolívar could not keep) speak to the persistence of revolutionary antislavery despite constitutional assurances to the contrary. In the case of Pétion there would have been an additional motive for explicit noninterference clauses, namely, his desire to gain diplomatic recognition from France—after all, an independence unrecognized by the major imperial powers is pretty worthless. As Haiti was forced to respond to international pressure to provide assurances that it would not try to export its revolution (remember that the Girondin wars of revolutionary France would have been on everybody's mind), it compensated by introducing constitutional clauses that would offer a right of residency to all people who had escaped slavery or genocide.

The constitutional provisions should also be read against the backdrop of a variety of practices that replaced direct revolutionary action with, for example, various immigration schemes. In 1818 Henri Christophe issued an edict that specified that a white man who had married a black woman anywhere in the world had right to settle in his kingdom and would even have his fare paid. The following decree by Dessalines is reprinted by Marcus Rainsford in his *Historical Account of the Black Empire of Hayti (338)*:

LIBERTY OR DEATH!
Government of Hayti.
*Head-Quarters, Jan. 14*
*1st Year of the Independence of Hayti.*
The Governor-General considering that a great number of Native Blacks, and Men of Colour, are suffering in the United States of America, for want of the means of returning,
Decrees,
That there shall be allowed to the Captains of American Vessels the sum of Forty Dollars for each Individual they may restore to this country. He orders that this Decree shall be printed, published, and posted up, and that a copy thereof be immediately forwarded to the Congress of the United States.
By the Governor-General,
Dessalines

Although some Haitians objected that this was the equivalent of engaging in the slave trade (Haiti was suffering from an acute labor shortage and thus had an active desire to replenish the population), Dessalines argued that those Africans on the ships were to be sold into slavery, while in Haiti they would be free.

The provisions regulating residency and citizenship in Haiti must thus be seen as directly linked to the provisions that regulate Haiti's relation to neighboring countries or colonies. We might say that the vagueness of the provisions was intentional, as even the asylum clauses could have been interpreted as interference in other countries' affairs. Apparently Henri Christophe, whose 1807 constitution features one of the most decidedly vague residence clauses as its first article, was strongly opposed to Pétion's 1816 provision on precisely those grounds. In any event, these clauses clearly point to the fact that Haiti's radical antislavery stance is not easily limited by state borders. The vagueness on citizenship in the early constitutions is a trace of the transnational nature of radical antislavery. That the early constitutions do not give criteria for citizenship should not be seen as an omission or oversight that is later amended. Rather, it is evidence that the revolutionaries did not think of the new state along the lines of a new nation finally liberated from the fetters of colonialism. Indeed, we may even go so far as to argue that the later specifications of citizenship are a measure of how far subsequent politicians had been pushed away from the original transnationalism of antislavery. Of course, they had no other choice—both internal and external pressures forced them to build a polity on the model of the modern Western nation-state.

Ironically, then, the idea of transnational liberation itself becomes part of a nationalistic rhetoric. The constitution of 1843, written after Boyer was deposed, further expands Article 44 of Pétion's constitution of 1816. Under the title "Of Haitians and Their Rights" we read:

> Art. 6—All individuals born in Haiti, or of African or Indian descent, and all those born in foreign countries to a Haitian man or a Haitian woman, are Haitian; also all those who up to this day have been recognized as Haitians.
>
> Art. 7—All Africans or Indians and their descendants may become Haitians. The law regulates the formalities of naturalization.

It seems that the inversion of Dessalines's declaration that all Haitians are black had finally become law: all descendants of Africans and Amerindians are Haitians. Now, in historical terms, we have to understand that by 1843 Haiti was no longer perceived as a threat to neighboring countries (with the sole exception of the former Spanish colony of Santo Domingo), and all immigration projects of the early years had failed. The original transnational radicalism had lost its concrete political meaning—note that the 1843 constitution no longer has a noninterference clause despite the bold claims of Articles 6 and 7. The transnational links that could have been an obstacle to nationalistic exclusivism become an ingredient of nationalism. It is transnationalism turned inward. This, I would argue, is the genealogical story of twentieth-century indigenist nationalism in Haiti, which gave a political and cultural articulation to the opposition against the American occupation in 1915 and in a unique move makes a certain kind of pan-Africanism the backbone of national resistance against American marines.

The trajectory we observe in the evolution of constitutional provisions can be confirmed in other cultural and political gestures. The most obvious incident of a political identification between the former slaves and Amerindians is, of course, the renaming of Saint Domingue as Haiti: like the resignification of all inhabitants of the new state as black, regardless of skin color, the renaming of Saint Domingue signals a violent break with the colonial past and a symbolic erasure of colonialism and colonial slavery. In keeping with this strategy, the insurgent slaves called themselves *indigène,* although at least half of the former slaves were born in Africa and some of the generals of the uprising were born on other Caribbean islands. Obviously, indigenism is used as a political rather than a racial, ethnic, or even geographic term, expressive perhaps of the idea that it is the slaves, not the masters, who have a rightful claim to the land.

We have seen the extraordinary efforts of intellectuals in Spanish Santo Domingo as they tried to produce a genealogy that would at the same time establish a nativist link to Indians as well as a familial link with the Spanish. In works such as Galván's *Enriquillo,* a quasi-mystical connection to Amerindian culture is transformed into an interpellation for nineteenth-century anti-Haitian nationalism. Now, as it turns out, Haitians lay claim to the same prehistory. How do the Haitians of the postindependence era imagine these links to the precolonial past?

One of the most telling texts is the *Histoire des caciques d'Haïti,* by Emile Nau (1812–1860), a mulatto writer and eminent figure in the local romantic movement, whose indigenism is rather different from the one we have seen on the Spanish side of the island. If Galván's *Enriquillo* was, in Doris Sommer's words, "the ideological shelter against the imputation of African (that is Haitian) identity in a country of dark people,"[18] Nau's *Histoire* is a vindication of a transgenerational and transcultural link between Africans and Amerindians that turns neither on cultural ties nor on religious belief and conversion; nor does it involve a complicated play of identitarian reflections. It is, rather, a link established through the struggle for liberty and justice. Both Galván and Nau tell the story of a rebellion led by an indigenous chieftain of mixed blood, somewhat condescendingly called Enriquillo by Galván, and Henri by Nau. But whereas Galván transposes the events into a story that turns by and large on romantic love and betrayal, Nau remains in the realm of political history, beginning with the history of discovery and ending with Henri's settlement with the Spanish. His introduction, moreover, situates the events surrounding the rebellion in the context of a history that is told from the point of view of those who become the victims of European expansionism: conquest and genocide, colonization and introduction of Africans, the Haitian Revolution, and finally the creation of Haiti.

Acknowledging that there are no blood ties between Indians and Africans, Nau argues that "the African and the Indian join their hands in chains." It is because of a "confraternité de malheur" [brotherhood of misfortune] and a "communauté de souffrances" [community of sufferings] that their destinies are linked and mixed (vol. 1, 12). In this picture, the Haitian Revolution is an act of vengeance: "To liberate a country this way means to take revenge for all those who have been oppressed and to take revenge for oneself and at the same time for the unfortunate Indians" (vol. 1, p. 13). Taking up the messianic rhetoric of the early days of the revolution, Nau's text no doubt means to evoke memories of Dessalines's epithet "avenger and liberator of his fellow citizens" (Article 20 of the constitution of 1805). When compared to the Dominican indigenism with its strong religious inflection, it is noticeable that the Haitian version is an expression of a very modern consciousness. It imagines loyalties and alliances without any need to appeal to transcendent justifications: politics here is not anchored in some otherwise guaranteed realm of values and traditions, but is something that happens when we pursue liberty and justice.

But Nau's argument does not stop at this point. Like the constitution of 1843, he turns the transethnic alliance between Amerindians and descendants of Africans into a basis for a new national belonging. "Having inherited their servitude, we have also inherited their fatherland" (vol. 1, p. 13). This act of inheriting is literarily performed in certain parallels between the indigenous chieftain Henri and the leaders of the Haitian Revolution. Like Toussaint Louverture in most conventional portraits, Henri is presented as a man born to lead: "To organize! That was his first concern, his first act. . . . This essential characteristic marked his whole career and to it he undoubtedly owed all his success" (vol. 2, p. 31). Henri is the one who dreamed up the slogan "Liberté ou mort" (vol. 2, p. 32), which of course figured prominently in Haitian revolutionary rhetoric. Like Toussaint, Henri never slept in the same place (vol. 2, p. 38). After first establishing a revolutionary alliance that was explicitly antimimetic and antitraditionalist, Nau slowly turns the story of Henri's uprising into an allegory of the Haitian Revolution, with one crucial difference: where Henri failed, the Haitians succeeded. In this final turn of the argument, the act of vengeance bestows quasi-native rights on Haitians and becomes grounds for a national interpellation. Indigenism is transformed from a mark of a radically transnational understanding of citizenship and residence into a ground for national identification. If the earlier idea was that of Haiti as a liberated territory—a kind of safe haven for anyone who was escaping genocide and slavery—the new idea of Haiti is the land of those who avenged the Indians and acquired a special right of residence.

Clearly, ideas of citizenship, nationality, and rights of residence undergo severe changes in the first half of the nineteenth century. Nau's historical essay confirms what we inferred from the transformation of the early constitutions. The juxtaposition of the non-interference clauses and the transmutations of the vague citizenship clauses express the same conflict that Gauthier traced in her study of the "death" of natural rights in post-Thermidor France. National interest has won the day, and natural rights can be acted on only to the extent that they do not conflict with the interests of the imperial powers (the Haitian constitutions are explicit that the assurances are directed at the colonial authorities, not at the peoples of those territories: noninterference concerns national interest, not popular sovereignty); revolutionary antislavery turns into humanitarian immigration laws. In the end, the dialectic between universalist aspirations and particularistic, identity-based claims is short-circuited by a conflation of the two in the apogee of the ideology of national interest.

Cut off from the world by a cordon sanitaire imposed by the imperial powers who feared a spread of the slave revolution, and fearful itself that whites might plot to take the territory back, Haiti is caught in a cold war of preventive measures and becomes increasingly isolated. Under pressure from European slaveholders and colonialists as well as peripheral Creole elites, the one state in the Western Hemisphere that came into being through a struggle for liberation which was not bound to issues of nationalism and nationhood is forced to sever its connections to the outside world.

# 12

## Life in the Kingdom of the North

Henri Christophe has not enjoyed a good press. To be sure, British abolitionists liked him well enough for his monarchical instincts and distaste for things French. That he announced plans to introduce English as the national language and to convert the country to Protestantism cannot have hurt, either.[1] There is a long correspondence between Christophe and Thomas Clarkson, who acted as his adviser at large and even facilitated a brief exchange of letters with Czar Alexander, who was rather taken with the idea of a black monarch on a tropical island.[2] In 1818 a British naval officer who was visiting Cap-Henry—the northern city that during colonial times had been known as Cap Français and later became Cap Haïtien—described Henri Christophe in a letter to a friend thus:

> The King is in his person what in England you would call a fine portly-looking man about 5 feet 10 inches. He is now growing stout, and on horseback, where he certainly looks his best, has much the appearance of old George. His dress, except on state days, is very like the Windsor uniform, without lace or star. He is quite black . . . very intelligent, pleasant and expressive—his features are much that of his countrymen—his nose rather long but flat at the nostrils—his lips are not thick—his eyes, except when in rage, rather small, but quick.[3]

British observers were generally impressed with the formality and strict protocol at Christophe's court. About the republican culture in the South, by contrast, they expressed dismay. It is difficult not to hear echoes of English disdain for French plebeian rituals and uncouth eating habits in the comments about the "lackadaisical southerners" whose state representatives were "shabbily dressed, inadequately rehearsed and slovenly" (209). To the minds of the Methodist missionaries John Brown and James Catt, the Republic was "a land . . . where Christianity is unknown, save through the disguise of Popery, and where no cheering sound of salvation breaks through the horrid silence" (240).

By 1818, when the British officer was comparing the Haitian king to "old George," Christophe's reign was in fact nearing its end. Barely two years later, in failing health and faced with growing popular discontent and a mutiny among his officers, he fatally shot himself. The experiment of a monarchy in Haiti had failed. His only surviving son, Jacques-Victor-Henry, was bayoneted to death by the conspirators, and his body was left to rot on a dung heap. His widow Marie-Louise and two daughters Améthyste-Henry and Anne-Athénaïre-Henry sought refuge in England, where they stayed at Clarkson's house for a while, before moving on to Italy. None of them ever returned to Haiti.[4]

British abolitionists and a faction of Haitian *noiriste* historians aside, Christophe's historical portrait is generally unflattering.[5] Leading French abolitionists such as Abbé Grégoire refused to endorse Christophe's regime. Historians, especially outside Haiti, have paid much more attention to the revolution and its main figures than to postrevolutionary Haiti and its leading political actors. Whereas Toussaint Louverture is often represented as a brilliant and far-sighted statesman, and Dessalines as a gifted general and father of Haitian independence, Henri Christophe's reputation has always been more dubious. His solution to the postcolonial predicament has often been seen as a mere curiosity or, the relentless severity of his regime notwithstanding, a picturesque footnote to history on the periphery. Even scholars who defend Christophe's program of self-improvement and hard work appear to be at a loss when it comes to assessing his legacy. An article that presents him as an "administrateur génial" raises the question "What school did Christophe form?" and concludes that "history remains silent on that question."[6]

This does not mean that Christophe has fallen into oblivion. But with the exception of Aimé Césaire's insightful *La tragédie du Roi Christophe* (1963), he is for the most part represented as someone who sought to satisfy his petty ambitions with crass displays of power and might—the symbol of the corruption of revolutionary principles. In C. L. R. James's play *Toussaint Louverture* (performed in London in 1936 with Paul Robeson in the role of Toussaint Louverture), Christophe is a somewhat dumb opportunist who only serves to illustrate the integrity and stern determination of the revolutionary heroes, especially, of course, Toussaint.[7] An expressionistic play by Eugene O'Neill titled *The Emperor Jones* (1920) takes up Christophe's story in a strangely ambiguous allegory of the U.S. intervention of 1915, in which a black American with a career as a petty criminal in the United States of Jim Crow laws ends up taking over the government of a black state in the West Indies—only to be hunted down by his own visions of an African crocodile god and a witch doctor.[8] An early novel by the Cuban writer Alejo Carpentier entitled *El reino de este mundo* (The kingdom of this world) (1949) is set in the North, in the shadow of Christophe's fortress. There, the story of the revolution is told, from the time of Mackandal's uprising to Christophe, from the perspective of Ti Noël, a lowly black man who experiences Christophe's brutal labor regime as a simple return of the abuses of slavery. Although not a character in the novel, Henri Christophe and his kingdom emerge as a sign of an elusive experiential and historical difference. While the novel is probably not Carpentier's most accomplished work, it does occupy a special place in Spanish American literary history. It was on the occasion of Carpentier's visit to the ruins of Henri Christophe's palace and fortress in the North that he developed the notion of *lo real maravilloso* (the marvelous real), which subsequently became a major influence for Spanish American writers of the so-called Boom as a novel conceptualization of historical experience on the periphery and an alternative to the dominant narratives of modernization and development. What struck Carpentier at the sight of Christophe's castle was what the German philosopher Ernst Bloch called the "simultaneity of the non-simultaneous"—a history shot through with discontinuities where the past appears to accumulate in layers rather than vanish into the present's prehistory.

### Constitution as Performance

Born in 1767 on the island of Grenada, which had been a French colony but was ceded to Britain in the Treaty of Versailles (1783), Henri Christophe was sent off as a cabin boy at a young age. There is some disagreement among his biographers about whether he was born free or a slave,[9] but the evidence appears to indicate that he was the son of free blacks or, more likely, a black and a mulatto. In Le Cap he entered the service of a French naval officer, for whom Christophe worked as a bootblack and mess boy. Barely twelve years old, Christophe joined a battalion of free blacks that was assembled by the French to give support to the American revolutionaries, and as a member of that battalion he apparently participated in the siege of Savannah, Georgia. On his return to Le Cap, he began to work as a waiter and later manager in a local hotel. During the revolutionary wars, he rose through the ranks of Toussaint Louverture's army. After the assassination of Dessalines in 1806, Christophe was designated to take over the leadership of the country. Fearful of Christophe's considerable power and ambitions, however, those who had conspired against Dessalines drafted a constitution that would have created a presidential system in which the president was little more than a figurehead, controlled by an all-powerful senate. Christophe rejected the proposal and declared himself president for life and supreme commander of the army, establishing a power base in the North. Pétion was eventually elected president for a four-year term.[10] With two heads of state claiming sovereignty over the territory of former Saint Domingue, civil war ensued. Only when the Senate reelected Pétion as president in 1811, thus putting an end to any hopes Christophe may have had of replacing Pétion in the second elections and so unifying the country under his leadership, Christophe decided to give up on his claim on the whole of the territory and instead create a separate state in the north. Civil war was over, but for almost a decade, Haiti was split into a northern monarchy and a republic in the West and South.

In March 1811 the Constitutional Law of the Council of State is promulgated. It is preceded by a preamble that briefly sketches the circumstances in which Christophe's first constitution of 1807 was born and argues for the need for constitutional change (*changement*). Although both Janvier and Mariñas Otero reprint the 1811 text as if it were a complete constitution, there are indications that it would be more appropriate to read it as an amendment to the 1807 constitution. There are no provisions concerning individual rights, slavery, or citizenship in the 1811 text. Yet we have no reason to assume that Christophe had weakened in his determination to keep slavery out of Haiti (even though he did not seem to have any qualms about forced labor). There is also no noninterference clause, yet we know that Christophe was very concerned about this issue and in fact objected, on the grounds that it was tantamount to interference with the affairs of foreign countries, to the provision in Pétion's constitution that practically offered a safe haven to runaway slaves. For these reasons it seems that we would have to read the 1807 and the 1811 constitutions together, in a narrative manner similar to that suggested by Dessalines's 1805 provisions that regulate Haitian citizenship in relation to skin color.

The explanatory preamble argues that the earlier text was born in the middle of civil strife, when there was no "social pact" in place, and that it therefore failed to establish the "only appropriate mode of government." Although the "small number of sublime principles" had been sufficient to guarantee the happiness and welfare of the people, it is now time to give the people a new constitution that will guarantee future stability:

Considering . . .

That it becomes us at present more than ever to establish a fixed order of things, a mode of government calculated to rule forever the country that gave us birth;

Considering that it is urgently necessary to invest the sovereign authority with a character great and august, so as to convey an idea of the majesty of power;

That the establishment of a hereditary throne is the consequence of this forcible consideration;

That the inheritance of power be vested only as to male legitimate children (at the exclusion of women) in an illustrious family that is faithfully devoted to the glory and the happiness of the fatherland which owes to it its political existence, is as much a duty as a signal mark of national recognition;

That it is the nation which now exercises, through us, its will and sovereignty; entrusting them to him who has rescued it from the abyss and the precipices where its most relentless enemies wanted to annihilate it, to him who governs now with such glory, that this nation has nothing to fear for its liberty, its independence, and its happiness;

That it is necessary also to establish high dignities, as well as to enhance the splendor of the throne as to reward eminent services rendered to the fatherland by officers who have devoted themselves to the happiness, the glory, and the prosperity of the State. The Council of State, therefore, enacts the Organic Law that follows.[11]

This declaration of intentions is followed by a constitutional text that is divided into eight titles, all of which concern issues of sovereignty, succession, and the structure of government. In every respect, the monarch is given supreme power.

In a proclamation signed by the Council of State and addressed to the "fellow citizens," the reasons for the change of state form are revisited. Taking up many of the phrases and arguments already present in the Preamble, they again assert that the previous constitution was devised at a time of turmoil, and that the work begun in 1807 needed to be concluded now that "the tempests have calmed down and the sky is more serene."[12] With the "State promising to last for eternity," they continue, "Les temps sont venus" [The time has come]. What follows are fairly familiar arguments about the advantages of concentrating state power in the hands of a single wise and heroic leader whose epic deeds in the war of liberation distinguish him as the person most apt to lead the country.

The interesting question here is not whether these arguments in favor of autocratic forms of government are persuasive. It is, rather, what was gained by making Christophe king? The constitution of 1807 already concentrated all power in the hands of a president for life. He already had quasi-dictatorial powers, supreme legislative and executive authority, and the right to appoint his successor. Why did the members of his council feel that the project of 1807 was left unfinished?

In light of the recurrent conflicts between the largely black rural population and the largely mulatto urban elites, we should not dismiss out of hand the concern with overcoming the splits within Haitian society and retaining political stability. It is not inconceivable that a hereditary monarchy, had it taken root in the country, would have prevented some of the civil strife that was the result of the recurrent attempts by one faction or another throughout the nineteenth century to seize state power. Christophe and his supporters may well have felt that popular identification with a dynastic family would have helped to reconcile the contradictions between the emerging nation's affective commitment to liberty from enslavement and a *raison d'etat* that demanded a disciplined workforce to guarantee survival of the state. The Preamble to the amendment of 1811 suggests that the council thought that an emotional attachment to a monarch who would be perceived as the epic hero of liberation and guarantor of liberty, and also as an embodiment of state authority, would solve the contradictions that indeed continued to haunt Haiti throughout the nineteenth and twentieth centuries.

A second consideration appears to have been a concern for international recognition. As the address from the Council of State to the fellow citizens says, one of the purposes of the constitutional change is to "gain international respect." There is clearly a contestatory intention behind the creation of a black monarchy—racial equality is asserted in the act of claiming the highest title and distinction for a black head of state.

A third element is not explicitly addressed but can be grasped when we read this text in the context of the earlier constitutions. By introducing a hereditary element in the rule of the state, the patriarchal and paternalistic element was strengthened considerably. Like the French dynastic principle,[13] Christophe's monarchical constitution explicitly excludes women from the succession to the throne (and it is worth remembering that Christophe also explicitly prohibited girls from attending the schools created with the help of British abolitionists). Whereas the dictatorial president of the constitution of 1807 had the right to appoint his successor (and thus could appoint his son, presumably), the monarchical constitution literally naturalizes the reproduction of power and thus shifts the patriarchy from a representational to a familial register. There are even provisions (Articles 4 and 5) which state that in the absence of male offspring, the king can adopt a son, but if he later has a biological son, that one has precedence over the one who was adopted. What we can observe here, then, is the subtle shift from a militaristic patriarchal model to a civilian patriarchal model, in which the reproduction of male power needs guarantees beyond mere rank, and where the ultimate expression of supreme power is precisely that the king *produces* his successor.

If there is any need to show to what extent Christophe adopted the role of the punitive father as his behavioral model and in the process erased any distinction between private and public role, reading the letters he sent to his wife and his son should suffice. As we know, Christophe never learned to write more than his name. The letters he sent to his family members are thus the result of dictation, and, in all likelihood, translation—a rather more public than private act. In very formal terms, most of these letters are orders of some sort or other, or mete out some form of censure, as for example a criticism of his son's handwriting, or his wife's failure to consult a doctor, or similar matters. What is at stake here is not Christophe's character, and certainly not whether he understood what good parenting might entail. Rather, it is the question of how Christophe envisioned power and what kind of reproduction of power he aspired to. And it seems obvious that his idea of unassailable power develops in the merging of the patriarchal family and the monarchical state, the punitive father and the absolute monarch.

Yet there is one more element to Christophe's monarchical constitution that deserves a closer look if we want to understand why he would have wanted to change from a dictatorial presidential system to a monarchical one. If the patriarchal model, combined with a hereditary monarchy, aims at closing the gap between the locus of power, abstractly conceived, and the actual embodiment of power, we may ask ourselves whether this leaves any role for constitutionality. If Christophe tried to produce absolute power as absolute presence, a constitution, which would necessarily inscribe the difference between that which legitimizes (i.e., the constitution) and that which is legitimized, would seem to be unwarranted. Now, raised in these terms, the issue refers us back to questions of popular sovereignty, democracy, and the familiar problems of authoritarianism.

But we could also pose the question from a different perspective and ask whether constitutionality poses any particular problems in the context of postrevolutionary Haiti.

In the preamble quoted earlier there is a phrase concerning the issue of how sovereignty is to be represented, which is repeated almost literally in the address of the Council of State to the citizens of Haiti, where we read that the intention is "to invest the sovereign authority with a great and imposing character which represents the idea of the majesty of power, which impresses that respect which is inseparable from royal power." Sovereign authority should be invested with imposing attributes which give a proper idea of the majesty of power. This phrase, it seems to me, goes right to the heart of a problem that Christophe, who himself could not read or write, must have felt rather deeply. How can authority be represented when the head of state and the vast majority of the citizens are illiterate? Constitutional regimes are supremely textual: they operate precisely by continuously measuring actual practices against a frame that exists only on paper. The point is precisely to keep the gap between any actual representative of state power and the idea of the state and its mode of operation open. It is in this gap that constitutional interpretation occurs and accumulates. Now, if only a very small number of people can interpret the founding text, can this text play its conventional role in imposing constraints on the exercise of power? Furthermore, the smaller the group of people who can check the founding text, the less likely it is that there could be an ongoing legal and political practice within which there is continuity of constitutional interpretation over time.[14]

These two problems, taken together, mean that the constitution would become an almost tautological document through which the small elite that can read can exercise power. In fact, we do not even have to assume that the small group of readers interpret the constitution in bad faith in order to see that problems might arise: if the second consideration is valid, interpretative problems would arise even if the small group of readers were doing their best to interpret the founding text. Practically, this means that far from imposing constraints on the exercise of power, the constitution would simply shift the site of power to where it can no longer be seen. Clearly, the pomp and circumstance at Christophe's court needs to be understood in this context, as well: power needs to be made visible; it needs to be seen and performed to be effective. This point is at least theoretically separable from the issue of *absolute* power and would presumably have had to be addressed by the republicans in the West and South as well, had they aimed for something other than a merely formal democracy. Christophe obviously aspired to absolute power, but even if he had not, the absence of a sizable and socially diverse group of literate citizens meant that a republican constitutional regime could not effectively impose constraints on the exercise of power. This in turn means that it would also not have produced legitimacy, since legitimacy flows from effective constraints. Perhaps Christophe had the constitutional texts of 1801, 1805, 1806, and 1807 read to him and decided that they did not bestow *enough* power on the ruler. But he may also have thought that in a country where hardly anyone could read or write, those texts provided no basis for power at all.

Returning to the question of what Christophe stood to gain by adopting a monarchical state form, we can now see that the hereditary nature of his regime fills precisely the place that a constitution cannot fill when the majority of people, including the head of state, cannot read or write. It provides a founding idea, a rule to be followed into the future about how the state should be governed. While it is somewhat paradoxical to establish a new monarchy which cannot derive any legitimacy from tradition (thus speaking to the modern, nontraditional nature of the monarchy), it is nevertheless possible to feel that some anticipatory benefit flows from the fact that "it will be like this from now on." Unlike the founding rule that is embodied in a written constitution, the rule of a hereditary monarchy can be deciphered and judged by anybody by virtue of a shared human experience of reproduction.

### Royal Culture

On March 28, 1811, Christophe is proclaimed King Henri I of Haiti. In the space of a few weeks, he forges a monarchy, with all its trappings. On April 5, he announces a hereditary nobility with four princes, eight dukes, twenty-two counts, thirty-seven barons, and fourteen knights. On April 7, a church hierarchy is established, with Toussaint Louverture's favorite chaplain as the king's grand almoner and archbishop of Haiti, and bishops in Les Gonaïves, Port-au-Prince, and Les Cayes (the last two, obviously, in Pétion's territory).[15] On April 12, Christophe issues a dress code for the nobility: a white tunic down to below the knee, white silk hose, red morocco shoes with golden square buckle, gold-hilted sword, and round hats for the princes and dukes, simpler attire for the lower ranks. On April 20, he creates the Order of the Garter or the Saint-Esprit, the Royal and Military Order of Saint-Henry. The coronation takes place on June 2, in a church newly constructed for the sole purpose of the ceremony.[16]

W. W. Harvey, a British observer of the events in Haiti, gives us a vivid description of Christophe's court and then remarks:

> Whatever may be thought of Christophe's bestowing these titles on the more distinguished part of his followers, the circumstance cannot but appear, at first sight at least somewhat absurd and ludicrous; and whether it arose from prejudice, or from any other feeling, Englishmen especially felt a reluctance to address a negro as his *Lordship*, or a mulatto as his *Grace*, which neither custom nor constraint could overcome.[17]

It is interesting that Harvey seems quite aware of the prejudicial element in the refusal to accept social distinction. It is in the aesthetic domain that he loses sight of the operations of prejudices:

> All the officers, whatever their rank or character, were fond of dress to an extravagant degree. They were required to possess good clothing, and were furnished with the means of procuring it: but in the expense of their garments, and the ornaments with which they were decorated, they far exceeded the desire of their sovereign, and often rendered their appearance ridiculous. Their coats were so bedecked with gold lace, that it was difficult to determine of what material they were made: their shoulders were burdened with epaulets of an enormous size: their caps were adorned, among other ornaments, with feathers nearly equalling their own height: and these articles, together with their beautiful white small-clothes and elegant silk hose, rendered their appearance supremely fantastical; nor was it possible for a European to behold a negro thus arrayed, without feeling amused to a degree which it would have been dangerous to manifest, yet difficult to conceal.[18]

In terms strongly reminiscent of those we saw operative in early-nineteenth-century Cuba, the aesthetic sense of former slaves is presented in a language of excess. Like Plácido, whose poetry was condemned as ostentatious for its use of erudite allusions, like the blackfaced buffoons of the Cuban comedies about negros catedráticos, the black aristocracy of Henri's kingdom has appropriated signs of distinction that render them "supremely fantastical" and ridiculous in the eyes of the British guest.

Now, it is not the case that Christophe and his court were naively unaware of the effect that the introduction of royalism in Haiti had on European witnesses. Indeed, Baron de Vastey, Christophe's main ideologue and, according to J.-F. Hoffmann, the first man of African descent in the New World to claim ethnic identity with the ancient

Egyptians,[19] made this effect more or less the raison d'être of the monarchy:

> A black king in St. Domingue! A crown on the head of a black man! That is what the French publicists, the journalists, the makers of systems of colonization cannot digest; according to them, a black king is a phenomenon that has never been seen in the world! . . . Scythian, Mongolian, and Ethiopian races; white, yellow, and black races, oppress! hate! Because you are not of the same color! Exterminate! The victorious color will reign absolute in the universe! These are the much extolled fruits of the enlightenment and of the civilization of the century that we live in.[20]

Unlike the constitutional texts considered in the previous chapter, Vastey proposes a direct link between the ideology of racial inequality and colonialism: the realm of equality is international, and international opposition against Christophe's kingdom is to be understood not as a response to his authoritarianism or, more generally speaking, as an opposition against a return to the monarchical state form but as a refusal to admit Haiti on equal footing with other countries. It is not surprising, then, that Vastey was in fact a staunch defender of inequality and tended to ridicule the idea that people were somehow "equal" except before the law.[21]

Economically, Christophe's state was rather successful, at least by some measures of success. Like Toussaint Louverture and Dessalines before him, Christophe imposed a harsh labor regime that guaranteed the continuation of the export-oriented plantation economy. Relatively quickly his state disposed of a huge economic surplus which allowed Christophe to maintain his army in a state of readiness against the much-feared return of French troops and to embark on various ambitious projects. He wrote a *code rural* that spelled out every detail of the workday.[22] At 3 A.M. a foreman would summon the field hands to take breakfast and say prayers. At 4:30 they were to go to the fields and do tidying jobs until it was light enough to begin the serious field work. At sundown they would gather again, say prayers, and return to the barracks. At midday, the field workers were allowed two hours of rest; Saturdays were reserved for work on the garden plots, and Sunday was a day of rest. The proprietors had to distribute one-quarter of theirs earnings to the workers. In fact, some have argued that the great difference between Christophe's reign and the colonial regime was that under Christophe the elites too were subject to the rules of a militarized agriculture. They could no longer enjoy their profits in the comfort of the cities but had to organize the rural labor force and spend their time on the plantation. Owners were also obliged to provide the workers with a nurse, a midwife, a weekly visit by a physician, and to take care of the children's education in the case of the parents' death.[23] Discipline was maintained through draconian penalties. Theft was punishable by death. Workers who had to travel during the week needed a pass. The agricultural operations were overseen by a military police, hired directly in Africa to ensure loyalty, who could enter the plantations at any time and punish anyone suspected of idleness on the spot, usually by flogging.

The economic surplus allowed Christophe to engage in considerable building activity. Along with an impressive fortress designed to withstand any foreign invasion on La Ferrière, Christophe also commissioned a number of charming châteaus for relaxation, receptions, and audiences. The little palaces had fanciful names: Victory, the Cloak, the Scepter, the Necklace, Embuscade, Belle-vue-le-Roi, and, most famously, Sans Souci, set at the foot of La Ferrière. W. W. Harvey gives a description of Christophe's palaces: there were highly polished floors of mahogany or marble, the walls were decorated with the most valuable paintings, and "every article of furniture was of the most costly kind; and whatever the most unbounded passion for splendour could suggest, was procured to decorate the habitations of—an uneducated negro."[24] For the purposes of public presentation, Christophe engaged the services of writers such as Juste Chanlatte, who provided theatrical pieces to be performed in Christophe's honor: *L'entrée du roi dans la capitale* (The entry of the king into the capital), *Nehri* (anagram of Henri), a play about the victory over Leclerc, and *La partie de chasse du roi* (The hunting party of the king), a comic opera in which, notably, a chorus of girls celebrates the merits of the king in Creole.[25]

Education posed a big problem for postrevolutionary Haiti. Like most postcolonial states in meridional America, Haiti was not in a position to create a state-funded public education system from one day to the next. In most of Spanish America, education continued to be in the hands of the Catholic clergy even after independence. Since the Vatican refused to recognize the black state, Haiti had to make do without church assistance, and the fact that literacy remained largely unchanged throughout the nineteenth century certainly has something to do with this. Christophe was able to rely on some help from British abolitionists, who promoted an educational system on the Lancasterian model and sent teachers to Haiti. Although travelers frequently commented on the enthusiasm of the students and the apparent success of these schools, it seems clear that they did not reach the populations who lived in rural areas and that access was largely limited to the children of the elite. Reading the enthusiastic accounts about black and mulatto children developing proficiency in English and Latin within a year of instruction (in a foreign language, namely, French, one has to assume), I cannot help but wonder whether these travelers were not somewhat blinded by a combination of abolitionist passions and racial prejudice according to which any display of learning among children of color seems miraculous.

Be that as it may, Christophe certainly spent considerable efforts on education and the arts. He created a philharmonic orchestra that would give concerts and play for dances at the court.[26] Eight painters worked at the palace. In 1816 the Englishman Richard Evans, to whom we owe the best-known portrait of Christophe—on horseback and very English—established an academy for drawing and painting at Sans Souci, which was directed by a Haitian artist named Charles. Several other schools of this kind remained active during Christophe's reign in the North.[27] From Santo Domingo he brought in Francisco Velázquez, a self-taught artist who in the eastern part of the island is usually quoted as the first Dominican painter, although I have never found him mentioned in accounts of Haitian culture and art. Velázquez apparently decorated Christophe's palace with scenes from Greek mythology in which the characters were represented as blacks.[28]

Literature did not play a large role in Christophe's kingdom; certainly it was much less important than in Pétion's republic. While Pétion secured the support of a handful of writers who would make it their task to attack the kingdom in the North, Christophe relied on a very small number of intellectuals such as Vastey and Chanlatte (who later switched alliance to Pétion), whose main output consisted of official declarations, essays, and, in the case of Chanlatte, the occasional theatrical piece or poem, like the following:

> Doux fruit d'une mâle fierté
> Compagne de la Liberté,
> Je te salue, Indépendence;
> De tes favoris la vaillance,
> Ici, t'élève des autels.[29]

> [Sweet fruit of a male pride
> companion of Liberty,
> I salute you, Independence;
> here the valor of your favorites
> erects altars for you.]

If in the years immediately following independence, writers were singing the heroic deeds of the war against the French, after the country split into two, writers devoted their skills to celebrating one state or the other and engaged in verbal battles, or *répliques,* in which insults and accusations were traded back and forth. Although the celebrations of liberty and independence continued, the two concepts now acquired a new meaning. In the Republic, "liberty" comes to mean liberty from political tyranny rather than slavery, as in the following poem by Dupré:

> Défenseurs de la liberté
> Quittons nos foyers, nos compagnes,
> Du Nord le tigre ensanglanté
> Paraît encore dans nos montagnes.[30]

> [Defenders of liberty,
> let us leave our hearths, our wives,
> from the North the bloody tiger
> appears again in our mountains.]

J. S. Milscent,[31] whose French father had fallen victim to the Terror in revolutionary France some twenty years earlier, exhorts his fellow republicans:

> Remplissons le même devoir,
> Brisons le joug du diadème,
> Que la loi ait du pouvoir.[32]

> [Let us fulfill our obligation,
> Let us break the diadem yoke,
> So that the law may have power.]

Despite this bellicose rhetoric, Christophe succumbed not to the militant love of liberty of the republicans, but to an insurrection among his own people. After his death, literary writing, which had gained some liveliness from the polemics between Monarchy and Republic, collapsed into an endless song in praise of Pétion and his successor Boyer.

Christophe's short-lived kingdom was a paradoxical creation: a nontraditional hereditary monarchy, with a head of state who championed education and the arts but could not himself do more than sign his name; a state in which the founding document acknowledges popular sovereignty only to propose that it be "entrusted" to the king. Under the heading of "stability" it adopts a traditionalism which can appeal to few traditions for legitimacy. Historians have tended to locate Christophe's modernity in his economic and agricultural policies, without noticing that his belief in the pliability of history, and his belief that one could simply start a new dynasty (and along the way change the national language and religion), speak far more eloquently to the oddly modern character of his regime.

Dessalines's constitution and the history of racial provisions in relation to the muted traces of the transnationalism of antislavery illustrated how emancipatory projects in the nineteenth century were pressed into the mold of the nation-state. They showed how an earlier universalism in which national boundaries played a minor role—at least from the perspective of the slaves—and which did not accord any special weight to national interest transmuted, under the pressures of colonialism and the continuation of slavery, into a particularism in which national interest and respect for national boundaries took precedence. We also observed how in the course of the nineteenth century the original emancipatory core of the Haitian Revolution—liberation from slavery and protection against genocide—became the backbone of a new form of nationalist discourse. The story of Christophe illustrates another aspect of the heterogeneous formation of a truncated modernity in the Caribbean. Of the early heads of state, Christophe is the only one who appears to have made a conscious effort to create a national culture. This is borne out both by his cultural politics and by the state form he adopts. He seemed to be aware of the difficulties that resulted from the fact that under the regime of colonial slavery, a solid counterhegemony had not developed. The Preamble to the 1811 constitution is explicit in this respect: the intention is to produce identificatory symbols which would allow for a reconciliation between the population's affective commitment to liberty and the rational need for economic development. Here again we can see how the special circumstances of the birth of Haiti produce a modern culture which is radically different from what Creole elites eventually imposed in most parts of meridional America. If all nations are in some sense imagined communities, and if print capitalism is the structural core of Creole nationalism, as Benedict Anderson has argued, we could see Christophe's kingdom of the North as an attempt to produce a stable community through an imaginary that can function even if 90 percent of the population cannot read and write and even if there is no local newspaper that would propagate the feeling of community and shared interests.

# 13

# Liberty and Reason of State

POSTREVOLUTIONARY CONSTITUTIONS II

In *From Rebellion to Revolution,* Eugene Genovese makes the following assessment of postrevolutionary Haiti:

> Toussaint, and after his death Dessalines and Henry Christophe, tried to forge a modern black state, based on an economy with a vital export sector oriented to the world market. The ultimate failure of their basically Jacobin program ushered in one of history's most grimly ironical counterrevolutions. Pétion's and Boyer's political relaxation and land reform replaced Henry Christophe's iron dictatorship and maintenance of the sugar plantations under rigorous work discipline. Haiti slowly became, in Sidney Mintz's words, "The Caribbean area's most thoroughgoing peasant country."[1]

After assigning a central place to the Haitian Revolution in the political history of the Western Hemisphere—we remember that for Genovese, the Haitian Revolution marked the turning point when slave uprisings took on the characteristics of bourgeois-democratic revolutions—he suddenly shifts gears from the political to the economic realm. Before the revolution, the historical process was driven by the revolutionary pursuit of liberty. And after the revolution? After the revolution, the truly revolutionary goal is modernization. One may of course wonder whether "bourgeois-democratic" was ever a felicitous term to describe the nature of the Haitian Revolution. But it is even more worrisome when the term "democracy" is simply discarded after the successful revolution. In a plot that bears alarming similarities to the Stalinist rhetoric of modernization and economic necessity, Pétion and Boyer are taken to task *not* for their role in the consolidation of minoritarian mulatto power, or for their failure to put in place institutions that would guarantee political participation of the largely illiterate rural population, but for "political relaxation" and "land reform." There is something almost gleeful in this account that assigns a severely curtailed space to liberty and equality: the revolutionary moment is reduced to a kind of switch, when in the name of liberty and equality a more modern, but equally oppressive, economic regime is ushered into being.[2] Genovese's admiration for the modern, albeit "iron," rule of Christophe, and his failure to distinguish between Christophe and Dessalines, can only be understood in the context of a historical perspective that sees progress as convergence toward "the mainstream of world history" and modernity,[3] now deprived of any cultural, political, or moral meaning, as inseparably linked to modernization.

It is a story that does not allow for discontinuity and disruption. Where Benjamin saw the failed emancipatory projects of the past which could be recalled in the present by the sudden spark of revolutionary energy, Genovese sees a process that is driven by a notion of historical necessity. Once the revolution happened, the project of emancipation strangely drops out of the picture. The hatred of slavery and the desire for individual liberty ignite revolution, as if by bodily reflex, but once the yoke is thrown off, progress is driven by technological and economic advances. For Genovese, Toussaint's great insight was the recognition that "European technology had revolutionized the world and forced all peoples to participate in the creation of a world culture at once nationally variegated and increasingly uniform."[4] If we leave aside the question of plausibility—I imagine that Toussaint's perspective was rather less concerned with the dynamics, directions, and shapes of world culture—Genovese's story is surprisingly simple: Toussaint, Dessalines, and Christophe are more, Pétion and Boyer less, progressive. And it is more specifically the breakup of the old plantations through what is one of the first, if not *the* first, land reform in the Americas that Genovese cites as "counter-revolutionary." (It should be mentioned too that because of Haiti's land reform, a historical process began that was the opposite of what happened in Spanish America, where after independence the land owned by the Spanish Crown and by indigenous populations passed into the hands of a minute Creole elite. It is certainly true that the breakup of the plantations in Haiti did not lead to the creation of a prosperous and egalitarian society. But neither did the preservation of the large-scale properties in Spanish America.) It seems that in Genovese's picture (which, of course, is not just his) the full array of human endeavors and perspectives only matters in the moment of revolution—prior to revolution, the process is driven by economic factors, and after revolution the same. It is as if an all-encompassing economic determinism can only be interrupted in the moment of violence.

Although Genovese invokes Sidney Mintz to support his diagnosis, Mintz actually offers a somewhat different account for Haiti's postrevolutionary predicament:

> Haiti was launched upon its independence with what might well have been the most pessimistic prognosis in modern world history: ravaged, hated, and feared by the slaveholding powers (including the United States); chained by economic indemnities to its former colonial master; and almost totally lacking in the skills, diplomatic contacts, and means necessary to build a modern nation. Surely the wonder of the second republic of the Hemisphere is not that it has fared badly, but that it has fared at all.[5]

While this is certainly not complete as an account of the difficulties Haiti faced after independence, Mintz hints at a story in which internal conditions and the operations of colonialism and neocolonialism combine to put Haiti in an extremely unstable position. Unlike Genovese, who appears to believe that Haiti's problems might have been solved through the iron rule of authoritarian modernization, Mintz's brief explanation here points toward the precarious place Haiti occupied in the nineteenth-century world system. Nevertheless, we should be careful not to overemphasize "Haitian underpreparedness" in relation to underlying structural problems. In my readings of the early constitutional texts, I try to show to what extent the difficulties of the new Haitian state were the result of issues that had more to do with the nature of the exploitative colonial regime and deficiencies in post-Enlightenment theories of liberation and the state than with the educational level of Haitians after independence. Western emancipatory thought did not offer a way of thinking about issues of racial equality in political terms. The "nation" emerged as the "point de capiton" (Mouffe/Laclau) in the early nineteenth century, and Haiti, where the struggle for liberation was not, first and foremost, a struggle for national liberation, had to fit into a mold that was ill suited, to say the least.[6]

I will return to this topic later on in this chapter. Suffice it to say now that Genovese's denunciation of Pétion and Boyer as counterrevolutionary (regardless of the fact that both embraced, at least formally, liberal principles of government) and his celebration of Christophe (regardless of the fact that he strove to re-create, at least formally, the Ancien Régime in the Caribbean) seem misguided. It is of course true that Pétion's constituency were the old affranchis, a class that had for a long time opposed abolition, had sided with the planters, and was always suspected of wanting to re-create the co-lonial caste system after independence. But should we consider Christophe revolutionary and modern on account of his implemen-tation of a project of authoritarian modernization alone? From the vantage point of twentieth-century history, Genovese's celebration of Christophe's authoritarian modernity as modernization cannot but seem ominous.

Genovese's account has been criticized for the most part on grounds of evidence. Historians such as Geggus and Fick have pointed out the extreme reductionism that underlies Genovese's bipartite model, the lack of evidence for the "bourgeois-democratic" nature of the Haitian Revolution and subsequent slave uprisings elsewhere, his failure to take into account the effects of creolization and local cultural developments, and so on. While these objections strike me as entirely justified, there is a certain danger in playing up the complexities and contingencies of historical records to such a degree that we lose sight of the theoretical dimensions of the issues and of the intellectual depth of the political thought of the founders of the Haitian state. With this, we would also lose the opportunity to see to what extent the struggle against racial subordination and thinking about racial equality was a challenge to post-Enlightenment political thought.

I will here again turn to the early Haitian constitutions as docu-ments that retain the contradictions between various political and ideological goals in the early years of the black state. Two issues will be addressed in what follows. The first one is particularly difficult, as it concerns the additional complications that arise when the relation-ship between liberty and equality is negotiated in connection with race. The second issue returns more directly to the problems raised by Genovese, that is, the relation between liberty and modernization.

In Toussaint Louverture's 1801 constitution, Title I is devoted to territorial definitions. Title II, "Of the Inhabitants," addresses the issue of liberty from slavery and racial equality:

Art. 3—Slaves may not exist in this territory, servitude is forever abol-ished. Here, all men are born, live, and die free and French.

Art. 4—All men, regardless of skin color, are here admissible to all employments.

Art. 5—There is no other distinction than that of virtues and talents, and no other superiority than that which the law bestows in the exercise of a public function. The law is the same for everybody, whether it punishes or protects.

The radical nature of these provisions can best be brought out by reading them against the backdrop of comparable provisions in the French constitutions between 1791 and 1799.[7] We may want to briefly recall the sequence of events here. In 1789 there was the Declaration of the Rights of Man and Citizen, which became the Preamble to the constitutions of 1791, 1793, and 1795 but was modified at each step. Only the post-Thermidorian constitution of 1795, which otherwise is far less radical than the Jacobin one of 1793, contains a ban on slavery. The constitution of 1799 no longer includes the Declaration of Rights and drops all references to free labor, let alone slavery and abolition, thereby clearing the way for the reintroduction of slavery in the French colonies in 1802.

The main influences on the Haitian text of 1801 are the constitution of 1791 and, especially, the Jacobin constitution of 1793. Unlike the French constitutions of 1791 and 1793, however, Toussaint's constitution does not contain a Bill of Rights. The issue of slavery is thus addressed not as part of a list of individual or social rights (as was the case in the French constitution of 1795) but as part of a title dealing with "inhabitants," that is, as an aspect of the political constitution of the colony. This is not just a minor detail in the vagaries of revolutionary constitutional history. Haiti, as a state founded to guarantee freedom from slavery and racial subordination, puts special pressure on the distinction between universal rights and contingent political arrangements. The changes in the Declaration of Rights between 1791 and 1795 show that far from offering indisputable guarantees, these lists of universal rights were very much open for debate. In the French constitution of 1793, Articles 21 and 22 of the Declaration of Rights had enshrined two rights that could be classified as "social": a right to assistance by the state and a right to education. According to Godechot's commentary, the provision that bans slavery in the French constitution of 1795 is the only social right that survived Thermidor.[8] Unsurprisingly, the 1799 constitution no longer contains any social rights.

From this perspective, it would seem only logical that the revolutionaries in Saint Domingue did not want to address the issue of slavery as part of a list of rights, which are more or less independent from each other and thus open to individual challenges. Indeed, it speaks to the radicalness of Toussaint's approach to the issue of slavery and racial equality that he chose to address it as part of the indispensable foundations of the geopolitical entity called Saint Domingue: Title I is "Of the Territory"; Title II, "Of the Inhabitants."

But we might go a step further and argue that once the elimination of racial subordination is at the center of the foundational agenda of the state, neither customary distinctions between "the social" and "the political" nor clear-cut distinctions between liberty and equality are persuasive.

From the perspective of contemporary political theory, Balibar has argued at some length that in fact there is no conflict at all between goals of liberty and goals of equality, and that liberal and libertarian political theory is simply wrong when it keeps producing this conflict as one of the crucial problems of the modern democratic state. Instead Balibar proposes that liberty and equality are mutually dependent on each other to a point where the distinction itself becomes doubtful, a thought he tries to capture with his coinage of "egaliberté."[9] Broadly speaking, I agree with his argument (even though I remain unconvinced by the proof he offers). However, I do think that the codependence of liberty and equality concerns is not just a structural invariant. Some issues put more pressure on the distinction than others: race is clearly one of them; gender, I would argue, is another. It is precisely because of the neglect in traditional political theory of issues of gender and race that the conflict between liberty and equality continues to command such respect. Clearly, in Saint Domingue, liberty (even in the restrictive sense of liberty from slavery) could only be guaranteed through racial equality: the heated controversies in the French Assembly of the 1790s over whether liberty should take precedence over equality or vice versa must have appeared disheartening in a situation where one could not exist without the other.

Another example for the subtle radicalization of the French texts in Saint Domingue is the ban of preferential treatment based on differences among people other than those of "virtues and talents." The phrase "virtues and talents" is found in the *Déclaration des Droits* of both the 1791 and 1793 French constitutions, but disappears with the Thermidorian Constitution. The constitution of 1799 goes so far as to revoke the rights of citizens for household employees:[10] if before Thermidor, no distinction among citizens was to be the basis for employment discrimination, now a distinction in employment becomes the basis for citizen rights. Obviously, Toussaint's constitution signifies a return to the more radical texts of the early 1790s.

If we did not read the clause about "virtues and talents" in the context of Toussaint's constitution, we might instead read it (as indeed it is often done) as touching on issues of class and somewhat anachronistically, "equal opportunity," and never realize that it is extremely pertinent to the question of slavery and free labor. But there is a subtle difference between the French texts and Toussaint's constitution which shows that the French were quite aware of the possible implications of this clause. Constitutions that do not contain a ban on slavery and indentured labor, and do not speak to the colonial question, but specify that the ban on employment discrimination applies only to citizens (Articles 1 and 5 in the 1791 and 1793 constitutions, respectively), in fact open a gap where slavery may be tolerated. Toussaint's constitution, by contrast, says: "All men, whatever their color, are here admissible to all employments."

While the French constitutions introduce a political limitation to the universal applicability of the clause—it applies only to French citizens—the Saint Domingue constitution gains a higher degree of universality by admitting territorial limitations. What emerges is a tendency we have already observed in previous chapters. We might say that a constitutional provision that is not a proclamation of a right and that is limited to "ce territoire" is more particularistic than a ringing Declaration of Rights. But to read it this way is not to see the underlying dialectic. It is through the unlinking of the rights of liberty from any question of citizenship that the universality lost in the first moment is restored in the moment that it applies to "all men." Although the 1801 constitution does not explicitly adopt the image of Saint Domingue as an "asylum," a "safe haven," or, as twentieth-century Spanish American resistance movements might have put it, a "liberated territory," the phrasing suggests precisely that. The provisions that guaranteed freedom from enslavement and racial discrimination in relation to employment thus prefigure the dialectic between universality and particularism we observed earlier in relation to the constitutions of Dessalines, Christophe, and Pétion and implicitly already open the territory as a safe haven for those who escape slavery and genocide.

Now, these provisions, which take off from an idea of liberty as liberty from slavery and end up radicalizing the idea of equality by unlinking it from (1) citizenship, thus making it available to all residents, and (2) color distinctions, are in stark contrast with later provisions which regulate the agricultural process in Saint Domingue.[11] Under Title VI, "About Cultivation and Commerce," one reads the following:

> Art. 14—The colony being essentially agricultural, it can not suffer the smallest disruption in the operation of its plantations.

Art. 15—Every plantation is a "manufacture" which requires the joining together of the planters and the workers; it is the tranquil home of an active and constant family, and the owner of the grounds or his representative is necessarily the father.

Art. 16—Every planter and worker is a member of the family and beneficiary of the revenues. Every change of domicile on the part of the planters brings about the ruin of the plantations.

In order to suppress a vice as disastrous for the colony as contrary to public order, the governor issues all police regulation that the circumstances make necessary and in accordance with the basis of the police regulation of the 20 Vendemiaire Year IX and the subsequent proclamation of 19 Pluviose by the General in Chief Toussaint Louverture.

A striking contradiction emerges between the provisions that guarantee individual liberty as freedom from slavery and equality as protection from racial discrimination, and the provisions that regulate agriculture. Indeed, we can already discern here what later came to be called *caporalisme agraire* (agrarian militarism). There can be no doubt that Toussaint Louverture was right to worry about the survival of the island and that measures were needed to get agricultural production back on track. After ten years of civil war, many of the white planters had fled the country or had been killed, and the former slaves had abandoned the plantations. With agriculture in shambles, the colony had no income and no source to feed the population. But the point here is not to assign blame or provide exculpatory explanations. It should be obvious that the problems the Haitian revolutionaries were facing were enormous and largely a result of ruthless colonial exploitation and abuse. The question I am trying to tackle is how these inherited problems translated into the foundations of a new state.

It is clear that authoritarian characteristics, which in Toussaint's constitution take on a paternalistic form, become increasingly prominent in later constitutions. Dessalines's 1805 constitution contains a statement to the effect that there could not be any color distinctions among the "members of the same family," whose father is the head of state, thus linking the claim of racial equality to a patriarchal image of state power. This is confirmed by the somewhat amusing provision that no one who is not "a good father, a good son, a good spouse, and especially a good soldier" (Article 9) is worthy of Haitian citizenship. What these texts suggest is an understanding of the state not as an abstract bureaucratic structure, in which positions could be filled by people of vastly different personal characteristics, but a structure built on the model of the patriarchal family, where the social hierarchy is entirely male and defined in terms of familial relatedness. Women remain excluded from consideration except as the implicit recipients of "good son" and "good spouse" behavior on the part of the men. If the Haitian constitutions operate as foundational fictions, the model is not, as in the nineteenth-century Spanish American novel, the heterosexual couple who stand at the beginning of a new family but rather the patriarchal clan which on the highest level coincides with the state itself.

In Dessalines's imperial Constitution of Haiti (1805), the paternalism of agricultural organization of Toussaint's constitution is replaced with a militaristic organization of the state. Under the heading "De l'Empire," Articles 15–18 provide the outline of the regional composition of the country in terms of military divisions. The section called "Du Gouvernement" establishes the Haitian Empire and Dessalines at its head:

> Art. 20—The People recognize as Emperor and Commander in Chief *Jacques Dessalines*, the avenger and liberator of his fellow citizens; he shall be addressed as Majesty; his august spouse, likewise, as Empress.
> Art. 21—The persons of Their Majesties are sacred and inviolable.

Subsequent articles specify that this is not a hereditary monarchy (Article 23), and that the emperor has the right to appoint his successor (Article 26). Articles 30 to 35 endow the emperor with vast authority: Article 30 gives him unrestricted legislative powers, Article 31 fiscal authority, and Articles 32 and 33 control over all issues concerning internal and external safety—in other words, over the police and the military. The only constraints on the emperor's powers are presented in Article 36, which, in keeping with the themes discussed in the previous chapters, specifies that the emperor will not engage in wars of conquest and will not disturb the internal peace in foreign colonies. The authoritarianism of Toussaint's and Dessalines's constitutions culminates in the constitution adopted by Henry Christophe in 1811, whose autocratic nature does not require further elucidation. Pétion's constitutions of 1806 and 1816 are less noteworthy in this respect, since they devise a fairly conventional republican state form on the French model that assigned sovereignty to the people, instituted separation of powers, and so on. The problem with Pétion was that he did not submit to the constraints of his own constitution and ruled outside of it for so many years that by 1816 he felt a *new* constitution was needed to restore legitimacy.[12]

Many more examples of the contradictions between the provisions guaranteeing liberty from slavery and those installing an authoritarian political regime could be listed, but the basic structure of the problem has, I think, become clear already. The tensions between provisions that radicalize the French revolutionary constitutions in their claims of liberty and equality and those that institute an authoritarian regime track a distinction Michel-Rolph Trouillot has proposed in *State against Nation*, a study that attempts to explain the origins of the Duvalierist regime. Trouillot presents us with what might be the most encompassing and theoretically sophisticated account of the complex relations in Haiti between political power, social formations, and divisions based on skin color. He argues that the political instability and rampant authoritarianism in Haitian history are due to the fact that "the Haitian state and the Haitian nation were launched in opposite directions."[13] Whereas the nation congealed around notions of liberty from slavery, the state in fact inherited the social and economic institutions from colonial times, which required a regimented labor force.

Although Trouillot's account aims specifically to produce an explanation of the totalitarianism of the Duvalier variety, the project leads him to produce a historical narrative of a much broader scope that addresses one of the most passionately debated issues in Haitian history: what is at the root of political and social conflict in Haiti, and, especially, what is the relationship between social and political splits along class lines and those that track skin color? The great merit of Trouillot's account is that it offers a structural explanation for a political scene that is, despite its small size, quite elusive and impenetrable (certainly for outsiders, but I suspect that the cliquishness of social and political life, and the partisan nature of most traditional scholarship, pose significant obstacles even to the insider). Trouillot neither reduces the color question to a mere epiphenomenon[14] nor takes the two competing epic narratives of national history, those of *noirisme* and of "mulatto historiography," at face value.[15] Rather, he offers an account that explains the various divisions and narratives as part of a deep fissure in the constitution of the Haitian state.

"State and nation were tied by the ideal of liberty, but the nation measured its liberty in Sunday markets and in the right to work on its gardenplots."[16] The leaders of the revolution and future heads of state, from Toussaint Louverture onward, however, felt it necessary to maintain the plantation system and the export-oriented economy. "The politicians and ideologues who emerged during the struggle were busy sketching the themes of a nationalist discourse while the emerging national community, pushed into the background, was beginning to shape a peasant world view of its own" (44–45). Given the former slaves' hatred of grueling work on the plantation, this continuation of the plantation regime could be achieved only through a paternalism that often deteriorated into extreme forms of authoritarianism. The Haitian state developed a form of agrarian militarism, while the former slaves wanted to have a plot of land to work on. Trouillot has offered a detailed analysis of the conflicts that resulted from this split between the nation and the state, a split that dovetailed with and magnified other splits such as that between *anciens libres* and *nouveaux libres,* mulattoes and blacks, or urban elites and rural masses. While Christophe's black monarchy in the North continued the system of caporalisme agraire instituted by Toussaint and Dessalines, the mulatto Pétion could not afford to alienate the mostly black masses through a forced-labor regime. To gain control of the state, he distributed land to the peasants. His plan succeeded: by the time he died, he was known by the nickname *Papa bon kè* (Father with a good heart), while Christophe committed suicide in the face of growing popular dissatisfaction with his agricultural policies. Still, all Haitian leaders since 1802 seemed to agree on two basic principles: first, that slavery was never to be allowed on Haitian soil; and second, that the large-scale export-oriented plantations be maintained and that land was to be distributed only for political advantage. Disagreement only emerged about who should control the remaining large estates and how the state could retain enough power to continue to impose the hated conditions of plantation work.

These considerations throw new light on the question why nineteenth-century Haitian literature appears strangely alien to the issues that emerge from nonliterary texts. Haitian literature clearly drew its inspiration from Europe, particularly France, where ever since the advent of romanticism, literature had become the venue for expressing the concerns of the nation. If the state was at the center of the classical and neoclassical tragedy—*Oedipus Rex* or *Prinz Friedrich von Homburg,* say—it somehow vanishes in the narrative literature that dominates the nineteenth century. To cast the desire for national consolidation as a desire for reconciliation between blacks and mulattoes, as does the first Haitian novel, *Stella,* thus turns out to be a highly ideological displacement whose main aim might well be to erase the evident conflict between the national imaginary, which centered around liberty, and the realities of a state, which had assumed distinctively authoritarian characteristics. Instead of articulating the yearning for a realization of the foundational dream of liberty, which Trouillot identifies as the heart of the national imaginary, *Stella* proposes that what is needed is racial reconciliation.

Unlike early literary texts such as *Stella*, then, those constitutions that did not simply adopt the French republican model are precise demarcations of the fissures that Haiti inherited from its colonial past and that could not be overcome by mere legal action. The tensions between the provisions that rearticulate a revolutionary conception of liberty and equality (a notion, incidentally, strangely absent from Trouillot's discussion) are neither the effect of a hasty constitutional process nor symptoms of what Marcelin called the "comic clash between dream and reality." Rather, they are indicators of a conflict that could perhaps not be solved at a time when slavery continued to be practiced everywhere else in the plantation zone and when the category of the nation operated as a de facto limit on universalist ideas of racial liberation. The political unconscious of radical antislavery was not the nation-state. We might say, expanding on the explanation Sidney Mintz offers for the difficulties that Haiti faced in the postrevolutionary period, that revolutionary antislavery in the Caribbean did not develop the kind of counterhegemony that would allow an elite to seize the state apparatus and establish itself in a hegemonic position the moment the colonial power withdrew. But while that is undoubtedly true, we also need to see that by virtue of being centrally concerned with racial slavery and racial subordination, the Haitian insurgents naturally developed a political vision in which the borders of the colonial territories had little significance. Yet freedom from slavery in Saint Domingue could be guaranteed only through independence. The transnational ideology that lay at the foundation of Haiti had to be disavowed even by those who owed their liberty from slavery to it.

# Conclusion

Haiti—in a sense the topic of this book—appears most concretely at its end, not the beginning. This reversal of customary procedure was a matter neither of choice nor of coincidence. At the core of the story of the Haitian Revolution and its impact is the fact of its suppression and denial. These acts of negation need to be accounted for specifically, in all concreteness and detail. Reductionism—whether of an economic-deterministic, epistemological, or psychoanalytic kind—will only further obscure the extent to which the disavowal of revolutionary antislavery became an ingredient in Creole nationalism and, eventually, in hegemonic conceptions of modernity. Yet simply to tell the story of the revolution, and then tell the story of its silencing, would also be to distort the historical landscape: to suggest that the facts are just there and that the silencing amounted to nothing more than some gaps in our historical narratives. Approaching Haiti through the records that have informed Western narratives—the records of Haiti's most immediate neighbors, Cuba and the Dominican Republic, but also the records in the European metropolises—allows for the kind of reflection on the operations of suppression and denial that purely structural or empiricist accounts would most likely preclude.

It is in light of the intellectual, political, and cultural efforts that were necessary to make the slave revolution of 1791 to 1804 vanish from respectable modernity that we can come to recognize what was really at stake. The conflicts that took place in the aftermath of the Haitian Revolution were partly conflicts over the shape and meaning of modernity, and about the kind of emancipation that modernity was supposed to bring about. This book thus also takes issue with the notion that modernity is an unfinished project that simply did not fully realize its emancipatory potential. As against that view, I argue that the modernity that took shape in the Western Hemisphere (in theoretical discourse as well as in cultural and social institutions) in the course of the nineteenth century contains, as a crucial element, the suppression of a struggle whose aim was to give racial equality and racial liberation the same weight as those political goals that came to dominate nineteenth-century politics and thought—most particularly, those relating to the nation and national sovereignty. Unless we submit the concept of modernity to a radical critique, our emancipatory goals and strategies will continue to reproduce the biases that came to shape modern thought in the Age of Revolution.

As the Haitian postrevolutionary constitutions show, any attempt to account for the social and political goals of radical antislavery—its claims of racial equality as well as its transnational and transimperial character—requires a thoroughgoing revision of the existing traditions of political and constitutional thought. The politics and ideology of radical antislavery ultimately ran up against the strictures imposed by the colonial world order; they were not to set the agenda. In the end, it is only through critical readings of the records, both canonical and marginal, that we can come to develop an understanding of the effects of disavowal on the concept of modernity that came to be dominant, and of a future that might have been different. It is in the accidental fragments that form the material of this book—in the trial records, in popular poetry, in the missing links of literary histories, as well as in the contradictions in historical and philosophical argument—that we can see how the disavowal of radical antislavery became constitutive for emerging national cultures in the Caribbean and metropolitan political discourse, while Haiti came to be considered the primitive backwater of Western civilization.

# Appendix A

## IMPERIAL CONSTITUTION OF HAITI, 1805

In the Imperial Palace of Dessalines, May 20, Year II:

We, H. Christophe, Clervaux, Vernet, Gabart, Pétion, Geffrard, Toussaint-Brave, Raphaël, Lalondrie, Romain, Capois, Magny, Cangé, Daut, Magloire Ambroise, Yayou, Jean-Louis François, Gérin, Férou, Bazelais, Martial Besse,

Acting in our own name and in that of the people of Haiti, who have constituted us legally as faithful organs and interpreters of their will,

In the presence of the Supreme Being, before whom all mortals are equal, and who has scattered so many species of beings over the surface of the earth, with the sole goal of manifesting his glory and his might through the diversity of his works;

Before the whole creation, whose disowned children we have so unjustly and for so long been considered:

We declare that the terms of the present Constitution are the free, spontaneous, and determined expression of our hearts and of the general will of our fellow citizens;

We submit it to the approval of His Majesty the Emperor Jacques Dessalines, our liberator, to receive its quick and complete implementation.

### PREFATORY DECLARATION

Article 1. The people who live on the island formerly called Saint Domingue agree to constitute themselves in a free and sovereign State that is independent from all other powers of the universe, under the name "Empire of Haiti."

Article 2. Slavery is abolished forever.

Article 3. The Haitian citizens are brothers to each other; equality in the eye of the Law is indisputably recognized; there cannot be any titles, advantages, and privileges other than those necessarily resulting from the regard and compensation for services rendered for liberty and independence.

Article 4. The law is the same for all, whether it punishes or protects.

Article 5. The law does not have retroactive effect.

Article 6. Property is sacred; any violation thereof will be rigorously prosecuted.

Article 7. Haitian citizenship is lost through emigration and naturalization in another country, as well as through afflictive and defamatory punishments. The former case brings with it the penalty of death and the confiscation of property.

Article 8. Citizenship is suspended as a result of insolvency and bankruptcy.

Article 9. Nobody deserves to be Haitian who is not a good father, a good son, a good husband, and, above all, a good soldier.

Article 10. Fathers and mothers cannot disinherit their children.

Article 11. Every citizen must have a trade.

Article 12. No white person, of whatever nationality, shall set foot on this territory with the title of master or proprietor nor, in the future, acquire property here.

Article 13. The preceding article shall not have any effect on white women who have been naturalized by the government, nor on their present or future children. Included in the present article are the Germans and Poles who have been naturalized by the Government.

Article 14. All distinctions of color will by necessity disappear among the children of one and the same family where the Head of State is the father; Haitians shall be known from now on by the generic denomination of blacks.

### OF THE EMPIRE

Article 15. The Empire of Haiti is one and indivisible; its territory is composed of six military divisions.

Article 16. Each military division shall be ruled by a divisional general.

Article 17. Each of these divisional generals shall be independent of the others and shall respond directly to the Emperor or the General in Chief designated by His Majesty.

Article 18. The following islands are integral parts of the Empire: Samana, La Tortue, La Gonâve, Les Cayemites, Ile-à-Vâche, Saôna, and the other adjacent islands.

### OF THE GOVERNMENT

Article 19. The Government of Haiti is entrusted to a first magistrate, who takes the title of Emperor and Commander in Chief of the armed forces.

Article 20. The people recognize as Emperor and Commander in Chief of the armed forces *Jacques Dessalines,* the avenger and liberator of his fellow citizens; he shall be addressed as Majesty, as shall be the Empress, his august spouse.

Article 21. The persons of Their Majesties are sacred and inviolable.

Article 22. The State assigns a fixed stipend to her Majesty the Empress, which she shall continue to receive, under the title of Princess Widow, after the death of the Emperor.

Article 23. The crown is elective and non-hereditary.

Article 24. The State assigns an annual stipend to the children recognized by His Majesty the Emperor.

Article 25. The sons recognized by the Emperor shall, like all other citizens, pass progressively through the military grades, the only difference being that their entry in the military service in the fourth semi-brigade shall be dated from the moment of their births.

Article 26. The Emperor designates his successor, and in the manner he sees most appropriate, either before his death or after.

Article 27. The State assigns an appropriate stipend to this successor, from the moment of his ascension to the throne.

Article 28. Neither the Emperor nor his successors shall have the right, under any circumstances or any pretexts, to surround himself with a special and privileged guard, whether under the name of guard of honor or any other title.

Article 29. Any successor who deviates from the dispositions of the previous article, from the path that shall have been indicated to him by the reigning Emperor, or from the principles enshrined in the present Constitution, shall be considered to be in a state of war against society, and declared to be such.

In that case, the councillors of State shall convene to declare his removal from office and to provide a replacement for him by that person among them whom they find most worthy; and in the case that the said successor resists the execution of this legal measure, the generals who are the councillors of State shall appeal to the people and the armed forces, who shall then give them their help and assistance in order to maintain liberty.

Article 30. The Emperor makes, seals, and promulgates the laws; he names and removes, at his will, the ministers, the general in chief of the armed forces, the councillors of State, the generals, and other agents of the Empire, the officers of the land and sea forces, the members of the local administrations, the governmental commissioners at the courts, the judges, and other public functionaries.

Article 31. The Emperor controls the income and expenses of the State and supervises the manufacture of currency; only he can order the distribution of money, and decide its weight and type.

Article 32. He has the exclusive right to make peace and declare war and to maintain political and contractual relations.

Article 33. He provides for internal security and the defense of the State and distributes the land and sea forces according to his will.

Article 34. In the case of a conspiracy against the security of the State, the Constitution, or his person, the Emperor shall have its authors or accomplices immediately detained; they shall be tried by a special council.

Article 35. His Majesty has the exclusive right to absolve a convict or to commute a sentence.

Article 36. The Emperor shall never embark on any enterprise that has the aim of making conquests or disturbing the peace and the internal regime of foreign colonies.

Article 37. Every public proclamation will be made in these terms: "The Emperor of Haiti and Commander in Chief of the armed forces, by the grace of God and the constitutional law of the State."

## OF THE COUNCIL OF STATE

Article 38. The divisional generals and the brigade generals are born members of the Council of State and compose it.

## OF THE MINISTERS

Article 39. The Empire shall have two ministers and one secretary of State:

The minister of finance shall be in charge of the department of the interior;

The minister of war shall be in charge of the department of the navy.

## OF THE MINISTER OF FINANCE AND OF THE INTERIOR

Article 40. The responsibilities of this minister include the general administration of the public Treasury; the organization of the local administrations; the distribution of the funds made available to the minister of war and other functionaries; public expenses; regulations that govern the book-keeping procedures and the paymasters of the divisional administrations; agriculture; commerce; public education; weights and measures; the gathering of public census data; territorial products; public lands—be it for their conservation or their sale; rural leaseholds; prisons; hospitals; road maintenance; ferries; saltworks; manufactures; customs; and finally the supervision and the manufacture of currency; and the implementation of laws and governmental decrees regarding the above subjects.

## OF THE MINISTER OF WAR AND OF THE NAVY

Article 41. The functions of this minister include the conscription, organization, inspection, supervision, discipline, policing, and movement of the land and sea forces; the personnel and matériel of the artillery and the corps of engineers; fortifications; fortresses; gunpowder and salpeters; the recording of the proclamations and decrees of the Emperor; their communication to the armed forces and the supervision of their implementation; he watches particularly that the decisions of the Emperor reach the military personnel promptly; he gives notice to the special councils of any military offenses that have come to his attention and supervises the commissioners of war and the officials of public health.

Article 42. The ministers are responsible for all offenses committed by them against public safety and the Constitution, for all assaults on property and individual liberty, for all waste of the funds entrusted to them; every three months they must present the following to the Emperor: a summary of projected expenditures, an account of the employment of the sums that were put at their disposal, and an account of the abuses that might have happened in the various branches of their administration.

Article 43. No minister can be criminally prosecuted in office or out of office, on the grounds of an administrative act, without the personal authorization of the Emperor.

## OF THE SECRETARY OF STATE

Article 44. The secretary of State is responsible for the printing, the registering, and the distribution of the laws, decrees, proclamations, and instructions of the Emperor; he works directly with the Emperor in matters of foreign relations; corresponds with the ministers, receives their requests, petitions, and other demands, which he shall submit to the Emperor; likewise, the matters the courts refer to him; he remits to the ministers the decisions and matters about which the Emperor has decreed.

## OF THE COURTS

Article 45. Nobody may infringe the right of the citizens to resolve disputes through private arbitration by arbiters of their own choice. Their decisions shall be legally recognized.

Article 46. There shall be a justice of the peace in every municipality; he cannot hear cases regarding more than one hundred Gourdes; when the parties cannot reconcile themselves in his court, they shall appeal to the courts with jurisdiction in their case.

Article 47. There shall be six courts with seats in the following cities: Saint Marc, Le Cap, Port-au-Prince, Les Cayes, L'Anse-là-Veau, and Port-au-Paix.

The Emperor determines their organization, the number of judges, their areas of competence, and territory of jurisdiction.

The courts hear all purely civilian cases.

Article 48. Military offenses are submitted to special councils and particular judicial procedures. The organization of these councils is determined by the Emperor, who shall decide appeals of judgments passed by the said special councils.

Article 49. Special laws shall be written for the notariate and with respect to the functionaries of the civil registry.

## OF WORSHIP

Article 50. The law does not recognize a dominant religion.

Article 51. Liberty of worship is tolerated.

Article 52. The State does not provide for the maintenance of any form of worship or any minister.

Article 53. In every military division, there shall be a principal administration, whose organization and supervision is essentially under the purview of the minister of finance.

## GENERAL DISPOSITIONS

Article 1. The Emperor and the Empress determine the choice, the stipend, and the upkeep of the persons who constitute their court.

Article 2. After the death of the reigning Emperor, when it might be considered necessary to revise the Constitution, the council of State will convene for this purpose, presided over by the most senior member of the council.

Article 3. Crimes of high treason and offenses committed by the ministers and the generals shall be tried by a special council which is appointed and presided over by the Emperor.

Article 4. The armed forces are by their nature obedient; no armed unit may deliberate.

Article 5. Nobody shall be tried without having had a legal hearing.

Article 6. The house of every citizen is an inviolable sanctuary.

Article 7. It can be entered in the case of a fire, a flood, in the case of a plea issuing from the inside, or in virtue of an order by the Emperor or any other legally constituted authority.

Article 8. He who kills another person deserves to be killed.

Article 9. All sentences that entail the penalty of death or afflictive punishment can be implemented only if confirmed by the Emperor.

Article 10. Theft is punished according to the circumstances that preceded it, accompanied it, and followed it.

Article 11. All foreigners who live in the territory of Haiti shall be bound by the country's laws of correction and punishment in the same way as Haitians.

Article 12. All property that formerly belonged to a white Frenchman is incontestably and by law confiscated for the benefit of the State.

Article 13. All Haitians who have acquired the property of a white Frenchman and who have so far paid only part of the price stipulated in the contract of sale shall be responsible to pay the remainder of the sum to the State.

Article 14. Marriage is a purely civil act and is authorized by the government.

Article 15. The law authorizes divorce in certain recognized and determined cases.

Article 16. A special law shall be issued regarding children born outside marriage.

Article 17. Respect of the superiors, subordination, and discipline are strictly necessary.

Article 18. A penal code shall be issued and strictly observed.

Article 19. In every military division a public school shall be established for the instruction of the youth.

Article 20. The national colors are black and red.

Article 21. Agriculture shall be honored and protected as the first, the most noble, and the most useful among the trades.

Article 22. Commerce, the second source of prosperity of States, neither needs nor admits fetters.

Article 23. In every military division, a commercial court shall be created, whose members shall be chosen by the Emperor from among the class of the merchants.

Article 24. In commercial interactions, honesty and good faith shall be scrupulously observed.

Article 25. The government guarantees the safety and protection of neutral and friendly nations who maintain with this island commercial relations, under the condition that they adjust to the regulations, practices, and customs of this country.

Article 26. The businesses and merchandise of foreigners shall be under the protection and guarantee of the State.

Article 27. There shall be national holidays to celebrate Independence, the Saint's Day of the Emperor and his august spouse, Agriculture, and the Constitution.

Article 28. At the first cannon-shot of alarm, the cities are evacuated and the nation rises up.

We, the representatives signed below, place the clear and solemn pact of the sacred rights of man and the duties of the citizen under the protection of the magistrates, the fathers and mothers of families, the citizens, and the armed forces;

We commend it to our descendants and render homage to the friends of liberty, to the philanthropists of all countries, as a sign of proof of the divine goodness, which through its immortal decrees has provided us with the opportunity to break our chains and to constitute ourselves as a free, civilized and independent people.

Signed as much in our own names as in that of our constituents:

*Signed:* H. Christophe, Clervaux, Vernet, Gabart, Pétion, Geffrard, Toussaint-Brave, Raphaël, Lalondrie, Romain, Capoix, Magny, Cangé, Daut, Magloire Ambroise, Yayou, Jean-Louis François, Gérin, Moreau [missing in opening], Férou, Bazelais, Martial Besse.

Note: This translation follows as closely as possible the text of Janvier, *Les Constitutions d'Haïti.*

# Appendix B

## CHRONOLOGY

| | |
|---|---|
| 1758 | Execution of François Mackendal |
| 1776 | Declaration of Independence of the United States of America |
| 1787 | Constitution of the United States of America |
| | Foundation of the Society for Effecting the Abolition of the Slave Trade, an unofficial extension of the Quaker slave trade committee, in England |
| 1788 | The Société des Amis des Noirs is formed in France |
| 1789 | Fall of the Bastille, July 14; Declaration of the Rights of Man and Citizen, August 26 (France) |
| 1791 | French Assembly extends political rights to freeborn men of color |
| | Insurrections in the Northern province of Saint Domingue, Cap Français burnt to the ground |
| 1792 | Fall of the French monarchy; proclamation of the Republic, Aug. 22 |
| 1792–93 | France at war with Austria, Prussia, Britain, Holland and Spain |
| 1793 | Saint Domingue rebels join Spanish side; Sonthonax publishes general emancipation decree in the North, August 29 (Saint Domingue) |
| | Girondin purge, trial and execution of Brissot (France) |
| 1794 | French Assembly passes law banning slavery, February 4; Toussaint switches sides from Spanish to French; execution of Robespierre, Saint Just, and fellow Jacobins, July 28 |
| 1795 | Treaty of Basle: Spain cedes Santo Domingo to France |
| | Thermidorian Constitution, Aug. 22; National Assembly dissolved; Directory established (France) |
| | Major slave rebellions in Venezuela, Cuba, Puerto Rico, Curaçao, Demerara; conspiracies in Santo Domingo, Trinidad, Louisiana, Bahamas |
| 1797 | Toussaint Louverture appointed governor-general, May 2 |
| 1799 | Civil war between Toussaint Louverture and Rigaud; Bonaparte overthrows Directory (France) |

| | |
|---|---|
| 1801 | Louverture proclaims new constitution and occupies Spanish Santo Domingo |
| 1802 | Bonaparte approves decree reestablishing slavery and the slave trade; Leclerc, leader of the French expeditionary force to retake Saint Domingue, enters Le Cap; Louverture surrenders, May 6; Louverture deported to France, June 7 |
| 1803 | Louverture dies at Fort de Joux, April 7 |
| | Slavery and color lines formally restored in the French colonies |
| 1804 | Dessalines declares Independence of Saint Domingue under the name of Haiti, January 1; massacre of the remaining white colonists; Dessalines crowned emperor of Haiti, October 8 |
| 1805 | Proclamation of first Haitian constitution, May 20 |
| 1806 | Dessalines assassinated, October 17; new Republican Constitution |
| 1807 | Henri Christophe proclaimed president of Haiti, February 17; issues his own constitution and establishes a capital in the North; Alexandre Pétion elected president of the republic of Haiti, with the capital in Port-au-Prince, March 11; Haiti is divided into two states, British Parliament abolishes the slave trade |
| 1808–26 | Spanish American revolutions |
| 1809 | Santo Domingo returns to Spanish rule |
| 1810 | Rigaud returns to Haiti and establishes an independent republic in the south; he dies within months and the southern republic rejoins Pétion's republic |
| 1811 | Henri Christophe transforms the North into a Kingdom and is crowned Henri I, June 2 |
| 1811–12 | Major slave rebellions and conspiracies in Louisiana, Martinique, Puerto Rico, Santo Domingo, including the Aponte Conspiracy of 1812 in Cuba |
| 1812–14 | Constitution of Cádiz (Spain); first constitutional period in Cuba |
| 1816 | Pétion declares himself president for life |
| | Simón Bolívar in Haiti |
| 1818 | Pétion dies and is succeeded by Jean-Pierre Boyer |
| 1819 | Congress of Angostura effectively rejects all measures of immediate slave emancipation |
| 1820 | Christophe commits suicide; Haiti is reunited |
| 1821 | "Ephemeral Independence" of Spanish Santo Domingo under leadership of Núñez de Cáceres, December 1 |
| 1822 | Boyer enters Spanish Santo Domingo, February 9; beginning of Haitian occupation of the former Spanish colony |
| | Denmarck Vesey's conspiracy in Charleston, South Carolina |
| 1826 | Boyer issues "Code Rural" |
| 1831 | Nat Turner's slave revolt in Virginia |
| 1833 | Emancipation Act passed by British parliament |

| 1836 | Slavery declared illegal in France |
| 1843 | Boyer resigns, March 13 |
| 1844 | Santo Domingo declares independence from Haiti |
| | Escalera Conspiracy in Cuba; Plácido executed |
| 1847 | General Faustin Soulouque president (Haiti) |
| 1848 | Slavery abolished in French and Danish Antilles |
| 1849 | President Soulouque declared Emperor Faustin I |
| 1861 | Santo Domingo becomes province of Spain |
| 1862 | Slave emancipation in the US; diplomatic recognition of Haiti by the United States |
| 1863 | Holland abolishes slavery |
| 1864 | Dominican Independence from Spain |
| 1865 | Thirteenth Amendment to the U.S. Constitution bans slavery |
| 1868–78 | Ten Year War in Cuba for independence from Spain (unsuccessful) |
| 1873 | Puerto Rico abolishes slavery |
| | Last known slave ship lands in Cuba |
| 1886 | Cuba is the last Caribbean territory to abolish slavery |
| 1895–98 | Cuba's second war of independence |
| 1899 | Treaty of Paris: Cuba ceded to the United States |
| 1902 | Cuban independence under Platt Amendment |
| 1915–34 | U.S. occupation of Haiti |
| 1916–24 | U.S. occupation of Dominican Republic |
| 1937 | Massacre of Haitian migrant workers in Dominican Republic under Trujillo |

Note: See also Joan Dayan, *Haiti, History, and the Gods* (Berkeley: University of Cailifornia Press, 1995), which includes a chronology of Haitian history and U.S.-Haitian relations; David Brion Davis, *The Problem of Slavery in the Age of Revolution 1770–1823* (New York: Oxford University Press, 1999), which includes a chronology of the history of abolitionism for the period 1770–1823; David P. Geggus, "Slavery, War, and Revolution in the Greater Caribbean," in *A Turbulent Time: The French Revolution and the Greater Caribbean*, ed. David B. Gaspar and David P. Geggus (Bloomington: Indiana University Press, 1997), which includes a chronology of slave rebellions and conspiracies; and Franklin W. Knight, *The Caribbean: The Genesis of a Fragmented Nationalism* (New York: Oxford University Press, 1978), which includes a general chronology of Caribbean history from Columbus to the 1980s, with a special focus on independence and antislavery movements.

# Notes

All translations are my own unless otherwise indicated.

INTRODUCTION

1   I borrow the period designation from E. J. Hobsbawm, *The Age of Revolution* (New York: Mentor, 1962), who offers 1791 to 1848 as beginning and end dates. There has been a great deal of discussion and disagreement among historians about Hobsbawm's approach to periodization, and about what characteristics need to be considered central for the time period in question. Most of this discussion focuses on Europe, and the issue of slavery is rarely, if ever, at the center of the debate. One of the purposes of this book is to explore the possibility of considering radical antislavery and its attendant cultures as part of the revolutionary environment. For an excellent survey of the revolutionary period in the Caribbean, with a stress on the impact of abolitionism and the French and Haitian Revolutions on the patterns of resistance, economic growth, and migration, see David P. Geggus, "Slavery, War, and Revolution in the Greater Caribbean, 1789–1815," in *A Turbulent Time: The French Revolution and the Greater Caribbean*, ed. David B. Gaspar and David P. Geggus (Bloomington and Indianapolis: University of Indiana Press, 1997), 1–50, which also includes generous bibliographical documentation and brief reviews of the scholarly literature. Studies coming out of Latin America tend to adopt a national rather than comparative or synoptic focus. For panoramic accounts of the revolutionary age in Spanish America, see François-Xavier Guerra, *Modernidad e Independencias* (México, D.F.: Fondo de Cultura Económica, 1993); John Lynch, *The Spanish American Revolutions, 1808–1826* (London: Weidenfeld and Nicolson, 1973); and Jaime E. Rodríguez O., *The Independence of Spanish America* (Cambridge: Cambridge University Press, 1998). Guerra points out that the attitudes toward France found within revolutionary antislavery differed significantly from those in Spanish American independence movements. While the latter were minoritarian elite movements that turned anti-French after the execution of the French king, revolutionary antislavery—for example, the uprisings in Coro, 1795; Maracaibo, 1799; and Salvador (Brazil), 1798—embraced as its slogan "libertad de los

franceses" [the liberty of the French]. For an analysis of the production of a discourse of Creole hegemony in Venezuela, especially in newspapers, see Alicia Rios, "La guerra y la prensa: Aparatos de captura del estado republicano (Venezuela, 1818–1822)," *Estudios* 6 (1998): 107–18. For a different panoramic account of the revolutionary age in the Americas and a comparative discussion of the revolutions that led to the independence of the United States, Haiti, and the Spanish American countries, see Lester D. Langley, *The Americas in the Age of Revolution, 1750–1850* (New Haven: Yale University Press, 1996), which suggests a typology of sorts to explain the different character of these revolutions. See also the work of Manfred Kossok, a historian in the former German Democratic Republic who along with a number of collaborators published numerous studies in comparative revolutionary history—a topic that was of considerable prestige in the G.D.R. and generated a wealth of scholarship which remains untranslated and is rarely taken into account in the academic debates in the "former West." See, for example, Kossok, ed., *Studien zur vergleichenden Revolutionsgeschichte, 1500–1917* (Berlin: Akademie-Verlag, 1974). For a brief sketch of Kossok's comparative approach, see his "Alternativen gesellschaftlicher Transformation in Lateinamerika: Die Unabhängigkeitsrevolutionen von 1790 bis 1830. Eine Problemskizze," *Jahrbuch für Geschichte von Staat, Wirtschaft und Gesellschaft Lateinamerikas* 28 (1991): 223–50.

2   The institution of slavery was of course not an invention of the New World colonies, and various forms of unfree labor continue to exist to this day. "Abolition" must not be mistaken as a happy end. It is clear that coercion, even extreme forms thereof, did not end when someone ceased to be a "slave." However, most scholars would agree that racial slavery in the plantation zone, despite significant regional and cultural variations, had certain common characteristics that distinguished it from slavery in the Ancient World, for instance, or from the coercive work situations of undocumented workers in contemporary Europe or United States. More contentious is the question of what lies at the heart of the practice of slavery: is it an issue of power—an issue to be understood in terms of violence, domination, and subordination—or is it, on the contrary, an issue of exploitation? In his classic *Slavery and Social Death: A Comparative Study* (Cambridge: Harvard University Press, 1982), Orlando Patterson, for instance, defines slavery broadly as "the permanent, violent domination of natally alienated and generally dishonored persons" (13). Similarly, David Brion Davis argues that the "main problem of slavery" is "a problem of dominance and submission" and that the complex relationship between antislavery and a free-labor ideology is related but perhaps not essential to the practice of slavery; see *The Problem of Slavery in the Age of Revolution, 1770–1823* (New York: Oxford University Press, 1999), 12–13. Clearly, this is directed against others, who by making exploitation the central feature assimilate slavery

to other labor arrangements in which the workers are prevented from enjoying the fruits of their labor and the surplus is appropriated by others.

These issues are complex and much beyond the purview of this book, which is mostly concerned with the ways in which the idea of racial equality was articulated, suppressed, and disavowed in cultural practices and attendant political discourses in the Age of Revolution. It should be noted, however, that both the "slavery as domination" hypothesis and the "slavery as exploitation" hypothesis assign only secondary importance to the issue of race, and that thinking through them about the topic at hand might lead us yet again to deny or disavow a significant part of the heritage of modernity.

3   If we find it difficult today to imagine such a historical moment, this is due, I suspect, to the influence of Marxist thinking—not a small irony, of course. In any event, the claim that requires further evidence is that this revolutionary expectation extended to include slavery and antislavery— in other words, that radical or revolutionary antislavery (as opposed to the "moderate" gradualism of mainstream abolitionism) has a rightful place on our maps of the Age of Revolution.

4   One of the most gripping and analytical accounts of the Haitian Revolution is, to this day, C. L. R. James's *The Black Jacobins* (1938; New York: Vintage, 1989). Even if some specific claims need to be revised in light of more recent research, the book is by no means obsolete. For an excellent, if no longer completely up-to-date, overview with extensive bibliographic references, see David P. Geggus, "The French and Haitian Revolutions, and Resistance to Slavery in the Americas: An Overview," in *La révolution française et les colonies,* ed. Jean Tarrade (Paris: Société française d'histoire d'outre-mer, 1989), 107–124. For a critical review of the various tendencies within the historiography of the Haitian Revolution (inside and outside Haiti), see Michel-Rolph Trouillot, *Silencing the Past: Power and the Production of History* (Boston: Beacon Press, 1995), 70–107. For a less critical but informative survey of Haitian historiography, see Catts Pressoir, Ernst Trouillot, and Hénock Trouillot, eds., *Historiographie d'Haïti* (Mexico City: Fournier, 1953). For Haiti's history from the revolution to the Duvalier regime, see David Nicholls, *From Dessalines to Duvalier: Race, Colour, and National Independence in Haiti* (New Brunswick: Rutgers University Press, 1996). For a more analytic account of the impact of the revolution on the Haitian state, see Michel-Rolph Trouillot, *Haiti: State against Nation. The Origins and Legacy of Duvalierism* (New York: Monthly Review Press, 1990). See David P. Geggus, "Haiti and the Abolitionists: Opinion, Propaganda, and International Politics in Britain and France, 1804–1838," in *Abolition and Its Aftermath: The Historical Context, 1790–1916,* ed. David Richardson (London: Frank Cass, 1985), 113–140, for a succinct account of the changing views of Haiti in the European and American metropolises.

Some of the specific issues in the literature on slave resistance and the Haitian Revolution will be discussed later.

5 For an exemplary study of the historical significance of collective affective states, particularly fear, see Georges Lefevre's well-known *The Great Fear of 1789: Rural Panic in Revolutionary France*, trans. Joan White (1932; New York: Random House, 1973).

6 For a fascinating account of the Atlantic from the sixteenth century to the early nineteenth, see Peter Linebaugh and Marcus Rediker, *The Many-Headed Hydra: Sailors, Slaves, Commoners, and the Hidden History of the Revolutionary Atlantic* (Boston: Beacon Press, 2000). Linebaugh and Rediker recover the anonymous masses of sailors, slaves, and others as revolutionary actors as well as many lesser-known political figures, such as Robert Wedderburn, a Jamaican whom they describe as "an intellectual organic to the Atlantic proletariat" and quote as warning Jamaica's rulers: "Prepare for flight, ye planters, for the fate of St. Domingo awaits you" (289, 320). For a highly imaginative account of the Caribbean at the time of the French Revolution, and particularly the transnational venues of communication in relation to slave resistance, see Julius Scott III, "The Common Wind: Currents of Afro-American Communication in the Era of the Haitian Revolution" (Ph.D. diss., Duke University, 1986). See Michel Hector, ed., *La révolution française et Haïti*, 2 vols. (Port-au-Prince: Société Haïtienne d'Histoire et de Géographie/Editions Henri Deschamps, 1995), for an excellent collection of brief historical essays by a great number of the important scholars in the field. Hector's collection, based on a conference held in Haiti on the occasion of the bicentennial of the French Revolution, is one of the very few volumes that transcend the usual geographic boundaries of scholarship and include researchers from the Caribbean, Latin America, Europe, and the United States. For an exceptionally interesting fictional account, see Alejo Carpentier, *El siglo de las luces*, trans. John Sturrock as *Explosion in a Cathedral* (Boston: Little, Brown, 1963). For the transnationalism of radical antislavery and the Haitian Revolution, see Geggus, "Haiti and the Abolitionists." Geggus points out that most European abolitionists thought that slaves needed a lengthy time of preparation before they would be ready for freedom, and that abolitionism was one of the fronts on which national rivalries between England and France were carried out. For an account of the relations between Haiti and the Spanish American revolutionaries, particularly Simón Bolívar, see Paul Verna's numerous studies, among them "Bolívar 'el haitiano': Revolucionario integral y libertador social," *Rev. Nacional de Cultura* 44 (1983): 145–59, and "La revolución haitiana y sus manifestaciones socio-jurídicas en el Caribe y Venezuela," *Boletín de la Academia Nacional de la Historia* (Venezuela) 67 (1984): 741–52.

7 In the late eighteenth century and the early nineteenth, neither Spain nor Portugal had a local abolitionist movement. In England, antislavery

activism started as early as the 1760s, with Sharp as one of the crucial figures. In 1772 there was a landmark court decision that there would be no slaves in England. In 1787 Sharp, Clarkson, and others formed an opposition group against slavery, later called Society for the Abolition of the Slave Trade. Although the long-term goal was abolition of slavery, the group focused first on abolition of the trade. After twenty years of massive popular agitation, led by Sharp and Clarkson, with Wilberforce leading the struggle in Parliament, the trade was abolished in 1807. However, it took another twenty-five years before slavery was abolished in the colonies.

In France, the Société des Amis des Noirs was founded in 1788. The organization was mostly the work of Brissot, who acted with Clarkson's encouragement and advice. The membership included Lafayette and Condorcet. The society decided to follow the British model, that is, aim at the abolition of trade first, then for the abolition of slavery itself. Unlike its British predecessor, the Amis des Noirs had only limited popular success. Once the revolution in France had started, it appears that people's interest turned to other matters, and only the Abbé Grégoire, Brissot, and a few others remained interested in the slavery issue. For an account of the ideology of the Amis des Noirs, see Robin Blackburn, *The Overthrow of Colonial Slavery* (New York: Verso, 1988), 169–73.

8   Blackburn, *The Overthrow of Colonial Slavery*, 548.

9   See Bruce Dairn, "Haiti and Egypt in Early Black Racial Discourse in the United States," *Slavery and Abolition* 14 (1993): 139–61; and Hollis R. Lynch, "Pan-Negro Nationalism in the New World, before 1862," in *Black Brotherhood: Afro-Americans and Africa*, ed. Okon Edet Uya (Lexington, Mass.: Heath, 1971), 41–62.

10  One of the most explicit statements in France about the possibility of a slave revolution is a utopian novel published in 1771 but set in the year 2440: "Nature has at last created this stunning man, this immortal man, who must deliver a world from the most atrocious, the longest, the most insulting tyranny. He has shattered the irons of his compatriots. So many oppressed slaves under the most odious slavery seemed to wait only for his signal to make such a hero. This heroic avenger has set an example that sooner or later cruelty will be punished, and that Providence holds in store these strong souls, which she releases upon earth to reestablish the equilibrium which the inequity of ferocious ambition knew how to destroy" (Louis-Sébastien Mercier, *L'an 2440*, quoted in Trouillot, *Silencing the Past*, 84 n. 21). In the author's imagination, a revolution that is barely twenty years away takes 669 years to occur. Trouillot quotes this novel in support of his claim that slave revolution was "unthinkable" at the time. I would argue that on the contrary, it shows that the idea of a slave revolution was perfectly available but expressed itself, for many different reasons, largely in utopias, fears, and

fantasies. For further discussion of the notion of the unthinkable in relation to the Haitian Revolution, see my "Unthinkable History? Some Reflections on the Haitian Revolution, Historiography, and Modernity on the Periphery," in *The Blackwell Companion to African American Studies,* vol. 2, ed. Lewis Gordon and Jane Gordon (Malden, Mass.: Blackwell, forthcoming).

11  There is considerable disagreement among historians about the role of the Haitian Revolution in the history of slave uprisings in the Caribbean. Geggus in particular has argued that the claims of Genovese, Yacou, and others who insist on a crucial role for the Haitian Revolution have been exaggerated, and that beyond the Aponte uprising in Cuba (1812) and a few others, it is difficult to document direct influence (e.g., "Slavery, War, and Revolution," 12). Even if Geggus is right (and his documentation usually seems impeccable), it is my contention that a very narrow notion of influence may unwittingly prevent us from recognizing the ideological and symbolic impact of the Haitian Revolution and thus make it impossible to recognize the cultural formation (which would include slaves and slave owners) in which knowledge of Haiti was taken for granted, and which we *know* existed.

12  Paris newspapers barely mentioned the death of Toussaint Louverture, and London papers only briefly alluded to it. The most extensive account was given in the London *Times* of April 27, 1803: "Toussaint L'Ouverture is dead. He died, according to letters from Besançon, in prison, a few days ago. The fate of this man has been singularly unfortunate, and his treatment most cruel. He died, we believe, without a friend to close his eyes. We never heard that his wife and children, though they were brought over from St. Domingo with him, have ever been permitted to see him during his imprisonment" (quoted in Marcus Rainsford, *An Historical Account of the Black Empire of Haiti: Comprehending a View of the Principle Transactions in the Revolution of Saint Domingo; with Its Ancient and Modern State* [London: James Cundee, 1805], 324).

13  José Luciano Franco, *Documentos para la historia de Haití en el Archivo Nacional* (Havana: Publicaciones del Archivo Nacional de Cuba, 1954), 70.

14  Franco, *Documentos para la historia de Haití,* 68.

15  See, e.g., Arthur L. Stinchcombe, "Class Conflict and Diplomacy: Haitian Isolation in the 19th-century World System," *Sociological Perspectives* 37 (1994): 1–23.

16  Jean Price-Mars, *La República de Haití y la República Dominicana,* quoted in Franklin Franco Pichardo, *Historia del Pueblo Dominicano,* vol. 1 (Santo Domingo: Instituto del Libro, 1992), 183–84. For a discussion of the impact of the Haitian Revolution on the United States, see Winthrop D. Jordan, *White over Black: American Attitudes toward the Negro, 1550–1812* (Chapel Hill: University of North Carolina Press, 1968), 375–402.

17  This is true, I submit, even though various forms of forced labor were reintroduced almost as soon as slavery was abolished. Among those who

have written about postrevolutionary Haiti there is a tendency to consider the abolition of slavery in Haiti as sadly unsuccessful, since it did not in fact bring about greater liberty for most former slaves (see, e.g., Carpentier's novel *El reino de este mundo* [The kingdom of this world], trans. Harriet de Onís [New York: Knopf, 1957]). What is lost in this view, which is in fact just an extension of the "slavery as exploitation" hypothesis, is that in Haiti, much like in revolutionary France, the exact meaning of "liberty" and "equality" were radically redefined. As the most urgent task was to integrate race within revolutionary thought, "liberty" came close to meaning "(racial) equality" (see chapters 12 and 13 in this volume for further discussion). By hastily subsuming the Haitian events under some teleology of freedom, we lose sight of the fact that the new state represented an astonishing rearticulation of revolutionary thought and thereby also foreclose all further thought about those aspects of modernity that were suppressed or disavowed as soon as they appeared.

18   Simón Bolívar, *Selected Writings*, comp. Vicente Lecuna, ed. Harold A. Bierck Jr., trans. Lewis Bertrand, vol. 2 (New York: Colonial Press, 1951), 562. It is clear that Bolívar found the institution of slavery repulsive and was acutely aware of the dangers that resulted from racial oppression of all forms. He tried various times—most importantly at the Congress in Angostura 1819—to persuade Creoles to abandon slavery, but he remained unsuccessful. Lynch calls Bolívar an abolitionist, although perhaps one who underestimated the difficulty of resolving racial problems in postindependence Spanish America (*The Spanish American Revolutions*, 211–12). However we assess Bolívar's attitude, it is clear that in his political vision, all forms of antislavery were subordinated to the primary political goal, independence from Spain.

19   Cuba received a total of 20,000 to 30,000 refugees from Saint Domingue (Blackburn, *The Overthrow of Colonial Slavery*, 387). For the effect on Louisiana, see Alfred N. Hunt, *Haiti's Influence on Antebellum America: Slumbering Volcano in the Caribbean* (Baton Rouge: Louisiana State University Press, 1988).

20   Franco, *Documentos para la historia de Haití*, 64.

21   David P. Geggus, "Slave Resistance in the Spanish Caribbean in the Mid-1790s," in Gaspar and Geggus, *A Turbulent Time*, 137.

22   Franco, *Documentos para la historia de Haití*, 139.

23   Franco, *Documentos para la historia de Haití*, 131. The Cuban governor was rightly skeptical about these claims and attached a note to that effect.

24   The reference to the "ancient record" of African military achievements carries a note by Rainsford to Leo Africanus, and the reference to "a writer of modern date" is to Adanson, *Voyage à Afrique*.

25   For a critical review of nineteenth- and twentieth-century French historians on the Haitian Revolution, from Mme. de Staël onward, see the

last chapter of Yves Bénot, *La révolution française et la fin des colonies* (Paris: Éditions La Découverte, 1988).

26  Samuel Huntington, *The Clash of Civilizations and the Remaking of World Order* (New York: Simon and Schuster, 1996), 136–37. Huntington rightly points out that Haiti has been isolated within the Western Hemisphere, but he takes that as an expression of Haiti's eternal essence. The possibility that it could be the effect of a geopolitics in which issues of alliance, cultural exchange, migration, economic assistance, and so on are subject to conscious decisions and thus to the operations of the usual set of strategic calculation, racial prejudice, and political constraints does not occur to Huntington. In support of his assessment of Haiti's status as a "lone country," he cites a 1995 article from the *Washington Post*: "Haiti's Traditions [*sic*] of Isolation Makes U.S. Task Harder" (137 n. 15).

27  François Furet and Mona Ozouf, eds., *Critical Dictionary of the French Revolution*, trans. Arthur Goldhammer (Cambridge: Harvard University Press, 1989). The only reference under "colonialism" in the index is to the entry for Barnave. Slavery fares a little better, as it is mentioned in the essays "The American Revolution," "Clubs and Popular Societies," "Condorcet," and "Kant," but in the end it turns out that none of these entries has more than the most cursory reference to slavery and abolitionism during the French Revolution.

28  See also Susan Buck-Morss, "Hegel and Haiti," *Critical Inquiry* 26 (2000): 822–25, who takes the historian Simon Schama to task for his account of the rise of Dutch culture in the sixteenth and seventeenth centuries in his recent *The Embarrassment of Riches*, which does not mention the fact that the Dutch were dominating the transatlantic slave trade and that it was there that much of Dutch wealth originated.

29  Hannah Arendt, *On Revolution* (1963; Harmondsworth: Penguin, 1990).

30  Although Arendt herself admits that "the social question" would be better and more simply called "the existence of poverty," she retains the old-fashioned terminology throughout her book, presumably to prevent the destructive forces of compassion from interfering with the reader's clear-sightedness. Her claim that the social question needs to be separated from politics is explicitly directed against Marx's claim that poverty is rooted in exploitation. Indeed, her whole effort to seal off the realm of politics from that of economics, moral sentiment, and the like needs to be understood as an anti-Marxist (as well as anti-Hegelian) move. Arendt wants to see the realm of politics as the realm of freedom, while poverty is "more than a state of deprivation, it is a state of constant want and acute misery whose ignominy consists in its dehumanizing force; poverty is abject because it puts men under the absolute dictates of their bodies, that is, under the absolute dictate of necessity" (60).

31  For Arendt, liberation is merely a necessary precondition of freedom. In

no way does it guarantee freedom. This is the exact obverse of a view such as Kojève's, who in his reading of Hegel's master-slave dialectic specifies that "freedom" means just "liberation" (49). See my reading of Kojève further on, in the section on Hegel's master-slave dialectic.

32 See David Brion Davis, *Slavery and Human Progress* (New York: Oxford University Press, 1984), 107–16. Davis sums up the prevalent view among nineteenth-century thinkers, from Benjamin Franklin to Friedrich Engels, as maintaining that modern slavery "was less of a moral evil than a senseless anachronism, an affront to social sciences" (113); similarly, late-nineteenth-century historians such as Ettore Ciccotti, J. K. Ingram, and many others considered slavery a "discrete and fundamentally premodern institution" (9).

33 For a discussion of how disciplinary and ideological affiliations have affected the debates over slavery in the European and North American academy since the time of the French Revolution, see Buck-Morss, "Hegel and Haiti."

34 James, *The Black Jacobins*, 85–86, 95.

35 James, *The Black Jacobins*, 392. Compare also Sidney Mintz: "On the whole, plantations were big enterprises for their time, and demanded large quantities of unskilled labor; their work schedules reduced jobs to a simple common denominator, and tended to treat the laborer as interchangeable; capital investment (though highly variable) was usually heavy, and cost accounting commonly made the plantation enterprise a business, its owner a business man more than a planter. . . . The effects of the domination of such enterprises were felt throughout the region, wherever men were brought together in large numbers, with more coercion or less, to plant, harvest, and process; such 'factories in the field' go back to the sixteenth century in the islands, and have continuously affected not only the economy of the region, but also the character of its communities and of the people in them" (*Caribbean Transformations* [New York: Columbia University Press, 1989], 257). From here Mintz goes on to point out the crucial differences between Caribbean societies and other, more "tribal" Third World societies and speculates that this may be the reason why the Caribbean has been "so rich a fount of political leadership" (258). See Stephan Palmié, *Wizards and Scientists: Explorations in Afro-Cuban Modernity and Tradition* (Durham: Duke University Press, 2002), for a defense of this thesis, albeit within a different theoretical paradigm.

36 There is a large literature on the question of slavery and capitalism, and specifically on the question whether the practice of slavery meant that a society was essentially precapitalist. Although positions continue to vary considerably, I think we can now with some degree of certainty say that slavery and capitalism were not in as strong an opposition as earlier historians had argued. Eric Williams, for instance, claimed that the slave trade provided "the capital which financed the Industrial Revolution"

while the institution of slavery was destroyed by "modern industrial capitalism" (*Capitalism and Slavery* [1944; Chapel Hill: University of North Carolina Press, 1994], ix). More recent work suggests that the best way to think about the relationship between slavery and capitalism is in terms of heterogeneous formations and contradictory but coexisting modes of production. A plantation's internal mode of operation may well be precapitalist, but its relations to the world market are capitalist. Recent data that suggest that inefficiency may not have been the decisive, or at least not the exclusive, reason for the abolition of slavery—in other words, that slavery was not abolished by capitalism—could also be read as an indirect confirmation that there was no strong antagonism between the two.

37 The issues I can only touch on here have produced an enormous literature. In the social sciences, there has been a consensus for a long time that Caribbean societies cannot be understood without the plantation, and Caribbean commonalities across the linguistic and cultural divisions are rooted in the plantation (Mintz, Ortiz, etc.). For an extensive study of the operations of the sugar plantation in all its aspects in Cuba, see Manuel Moreno Fraginals, *El ingenio* (Havana: Editorial de Ciencias Sociales, 1986). Although recent work tends to be less interested in the plantation as a causative factor, the basic claims of the earlier work still hold. See also Antonio Benítez Rojo, *La isla que se repite* (Barcelona: Editorial Casiopea, 1998), for a more literary interpretation of the effects of the plantation on Caribbean culture.

The concept of transculturation, originally suggested by Fernando Ortiz in *Cuban Counterpoint: Tobacco and Sugar,* trans. Harriet de Onís, with a new introduction by Fernando Coronil (1940; Durham: Duke University Press, 1995), as an alternative to the concept of acculturation in functionalist anthropology, has been given vastly different meanings. While Angel Rama, for instance, uses it in an unabashedly high-cultural sense (*Transculturación narrativa en América Latina* [México, D.F.: Siglo Veintiuno Editores, 1987]), others, like Mary Louise Pratt, who work close to the border between literature and anthropology, have given it a more contestatory meaning (*Imperial Eyes: Travel Writing and Transculturation* [London: Routledge, 1992], 5–6).

Ortiz's account of Cuban history as one of "intermeshed transculturations" (98) is a particularly interesting example in the present context and as such merits some comment here. The great advantages of Ortiz's formulation over other attempts to account for cultural processes in the Caribbean are well known (see Coronil's introduction for a discussion that tries to defend Ortiz's concept against objections of the kind I am presenting here). The problem is, to put it succinctly, that Ortiz's description of the interactions between the various transplanted cultures in colonial Cuba assimilates different forms of oppression in a way that depoliticizes them radically: "Everybody, those above and those below, lives together in the same atmosphere of terror and oppression, the oppressed in terror of punishment, the oppressor in terror of reprisals; everybody outside justice, unadjusted, beside themselves. And everybody [is caught] in the painful process of transculturation in a new cultural environment" (102; translation amended). The antagonisms that separate various kinds of Cubans are sublated in the pain and struggle they share. By overriding and transcending the divisions of class and ethnicity, transculturation is the medium in which slaveholders and slaves, and Cubans of all colors, are linked and integrated—a transhistorical force quite beyond the reach of particularistic interest. There is no outside to transculturation: even the genocide of the indigenous populations in the Caribbean is designated, disconcertingly, as a "transculturación fracasada" [failed transculturation] (100). Where a more politically nuanced narrative would have pointed to antagonisms, victories, and losses, the culturalist narrative suggests an imagery of absorption and incorporation: within the national territory, culture has taken on the role of politics as the vehicle for resolving divisions.

38 Davis's argument that the British abolitionist movement was, in important respects, a strategy for disciplining the British labor force is a case in point. It was against the backdrop of the horrors of colonial slavery that the British workers submitted to the increasingly repressive labor regime at home. Marx's use of the term "wage slavery" not only signals the connection between unfree labor in the colonies and so-called free labor in Europe but also suggests the possibility that wage labor may in some ways be understood as derived from slave labor.

39 Sidney Mintz, *Caribbean Transformations*, 257.

40 Jonathan Rée, "The Brothers Koerbagh," review of *Radical Enlightenment: Philosophy and the Making of Modernity, 1650–1750*, by Jonathan Israel, *London Review of Books*, 24 January 2002, 21.

41 *Toussaint Louverture: La révolution française et le problème colonial* (Paris: Le club français du livre, 1960).

42 Eugene Genovese, *From Rebellion to Revolution: Afro-American Slave Revolt in the Making of the Modern World* (Baton Rouge: Louisiana State University Press, 1979), xxi–xxii, xix–xx. For a more detailed critique of Genovese's thesis, see chapter 13 in this volume.

43 It is worth remembering that the historiography of abolitionism—at least in England—begins with the writings of the abolitionists themselves (see Clarkson's two-volume *History of the Rise, Progress, and Accomplishment of the Abolition of the African Slave-Trade by the British Parliament* of 1808) and was dominated by Clarksonians for a long time. For an analysis of Clarksonian ideology and rhetoric, see Davis, *Slavery and Human Progress*, 116–19.

44 Carolyn E. Fick, *The Making of Haiti: The Saint Domingue Revolution from Below* (Knoxville: University of Tennessee Press, 1990).

45 Michel-Rolph Trouillot charges Fick with being "overly ideological" and

too much in awe of the "heroism" of the revolutionary slaves, thus failing to transcend the limitations of what he calls the "epic tradition" in the historiography of the Haitian Revolution (*Silencing the Past*, 175 n. 65). Although there may be some truth in that, it should not distract us from the novelty and interest of the materials she adduces, largely due to her subalternist approach.

46   Blackburn, *The Overthrow of Colonial Slavery*, 259. See also Robert L. Paquette, *Sugar Is Made with Blood: The Conspiracy of La Escalera and the Conflict between Empires over Slavery in Cuba* (Middletown, Conn.: Wesleyan University Press, 1988), for similar views. Blackburn's position is a sophisticated response to the common view that French abolitionism was weak and short-lived, and that it was the generally more conservative British abolitionism, which was not entangled in revolutionary culture, that proved politically effective. See, e.g., Daniel P. Resnick, "The Société des Amis des Noirs and the Abolition of Slavery," *French Historical Studies* 7 (1972): 558–69. For a discussion of the various positions and interesting additional documentation, see Geggus, "Racial Equality, Slavery, and Colonial Secession during the Constituent Assembly," *American Historical Review* 94, no. 5 (Dec. 1989): 1290–1308.

47   Blackburn, *The Overthrow of Colonial Slavery*, 259.

48   Blackburn, *The Overthrow of Colonial Slavery*, 27.

49   Interestingly, the origins of the suffrage movement in abolitionism are a mainstay in any handbook of women's studies. As we have seen before in relation to other historical events, here again politically highly significant lacunae in our knowledge of the emancipatory politics of modernity are reproduced and perpetuated, at least in part, by disciplinary fragmentation and disciplinary hierarchies. Not mentioning the segue of the abolitionist movement into the suffrage movement and assigning it to courses in women's studies perpetuates an understanding of issues of gender and sexuality as irrelevant to politics, and impervious to a revolutionary dynamic.

50   See Amy Dru Stanley, *From Bondage to Contract: Wage Labor, Marriage, and the Market in the Age of Slave Emancipation* (Cambridge: Cambridge University Press, 1998), esp. 1–59, for an excellent account of some of the connections. See also Nancy Isenberg, *Sex and Citizenship in Antebellum America* (Chapel Hill: University of North Carolina Press, 1998); and, for Great Britain, Adriana Craciun and Kari E. Lokke, eds., *Rebellious Hearts: British Women Writers and the French Revolution* (Albany: State University of New York Press, 2001).

51   Blackburn, *The Overthrow of Colonial Slavery*, 153, 423.

52   See chapter 4 in this volume for details.

53   For details about some films about slavery, including Pontecorvo's *Queimada* (distributed in the United States as *Burn!*), see Natalie Zemon Davis, *Slaves on Screen: Film and Historical Vision* (Cambridge: Harvard University Press, 2000).

54 We might even read Davis's argument in *Slavery in the Age of Revolution*, according to which abolitionism was a means for disciplining the workforce in the metropolis by contrasting supposedly benevolent free labor with the horrors of slave labor on the plantations, as a sophisticated version of this point. See Thomas Bender, ed., *The Antislavery Debate: Capitalism and Abolitionism as a Problem in Historical Interpretation* (Berkeley and Los Angeles: University of California Press, 1995), for an excellent collection of essays on the relationship between capitalism and abolitionism in the English-speaking world.

55 For Creole nationalism, see Benedict Anderson, *Imagined Communities: Reflections on the Origin and Spread of Nationalism* (New York: Verso, 1983), 50–61.

56 Joaquim Maria Machado de Assis, *Memorial de Aires*, trans. as *The Wager: Aires' Journal*, by P. L. Scott-Buccleuch (London: Peter Owen, 1990), 43. It may be worth quoting the Portuguese original here, since the text is quite obscure: "A Poesia falará dela [a escravidão], particularmente naqueles versos de Heine, em que o nosso nome está perpétuo. Nêles conta o capitão do navio negreiro haver deixado trezentos negros no Rio de Janeiro, onde 'a Casa Gonçalves Pereira' lhe pagou cem ducados por peça. Não importa que o poeta corrompa o nome do comprador e lhe chame Gonzalez Perreiro; foi a rima ou a sua má pronúncia que o levou a isso. Também não temos ducados, mas aí foi o vendedor que trocou na sua língua o dinheiro do comprador" (*Obra Completa*, vol. 1 [Rio de Janeiro: J. Aguilar, 1959], 1118). The reference to Heine (a writer who, not unlike Machado, was much denounced because of his lack of national enthusiasm, his "bad character," and, more or less explicitly, because of his race) is to one of his last works, a long poem entitled "Das Sklavenschiff" (The Slave Ship). (The third edition of *Obra Completa* has "Gonçalves" instead of "Gonzalez"; earlier editions, the English translation, and the Heine poem itself have "Gonzalez"; I have therefore restored "Gonzalez" to the Portuguese quote.)

57 For an exploration of the similarities and differences between different forms of slavery, from antiquity to the nineteenth century, and in societies around the globe, see Patterson, *Slavery and Social Death*.

58 Néstor García Canclini, *Hybrid Cultures: Strategies for Entering and Leaving Modernity*, trans. Christopher L. Chiappari and Silvia L. López, with a foreword by Renato Rosaldo (Minneapolis: University of Minnesota Press, 1995).

59 Renato Rosaldo, foreword to García Canclini, *Hybrid Cultures*, xvi.

60 Tomás Gutiérrez Alea's 1976 *La última cena* (The last supper), with its depiction of slaves from vastly different cultural and social backgrounds, is an astonishingly successful illustration of this point.

61 Trouillot, *Silencing the Past*, 58–69. According to Dahomean oral history, Tacoodonou "put Da to death by cutting open his belly, and placed his body under the foundation of a palace that he built in Abomey, as a

memorial of his victory; which he called Dahomey, from the unfortunate victim, and Homy his belly: that is the house built in Da's belly"
(65).

62 Julio Ramos, *Desencuentros de la modernidad en América Latina* (México:
Fondo de Cultura Económica, 1989).

63 It should be remembered, however, that continental European countries
were not modernized and homogeneous in the late eighteenth century
and the early nineteenth, either. Historical scholarship on the French
Revolution, for example, has long shown to what extent France was
linguistically diverse and largely illiterate before the revolution. In fact,
the imposition of French as the lingua franca of France and the rise of
literacy need to be seen as effects of the revolution, not the other way
around.

64 Compare the following passage from *Der Auftrag*, a 1979 play by Heiner
Müller, the most celebrated playwright of the former G.D.R., about a
(fictional) failed slave uprising in Jamaica, planned by three emissaries
from revolutionary France who are called back after Napoleon's rise to
power. The play is based on Anna Seghers's story "Das Licht auf dem
Galgen" (The Light on the Gallows): "Und wir brauchen unsre Zeit jetzt,
um die schwarze Revolution abzublasen, die wir so gründlich vor-
bereitet haben im Auftrag einer Zukunft, die schon wieder Vergangen-
heit ist wie die anderen vor ihr. Warum kommt die Zukunft in unsrer
Sprache nur einzeln vor, Galloudec. Bei den Toten ist es anders" [And
we need all the time we have now to call off the black revolution which
we prepared so thoroughly in the name of a future which is already a
past just like the others before. Why does future only occur in the
singular in our language, Galloudec. It's different among the dead]
(Heiner Müller, *Germania: Tod in Berlin, Der Auftrag*, ed. Roland Clauß
[Stuttgart: Klett, 2002], 71).

65 For the political aspects, see Davis, *Slavery in the Age of Revolution*, and
Bénot, *La révolution française;* for the economic aspect, see Williams,
*Capitalism and Slavery.*

66 Joan Dayan's *Haiti, History, and the Gods* (Berkeley and Los Angeles:
University of California Press, 1995), shows that a lot can be achieved
with literary interpretation of materials that are not high literary, and
that an attempt to reconstruct subaltern subjectivity with cultural and
literary imagination is well worth the effort.

67 See Mary Wollstonecraft, *Vindication of the Rights of Woman* (1792; Harmondsworth: Penguin, 1975): "if they [women] are really capable of
acting like rational creatures, let them not be treated like slaves"; "liberty
is the mother of virtue, and if women be, by their very constitution,
slaves, and not allowed to breathe the sharp invigorating air of freedom,
they must for ever languish like exotics" (120–22). The most extensive
and explicit appropriation of the language of slavery to describe the
situation of women is the Saratoga Declaration of Sentiments of 1848.

68  G. W. F. Hegel, *Phänomenologie des Geistes* (1807; Frankfurt: Suhr-
kamp, 1981), 137–55; *Phenomenology of Spirit*, trans. A. V. Miller (Oxford:
Oxford University Press, 1977), 104–19. Most Hegel scholars agree
that even though Hegel uses the terms "Herr" (master) and "Knecht"
(knave, bondsman) in the *Phenomenology*, he uses these terms inter-
changeably with the vocabulary of slavery. In support of this view, we
might point to earlier instantiations of Hegel's idea of a master-slave
dialectic, for instance in Rousseau, or to parallel texts, e.g., in Hegel's
*Encyclopedia;* see Michael N. Forster, *Hegel's Idea of a Phenomenology of
Spirit* (Chicago: Chicago University Press, 1998), 320, for a discussion
of the relevant passages in the *Encyclopedia*.

69  Obviously these questions touch on one of the central issues in the
American Revolution—what David Brion Davis called the "dilemma of
slaveholding revolutionaries." This is not a topic that can be addressed
in a footnote. Still, it may be worth referring the reader to Bernard
Bailyn's highly influential book *The Ideological Origins of the American
Revolution*, enlarged ed. (Cambridge: Harvard University Press, 1992).
Slavery is barely mentioned in Bailyn's account of the revolution. When
he does turn to the topic, his argument is mostly concerned with defending the view that slavery was an appropriate and indeed politically progressive metaphor for colonial oppression. The continuation of actual
slavery is just an inconsistency that was resolved in due course. The
American revolutionaries began by claiming the language of enslavement for themselves only to end up realizing that it would also apply to
racial slavery. "The degradation of chattel slaves—painfully visible and
unambiguously established in the law—was only the final realization of
what the loss of freedom could mean everywhere; for there was no such
thing 'as *partial* liberty': he who has authority 'to restrain and control my
conduct in any instance without my consent hath in all.' From this point
of view it made little difference whether one's bondage was private or
public, civil or political, or even whether one was treated poorly or well"
(234). At the center of Bailyn's view is the hypothesis of an ideological
and historical continuity and progress—a forever expanding American
freedom, first articulated by the revolutionaries and eventually extended
to their slaves. "The identification between the cause of the colonies and
the cause of the Negroes bound in chattel slavery—an identification built
into the very language of politics—became inescapable" (235). Antislavery is, in other words, a mere application or extension of a moral and
political view that was conceived in the more properly political realm of
the struggle for independence.

70  Paul Gilroy, *The Black Atlantic* (Cambridge: Harvard University Press,
1993), 54–55. Gilroy does not explain how he can enlist Hegel, of all
European philosophers, as an ally against the idea of history as progress.
Later on, when discussing Frederick Douglass's autobiographical narrative, Gilroy suggests that when Douglass violently confronts the slave

breaker he had been sent to, we encounter an "alternative" and "inversion" of Hegel's allegory (60–61). The exact relation between these two appeals to Hegel remains obscure.

71  Davis, *Slavery in the Age of Revolution*, 12–13. I suspect that this emphasis on Hegel in Davis's 1998 preface to a book written in 1975 is in part due to a subtle change of position: whereas the book of 1975 seems to be at least in part motivated by a concern with exploitation (of the white working class as well as of slaves), Davis in 1998 seems more concerned with questions of power. The changed ideological landscape and the loss of prominence of Marxist theory in scholarly argument may have a lot to do with this shift.

72  This agreement regarding the meaning of the dialectic vanishes quickly when it comes to the arguments that support this view, since they turn on the question what role history plays in the *Phenomenology* in general. While some Hegel scholars have argued that history plays no role, others, like Georg Lukács, maintained that on the contrary, the *Phenomenology* is a "grand threefold treatment of history and is structured accordingly" (quoted in Forster, *Hegel's Idea*, 292). It is striking, then, that it is *only* regarding the absence of any reference to modern slavery that critics and scholars agree. See Forster, *Hegel's Idea*, 290–500, for an exhaustive discussion of the problem of history and historicism in the *Phenomenology*.

73  The adequacy of Hegel's lordship and bondage section has been criticized from a number of perspectives. The best-known objection is perhaps that of Sartre, who argues that the pronounced dualism of the dialectic means that the equally crucial dialectic between one master and another cannot be accounted for (*Critique of Dialectical Reason: Theory of Practical Ensembles*, trans. Alan Sheridan-Smith, ed. Jonathan Rée, vol. 1 (London: NLB, 1976), 158. Robin Blackburn picks up on this objection, adding that it also fails to address "the problem of how *inter-subjectivity* could develop between slaves in differing situations and of different extraction," as well as the important role of people who were neither slaves nor slaveholders and nevertheless played a crucial role in the struggle against slavery (*The Overthrow of Colonial Slavery*, 530). Frantz Fanon appears to be raising even more fundamental issues regarding the applicability of the dialectic to situations of racial subordination in a footnote to his brief chapter on Hegel: "I hope I have shown that here the master differs basically from the master described by Hegel. For Hegel there is reciprocity; here the master laughs at the consciousness of the slave. What he wants from the slave is not recognition but work" (*Black Skin, White Mask*, trans. Charles Lam Markmann [New York: Grove, 1967], 220).

74  Forster, *Hegel's Idea*, 317–22.

75  Forster, *Hegel's Idea*, 317.

76  It is in fact very difficult to read Forster's account of Reitemeier and not

think of Europe's colonial expansion into the Caribbean. Forster says: "As a result of Athenian victory in the Persian Wars early in the fifth century, and the consequent expansion and change in the character of the Athenian economy (particularly from a rural and agrarian to an urban and manufacturing/trading emphasis), slavery had undergone a dramatic expansion and transformation for the worse in quality in fifth-century Athens" (*Hegel's Idea*, 320). Later, when adding the second layer to his account of historicity in the *Phenomenology*, he makes the same argument for Rome: "the *Lordship and Bondage* section also refers to the substantial growth in Roman slavery which occurred after and as a result of Rome's success in that war [the Second Punic War] and the consequent great increase in Roman prosperity" (322). Are we really not to think of the links between wealth accumulation in France, England, and Holland, the expansion overseas, and the enormous expansion of slavery?

77  For an extensive study of the German press about the Haitian events, see Karin Schüller, *Die deutsche Rezeption haitianischer Geschichte in der ersten Hälfte des 19. Jahrhunderts: Ein Beitrag zum deutschen Bild des Schwarzen* (Cologne: Böhlau, 1992); and "From Liberalism to Racism: German Historians, Journalists, and the Haitian Revolution from the Late Eighteenth to the Early Twentieth Centuries," in *The Impact of the Haitian Revolution in the Atlantic World*, ed. David P. Geggus (Columbia: University of South Carolina Press, 2001), 23–43.

78  I would like to thank Fred Neuhauser for his help with the Hegel text.

79  In a note Buck-Morss defends Hegel against the Marxist criticism that maintains that Hegel failed "to take the next step to revolutionary practice," reiterating that "the slaves of Saint Domingue were, as Hegel knew, taking that step for him" ("Hegel and Haiti," 848 n. 84). Again, she probably wants to say that we should realize the veiled allusions in the text, but she chooses language that suggests that somehow historical actors can finish what the writer omits.

The problem becomes most clear, perhaps, when Buck-Morss quotes Hegel as saying "it is solely by risking life that freedom is obtained. . . . The individual, who has not staked his life, may, no doubt, be recognized as a Person [the agenda of the abolitionists!]; but he has not attained the truth of this recognition as an independent self-consciousness" (849). Now, these sentences certainly resonate with the Haitian Revolution and the issue of moderate abolitionism. However, within the dialectic, they occur at the beginning, when Hegel explains the life-and-death struggle, as a result of which the master-slave dualism comes into being. Hegel does not say that a life-and-death struggle can also *resolve* the dualism. As I will argue in the following, this is a highly significant difference.

80  Judith Butler, *The Psychic Life of Power: Theories in Subjection* (Stanford: Stanford University Press, 1997), 31.

81  Alexandre Kojève, *Introduction to the Reading of Hegel: Lectures on the*

*Phenomenology of the Spirit,* trans. James H. Nichols Jr. (1947; Ithaca: Cornell University Press, 1980).

82    This is also true for Davis's account. His appeal to Hegel calls for some comment. In the 1998 preface to *Slavery in the Age of Revolution,* he acknowledges the contributions of those who took part in the debate that ensued after the work's publication, but then says that the book was, in some crucial respects, misunderstood or, at the very least, that in the heat of the "antislavery debate," the "core of the book" was neglected (13). He charges that historians failed to see what was really at stake: "the dilemmas of *slaveholding revolutionaries*" (13). Using Jefferson's ambiguous position as his example, Davis says that "the main 'problem of slavery'" is "a problem of dominance and submission, which I tried to illuminate in the concluding pages with a partly imaginary struggle, against a Hegelian backdrop, between Napoleon and Toussaint L'Ouverture" (12). I have already pointed out that this "return" to Hegel may well be connected to the question of whether slavery should be understood in terms of exploitation or domination. But there is another aspect to this as well. What exactly is illuminated by Hegel's master-slave dialectic? And why does Hegel's dialectic illuminate Jefferson's dilemma?

There are two curious moments in his discussion: in the imaginary one-on-one struggle between Toussaint Louverture and Napoleon, it is the "life-and-death struggle" that they are acting out. "Toussaint finally submits—as he did in history—because he prefers Napoleon's vision of truth to his own death. Napoleon accepts the submission—as he did in history—because it validates his own sense of omnipotence. . . . Toussaint's bondage is an objective proof that Napoleon's freedom is no illusion" (560). There are a number of problems to be noted here. First, Napoleon never even answered Toussaint Louverture's famous letter "From the First of the Blacks to the First of the Whites," and it is a little hard to imagine a life-and-death struggle between two people if one of them refuses to even acknowledge the existence of the other. Second, can we really maintain that Toussaint Louverture submitted to Napoleon? After all, he was steadfast in his antislavery stance, he had risked his life plenty of times during the guerrilla war against the French, and he certainly did not submit to incarceration in France to save his life.

What did Davis hope to establish with his parable? Surely something odd is happening when a historian ends a finely nuanced and amply researched historical study with an imaginary fight between two historical figures and then claims—against historical fact—that one loses because he valued his life more than his freedom. And it is even more odd to return to this seemingly marginal part of the book, almost twenty-five years later, and to claim that it represents the core. Compare the following statement, later on in the original epilogue: "[Toussaint] thought he had established his people's independence without dooming their future by a rash and total break with France. Hence his professions of loyalty to France were not without some truth. They were a mark, to be shared by many future black leaders, of his own supreme tragedy" (563). Toussaint submitted only in the sense that he failed to declare independence from France. The failure to make the crucial move—the declaration of independence—is not just contingently related to the project of revolutionary slave emancipation. It is *the* failure of that project.

Now, as a matter of historical fact, Davis is right about this. Napoleon's attempts to reintroduce slavery in Saint Domingue leave no doubt about that. Clearly, it would have been more prudent if Toussaint had declared independence. And Davis is not the first to have made this argument—James, for one, argued the same point in *The Black Jacobins*. In the case of James, the motivations for such a view are clear enough. As his preface and footnotes to the second edition of 1963 explain, he thought of the Haitian Revolution as a model and a cautionary tale for the independence struggles in Africa. But in the case of Davis, the question of motivations must be answered in a different way.

What is really at stake, I think, are the paradoxes that result from the conflicts at the heart of the American Revolution. The odd allegorical tale of the struggle between Toussaint Louverture and Napoleon is best understood as a displacement of the troublesome fact that American independence, with its high-flying rhetoric of freedom and individual rights, did not bring about the abolition of slavery. By choosing Toussaint Louverture and Napoleon—two figures who do not play a major role in the main body of the book—as protagonists, Davis suddenly focuses on the one struggle for emancipation that actually involves a struggle both against slavery and against colonial rule, thus suggesting a natural affinity or even continuity between the two projects. Toussaint did not receive the recognition he desired because he did not declare independence from France. Davis does not give us a theoretical account here, but ultimately he seems to suggest that liberty is achieved only through independence. That in turn raises the question whether Davis means to suggest that the Rights of Man can be realized only as the Rights of Citizens, an argument that might turn on the idea of popular sovereignty; or, on the contrary, that the Rights of Man and Citizen are somehow an effect of national sovereignty—an argument in which sovereignty is an effect of geopolitical arrangements. In the first case, the abolition of slavery might be understood as implied in the concept of popular sovereignty; in the second case, the abolition (or continuation) of slavery is part of the claim of sovereignty of the state. None of this is spelled out in Davis's texts, but it seems to me that it is the latter claim that attracts Davis and compels him to keep returning to the "dilemma of slaveholders." In *Slavery and Human Progress* (1984) he thus argues, again appealing to Hegel's master-slave dialectic, that it makes sense to "speak of slave emancipation's 'enslaving' the British West Indies" (127).

While not as overtly apologetic as the consistency argument we saw earlier in the discussion of Bailyn, Davis's argument ultimately suggests that abolition without independence would have produced a freedom as imaginary as independence without abolition. Perhaps from the perspective of a Hegel, but I am sure the slaves would have seen it differently. In the end, radical antislavery is denied as a possible way to liberation. The original transnationalism of the revolutionary movement has vanished (or become illusionary?), and the historical path chosen by the American revolutionaries merely one (and not the worse) of two revolutionary options rather an instance of revolution turning into counterrevolution.

83  A mere look at Kojève's rendition of the structure of the *Phenomenology* at the back of his commentary confirms this point. Where Hegel consistently uses a fairly technical language as developed in the context of German idealism, Kojève provides translations into concrete political and historical terms. For example, where Hegel, in the chapter entitled "Vernunft" [Reason], lists as a subheading "Beobachtende Vernunft" [Observing Reason], Kojève writes "The Scientist" (269); where Hegel says "Die Individualität, die an und für sich reel ist" ["the individuality which is in and for itself real"], Kojève says "The Man of Letters" (273); and for a section entitled "Die Tugend und der Weltlauf" [Virtue and the Way of the World], Kojève writes "The individual who wants to *improve* the World: Reformism and the impotence of non-revolutionary intervention" (273).

84  For a plausible and well-contextualized account of Kojève's amendments to Hegel's story, see Michael S. Roth, *Knowing and History: Appropriations of Hegel in Twentieth-Century France* (Ithaca: Cornell University Press, 1988), 94–124.

85  *Genesis and Structure of Hegel's Phenomenology of the Spirit*, trans. Samuel Cherniak and John Heckman (Evanston: Northwestern University Press, 1974), 77.

86  As Hegel puts it in a succinct restatement in the *Encyclopedia*: "All peoples in order to become free . . . have had first to go through the strict discipline of subjection to a lord. . . . Bondage and tyranny are therefore a necessary step in the history of peoples and therefore something *relatively* justified" (quoted in Forster, *Hegel's Idea,* 254). Bondage and unfree labor, far from being an aberration or an accident in the history of unfolding of freedom, are a necessary part of it. This is incidentally also true in Rousseau, who thought that the process of subjugation is necessary for a true community or general will, and thus freedom.

87  Charles Taylor, *Hegel* (Cambridge: Cambridge University Press, 1975), 157. Compare also Hyppolite's more esoteric account of the problematic transition, which seems to agree with Taylor's summary in matter of substance, if not language: "But while, by dint of courage, the master's consciousness posed itself above life, only the slave's conscious-

ness proved able to dominate that objective being—the substance of being—and to transpose the I of self-consciousness into the element of being-in-itself. Tested through anguish and disciplined by service, self-consciousness became *form* which found its *matter* in being-in-itself and inscribed itself therein. . . . Self-consciousness now gains not only living independence but also liberty, which pertains to thought. The concept of liberty presents itself in stoicism and is further developed in skepticism" (*Genesis and Structure* 178).

88  The striking rhetorical and narrative intensification in Kojève clearly needs to be considered in the historical context of his lectures between 1933 and 1939 in Paris, a time when the Nazi threat had become an undoubtable fact, fascism was on the rise in almost every European country, and the Popular Front was taking shape in France. Both the urgency of the text and the rhetoric that some commentators have traced back to writers such as Carl Schmitt, on the opposite end of the political spectrum, need to be seen as a response to the catastrophes looming on the horizon.

89  Peter Brooks, "The Melodramatic Imagination," in *A New History of French Literature,* ed. Denis Hollier (Cambridge: Harvard University Press, 1989), 605–6. See also chapter 9 in this volume, where I discuss an example of revolutionary theater.

90  See G. A. Kelly's influential "Notes on Hegel's 'Lordship and Bondage,'" in *Hegel: A Collection of Critical Essays,* ed. Alasdair C. MacIntyre (Notre Dame: University of Notre Dame Press, 1976), for a critique of Kojève's interpretation.

91  Marshall Berman, *All That's Solid Melts into Air* (Harmondsworth: Penguin, 1982).

92  Walter Mignolo, *The Darker Side of the Renaissance* (Ann Arbor: University of Michigan Press, 1995), 317.

93  Edward Said, *Culture and Imperialism* (New York: Knopf, 1993), 278; Gilroy, *The Black Atlantic,* 49; Néstor García Canclini, *Hybrid Cultures: Strategies for Entering and Leaving Modernity,* trans. Christopher L. Chiappari and Silvia L. López (Minneapolis: University of Minnesota Press, 1995), 13–14.

94  Joan Dayan further develops similar points in her excellent "Paul Gilroy's Slaves, Ships, and Routes: The Middle Passage as Metaphor," *Research in African Literatures* 27 (1996): 7–14. See also Neil Lazarus, "Is a Counterculture of Modernity a Theory of Modernity?" *Diaspora* 4 (1995): 323–39.

95  Jean Laplanche and J.-B. Pontalis, *The Language of Psychoanalysis,* trans. Donald Nicholson-Smith (New York: Norton, 1973), s.v. "Disavowal (denial)." In Freud, disavowal *(Verleugnung)* is usually linked to castration anxiety. Noticing the absence of a penis in females, children "disavow the fact and believe that they *do* see a penis, all the same" (*The Standard Edition of the Complete Psychological Works of Sigmund Freud,* trans.

James Strachey, vol. 19 [London: Hogarth Press, 1953–1974], 143–44). Freud discusses the notion of disavowal usually in relation to fetishism, where the fear of castration leads to the creation of a fetish that operates as a substitute of sorts for the absent penis. In the famous case of the Wolf Man, Freud further analyzes the defense mechanisms for dealing with external reality: "In the end there were to be found in him two contrary currents side by side, of which one abominated the idea of castration, while the other was prepared to accept it and console itself with femininity as a compensation" (*Standard Edition*, vol. 27, 85). But Freud also links disavowal to other scenarios. In the case of traumatic neuroses that can emerge after experiences of shock in war, accidents, and so on, disavowal is linked to the fear not of castration but of death. As in the first case, it functions as a defense mechanism against a "traumatic perception," but now of a different nature. It is quite clear that Freud never resolved the tension between his accounts of internal and external trauma (see Ruth Leys, *Trauma: A Genealogy* [Chicago: University of Chicago Press, 2000], 18–40, for an excellent discussion). In my usage of the term, I rely on the second meaning, admitting the first meaning only at times when the historical evidence suggests that the external trauma may have been fantasized in terms of castration.

96  Freud, *Standard Edition*, vol. 23, 204.

## I. THE TRIAL OF JOSÉ ANTONIO APONTE

1  José Luciano Franco, *Las conspiraciones de 1810 y 1812* (Havana: Ciencias Sociales, 1977), 185. Franco's book includes a transcript of part of the proceedings. Throughout this chapter, all page references without further indication of author and title are to Franco's text. Many aspects of the Aponte Conspiracy are still mysterious. For an excellent step-by-step account of the Aponte Conspiracy and a detailed discussion of the importance of Haiti to the conspirators, see Matt Childs, " 'A Black French General Arrived to Conquer the Island': Images of the Haitian Revolution in Cuba's 1812 Aponte Rebellion," in *The Impact of the Haitian Revolution,* ed. David P. Geggus (Columbia: University of South Carolina Press, 2001), 135–56, which is based on archival work in Cuba and Spain and draws on materials not included in Franco's edition. For Cuban fears relating to Haiti, see also Alain Yacou, "Le péril haitien à Cuba: De la Révolution nègre à la reconnaissance de l'independence (1791–1825)," in *La révolution Française et Haiti,* ed. Michel Hector, vol. 2 (Port-au-Prince: Société Haïtienne D'Histoire et de Géographie/Editions Henri Deschamps, 1995), 186–99; and Clarence J. Munford and Michael Zeuske, "Black Slavery, Class Struggle, Fear, and Revolution in St. Domingue and Cuba, 1785–1795," *Journal of Negro History* 73 (1988):

12–32. For an extensive discussion of the historiography on the Aponte Conspiracy and the epistemological and methodological challenges it poses, see Stephan Palmié, *Wizards and Scientists: Explorations in Afro-Cuban Modernity and Tradition* (Durham: Duke University Press, 2002), 79–157. Unlike most historians, Palmié remains skeptical regarding Aponte's involvement in an uprising "of major proportions" (132). As an alternative to the teleological appropriation of Aponte as a "Creole revolutionary" by Genovese and José Luciano Franco, among others, Palmié reads him as a "theorist" of Afro-Cuban history and culture (126).

2   When asked about the purpose of his book, Aponte at one point says that he meant to give it to the Spanish king. The interrogators clearly do not believe him. In the absence of further evidence, we can only speculate about this question. I am inclined to think that the book probably served a number of purposes, from entertainment to instruction and legitimization of authority. It is obviously possible that Aponte was simply being sarcastic when he pointed to the Spanish king as the book's intended recipient. However, given that kings and people in high authority clearly occupy an important place in the book, it seems more plausible to think that Aponte indeed entertained some such idea. It speaks to the inability of the interrogators even to conceive of a politics that places racial liberation at the center of political action that they could not imagine that Aponte's antagonism was really not toward the Spanish king but toward local slaveholders and slave traders. (This is, incidentally, also true both for those who cast Aponte as a "leader of the vanguard" and for Palmié, who opposes this view and suggests "theory" as an alternative.)

3   See José Luciano Franco, "La conspiración de Aponte," in *Ensayos históricos* (Havana: Ciencias Sociales, 1974), 25, for a brief discussion of the role and character of these various societies of African origin. For a trenchant critique of Franco's claims, see Palmié, *Wizards and Scientists*, 89–92.

4   I would like to thank David Brown for this observation.

5   This argument could be taken as further evidence against Genovese's thesis of the bourgeois-democratic character of slave uprisings after 1804. It would lend support instead to my sense that the issue of state form was somewhat alien to the issue of liberty from slavery, and that any account that focuses on the institutional aspects of the "foundation of liberty" (Arendt) almost necessarily misses the political aspects of the struggle against slavery and the specificities of revolutionary antislavery. It is for the same reason, I think, that Palmié's spirited polemic against a rationalist appropriation of Aponte for the cause of Third World revolution by José Luciano Franco, Philip Foner, and others remains caught in arguments that seem to pull in very different directions. I think Palmié is quite right to insist that in assimilating Aponte to later models of revolutionaries, we lose sight of the true radicalness of his enterprise.

Yet instead of reconfiguring the political ground on which Aponte's activity took place, Palmié offers us an Aponte whose revolutionary intent is largely epistemological and historiographical.

6 For a list of the books that were found in Aponte's possession, plus attempts to identify them, see Palmié, *Wizards and Scientists*, 290–93. Bruce Dairn, in "Haiti and Egypt in Early Black Racial Discourse in the United States" (*Slavery and Abolition* 14 [1993]: 139–61), argues that Afrocentrist ideas spread from Haiti to the United States. One possible explanation for this (and thus Aponte's knowledge) is Napoleon's expedition to Egypt in 1798, which marked the beginning of an Egyptomania in Europe. Apparently the debates surrounding Egypt were well known among the Haitian revolutionaries.

7 Jean François was an early leader of the Haitian Revolution who, like Gil Narciso and Georges Biassou, had fought with the Spanish troops against the French and was eventually forced into exile by Toussaint Louverture. In 1796, these three, along with their troops, had tried to settle in Cuba. They were prohibited from entering Havana when the authorities learned that the population of color was preparing festivities in anticipation for their arrival, and the exiles eventually left for various other locations. See Childs, "A Black French General," 145–47, for a fascinating account of how Jean François, who had been less than enthusiastic about slave emancipation, was transformed in the popular imagination into the distinguished admiral Juan Francisco, supposedly serving Henri Christophe. At the time of the Aponte uprising, the historical Jean François was already dead.

In late 1811 another contingent of former combatants of the Haitian Revolution arrived in Havana, including, again, Gil Narciso and former troops of Jean François. Fearing the impact of the black generals in Cuba, the colonial authorities ordered the officials to be housed outside the city. It remains unclear to what extent they had contacts with the Cuban conspirators. It appears that the presence of the black soldiers was used by the conspirators to project the idea that the 1812 uprising was a powerful movement that counted on the support of the neighboring independent black state. Narciso managed to escape prosecution and continued his voyage to Santo Domingo, where he was involved in another slave revolt (Childs, "A Black French General," 146–48).

8 Citing archival materials, Childs gives a slightly different version of the event ("A Black French General," 143). My account is based on the materials edited by Franco.

9 For a different genealogy of Egyptocentrism from biblical sources, see Theophus Harold Smith, *Conjuring Culture: Biblical Formations of Black America* (New York: Oxford University Press, 1994).

10 Martin Bernal, *Black Athena: The Afroasiatic Roots of Classical Civilization* (New Brunswick, N.J.: Rutgers University Press, 1987).

11 For the debates surrounding Bernal's thesis, see Mary R. Lefkowitz, *Not Out of Africa* (New York: Basic Books, 1997); and Martin Bernal, *Black Athena Writes Back: Martin Bernal Responds to His Critics,* ed. David Chioni Moore (Durham: Duke University Press, 2001).

12 Bernal, *Black Athena,* 160–88.

13 Susan Buck-Morss points out that there are certain striking similarities between the *vèvè* drawings in vodun and Masonic iconography. She also points out that Ogé and some of his mulatto allies were Freemasons ("Hegel and Haiti," *Critical Inquiry* 26 [2000]: 854–86). Léon-François Hoffmann, in his *Essays on Haitian Literature* (Washington: Three Continents Press, 1984), 55, claims that Vastey, the chief ideologue at Henri Christophe's court, was the first black man in the New World to claim ethnic identity with ancient Egyptians, but does not offer any thoughts on the origins of Vastey's account.

14 André Combes, "La Franc-Maçonnerie aux Antilles et en Guyane Françaises de 1789 à 1848," in *La Période Révolutionnaire aux Antilles: Images et Résonnances,* Actes du Colloque International Pluridisciplinaire, 26–30 November 1986, ed. Roger Toumson (Faculté des Lettres et des Sciences Humaines, Université des Antilles et de la Guyane: GRELCA, n.d.), 162. Perhaps due to his affiliation, Combes is reticent to disclose the sources of his information and perhaps a little too concerned with bringing out the progressive elements in Masonic culture, so a degree of skepticism regarding some of his data may be in order. For a discussion of Freemasonry in Cuba, especially its role in the conspiracy of 1810 (which involved some people of color and is usually seen as a precursor to the Aponte Conspiracy), see José A. Ferrer Benimeli, "Révolution française et littérature clandestine à Cuba: La Franc-Maçonnerie comme élément conspirateur," in Toumson, *La Période Révolutionnaire aux Antilles,* 29–48.

15 Combes, "La Franc-Maçonnerie aux Antilles," 176.

16 Wilson Jeremiah Moses, *Afrotopia: The Roots of African American Popular History* (Cambridge: Cambridge University Press, 1998), 7.

17 Of course, the opposite is a definite possibility, too. As Palmié suggests, Aponte may have been attracted to Masonry precisely because it was yet another "hermetic system of knowledge production" that would assist him in his project of reconfiguring history (*Wizards and Scientists,* 131).

18 David Nicholls, *From Dessalines to Duvalier: Race, Colour, and National Independence in Haiti* (New Brunswick: Rutgers University Press, 1996), 130.

19 Wilson Jeremiah Moses, ed., *Classical Black Nationalism: From the American Revolution to Marcus Garvey* (New York: New York University Press, 1996), 53–67.

20 See Dairn, "Haiti and Egypt"; and Hollis R. Lynch, "Pan-Negro Nationalism in the New World, before 1862," in *Black Brotherhood: Afro-*

*Americans and Africa,* ed. Okon Edet Uya (Lexington, Mass.: Heath, 1971), 41–62.

21 I would like to thank Scott Trafton for alerting me to the scientistic frame in which the debates in the later nineteenth century took place.

22 I have not been able to find out whether the Cuban Teatro Bufo is connected to minstrel shows in the United States. The similarities are certainly striking, since the minstrel shows also ridiculed pretentious styles of speaking and megalomaniacal ambitions. See William J. Mahar, *Behind the Burnt Cork Mask: Early Blackface Minstrelsy and Antebellum American Popular Culture* (Urbana: University of Illinois Press, 1999), 62, who mentions as typical examples of this critique of pretension the pronunciation of "elegant" as "hellygunt," and a vocabulary that included terms such as "spiritable" and "temporalities." See also "A Negro Lecture on Locomotion: As Recited by Great Western and R. Edwards," in Mahar, *Behind the Burnt Cork Mask.* Dale Cockrell, in *Demons of Disorder: Early Blackface Minstrels and Their World* (Cambridge: Cambridge University Press, 1997), 55, quotes the definition of the black dandy as "a larn'd skolar." Both Mahar and Cockrell argue that the minstrel show did not in fact aim at ridiculing black culture but rather reflects a marginal white perspective on white high culture (e.g., opera).

23 Francisco Fernández, "Los negros catedráticos," in *Teoría y práctica del catedratismo en "Los negros catedráticos de Francisco Fernández,"* ed. Matías Montes Huiobro (Miami: Persona, 1987), 61–106. I am quoting the Spanish original, since it is impossible to give a good sense of the text in translation.

24 Antonio de Nebrija (1444–1522) was one of Spain's great Renaissance humanists. The text referred to in the play (and the book found in Aponte's house) could be either *Aelij Antonij Nebrissensis gramatici introductionis latinae explicatae,* one of many Spanish commentaries of that text (which often had "Arte Nebrija" in the title), or Nebrija's famous *Gramática castellana* (Palmie, *Wizards and Scientists,* 291).

25 Francisco Calcagno, *Aponte* (Barcelona: Tip. de Francisco Costa, 1901), 8. Of course, 1902 was neither the first nor the last time that the "specter of Haiti" has been invoked. Similar things happened in 1844, during the so-called Escalera Conspiracy (see chapter 3 of this volume), and in 1912, during the massacre of the Partido Independiente de Color. During the Ten Year War (1868–1878), Antonio Maceo, one of the leaders of the insurgents, became the victim of a sinister smear campaign, according to which he wanted to set up a black republic after the example of Haiti; see Leopoldo Horrego Estuch, *Maceo, héroe y carácter* (Havana: La Milagrosa, 1952); and Philip Sheldon Foner, *A History of Cuba and Its Relations with the United States,* vol. 2 (New York: International Publishers, 1962–1963), 258–62.

## 2. CIVILIZATION AND BARBARISM

1   Julius Scott III, "The Common Wind: Currents of Afro-American Communication in the Era of the Haitian Revolution" (Ph.D. diss., Duke University, 1986).

2   For an extensive compilation of sources about preacademic painting in Cuba, see Jorge Rigol, *Apuntes sobre la pintura y el grabado en Cuba: De los orígenes a 1927* (Havana: Editorial Pueblo y Educación, 1971); Adeleida de Juan, *Pintura cubana: Temas y variaciones* (Mexico, D.F.: UNAM, 1980); and *Pintura y grabado coloniales cubanos: Contribución a su estudio* (Havana: Instituto Cubano del Libro, 1974). See also Jorge Mañach, "La pintura en Cuba: Desde sus orígenes hasta 1900," in *Las Bellas Artes en Cuba,* ed. José Manuel Carbonell y Rivero (Havana: El Siglo XX, 1928), 225–66; and Guy Pérez Cisnero, *Características de la evolución de la pintura en Cuba* (Havana: Dirección General de Cultura, Ministerio de Educación, 1959).

3   By contract, the most comprehensive study of nineteenth-century painting in Haiti, Michel Philippe Lerebours's *Haiti et ses peintres de 1804 à 1980: Souffrances & Espoirs d'un Peuple,* 2 vols. (Port-au-Prince: L'Imprimeur II, 1989), argues for a continuity between colonial, anonymous, and postrevolutionary art on the basis of stylistic characteristics.

4   In this I disagree with Luz Merino's argument in her excellent "Apuntes para un estudio de la Academia San Alejandro," *Revista de la Biblioteca José Martí* 18 (1976): 117–42. Merino argues that the focus on drawing indicates that San Alejandro was not conceived as an academy of fine arts, not as a space for autonomous art, but rather as a school with utilitarian purposes. I would argue that the distinction between utilitarian and autonomous art had simply not been made. If we subsume San Alejandro under the heading of utilitarian art, we effectively lose sight of what distinguished academic art from the popular arts. Distinctions such as good taste/bad taste, drawing/painting, perspectival/nonperspectival painting, and realistic representations/humorous, satirical, or expressivist distortions produce aesthetic hierarchies that set apart "real art" from "popular crafts" and that cannot be justified on purely utilitarian grounds. The fault lines that emerge in these distinctions clearly track distinctions of color, and it is partly for that reason, I think, that the discussions of "good taste" that we typically associate with eighteenth-century aesthetics carry well into the nineteenth century in Cuba.

5   As evidence for the lost tradition of wall paintings, Rigol also lists street names in Havana—for example, the Calle del Aguilar (where a picture of an eagle was painted in a tavern), Calle de los Angeles (angels painted on a street corner), Calle de Jesús Peregrino (which referred to an altar that Aponte had there), the Plaza del Vapor (referring to a painting of the first

steamboat, *Neptuno,* that came to the island and made trips between Matanzas and Havana), and so on (*Apuntes,* 12). Unfortunately Rigol does not give documentation for his claims.

6 Quoted in Rigol, *Apuntes,* 45.

7 Quoted in Rigol, *Apuntes,* 49.

8 Frederika Bremer, *Cartas de Cuba* (Havana: Arte y Literatura, 1981), 157–58.

9 *Papel Periódico,* 10 February 1791, 46–47.

10 *Papel Periódico,* 31 May 1792, 174–75.

11 *Papel Periódico,* 3 June 1792, 178.

12 Quoted in Rigol, *Apuntes,* 45–46.

13 Cirilo Villaverde, *Excursión a Vuelta Abajo* (Havana: Letras Cubanas, 1981), 84–85.

14 Note, for instance, that Joaquín E. Weiss's extraordinarily detailed and well-documented *La Arquitectura colonial cubana: Siglos XVI al XIX* (Havana: Instituto Cubano del Libro, 1996) does not mention murals, even though on close scrutiny of the historical photographs that are reproduced in the book, it seems that some of the buildings where murals have been restored recently (e.g., on the Plaza Vieja) show faint murals on the facade.

15 There may be multiple reasons for this discrepancy. Large structures and public buildings are more likely to survive than popular dwellings, and as a result, the examples of the folk tradition disappeared while the more restrained decorations of the mansions of the elite survived. It might also be the case that the cultural critics at the time felt that in order to denounce muralism *tout court* as barbaric, it was strategically better to pick up on popular examples.

16 I owe all specific archaeological information on murals in this chapter to conversations and interviews with Roger Arrazcaeta Delgado, director, Antonio Quevedo Herrero, conservationist, and Ivalú Rodríguez Gil, restorer, Gabinete de Arqueología de la Oficina del Historiador, 3–10 June 1997. Their generous help with my research is gratefully acknowledged. Although Nicolás de Escalera is occasionally identified as a man of color, it seems that there is no evidence that he was not white. He is one of the first documented Cuban painters and is particularly known for his religious art. Twentieth-century critics tend to have a rather dim view of his style on account of his "facile mysticism."

17 Today c/Tacón 8, La Havana Vieja.

18 Today c/Amargura 65, La Havana Vieja.

19 One of the difficulties in analyzing the styles is that these paintings cannot be dated except in relative terms or in relation to architectural changes.

20 The similarity between some of the ornamental patterns of wall paintings in Havana and Pompeian patterns is quite striking. Given that murals appear to have originated in the late eighteenth century in Cuba,

when the discovery of Pompeii was only recent memory, it is quite likely that there was some kind of influence. This hypothesis was confirmed by Eusebio Leal, historian of the City of Havana (personal interview, 9 June 1997), although he could not offer any explanation of how Pompeian iconography arrived in Cuba, either.

21 Nieves Benítez Castillo, director of the Museo de Arte Sacro, La Havana Vieja, personal interview, 4 June 1997.

22 Nieves Benítez Castillo, personal interview, 4 June 1997; Father Rafael, archivist of the Convento de los Franciscanos, Guanabacoa, personal interview, 1 June 1997.

23 Jorge Bermúdez Rodríguez, "Vicente Escobar, nuestro pintor preliminar," *Revista de la Biblioteca Nacional José Martí* (January–March 1984): 141–51. Although Bermúdez's article is one of the most interesting pieces written about Escobar in that the author does not take the negative aesthetic judgment on Escobar for granted, he ends up justifying it on moral and political grounds. What he does not consider is the possibility that people of color may have seen little cause for siding with the emerging criollo bourgeoisie against the colonial authorities, especially since it was the local bourgeoisie that engaged in a struggle for cultural hegemony, while the Spanish authorities were usually unconcerned with the details of cultural developments in the territory as long as they did not feel threatened in their position as colonial rulers.

24 Evelio Govantes, "Vicente Escobar, uno de los precursores de la pintura en Cuba," conferencia leída el 17 de febrero de 1937 (Havana: Imprenta Molina y Cía., 1937), 16.

25 The following account of Espada's activities is based on Torres-Cueva's long introductory essay in *Obispo Espada: Ilustración, reforma y antiesclavismo*, ed. Eduardo Torres-Cuevas (Havana: Ed. Ciencias Sociales, 1990); the three quotations that follow can be found on pp. 68–74.

26 José Fernández de Castro, "El aporte negro en las letras de Cuba," *Revista Bimestre Cubana* 38 (1936): 62.

27 Félix Varela, "Memorandum about Slavery," in *Escritos políticos* (Havana: Ciencias Sociales, 1977), 263.

28 José Antonio Saco López, *Memoria sobre la vagancia en la isla de Cuba* (Santiago de Cuba: Instituto Cubano del Libro, 1974). The famous essay won a competition on the topic of idleness organized by the Real Sociedad Patriótica in 1831 and was published twice, in 1832 and 1834. See also his "The Suppression of the African Slave Trade on the Island of Cuba" (1845), in *Obras*, vol. 1 (New York: Librería Americana y Estrangera, 1853), 177–232, which contains lengthy discussions of the similarities and differences between Cuba, Haiti, and other Caribbean islands.

29 Juan Bautista Vermay, "Discurso leído por el director de la academia de dibujo D. Juan Bautista Vermay en los exámenes públicos de sus alumnos el dia 12 de febrero," *Memorias de la SE de La Havana*, no. 51, distr. en marzo de 1824, 383–89.

30 See, for instance, Serge Gruzinski, *La Colonisation de l'imaginaire* (Paris: Gallimard, 1988), on transcultural painting in Mexico.

31 Rigol may be referring here to affirmations made, for instance, by Guy Pérez Cisneros, who cites Serafín Ramírez and Saco to the effect that the clergy trained the painters of color, and that this was in keeping with strategies we know from the Spanish American mainland—Cuzco, Quito, et cetera. Yet Pérez Cisneros also admits that no direct data or documentation has been found that would confirm this hypothesis (*Características de la evolución de la pintura en Cuba* [Havana: Dirección General de Cultura, Ministerio de Educación, 1959], 30).

32 Rigol, *Apuntes*, 6.

33 Junta Ordinaria, 17 November 1817, in *Acuerdos de la Junta Ordinaria de la Real Sociedad Patriótica*, book 6, MS sheets 67–68. I have not been able to find this passage in the printed minutes of the Sociedad Patriótica.

34 According to Jean Lamore, students had to provide a certificate that proved the "limpieza de sangre" [purity of blood] in order to enter the academy, but he does not offer documentation; see Lamore's introduction to *Cecilia Valdés o La Loma del Angel*, by Cirilo Villaverde, ed. Jean Lamore (Madrid: Cátedra, 1992), 11.

35 Junta Ordinaria, 26 March 1821, in *Acuerdos de la Junta Ordinaria de la Real Sociedad Patriótica*, book 6, MS sheet 140.

36 Junta Ordinaria, 2 August 1821, in *Acuerdos de la Real Sociedad Patriótica*, book 6, MS sheet 447.

37 Antonio Bachiller y Morales, *Apuntes para la historia de las letras y de la instrucción pública de la isla de Cuba* (Havana: P. Massana, 1859), 89.

38 Antonio Bachiller y Morales, *Los negros* (Barcelona: Gorgas, n.d.), 109; italics mine.

39 Francisco Calcagno, *Poetas de color* (Havana: Imp. Militar de la V. de Soler, 1878), 11.

40 Bernardo G. Barros, "Discurso de ingreso como miembro de numero de la sección de literatura presentado a la academia pocos días antes de morir por el sr. Bernardo G. Barros," Academia Nacional de Artes y Letras, *Discursos pronunciados en la sesión celebrada por esta corporación a la memoria del académico fallecido sr. Bernardo G. Barros y Gómez, el día 12 de mayo de 1924* (Havana: El Siglo XX, 1924), 25.

41 See Carlos Venegas Fornias, *La urbanización de las murallas: Dependencia y modernidad* (Havana: Letras Cubanas, 1990), 9–37, on the introduction of neoclassicism in early-nineteenth-century urban planning and architecture in Havana.

42 One might argue that the construction of pastoral landscapes and tranquillity of rural scenes in Europe required just as much artifice and was just as politically operative in Europe as it was in the New World. The problem for Villaverde's painter would be, it seems, that pictorial conventions developed in, say, England to resolve class conflicts and transform the rural poor into objects of aesthetic consumption could not

readily be applied to landscapes marked by industrial agriculture and slavery. For a discussion of the political implications and intentions of landscape painting in late-eighteenth- and early-nineteenth-century England, see John Barrell, *The Dark Side of the Landscape: The Rural Poor in English Painting, 1730–1840* (Cambridge: Cambridge University Press, 1980).

## 3. BEYOND NATIONAL CULTURE, THE ABJECT

1   Leopoldo Horrego Estuch, *Plácido, el poeta infortunado* (Havana: Dirección General de Cultura, Ministerio Educación, 1960), 296, cites the following titles: Larramendi, *El mulato Plácido* (Spain, 1846); Lamoine, *Plácido* (Chile, 1871); Casimiro Delmonte, *La conspiración de la Escalera* (novel); Diego Vicente Tejera, *La muerte de Plácido* (theater play); Crescencio Rodríguez, *Plácido* (historical-dramatic episode). I have not been able to find further information about any of these titles.

2   According to Domingo Figarola-Caneda, *Placido (Poeta cubano): Contribución histórico-literaria* (Havana: Imprenta "El Siglo XX," 1922), 71–141, the first edition of his work was published in Palma de Mallorca by a Spaniard who had met Plácido in Havana and taken his early poems back to Spain. An edition by Plácido's mentor Sebastián Alfredo de Morales (1838–1842) was followed by seventeen collections, without counting the major or minor collections in various anthologies in Europe and the Americas. Editions include Mexico (1842, 1856), Barcelona (1845), New Orleans (1847), New York (1855, 1857, 1860), Mexico City (1856), Paris (1862), and a translation into French (1863). In 1875 Plácido's poetry formed the first volume of the *Colección de los Mejores Autores Americanos* (1875). His "Plegaria a Dios" was translated into English by Longfellow in 1849, as well as into French and German, where it was quoted in the biographical *Placido: Dichter und Märtyrer, Eine Biographie* (1865). Many of the earlier editions are extremely unreliable and include false information. To this day, there is no reliable edition that would establish the texts and variants, and one is left to guess which grammatical errors are due to the poet's lack of formal education, and which we owe to the typesetters.

3   See, for instance, the compilation *Placido (Poeta cubano)*, by Figarola-Caneda, or Francisco González del Valle's lecture "Es de Plácido la plegaria a Dios?" (Is the "Plegaria a Dios" written by Plácido?). González del Valle offers an extensive review of the literature about whether the "Plegaria" is authentic and concludes that there are no good reasons for doubting it. His lecture is followed by a response by Figarola-Caneda, who argues that Cuba's history "demands" and "requires" an answer to the question of authenticity. He concludes by saying that "nobody can predict for how long we will remain ignorant and condemned to not knowing more about Plácido's life and work. Probably it will have to be

forever." The discussion has thus come full circle: González del Valle joins the Academy of History because of the merits of his work on Plácido, but the end of the ceremony already prepares the audience for another "return" of Plácido (*Es de Plácido la plegaria a Dios? Discursos leídos en la recepción pública del doctor Francisco González del Valle, la noche del 16 de julio de 1923; contesta en nombre de la corporación el señor Domingo Figarola-Caneda* [Havana: El Siglo XX, 1923]).

4  See Robert L. Paquette, *Sugar Is Made with Blood: The Conspiracy of La Escalera and the Conflict between Empires over Slavery in Cuba* (Middletown, Conn.: Wesleyan University Press, 1988), 16.

5  Giral's films have caused consternation in Cuba because of their racial politics, and his *Techo de Vidrio* (Glass Roof, 1982), for instance, was completed with ICAIC funding but then withdrawn from distribution.

6  Abelardo Estorino, *La dolorosa historia del amor secreto de José Jacinto Milanés* (1974; first performance, 1985), in *Teatro Cubano Contemporáneo: antología,* ed. Carlos Espinosa Domínguez (Madrid: Sociedad Estatal Quinto Centenario, Fondo de Cultura Económica, Centro de Documentación Teatral, 1992).

7  Horrego Estuch, *Plácido*, 345.

8  Historians disagree about the political role of the free population of color. Although many claim that the free population was indeed where antislavery activities congealed (in *Sugar Is Made with Blood*, Paquette considers it the crucial element in the Escalera Conspiracy, for instance), Walterio Carbonell ("Plácido ¿conspirador?" quoted in Paquette, *Sugar Is Made with Blood*, 20) and others have argued that the true revolutionary class was the field slaves and that the free population was largely co-opted by the whites and exhausted their energies in imitating white culture.

I am inclined to think that in some sense, both views are correct. On the one hand, the free population of color—most of them mulattoes— occupied an intermediate position between black slaves and free whites, which meant that their foremost concern may have been to distinguish themselves from slaves. On the other hand, it also appears that as a matter of empirical fact, almost all large-scale, coordinated slave uprisings in the slaveholding Atlantic involved the free population of color. For an excellent analysis of the complex and constantly shifting relations between free people of color and slaves in Saint Domingue, see C. L. R. James, *The Black Jacobins* (1938; New York: Vintage, 1989). The argument I am pursuing here does not require that we decide this issue—the fact that whites *thought* of the free population of color as a great danger is what matters the most.

9  For a detailed discussion of the professional activities of the free population of color, see Pedro Deschamps Chapeaux's groundbreaking studies, especially *El negro en la economía habanera del siglo XIX* (Havana: Instituto Cubano del Libro, 1971).

10   Quoted in Paquette, *Sugar Is Made with Blood*, 127.

11   Quoted in Paquette, *Sugar Is Made with Blood*, 105. Although Vives would have preferred to expel the entire class from Cuban soil, he realized that such a radical measure might bring about precisely the upheaval he was fearing. In the end his recommendation came down to the suggestion that at least those convicted of a crime should be deported and incarcerated in the Spanish prisons on the North African coast.

12   Quoted in Paquette, *Sugar Is Made with Blood*, 142.

13   Ramiro Guerra's figures are fairly conservative (4,000 whites and mulattoes accused, 78 executed, 600 imprisoned, and 400 expelled from the island) but apparently do not include black slaves and those killed without trial (*Manual de la historia de Cuba*, vol. 1, *De su descubrimiento hasta 1868* [Madrid: Ediciones ERRE, 1975], 454–55). José Luciano Franco ("La conjura de los negreros," in *Ensayos históricos* [Havana: Ciencias Sociales, 1974], 198) puts the figure at 7,000 mulattoes and blacks beaten to death, but others have come up with numbers anywhere between 15,000 and 35,000 (see William Luis, *Literary Bondage: Slavery in Cuban Narrative* [Austin: University of Texas Press, 1990], 16).

14   Paquette, *Sugar Is Made with Blood*, 196–205; Daisy Cué Fernández, "Plácido y la Conspiración de la Escalera," in *Acerca de Plácido*, ed. Salvador Bueno (Havana: Letras Cubanas, 1985), 440–46.

15   Paquette, *Sugar Is Made with Blood*, 263.

16   Guerra, *Manual*, vol. 1, 454–56.

17   One of Turnbull's ideas appears to have been to engage the support of Haiti in the event that war between the United States and Britain broke out: Haitian troops could raise Louisiana's slaves and the free people of color and thus help break up the United States by intervening at the strategic location of New Orleans (Paquette, *Sugar Is Made with Blood*, 247).

18   For an excellent contextualized review of the historiography of the conspiracy, see the introduction to Paquette, *Sugar Is Made with Blood*. Interestingly, the Cuban Revolution of 1959 did not change the view of the conspiracy as a fabrication and instead favored a narrative of victimization.

19   Jorge Castellanos, *Placido: Poeta social y politico* (Miami: Ediciones Universal, 1984).

20   Ultimately, however, Castellanos's account depends on a good deal of psychological speculation, particularly on the assumption that Plácido was deeply religious. To my mind it is equally plausible to think that Plácido felt he was innocent because he thought the Cuban law of slavery illegitimate and was appealing to what legal scholars would call "natural law."

21   Domingo Del Monte was unquestionably at the center of these efforts. In a letter to Figarola-Caneda (1886), Federico Milanés gives an interesting account of Del Monte's project of the 1830s: "to give those who

aspired to distinguish themselves through their love of letters a tone of dignity and decorum which would elevate them in the eyes of the common people who until then habitually confused the intentions of those who wanted to represent the culture of the country in verse or prose with the intentions of those lampoonists and vulgar poetasters who are swarming at our fiestas and gatherings." This being his project, Del Monte was naturally severe with those who did not develop their natural talents and instead continued to play the humiliating role of the "cheerful improviser" (Figarola-Caneda, *Placido (Poeta cubano)*, 199).

22  Pedro José Guiteras, "Gabriel de la Concepción Valdés" (1874), in Bueno, *Acerca de Plácido*, 93. In his excellent prologue, Bueno gives a concise summary of the critical literature about Plácido and contextualizes in detail the changes in the critical evaluation of the poet (5–29). For a more combative account, see José Luciano Franco, "Plácido: Una polémica que tiene cien años," in Bueno, *Acerca de Plácido*, 379–93.

23  In close readings of some of Plácido's better poems, Vera M. Kutzinski shows that the issue of race and color is by no means as absent from the texts as some readers have claimed; see *Sugar's Secrets: Race and the Erotics of Cuban Nationalism* (Charlottesville: University Press of Virginia, 1993), 101–33.

24  Quoted in Figarola-Caneda, *Placido (Poeta cubano)*, 185–86.

25  See Figarola-Caneda, *Placido (Poeta cubano)*, which reprints many essays and letters from the extensive polemic surrounding the Morales edition.

26  Horrego Estuch, *Plácido*.

27  In the Morales edition, the verses "Caramba, qué sabio, cuánta ilustración" precede the poem as an epigraph attributed to "Lince" and are then repeated as the chorus of the poem. Lince (lynx) was a pseudonym used by Morales himself. It seems, then, that Plácido appropriated verses by his supporter (and editor) here. In a note, Morales explains that the poem alludes to a polemic, but he does not explain what the polemic was about. Plácido (Gabriel de la Concepción Valdés), *Poesías Completas con doscientas diez composiciones inéditas*, su retrato y un prólogo por Sebastián Alfredo de Morales (Havana: La primera de papel, 1886), 255.

28  This is the version of 1837 as quoted in Figarola-Caneda, *Placido (Poeta cubano)*, 224, 226.

29  Domingo Del Monte, *Escritos*, vol. 2 (Havana: Cultural, 1929), 149–50.

30  Quoted in Figarola-Caneda, *Placido (Poeta cubano)*, 199. Fernández de Castro, who shares the common disdain for Plácido, mentions in "El aporte negro" several other poets of color: A. Baldomero Rodríguez, Ambrosio Echemendía (both freed through the intervention of white intellectuals), A. Medina, J. B. Estrada, Vicente Silveira, and José del Carmen Díaz. According to Fernández de Castro, their work is only partially preserved, and of third or fourth category.

31  Quoted in Figarola-Caneda, *Placido (Poeta cubano)*, 200.

32  According to Corominas's *Diccionario etimológico*, *vil* comes from Latin *vilis*, which means cheap or without value. Casares's *Diccionario ideológico* defines *vil* as *ruin* (petty, despicable, mean), *bajo* (low), *despreciable* (abject, despicable), and adds that when used as an adjective it means "a disloyal person." Corominas also cites a variant for 1739 *en vilo* and explains that the original meaning is "without firmness" or "without stability."

33  Julia Kristeva, *Powers of Horror: An Essay on Abjection*, trans. Leon S. Roudiez (New York: Columbia University Press, 1982), 4.

34  Enrique Piñeyro, "Gabriel de la Concepción Valdés, *Plácido*," in Bueno, *Acerca de Plácido*, 207–27.

35  The well-known "Despedida a mi madre" (Goodbye to my mother), a poem Plácido wrote while awaiting his execution, can also be read as a response to the discourse of the abject, albeit not in an ironic key. Referring to his fate as "sangrienta historia" [bloody history], he adopts the perspective of the afterlife: "ya moro en la gloria, / Y mi plácida lira a tu memoria / Lanza en la tumba su postrer sonido. / Sonido dulce, melodioso, santo, / Glorioso, espiritual, puro, divino. / Inocente, espontáneo" [Already I dwell in the glory, / And my calm lyre sends in your memory / in the grave its last sounds. / A sweet, melodious, saintly sound, / Glorious, spiritual, pure, divine. / Innocent, spontaneous] (in *Poesías Completas*, ed. Morales, 37). The list of attributes he promises for his posthumous poetry reflects precisely what his contemporaries denied him, and what he ironically attributed to Milanés.

36  Manuel Sanguily, "Un improvisador cubano," in Bueno, *Acerca de Plácido*, 160–76.

37  Marcelino Menéndez Pelayo, "De 'Historia de la poesía hispanoamericana,'" in Bueno, *Acerca de Plácido*, 153.

38  Quoted in Figarola-Caneda, *Placido (Poeta cubano)*, 139.

39  Cintio Vitier, a member of the Orígenes group around Lezama Lima and an important figure in Cuba's cultural life of the twentieth century, argues the exact opposite. In "Cubanía de Plácido," a chapter from his *Lo Cubano en la poesía* (1958; reprinted in Bueno, *Acerca de Plácido*, 346–56), he writes: "Plácido's poetry lives and dies with the author; it does not continue anything, nor does it announce anything, it does not belong to the historical becoming." Now, Plácido clearly belongs to a period when what might count as "Cuban" was far from established. In fact, I would argue that it was not until after the suppression of the cultures of radical antislavery that "Cubanity" in Vitier's sense came into being. It is only within a Creole teleology that considers the expression of Cubanity the goal of history that Plácido vanishes into abject singularity. While ostensibly explaining why Plácido disappeared, Vitier's observation in fact allows us to understand why Plácido has not vanished: once we erase from historical memory the contexts that produced

a certain violent event, we lose all means for integrating this event into our explanatory narratives and transforming this event into patterns of experience—hence Plácido's returns.

40  Jorge Mañach, *Indagación del choteo* (Miami: Mnemosyne, 1969), 26. Thanks to Hortensia Calvo for alerting me to the choteo in relation to Plácido.

41  Albert Bates Lord, *The Singer of Tales* (Cambridge: Harvard University Press, 2000).

42  Eugenio María de Hostos, "Placido," in Bueno, *Acerca de Plácido*, 71. Hostos was one of the leading Spanish American critics, pedagogues, and writers of the nineteenth century, who in literary histories is often credited for being a truly modern figure who lived "at the height of his time" and "taught Spanish America how to think"; see Luis O. Zayas Micheli, "Eugenio María de Hostos," in *Historia de la Literatura hispanoamericana*, ed. Luis Iñigo Madrigal, vol. 2 (Madrid: Cátedra, 1987), 459. Puerto Rican by birth, Hostos was naturally interested in the question of colonialism and nationalism and favored an Antillean confederation as an alternative to Spanish rule (see his novel *Peregrinación de Bayoán*).

43  This is an interesting reversal of David Brion Davis's account of the symmetries between slavery and colonialism, and antislavery and the struggle for independence. Where Davis thinks that it makes sense to think of abolitionism "enslaving the British West Indies" in the early nineteenth century (see Introduction, this volume), Plácido seems to suggest that national independence means (continued) slavery for some of those ostensibly liberated.

44  "A Venecia," in *Poesías Completas*, ed. Morales, 33.

45  In 1830 Russia had brutally suppressed a Polish uprising and abandoned its earlier policy of tolerating a Polish monarchy loyal to the czar. It is quite likely that reports of these events prompted Plácido to write about the remote Eastern European nation. Because he closely collaborated with Morales, the chief editor of a Matanzas newspaper, Plácido would thus have had relatively easy access to political information.

46  See Christopher Schmidt-Nowara, *Empire and Antislavery: Spain, Cuba, and Puerto Rico, 1833–1874* (Pittsburgh: University of Pittsburgh Press, 1999), 1–36, for a more detailed account of the events in Spain and their impact on the colonies.

47  Recent work on the Carlist War has tended to pay more attention to the popular and regional aspects behind the uprising rather than the constitutional and dynastic issues. See Francisco Asín and Alfonso Bullón de Mendoza, *Carlismo y sociedad, 1833–1840* (Zaragoza: Librería General, 1987). As far as Cuba was concerned, however, the constitutional question was clearly central, and it is doubtful that Plácido's account was intended to allude to any other underlying conflicts.

48  "Quien lleva santos y esgrime espada / Acrecentando la rebelión, / Y

cruel seduce los infelices / Bajo pretexto de religión; / Es una fiera voraz, inícua, / Maligno miembro de la Nación, / Monstruo execrable, que con mil vidas / No paga el colmo de su traición" [Those who carry statues of saints and fight with swords / Thus increasing the rebellion / And cruelly seduce the unfortunate / Under the pretext of religion / Are ravenous wicked beasts, / Malignant members of the Nation, / Abominable monsters who do not with a thousand lives / pay for the extent of their betrayal].

49   Guerra, *Manual*, 396. It is doubtful that the Spanish presented this reason in good faith, but that does not make it a bad argument. Guerra is quick to dismiss it, but it strikes me as remarkable that this is a repeat of arguments that in the case of France and Saint Domingue led to the Haitian Revolution (see part 3 in this volume).

50   Quoted in Zayas Micheli, "Eugenio María de Hostos," 462.

51   Hostos, "Plácido," in Bueno, *Acerca de Plácido*, 75–76.

### 4. CUBAN ANTISLAVERY NARRATIVES

1   Gertrudis Gómez de Avellaneda, *Sab*, ed. Mary Cruz (Havana: Instituto del Libro Cubano, 1973).

2   Del Monte started his *tertulia* in Matanzas in 1834 and moved it to Havana in 1835, where it continued to function until he left Cuba in 1843. On Del Monte and his circle, see José Zacarías González del Valle y Ramírez, *La vida literaria en Cuba (1836–1840)* (Havana: Publicaciones de la Secretaría de Educación, 1938), a historical account by a member of Del Monte's salon. See also Urbano Martínez Carmenate, *Domingo Del Monte y su tiempo* (Havana: Ediciones Unión, 1997); and Elías Entralgo, *Domingo Delmonte* (Havana: Cultural, 1940). For a discussion of nineteenth-century Cuban literature and culture in general, see Reynaldo Gonzáles, *Contradanzas y latigazos* (Havana: Letras Cubanas, 1983) and Roberto Friol, "La novela cubana en el siglo XIX," *Unión* 6, no. 4 (1968): 179–207; for the history of printing in Cuba, see Ambrosio Fornet, *El libro en Cuba: siglos XVIII y XIX* (Havana: Editorial Letras Cubanas, 1994).

3   Juan Francisco Manzano, *Obras* (Havana: Instituto Cubano del Libro, 1972).

4   Apart from Manzano's *Autobiografía*—the only known autobiography of a slave written in Spanish America—Madden's dossier included various fictional narratives, poems, and interviews with Del Monte. See William Luis, *Literary Bondage: Slavery in Cuban Narrative* (Austin: University of Texas Press, 1990), 35–40, for further details and references.

5   Salvador Bueno, ed., *Cuentos cubanos del siglo XIX: Antología* (Havana: Editorial Arte y Literatura, 1975), 103–32.

6   Anselmo Suárez y Romero, *Francisco: El ingenio o Las delicias del campo (Las escenas pasan antes de 1838)*, ed. Eduardo Castañeda (Havana: In-

stituto del Libro, 1970). The novel was written during a stay on a plantation owned by Suárez y Romero's family; it was not published until 1880.

7   Iván A. Schulman, "Reflections on Cuba and Its Antislavery Literature,"
    *SECLOLAS Annals* 7 (1976): 65.

8   Miguel Barnet, *Biografía de un cimarrón* (Havana: Academia de Ciencias
    de Cuba, Instituto de Ethnología y Folklore, 1966); César Leante, *Los
    guerrilleros negros* (Mexico City: Siglo Veintiuno, 1979); Reinaldo Arenas,
    *La loma del ángel* (Miami: Ediciones Universal, 1995).

9   See Mary Louise Pratt, *Imperial Eyes: Travel Writing and Transculturation*
    (London: Routledge, 1992), 86–107, for an exploration of the link be-
    tween the sentimental love stories and abolitionism.

10  Quoted in Lorna Vera Williams, *The Representation of Slavery in Cuban
    Fiction* (Columbia: University of Missouri Press, 1994), 2.

11  Schulman, "Reflections," 66 n. 4.

12  Quoted in Williams, *Representation of Slavery,* 8.

13  Orlando Patterson, *Slavery and Social Death: A Comparative Study* (Cam-
    bridge: Harvard University Press, 1982), 45.

14  Félix Varela, who in 1822 had been sent to Spain to represent Cuba in
    the Cortes with instructions to call for a repudiation of the slave trade
    treaty with Britain, instead introduced a resolution strengthening the
    ban and signaling gradual abolition. After the royalist coup and the
    dissolution of the Cortes, his project simply vanished (Robin Blackburn,
    *The Overthrow of Colonial Slavery* [New York: Verso, 1988], 394–95).

15  Schulman, "Reflections," 60.

16  Franklin W. Knight, *Slave Society in Cuba during the Nineteenth Century*
    (Madison: University of Wisconsin Press, 1970), 365, table 3. I have
    rounded the figures.

17  María Pilar Pérez Cantó, "Intentos de colonización blanca en Cuba du-
    rante el s. XIX," *Revista Internacional de Sociología* 42 (1984): 491–516.

18  José Fernández de Castro, "El aporte negro en las letras de Cuba,"
    *Revista Bimestre Cubana* 38 (1936): 41.

19  Del Monte, *Escritos,* vol. 1 (Havana: Cultural, 1929), 231. Compare also
    the following account of the political and demographic situation of Cuba
    in an essay entitled "Estado de la población blanca y de color de la isla de
    Cuba, en 1839" (State of the white population and that of color on the
    island of Cuba in 1839): "There are so many black slaves here and we are
    surrounded by them everywhere, and [one day] they will rise up against
    the whites and kill them and the island will be ruined, but when an
    illustrious patrician forcefully calls out that we have a lot of blacks who
    in the end will make themselves the owners of the island if we continue
    to introduce African-born slaves, and that the only remedy that we have
    is to prohibit once and for all the trade, and to punish those who break
    the law, then that person is regarded with contempt, as if he were a
    visionary" (Del Monte, *Escritos,* vol. 1, 154–55). Like Saco, Del Monte
    points to silence as the political problem of the Creole elite.

20  See Williams, *Representation of Slavery*, 5–7, for a brief account of the vicissitudes of the academy.

21  As early as 1792 we find discussions of the affective benefits and dangers of novels in the *Papel Periódico* (29 January) under the title "A las señoritas de la Havana" (To the young ladies of Havana): "Some people believe that the reading of novels, far from being dangerous, is useful; but if I have to give my view on this matter, I confess that those novels that do not transgress the limits of decency serve the good purpose of softening hard souls, yet very harmful for the sensible ones." In Cuba, as in most other places in Spanish America, the notion that fiction, and particularly the novel, was dangerous slowly vanished in the first decades of the nineteenth century.

22  Julio Ramos, in "Cuerpo, lengua, subjetividad," *Revista de Crítica Latinoamericana* 19 (1993): 225–37, proposes an alternative to the realist assessment of the narratives, although he does not link the antislavery novels to any specific historical constellation. He shows that the antislavery narratives essentially do two things: on the one hand, they integrate the slave in what he calls "the rationality of language," that is, they change the discourse about slaves from a discourse about mere physical bodies into a discourse about human subjects; on the other, they hierarchize forms of speech in a way that the vernacular Spanish of the slaves is devalorized vis-à-vis other, more educated forms of speech.

23  Quoted in Mary Cruz, "*Sab*: Su texto y contexto," in *Sab*, by Gertrudis Gómez de Avellaneda, ed. Mary Cruz (Havana: Instituto del Libro Cubano, 1973), 43.

24  This reading turns on a normative interpretation of the first occurrence of the term *poesía* as referring not to a literary genre but to certain pleasing and noble qualities that can be embodied by reality, prose, or, of course, poetry in the more narrow sense. Both usages were customary in the nineteenth century, and the immediate context justifies this reading (after all, Hugo's text is not poetry but a novel). Tanco y Bosmeniel's reference has often been taken out of context and used as evidence that the identitarian ideal of la Cuba mulata originates with the antislavery novel. The context, however, shows quite clearly that Tanco y Bosmeniel was rather more ambivalent about this "poetry" than the sentence by itself lets on.

25  Gómez de Avellaneda, *Sab*, 243.

26  For a reading of the issue of race in *Sab* as an allegory for gender, see Doris Sommer, *Foundational Fictions: The National Romances of Latin America* (Berkeley and Los Angeles: University of California Press, 1991), 114–37.

27  Quoted in Eric J. Sundquist, *To Wake the Nations: Race in the Making of American Literature* (Cambridge: Harvard University Press, 1993), 33.

28  Francisco Arango y Parreño, "Letter to the Spanish King," 20 November

1791, in *Obras*, vol. 1 (Havana: Dirección de Cultura, Ministerio de Educación, 1952), 109–12.

29  Slavoj Žižek, *The Sublime Object of Ideology* (London: Verso, 1989), 33.

30  Žižek's argument remains strangely underdeveloped in this respect. His use of Kafka as his example for the operations of ideology "on the side of reality" may serve as an illustration here: Kafka's nightmarish tales of an all-powerful and omnipresent bureaucracy should not be read, Žižek argues, as exaggerations of a subjectively distorted experience; they merely show that we always already relate to bureaucracy as if it were omnipresent and all-powerful. This *as if* is located not on the level of conscious belief but in the material practices that are themselves constitutive of a social field.

The reason for the wide popularity this account of the operations of ideology enjoys is that it seems to avoid using notions of truth, reflection, misrepresentation, or the false consciousness of classical Marxist theory, and their objectivist or realist correlatives. By locating fantasy on the side of reality, Žižek seems to be able to produce a theory of ideology that does not immediately fold into an unpromising return to some of the most controversial issues in the history of philosophy and political theory. The problem is that Žižek does not appear to differentiate between ideology as that which informs our material or social practices and the representation of an ideological fantasy in a literary text. As a result, it seems almost impossible to distinguish the unconscious enactment of an ideological fantasy from its critical representation. Are Kafka's stories simply another instantiation–perhaps even a reinscription—of our way of relating to an omnipotent bureaucracy?

31  We find this version of the argument from realism, for instance, in the memoirs of a Spanish merchant in Cuba who wrote that "the treatment given to the slaves, except for rare instances, is not as rigorous as the novelists paint it" (quoted in Fernández de Castro, *El aporte negro*, 41).

32  Villaverde first wrote a brief novella in 1839 and in the same year reworked it into a longer text that eventually became the basis for the first two chapters of the 1882 text. For an account of the differences between these versions, see Luis, *Literary Bondage*, 102–18. See also my introduction to a new translation of the 1882 novel: Cirilo Villaverde, *Cecilia Valdés, or El Angel Hill*, trans. Helen Lane, ed. Sibylle Fischer (New York: Oxford University Press, 2004).

33  Cirilo Villaverde, *Cecilia Valdés o La Loma del Angel* (Madrid: Cátedra, 1992).

34  Although the incest theme also appears in some other early Cuban narratives (see especially the early fiction of Villaverde), it is indicative that it also appears in several texts that are usually counted among the Spanish American indigenist tradition, for example, *Cumandá* (1879), an Ecuadorian novel by Juan León Mera, and *Aves sin nido* (1889), a novel by the Peruvian Clorinda Matto de Turner, further supporting the

hypothesis that incest is somehow a particularly suitable fantasy for the negotiation of racial anxieties.

35 Martín Morúa Delgado, *Sofía* (Havana: Instituto Cubano del Libro, 1972). See also Morúa Delgado's essay "Las novelas del Sr. Villaverde" (The novels of Mr. Villaverde) (1891), in which he accuses Villaverde of having failed to transcend the "malignant spirit of those times"; *Impresiones literarias y otras páginas*, vol. 5 of *Obras Completas* (Havana: Edición de la Comisión Nacional del Centenario de Martín Morúa Delgado, 1959), 24. For a detailed discussion of Morúa Delgado's novel, see Vera M. Kutzinski, *Sugar's Secrets: Race and the Erotics of Cuban Nationalism* (Charlottesville: University Press of Virginia, 1993), 101–33; and Luis, *Literary Bondage*, 139–61.

36 Lino Novás Calvo, *El negrero, vida novelada de Pedro Blanco Fernández de Trava* (Madrid: Espasa-Calpe, 1933).

37 Cirilo Villaverde, *La primitiva Cecilia Valdés de Cirilo Villaverde* (Havana: Imprenta de Cuba Intelectual, 1910), n.p.

38 For example, Patterson's comparative analysis of slavery in *Slavery and Social Death*, which covers slaveholding practices from antiquity to the nineteenth century around the globe, mentions incest just once, in relation to sacralizing rituals that shore up royal authority in various parts of the world, but makes no mention of it as a possible effect of treating slaves as nonsocial beings. Verena Martínez-Alier's *Marriage, Class, and Colour in Nineteenth-Century Cuba: A Study of Racial Attitudes and Sexual Values in a Slave Society* (Ann Arbor: University of Michigan Press, 1989) does not mention it at all.

39 Luis, *Literary Bondage*, 117–18. See Claude Lévi-Strauss, *The Elementary Structures of Kinship*, trans. James Harle Bell and John Richard von Sturmer, ed. Rodney Needham (Boston: Beacon Press 1969), for a critical review of the nineteenth- and early-twentieth-century literature on this topic.

40 Doris Sommer, *Proceed with Caution, When Engaged by Minority Writing in the Americas* (Cambridge: Harvard University Press, 1999), 209.

41 Kutzinski, *Sugar's Secrets*, 27.

42 Werner Sollors, *Neither Black nor White yet Both: Thematic Explorations of Interracial Literature* (Cambridge: Harvard University Press, 1997), 314. His examples range from Brazil to Cuba and the U.S. South and include *Cecilia Valdés*, but not the other Cuban antislavery narratives I discuss in this chapter.

43 Lévi-Strauss points out that what is universal is the very fact of an incest taboo. What does and does not count as incest, beyond the case of parent/child, varies considerably from culture to culture. In the case of the Cuban antislavery novels, it is thus significant that the infractions of the taboo are not of the most paradigmatic kind, thus leaving room for moral ambiguity.

44 Luis glosses Leante as saying that "Cecilia and Leonardo had to be

brother and sister because so are the two races which they represent" (*Literary Bondage,* 117). But Leante's position may actually be a little more ambivalent than is obvious at first sight, since he seems also to reject the incest theme as the central axis of the novel: the "tragedy does not lie in the incestuous love affair of Leonardo and Cecilia, but in the historical space" (César Leante, "Cecilia Valdés, espejo de la esclavitud," *Casa de las Américas* 15 [1975]: 20).

45  This is David Grene's translation: Sophocles, *Oedipus the King,* 2d ed. (Chicago: University of Chicago Press, 1991), 52.980–83.

46  The term "miscegenation" (derived from Latin "miscere" to mix, and "genus," which can mean anything from "sort" and "kind" to "gender," but is here intended to mean "race") was invented in 1864 in a pamphlet against Abraham Lincoln, who was at the time running for re-election (Werner Sollors, *Neither Black nor White Yet Both: Thematic Explorations of Interracial Literature* [Cambridge: Harvard University Press, 1997], 287). The terms commonly used in Cuba to signify conceptions of racial, ethnic, and cultural mixture, from "mestizaje" and "mulatez" to Fernando Ortiz's anthropological concept of "transculturation" (*Cuban Counterpoint of Sugar and Tobacco* [1940], Durham: Duke University Press, 1995) tend to have less of a pejorative tone.

47  Sollors, *Neither Black nor White,* 316–19.

48  For a very suggestive reading of the incest theme in relation to the political and philosophical problem of recognition, see Judith Butler, *Antigone's Claim: Kinship between Life and Death* (New York: Columbia University Press, 2000), esp. 12–13.

### 5. MEMORY, TRAUMA, HISTORY

The poem in the chapter epigraph is quoted in Franklin J. Franco, *Los negros, los mulatos y la nación dominicana,* 8th ed. (Santo Domingo: Editora Nacional, 1989), 74.

1  Antonio del Monte y Tejada, quoted in Frank Moya Pons, *Manual de Historia Dominicana* (Santo Domingo: Caribbean Publishers, 1992), 192.

2  There is a noticeable variation in terminology used by historians in relation to the changes of political regime in eastern Hispaniola, obviously reflecting the ideological positions of the authors. The period between 1822 and 1844 is most commonly called "Haitian occupation," even though the annexation happened through a treaty and not through military force. Some more pro-Haitian authors such as Franklin Franco Pichardo thus refer to it as the "period of integration with Haiti." Toussaint Louverture's and Dessalines's attempts to incorporate Santo Domingo within the Haitian Republic are typically referred to as "invasions," although that also gives a somewhat misleading picture. It would seem more accurate to describe the situation in terms of colonial warfare and revolutionary civil war.

3   Etienne Balibar, "The Nation Form: History and Ideology," trans. Chris Turner, in *Race, Nation, Class,* by Etienne Balibar and Immanuel Wallerstein (New York: Verso, 1991), 87.

4   For an excellent critique of the developmentalist narrative, see Dominick LaCapra's discussion of Charles Taylor's *Sources of the Self* in LaCapra's collection of essays *Representing the Holocaust: History, Theory, Trauma* (Ithaca: Cornell University Press, 1994), 183–87. LaCapra draws a clear connection between what he calls "redemptive narratives" (of a group of people or, as in the case of Taylor, the whole of Western history and philosophy) and the inability to perceive historical discontinuities, the operations of historical trauma, and the problematic and contested constitution of historical subjects.

5   I would like to thank Julia Hell for bibliographical help, and, especially, endlessly interesting conversations about the topic of memory and trauma.

6   Jacqueline Rose, *States of Fantasy* (Oxford: Clarendon, 1996), 3. Fantasies are not just "psychical facades which bar the way to memories" (Freud in a letter to Fliess, quoted by Rose, p. 5), she argues, but bear the imprint of the event that is being displaced. While for Rose they are reelaborations of memories, Žižek goes so far as to consider them the core structure that gives support and coherence to social reality itself (*The Sublime Object of Ideology* [London: Verso, 1989], 36, 44), whereas Lacan appears to have put more emphasis on the protective function of fantasies.

7   Edouard Glissant, *Caribbean Discourse: Selected Essays,* trans. Michael Dash (Charlottesville: University Press of Virginia, 1989), 64.

8   One may of course wonder whether assigning such paradigmatic status to the Holocaust is in itself appropriate. But whatever we might think regarding this question, the fact remains that claiming the Holocaust and the memory of the Holocaust has become an extremely common gesture of vindication. See, for instance, Paul Gilroy, *The Black Atlantic* (Cambridge: Harvard University Press, 1993), which draws strongly on a perceived similarity between slavery and the Holocaust, and between Jewish and African diasporas.

9   Shoshana Felman, "After the Apocalypse: Paul de Man and the Fall to Silence," in *Testimony: Crises of Witnessing in Literature, Psychoanalysis, and History,* by Shoshana Felman and Dori Laub (New York: Routledge, 1992), 140, 139. LaCapra offers a trenchant critique of this essay in "Paul de Man as Object of Transference," in *Representing the Holocaust,* 116–25.

10  Sigmund Freud, *Moses and Monotheism,* in *The Standard Edition of the Complete Psychological Works of Sigmund Freud,* trans. James Strachey, vol. 23 (London: Hogarth Press, 1953–1974), 7–137.

11  Cathy Caruth, *Unclaimed Experience: Trauma, Narrative, and History* (Baltimore: Johns Hopkins University Press, 1996), 11.

12  There is something puzzling about the fact that Caruth foregrounds the issue of referentiality quite so much. I suspect that the imaginary opponent is some benighted Rankian who claims that history "speaks of its own accord." Of course, there are some such people, but much innovative recent historical work gives ample room to issues of interpretation, historical memory, and the repression thereof; one only needs to think of Guha's work on Indian peasant uprisings, or the recent debates on slavery and antislavery, with their strong appeal to counterfactual forms of reasoning, and their attempts to read texts against the grain. No doubt historians of all sorts, anthropologists, cultural critics, and others frequently differ as to how much weight to give to claims that can be made only by inference and cannot be verified. But the real issue here is not some crude positivism but what *kind* of interpretation is most appropriate. By making the argument turn on the issue of referentiality, Caruth in fact misses the opportunity to show how skillful analytic readings, of the sort she herself practices, can indeed illuminate aspects of the historical experience that other forms of argument overlook. Perhaps the issue here is a dispute over domains: if history is referential, it is in the domain of the historian; if it is not straightforwardly referential, it is the domain of the analytic critic. But this is precisely what we should not argue. Instead, we need to show how the territory of the historian is profoundly shaped by subjective factors, even if it is in some sense referential.

13  Caruth, *Unclaimed Experience*, 136 n. 22.

14  Although Žižek does not say so, it seems to me that he is drawing here on Freud's thesis of the murder of the primal father by the group of disempowered sons, which leads first to the repression of the deed and eventually to its compulsive repetition in the future. See *Moses and Monotheism*, 23 and esp. 81–89. See also *Totem and Taboo*, in *Standard Edition*, vol. 13, pp. 1–161.

15  Žižek goes to some lengths to establish the parallelism between Benjamin and Hegel here. Having argued that Hegel is a far cry from the historicist objectivism that some attribute to him, Žižek proceeds to suggest (and then refute) the idea that Benjamin, in the *Theses*, comes dangerously close to Stalinism (*Sublime Object of Ideology*, 142–43). In this account, both have been misunderstood as totalitarian—clearly a dubious claim in the case of Benjamin—which only further illustrates that there must be an unspoken agenda behind the argument here.

16  It is interesting in this respect that Žižek seizes the concept of transference to explain the possibility—not the necessity—of repetition: yet in the classical Freudian analytic process, it is transference through which the subject breaks through the cycles of compulsive repetition. And although transference works differently for Lacan, it is when the analysand abandons transference that "acting out" gives way to "working

through." It seems that Žižek has a greater investment in keeping the concept of repetition in place than in trying to give a political content to transference as that which might put an end to repetition.

17 Although the secret society that drove the struggle toward independence in 1844—the so-called Trinitarios—were in their vast majority white, some prominent blacks, most importantly the three brothers Puello, eventually joined their forces. This was invaluable for the society, since their pro-Haitian opponents had been arguing that the Trinitarios would reintroduce slavery.

18 For an excellent discussion of the writings of Peña Batlle and Balaguer, and Dominican anti-Haitianism in general, see Pedro L. San Miguel, *La isla imaginada: Historia, identidad y utopía en La Española* (Santo Domingo: Isla Negra/La Trinitaria, 1997), esp. 82–100.

19 In 1801 an armed confrontation between the forces of Toussaint Louverture and the authorities in Santo Domingo was avoided through last-minute negotiations. Louverture's forces entered the town of Santo Domingo unopposed, a Te Deum was performed for him in the cathedral, and he received the keys of the city, after which he went straight to the main square and proclaimed all people in Santo Domingo free, in accordance with the principles of liberty, equality, and fraternity and the Declaration of the Rights of Man and Citizen. Similarly, in 1822, the Haitian takeover was preceded by negotiations between Núñez de Cáceres—who realized that his declaration of independence was not going to last—and the Haitian president Boyer. Not a single shot was fired that time. Haitian incursions into Dominican territory under Soulouque were of a different order and took place without diplomatic backup. However, the experiential patterns were set, I would argue, by the events in the early nineteenth century, and it was according to those patterns that the later events were interpreted.

20 Emilio Rodríguez Demorizi, ed., *Poesía popular dominicana* (Santo Domingo: UCMM, 1973), 85. Rodríguez Demorizi points out that some of the virulently anti-Haitian "poetry" published in newspapers at the time of the War of Restoration was in fact planted by pro-Spanish annexationists who tended to benefit from arousing and manipulating anti-Haitian feelings. The "nationalist" position at this point would probably have played down latent anti-Haitianism; in fact, Haiti supported the anti-Spanish side of the war.

21 One of the most exhaustive Dominican treatments of the event is that of Bernardo Vega, *Trujillo y Haiti*, vol. 1 (1930–1937; Santo Domingo: Fundación Cultural Dominicana, 1988). See also Edwidge Danticat, *The Farming of the Bones* (New York: Soho Press, 1998); and Mario Vargas Llosa, *La fiesta del chivo* (Mexico City: Alfaguara, 2000).

22 Joaquín Balaguer, *La isla al revés: Haití y el destino dominicano* (Santo Domingo: Fundación José Antonio Caro, 1983), 36.

23  Quoted in Vega, *Trujillo y Haiti*, 25. What becomes clear in these linguistic manipulations is the deeply political nature of any vocabulary of color and race.

24  See Moya Pons, *Manual*, for a detailed account of the changing alliances, Dessalines's invasion, and Dominican resistance to French rule in the aftermath of Napoleon's invasion of Spain. See Emilio Cordero Michel, *La Revolución Haitiana y Santo Domingo* (Santo Domingo: Editora Nacional, 1968), for an account of Ferrand's pro-slavery activities.

25  Historians vary in their assessment of Boyer's motivations. While some argue that the main motive for occupying Santo Domingo was a justified desire to protect Haiti against French aggression (e.g., Franco Pichardo, *Historia del pueblo dominicano;* Vega, *Trujillo y Haiti;* Cordero Michel, *La revolución haitiana*), others also point to internal problems in Haiti, having to do with controlling the veterans of the revolutionary war in Haiti (e.g., Moya Pons, *Manual*, 219–20).

26  Moya Pons, *Manual*, 223.

27  The Haitian legal code had been established by Pétion and entailed, like the Napoleonic reforms that had inspired it, a radical rationalization and unification of the civil code.

28  The abolition of traditional forms of collective landownership and the institutionalization of individual property rights were crucial for the development of an export-oriented capitalist economy everywhere on the periphery. Boyer's land reform had the additional purpose of making land available for distribution among former Dominican slaves and among Haitians who had rendered services to Boyer or the Haitian state.

29  Despite the taxes, the economy in the eastern part picked up considerably, in part because of land distributed to *libertos* and former slaves, which created an internal market. According to some calculations, almost half of the families in the eastern part benefited from the redistribution of land. Boyer also benefited landowners by reducing debts incurred during the colonial period to the cathedral and other religious institutions (the prime lenders) to one-third of the original sum. Then in 1836 the economic crisis in Europe made prices rise and set off an inflationary spiral that did not stop for years and led to a severe monetary crisis in the West; see Franco Pichardo, *Historia del pueblo dominicano*, vol. 1 (Santo Domingo: Instituto del Libro, 1992), 185–88.

30  David Nicholls, *From Dessalines to Duvalier: Race, Colour, and National Independence in Haiti* (New Brunswick: Rutgers University Press, 1996), 69. Twentieth-century Haitian nationalism typically presents a very different image of Haiti. Price-Mars's famous anthropological study *Ainsi parla l'oncle*, conceived in the context of the U.S. occupation of Haiti and clearly intended as a statement of national culture, for instance, documents and memorializes the African roots of Haitian peasant culture.

Price-Mars's charge of "Bovaryism" against a postcolonial elite with continuing attachment to French metropolitan culture clearly aims to promote a popular culture whose main values were not modernization and secularism. However, the fact that Haitian elites have tended to devalorize popular culture of syncretic or African roots should not lead us to overlook that the white Creole elite all over the Caribbean were either unable or unwilling to recognize the Haitian political project as a modern one, and, moreover, one that might offer an alternative to their own idea of modernization and progress.

31  See Franco, *Los negros, los mulatos y la nación dominicana:* "The unification of the East with the Western part meant a definite leap forward in the process of the development of the social and economic forces" (135). Franco points out that Dominican historians traditionally insist that the "flor y nata" [crème de la crème] of Dominican families fled the country, and that there was widespread resistance against the Haitians; against this view, Franco argues that resistance remained ineffective, largely because it lacked the support of the majority of the population (136).

32  In Spanish American literature, *indigenismo* is customarily distinguished from *indianismo.* The latter usually refers to depictions of the aboriginal population of the Americas that borrow so heavily from European romantic imagery that the portrait in the end has little to do with native Americans. The term "indigenismo" is typically reserved for more culturally correct and politically engaged depictions (e.g., Arguedas or Scorza in Peru) of the indigenous population. Dominicans have traditionally referred to their homegrown literary style as indigenismo, although it is obviously much closer to what in Spanish America would normally be called indianismo. It is for that reason that I often use the English term "Indians" rather than "indigenous" or "native" in my discussions: the protagonists of the Dominican stories and poems had little in common with the aboriginal population and are better referred to with the quasi-fictional name of "Indians."

### 6. GUILT AND BETRAYAL IN SANTO DOMINGO

1  Manuel de J. Galván, *Enriquillo* (Mexico City: Editorial Porrúa, 1986), translated as *The Cross and the Sword* by Robert Graves, UNESCO collection of representative works, Latin American series (Bloomington: Indiana University Press, 1954).

2  See Doris Sommer, *Foundational Fictions: The National Romances of Latin America* (Berkeley and Los Angeles: University of California Press, 1991), 233–56, for a critical contextual reading of *Enriquillo.* See also Concha Meléndez, *La novela indianista en hispanoamerica (1832–1889)* (Río Piedras, P.R.: Ediciones de la Universidad de Puerto Rico, 1961), for an example for earlier interpretations of indianismo.

3 See José Joaquín Pérez's prologue to Javier Francisco Angulo y Guridi's historical drama *Iguaniona: Drama histórico en verso y en tres actos* (1882; Santo Domingo: Publicaciones América, 1978).

4 See, for instance, Rodríguez Demorizi's *Poesía popular dominicana*, or Max Henríquez Ureña's chapters on folklore in his *Panorama historico de la literatura dominicana* (Santo Domingo: Editorial Libreria Dominicana, 1965). The only affirmation of an ethnic filiation of Dominicans and the indigenous population I have found is, ironically, in a book written by a nineteenth-century Haitian intellectual: Emile Nau, in *Histoire des Caciques d'Haïti*, 2 vols. (Port-au-Prince: Panorama, 1963), appears to have found some plausibility in that claim.

5 Javier Francisco Angulo y Guridi, *La fantasma de Higüey* (Havana: Davila, 1857).

6 José Joaquín Pérez, *Fantasías indígenas y otros poemas*, with an introduction and notes by José Alcántara Almánzar (Santo Domingo: Fundación Corripio, 1989).

7 See, for instance, Alcántara Almánzar, who in his notes to the 1989 edition of Pérez, *Fantasías indígenas*, charges that Pérez's chronology is faulty (31).

8 Alejandro Llenas, "La boca del indio," in *Tradiciones y cuentos dominicanos*, ed. Emilio Rodríguez Demorizi (Santo Domingo: Julio D. Postigo e hijos Editores, 1969), 133–38.

9 Other texts that have some or all of these features include not only Angulo y Guridi's *La fantasma de Higüey* (1857) but also Félix María Del Monte's zarzuela, *Ozema o la joven indiana* (1867), Angulo y Guridi's *Iguaniona* (written in 1867 and published in 1881), and Salomé Ureña de Henríquez's epic poem *Anacaona* (published in 1880). The remarkable short story by the Cuban general of the Ten Year War, Máximo Gómez, "El sueño del guerrero" (The warrior's Dream) (1889) also touches on many of the issues raised by Dominican indigenismo (in *El cuento en Santo Domingo*, ed. Sócrates Nolasco [Ciudad Trujillo: Librería Dominicana, 1957], 105–9). There is an 1843 novel entitled *Los amores de los indios*, by Alejandro Angulo y Guridi, written in exile in Cuba, which I have been unable to locate (see chapter 8 in this volume). The same applies to *Escenas aborígenes*, by Francisco Javier Angulo y Guridi (1872). By far the most reliable and well-researched bibliographical documentation is in Catharina Vallejo, *Las madres de la patria y las bellas mentiras: Imágenes de la mujer en el discurso literario nacional de la República Dominicana, 1844–1899* (Miami: Ediciones Universal, 1999), 309–18, which focuses on the role of gender in some of the better-known indigenista texts.

A story that is in many ways similar to "La boca del indio" is "La Ciguapa" by Francisco Angulo y Guridi (in Rodríguez Demorizi, *Tradiciones y cuentos dominicanos*, 85–96). Framed as an example of the depth of popular superstition, it is the story of the *ciguapas*, a species of tiny people of perfect beauty and fierce loyalty, physically resembling the Indians in every detail except for their size and endowed with the same affects as humans, although incapable of speech. The ciguapas are so passionately jealous that when a male ciguapa discovers a couple of humans in amorous conversation, he will show himself to the woman, and the woman who catches his sight will die, as will the ciguapa himself. If the ciguapa is female, she will kill the man in the same way. Obviously, this story could be read in many ways, and the version Angulo y Guridi gives clearly has a lot to do with the denial of female sexuality. (A young man declares his love to a girl, who insists that she does not understand what he is talking about; at the moment she finally understands, the ciguapa shows up and kills her.) The structural similarities with "La boca del indio" consists in the fact that here again, "Indians" exist as a kind of double of the Dominicans. There is a shadowland, a remnant of the indigenous past, that duplicates everyday reality. But unlike "La boca del indio," here the past wreaks havoc when it intrudes into reality.

10    See chapter II in this volume on the Haitian version of *Enriquillo*, Emile Nau's *Les caciques d'Haiti*.

11    I am relying here on the basic elements of Lacanian psychoanalysis, as they seem most able to elucidate the relationship between identity formation on the most abstract level and specific psychic and affective experiences and goals that are clearly present in the literary text. However, other theoretical vocabularies might produce similar results. The Hegelian notion of recognition in the process of subject constitution comes to mind. But we could also think of Neoplatonic speculations about the possibility (necessity) of the God of monotheism being a Trinity.

12    The uncertain status of Freud's text has produced a long history of argument. If we read the text literally, as an account of "what actually happened," one of the questions that becomes pressing is how we are to imagine a continuing, transgenerational memory trace of which no conscious knowledge could exist. Freud wavered between claiming that the argument was "in analogy" to the structures familiar from the genesis of individual neurosis, and claiming that groups too had a collective memory. But what would be the site for an unconscious that would survive centuries? Freud realized that by claiming a transgenerational unconscious, he contradicted one of evolutionary biology's most strongly held beliefs, namely, that acquired characteristics cannot be inherited, but he concluded that "the audacity cannot be avoided" (100). See Eric Santner, "Freud's *Moses* and the Ethics of Monotropic Desire," *October*, no. 88 (spring 1999): 3–43, for an extensive discussion of the underlying problem of whether "trauma is ultimately a historical event available to an archaeological gaze" or "a structural impasse, antagonism, or

'bind' internal to the mental life of an individual or the cultural 'archive' of a collectivity."

13  Jacqueline Rose, *States of Fantasy* (Oxford: Clarendon, 1996), 48.

### 7. WHAT DO THE HAITIANS WANT?

1  Slavoj Žižek, *The Sublime Object of Ideology* (London: Verso, 1989), 114–15. Now, of course, as is often the case with Žižek's arguments, his account explains the operations of a social or political phenomenon better than its sociopolitical or sociopsychological origins. In the case of Lacan's "Che vuoi?", for instance, Žižek claims that anti-Semitism is the clearest articulation of the problem and adduces as a supporting argument the inscrutability of the Jewish God. Leaving aside the fact that this strikes me as a hopelessly thin and epistemologistic account of the origins of anti-Semitism, it also raises the question why the equally inscrutable Protestant God did not generate similar anti-Protestant fantasies. By saying that "the Other wants something from us, but we are at the same time incapable of translating this desire of the Other into a positive interpellation, into a mandate with which to identify," Žižek gives us a persuasive description of the impasse from which racist or anti-Semitic fantasies arise, but it does not explain why we are in some cases capable, and in some cases incapable, of translating the desire of the Other into a positive mandate. This is all the more troubling because Žižek wants to use symbolic identification and its regulatory function of the subject's imaginary identification as an account of the subject's interpellation into a sociopolitical field. In other words, it is in the notion of symbolic identification that politics and ideology become fundamental in a psychoanalytic account of subject constitution.

What Žižek cannot explain—and this ultimately brings us back to the issues discussed in chapter 5—is why, if we are principally incapable of knowing the desire of the Other, this incapability sometimes leads to pathologies such as misogyny and racism, and sometimes it does not. Žižek's account seems to suffer from what I might call the Kantian disease: the dream of creating something from nothing, the whole world from pure reason, or, in this case, the whole catastrophe of human history and its pathologies from the floor plan of the psyche. But pulling a rabbit out of a hat usually requires some diversionary tactics . . . The case study at hand shows that without an account of substantive political, social, and moral commitments and goals, and all the messy stuff of historical experience, we end up naturalizing pathologies such as racism, anti-Semitism, or sexism and obscuring rather than elucidating the operations of domination and hegemony that produced oppressive societies and oppressive social orders and allow them to reproduce themselves.

2  Emilio Cordero Michel, *La Revolución Haitiana y Santo Domingo* (Santo Domingo: Editora Nacional, 1968), 59.

3    Franco Pichardo, *Historia del pueblo dominicano*, vol. 1 (Santo Domingo: Instituto del Libro, 1992), 181.

4    Balaguer attributes this fact to the skillful machinations of Boyer's agents rather than true popular sentiment (*La isla al revés: Haití y el destino dominicano* [Santo Domingo: Fundación José Antonio Caro, 1983], 22–23).

5    Quoted in Cordero Michel, *La revolución haitiana y Santo Domingo*, 60.

6    The poem is entitled "Lamentos de la Isla Española de Santo Domingo" (Laments of the Spanish Island of Santo Domingo) and is cited by Menéndez Pelayo as very bad poetry, though expressive of sincere Spanish sentiment, and reprinted by Rodríguez Demorizi in *Poesía popular Dominicana*. According to the latter, it was probably written by a popular poet by the name of Maestro Mónica in the 1790s. Here is a more extensive version: "¿Cuándo pensé ver mi grey / sin Rey? / ¿Cuando mi leal y fiel porte / sin norte? / . . . La primera en Indias que / fé / tuve; y con igual privanza, / esperanza / en mi Dios, y en realidad / caridad; / y ahora, igualdad, libertad, / y Fraternidad profana, / me dan por la soberana / Fé, Esperanza y Caridad" [When did I expect to see my flock / without King? / When my loyal and faithful behavior / without guidance? . . . As the first in the Indies / such faith / I had; and with equal loyalty / hope / in my God, and in reality / charity; / and now, I am given equality, liberty, / and profane fraternity / instead of the superior / Faith, Hope, and Charity] (21–22).

7    Quoted in Rodríguez Demorizi, *Poesía popular dominicana* (Santo Domingo: UCMM, 1973), 267–86. The date of composition is uncertain. Juan Antonio Alix (1833–1918) is usually referred to as the most productive and accomplished of the "popular poets." He left behind hundreds of *décimas*—the most popular verse meter in the Caribbean and Spanish America—many of them satirical, erotic, or scatological. His politics seem to have been somewhat opportunistic, with Alix changing back and forth between the Restorationist and the Spanish forces.

8    In Rodríguez Demorizi, *Tradiciones y cuentos dominicanos* (Santo Domingo: Julio D. Postigo e hijos Editores, 1969), 107–12.

9    Bonilla y España's story may well be inspired by some actual events. Robert Cornevin, in *Le théâtre haïtien des origines à nos jours* (Ottawa: Editions Leméac, 1973), 40–41, for instance, relates that when after Dessalines's declaration of independence the French general Ferrand had fled from the French part of the island to Spanish Santo Domingo, the troops asked to be given a space to put on comedies. It was decided to erect a stage in the old Convent of Santa Regina, which had served as an arsenal. The figure of the saint was replaced with the word "theater," and the former sacred space was transformed into a site for soldiers' entertainment. Cornevin comments that these sorts of cultural activities by the French had no influence on the culture of the Dominican elites. Undoubtedly he is right if we entertain a narrow notion of "influence." I suspect, however,

that events of this sort may well have contributed to the development of a cultural imaginary that allowed future generations to cast the difference between Dominicans and Haitians in terms of secularism and religiosity.

10  *Cosas Añejas* (Santo Domingo: Ediciones de Taller, 1982). Penson acknowledges his debt to Bonilla and explains that he had received permission from the author to rewrite the story.

11  For an account of Del Monte's intellectual and political activities, see Catharina Vallejo, *Las madres de la patria y las bellas mentiras: Imágenes de la mujer en el discurso literario nacional de la República Dominicana, 1844– 1899* (Miami: Ediciones Universal, 1999), 96–104.

12  See Emilio Rodríguez Demorizi, *Pintura y escultura en Santo Domingo* (Santo Domingo: Librería Hispaniola, 1972). According to Rodríguez Demorizi, Bonilla based his painting on Del Monte's poem. Unfortunately, I have not been able to trace the painting and have not found any reproductions of it.

13  Penson felt compelled to include as an appendix the transcript of the proceedings against the Dominicans in his *Cosas Añejas*.

14  Laura Mulvey, *Visual and Other Pleasures* (Bloomington and Indianapolis: Indiana University Press, 1989), 15. Mulvey argues that the display of women's bodies for the gaze and enjoyment of men means that it potentially invokes the scene of castration. The fear of castration is thus at the root of the fetishization of the female body in film. In Penson's story, the fetishization of Agueda's body seems almost overdetermined, as it could be explained both by the familiar psychoanalytic account of the role of the castration threat in psycho-sexual development and by a more historical, contingent account where castration is the effect of competition between two males. For an excellent discussion of Mulvey, see Linda Williams, *Hard Core: Power, Pleasure, and the "Frenzy of the Visible"* (Berkeley: University of California Press, 1989), 41–46.

15  There are striking similarities between the structure of "The Virgins of Galindo" and what O. Mannoni called the Prospero complex—the sum of psychic dispositions that characterize both the figure of colonial paternalism and the racist whose daughter has been subject to an imaginary rape by inferior beings (*Psychologie de la colonisation* [Paris: Seuil, 1950], 71). See also Fanon's critique in *Black Skin, White Mask,* trans. Charles Lam Markmann (New York: Grove, 1967).

16  Sigmund Freud, *The Standard Edition of the Complete Psychological Works of Sigmund Freud,* trans. James Strachey, vol. 26 (London: Hogarth Press, 1953–1974), 305–6.

## 8. FICTIONS OF LITERARY HISTORY

1  Marcio Veloz Maggiolo, "Biblioestadística," in *Ponencias del Congreso Crítico de Literatura Dominicana,* ed. Diógenes Céspedes, Soledad Alvarez, and Pedro Vergés (Santo Domingo: Editora de Colores, 1994).

Because of the turbulent history of the territory, numerical accounts vary quite a bit, depending on what is counted as "Dominican": texts written by people living in the eastern part of Hispaniola at the time, by writers in exile, or by descendants of Dominicans in exile, texts written in French, texts published abroad, and so on. Whatever criterion we adopt, however, it is obvious that literary production is extremely thin compared to, say, Cuba, and in particular, it does not show the exponential increase in the last two or three decades of the nineteenth century that we observe in many other Spanish American countries with the arrival of *modernismo*. For a well-documented account of women writers, see Catharina Vallejo, *Las madres de la patria y las bellas mentiras: Imágenes de la mujer en el discurso literario nacional de la República Dominicana, 1844–1899* (Miami: Ediciones Universal, 1999).

2  See Emilio Rodríguez Demorizi, *La imprenta y los primeros periódicos de Santo Domingo* (Santo Domingo: Ed. Taller, 1944).

3  *El Telégrafo Constitucional de Santo Domingo* and *El Duende*. In June the *Telégrafo* even published some articles on the rights of citizens, but by July it appears to have shut down its operations.

4  Henríquez Ureña, in *Panorama histórico de la literatura dominicana* (Santo Domingo: Editorial Librería Dominicana, 1965), mentions an elegiac poem written by Napoléon Guy Chevremont d'Albigny, a French professor who was working as a teacher in Santo Domingo from 1830 onward.

5  Henríquez Ureña, *Panorama histórico*, 112.

6  Rodríguez Demorizi, *Poesía popular dominicana* (Santo Domingo: UCMM, 1973), 52–53.

7  José Joaquín Pérez, prologue to *Iguaniona: Drama histórico en verso y en tres actos*, by Javier Francisco Angulo y Guridi (1881; Santo Domingo: Publicaciones América, 1978), 12–13.

8  Salomé Ureña de Henríquez, "Impresiones," in *Fantasías indígenas y otros poemas*, ed. José Joaquín Pérez (Santo Domingo: Fundación Corripio, 1989), 15–17.

9  Sigmund Freud, "Mourning and Melancholia," in *The Standard Edition of the Complete Psychological Works of Sigmund Freud*, trans. James Strachey, vol. 14 (London: Hogarth Press, 1953–1974), 244.

10  Salomé Ureña de Henríquez, "Ruinas," in *Antología mayor de la literatura dominicana (siglos XIX-XX): Poesía I*, ed. Manuel Rueda (Santo Domingo: Ediciones de la Fundacíon Corripio, 1999), 191–93. There is also a biographical sketch on pp. 189–91. On Ureña de Henríquez's significance in Dominican literature, see Vallejo, *Las madres de la patria*, 167–77.

11  The second half of this verse is obscure or possibly corrupt.

12  Rodríguez Demorizi, *La era de Francia en Santo Domingo: Contribución a su estudio* (Ciudad Trujillo: Editora del Caribe, 1955), 59, 61.

13  Pedro F. Bonó, "Apuntes sobre las clases trabajadoras dominincanas,"

in *Papeles de Pedro F. Bonó: Para la historia de las ideas políticas en Santo Domingo*, ed. Emilio Rodríguez Demorizi (Santo Domingo, Editora del Caribe, 1964), 190–245. For an excellent reading of Bonó's essay, see Pedro L. San Miguel, *La isla imaginada: Historia, identidad y utopía en La Española* (Santo Domingo: Isla Negra/La Trinitaria, 1997), 76–82.

14 Bonó, "Apuntes," 218–21.

15 Jean Laplanche and J.-B. Pontalis, *The Language of Psychoanalysis*, trans. Donald Nicholson-Smith (New York: Norton, 1973), s.v. "Working-through."

16 See, for instance, Emilio Rodríguez Demorizi, ed., *Del romancero dominicano* (Santiago, R.D.: Editorial El Diario, 1943), and his *Poesía popular dominicana*.

17 Pedro F. Bonó, *El montero* (1856; San Francisco de Marcorís: Comisión Organizadora Permanente de la Feria Nacional del Libro, 1989).

18 Manuel Arturo Peña Batlle, ed., *Antología de la literatura dominicana*, Colección Trujillo, Centenario de la república, 1844–1944, 17–18, ser. 4, Literatura, vols. 1–2 (Santiago: Editorial El Diario, 1944); Frank Moya Pons, *Bibliografía de la literatura dominicana, 1820–1990* (Santo Domingo: Comisión Permanente de la Feria Nacional del Libro, 1997); José Alcántara Almánzar, ed., *Dos siglos de literatura dominicana (s. XIX–XX): Prosa* (Santo Domingo: Comisión Oficial para la Celebración del Sesquicentenario de la Independencia Nacional, 1996).

19 See San Miguel, *La isla imaginada*, 72.

20 For different reasons, other critics have actually tried to link nineteenth-century indigenismo to early writings, most importantly to colonial texts. Galván's reliance on colonial chronicles, for instance, has been interpreted as evidence for a certain continuity.

21 For an example of the arduousness of identifying and locating early literary texts, see Vallejo's annotated bibliography in *Las madres de la patria*.

22 See Vallejo, *Las madres de la patria*, 43–44, for a comparative reading of *Facundo* and *El Montero*.

23 Bonó, *Papeles*, 89–90.


## 9. LITERATURE AND THE THEATER OF REVOLUTION

1 It may be of interest to read this extraordinary text in the French original: "Pour dresser l'acte d'indépendance, il nous faut la peau d'un blanc pour parchemin, son crâne pour écritoire, son sang pour encre et une baïonette pour plume. . . . Le nom Français lugubre encore nos contrées." Quoted in Maximilien Laroche, *La littérature haïtienne: Identité, langue, réalité* (Montréal: Leméac, 1981), 45. The imagery of the Declaration of Independence itself is not quite as virulent, but, as Maximilien Laroche rightly points out, there is an undercurrent of violence, "an intense vibration" of belligerence and an unforgiving hostility toward

those who installed the slaveholding regime in the former colony that extends even to the use of language in the foundational text. For a narrative of the situation that preceded Boisrond Tonnere's appointment as the drafter of the declaration, see Thomas Madiou, *Histoire d'Haïti*, vol. 3 (Port-au-Prince: Henri Deschamps, 1985), 144–45. For a translation of the Haitian Declaration of Independence see Charles Arthur and Michael Dash, eds., *Libète: A Haiti Anthology* (Princeton: Marcus Wiener Publishers, 1999), 44.

2  Price-Mars's term "Bovarysme collectif"—after Gustav Flaubert's literary creation Emma Bovary—takes aim at what he considered the elite's failure to recognize the true nature of their country and their aspirations to a more notable life, in this case, the life of Frenchmen of color. See Nicholls, *From Dessalines to Duvalier*, 156–58, for further discussion of Price-Mars's writings.

3  The double contradiction between oral and written traditions and between French and Creole has led to considerable discussion among Caribbeanists as to which problem is structurally more important. For some, the real problem is not the contradiction between literature written in French and in Haitian Creole but the contradiction between written and oral literature, which has led to the coinage of the neologism "oraliture." See, for example, Maximilien Laroche, *Double scène de la représentation: Oraliture et Littérature dans la Caraïbe* (Sainte-Foy, Québec: GRELCA, 1991), esp. 15–31; or Edouard Glissant, *Caribbean Discourse: Selected Essays*, trans. Michael Dash (Charlottesville: University Press of Virginia, 1989), 182–94.

4  Laroche, *La littérature haïtienne*, 113.

5  Doris Sommer, *Foundational Fictions: The National Romances of Latin America* (Berkeley and Los Angeles: University of California Press, 1991).

6  See Ulrich Fleischmann, *Ideologie und Wirklichkeit in der Literatur Haitis* (Berlin: Colloquium Verlag, 1969), 92–95, for an equally trenchant critique of Hénock Trouillot's account of Haitian literature. While acknowledging the empirical merits and the excellent documentation compiled by Trouillot, Fleischmann rejects Trouillot's critical orientation as overtly ideological and blinded by antimulatto prejudice.

7  Hénock Trouillot, *Les origines sociales de la littérature haïtienne* (Port-au-Prince: N. A. Théodore, 1962), 98.

8  See Trouillot, *Les origines sociales*, 20–21, for examples of celebrations of Independence and the poetry of flattery.

9  See Léon-François Hoffmann, "En marge du premier roman haïtien: *Stella*, d'Emeric Bergeaud," in *Haïti: Lettres et l'être*, by Léon-François Hoffmann (Toronto: GREF, 1992), 147–65, for a detailed account of the novel, which is very difficult to locate.

10  Ghislaine Rey, *Anthologie du roman haïtien de 1859 à 1946* (Sherbrooke, Québec: Naaman, 1982).

11   Maximilien Laroche, *La littérature haïtienne*, 47–48.

12   Cornevin, *Le théâtre haïtien des origines à nos jours.* (Montréal: Leméac, 1973), 50.

13   Trouillot, *Les origines sociales*, 58.

14   Jean Fouchard, *Le théâtre à Saint-Domingue* (Port-au-Prince: Imprimerie de l'Etat, 1955), 303–44.

15   Jean Fouchard, *Artistes et repertoire des scènes de Saint-Domingue* (Port-au-Prince: Imprimerie de l'Etat, 1955).

16   See Cornevin, *Le théâtre haïtien*, 24–25.

17   Alfred de Laujon, *Souvenirs de trente années de voyage à St-Domingue*, quoted in Cornevin, *Le théâtre haïtien*, 32.

18   Médéric Moreau de Saint-Méry, *Description topographique, physique, civile, politique et historique de la patrie française de l'Isle Saint-Domingue*, vol. 1, p. 360, quoted in Joan Dayan, *Haiti, History, and the Gods* (Berkeley and Los Angeles: University of California Press, 1995), 184.

19   Peter Brooks, *The Melodramatic Imagination: Balzac, Henry James, Melodrama, and the Mode of Excess* (New Haven: Yale University Press, 1976), 15.

20   The French text is somewhat obscure, and neither Dayan (*Haiti, History, and the Gods,* 184) nor Fouchard (*Le théâtre à Saint-Domingue,* 251) takes notice of the fact that it only makes sense if we assume that the title *Héros Américain* refers to a second play as different from the first. Fouchard remains silent on the issue, and Dayan's translation suggests that she believes *The American Hero* and *The American Heroine* to be one and the same.

21   Ribié, quoted in Fouchard, *Le théâtre à Saint-Domingue*, 251.

22   For further details on Abbé Raynal's *Histoire* see Srinivas Aravamudan, *Tropicopolitans: Colonialism and Agency, 1688–1804* (Durham: Duke University Press, 1999), 290–325.

23   C. L. R. James, *The Black Jacobins* (1938; New York: Vintage, 1989), 24–25. Without mentioning James, Michel-Rolph Trouillot objects to this use of the passage in the *Histoire*, arguing that the reference was to Jamaica rather than Saint Domingue and that the invocation of Spartacus was meant as a warning. Ultimately Trouillot wants to reduce Abbé Raynal's (and Diderot's) stance to a rhetorical device or a strategic argument that loses significance in light of the plentiful contradictions in the *Histoire*, which are taken to be further support for the claim that the Haitian Revolution was simply "unthinkable" (Michel-Rolph Trouillot, *Silencing the Past: Power and the Production of History* [Boston: Beacon Press, 1995], 84–87). One of the problems with this view is that it has to consider a thought contained in a warning to be a nonthought. More generally, it seems to me that by subtracting all political views involved in contradictions from our accounts of the Enlightenment and modernity, we actually lose sight of the political process that cemented white hegemony in the Caribbean and became one of the pillars of Creole

national cultures in many places. In the end, this could lead us to unwittingly reproduce the Eurocentric and racially exclusivist concept of modernity we set out to revise.

24 The only French revolutionary play with a title that would suggest the events in the colony as the theme I have come across is the anonymous *La révolte des nègres*, which is mentioned in both Maurice Albert, *Les théâtres des boulevards (1789–1848)* (Paris: Société Française d'Imprimerie et de Libraire, 1902), 76; and Marvin Carlson, *The Theatre of the French Revolution* (Ithaca: Cornell University Press, 1966), 161; but I have been unable to find any further information on it. This should not be taken to imply that there were not more plays taking up the issue of slavery and the revolution in Saint Domingue. The theatrical frenzy of the days after the lifting of the restrictions is well documented, but many of the popular plays were never published, and many titles were lost. However, it is worth noting that both Carlson and Albert put *La révolte des nègres* in the company of titles like *Les Capucins à la frontière* and *La guillotine d'amour* and describe them as part of a "series of bizarre pantomimes and ballets" (Carlson), conceived to "attract the public and pique its curiosity through the *bizarrerie* of the announcements" (Albert). Here again we see a connection between the colonial theme and the genre of pantomime, mixed with dance. And again we see how the genre is dismissed as merely bizarre from the standpoint of high culture.

25 See Albert, *Les théâtres des boulevards*, 19–21; and Brooks, *The Melodramatic Imagination*.

26 Dayan, *Haiti, History, and the Gods*, 186.


## 10. "GENERAL LIBERTY, OR THE PLANTERS IN PARIS"

1 Fouchard, *Le théâtre à Saint-Domingue* (Port-au-Prince: Imprimerie de l'Etat, 1955), 231; and Cornevin, *Le théâtre haïtien des origines à nos jours* (Montréal: Lemére, 1973), 39. Since the play is not available in print, I include the original French text with all quotes.

2 See especially Yves Bénot, *La révolution française et la fin des colonies* (Paris: Éditions La Découverte, 1988); and Florence Gauthier, *Triomphe et mort du droit naturel en révolution 1789–1795–1802* (Paris: PUF, 1992).

3 C. L. R. James, *The Black Jacobins* (1938; New York: Vintage, 1989), 192.

4 James, *The Black Jacobins*, 185–93.

5 *Revêche* means contrary, disagreeable; *minaudière* lackadaisical, full of airs.

6 Page and Bruley had led a smear campaign against Sonthonax and Povorel in 1793, accusing them variously of trying to have themselves declared kings of Saint Domingue (the implication being that they were royalists and thus counterrevolutionaries) and wanting to deliver the colony to England (Gauthier, *Triomphe et mort*, 226). Verneuil was one of the leaders of the *colons enragé* who rose against Sonthonax in Le Cap on

December 2, 1792, and was deported to France in the aftermath (Bénot, *La révolution française*, 163, 272). Bruley took on the mantle of republicanism once in France, without changing his mind about the issue of slavery. As late as 1814, he argued for the reconquest of Haiti and reintroduction of slavery (256).

7   The longer phrases in italics are preceded by numbers that refer to footnotes, which explain that the phrases are literal quotes from the plan signed by Page and Bruley, submitted to the Committee for Public Health in 1793.

8   Gauthier, *Triomphe et mort*, 236.

9   Gauthier, *Triomphe et mort*, 231–36.

10  Her strong partiality toward Robespierre seems to prevent her from properly assessing some of the debates at times; her account of Robespierre's position vis-à-vis the Brissotin war, for instance, does not even consider the possibility that his opposition may have been a question of strategy as much as a matter of principle.

11  Italics in the original (26).

12  See, for instance, Jean Tarrade, who argues, much like many historians of the American Revolution, that it simply took a while for the French to recognize all the implications of the Declaration of the Rights of Man and Citizen. For Tarrade, it is only too understandable that it was not until the Second Republic and the activities of Schoelcher that France finally abolished slavery for good (1848). Instead of a movement of active suppression of a heterogeneous revolutionary culture centered in the Caribbean, Tarrade thus sees only a progressive clarification of emancipatory ideas, which are considered in abstraction from any notion of agency and are clearly located in the metropolis rather than the remote plantation zone ("Les colonies et les principes de 1789: Les assemblées révolutionnaire face au problème de l'esclavage," in *La révolution française et les colonies*, ed. Jean Tarrade (Paris: Société Française d'Histoire d'outre-mer, 1989), 9–33.

13  During the Revolution, Brissot devoted most of his efforts to the recognition of the political rights of mulattoes and fought for the abolition of the slave trade rather than slavery itself. However, this was the strategy first inaugurated by the British abolitionists and adopted by most antislavery activists in Europe, and it does not necessarily imply the belief that slavery itself could or should be continued. Brissot's writings before the Revolution go so far as to justify armed revolt by slaves and present vigorous arguments for the equality of all humans, regardless of skin color (Bénot, *La révolution française*, 40). For an excellent account of Brissot's politics in the context of the volatile revolutionary process in France, see David Geggus, "Racial Equality, Slavery, and Colonial Secession during the Constituent Assembly," *American Historical Review* 94, no. 5 (Dec. 1989): 1290–1308. For a different assessment, see Michel-Rolph Trouillot, who cites Brissot as saying that a slave revolution was

simply unthinkable (*Silencing the Past: Power and the Production of History* [Boston: Beacon Press, 1995], 90).

14　Ozouf does return to the issue at the end of the essay, asking: "How can one explain why Girondins such as Ducos and Boyer-Fonfrède, who owned property in Santo Domingo, actively supported a revolt of the black population that threatened to cost them their fortunes?" (361). Instead of further investigating this admittedly surprising constellation, she simply returns to the rather abstract view that the political is not determined by the social.

15　See François Furet, "The French Revolution Is Over," in *Interpreting the French Revolution*, by François Furet, trans. Elborg Forster (Cambridge: Cambridge University Press, 1981), 1–80.

16　Robin Blackburn, *The Overthrow of Colonial Slavery* (New York: Verso, 1988), 195.

17　Bénot, *La révolution française*, 190.

18　Blackburn, *The Overthrow of Colonial Slavery*, 173.

19　For a very interesting, if elliptical, theoretical consideration of the issues, see Susan Buck-Morss, *Dreamworld and Catastrophe* (Cambridge: MIT Press, 2000), 9–15 (hypertext). Buck-Morss concludes that the "double legacy of the French Revolution" is popular sovereignty and the democratic nation-state, each with its specific form of devolution into violent infringement of forms of sovereignty—revolutionary terror and military aggression. Although I cannot here enter into the specific argument, I think that this is overall a more promising approach than any attempt at defending this or that revolutionary faction.

## II. FOUNDATIONAL FICTIONS

1　It should be noted that this account, which assigns primacy to the slave revolt in the Caribbean, is not universally accepted. David Geggus, for instance, has argued that Toussaint did not openly adopt the cause of general liberty until after Sonthonax's decree of August 1793 and the Declaration of the French Assembly of February 1794 (David P. Geggus, "The French and Haitian Revolutions, and Resistance to Slavery in the Americas: An Overview," in *La révolution française et les colonies*, ed. Jean Tarrade [Paris: Société française d'histoire d'outre-mer, 1989], 118). While I find this aspect of Geggus's argument somewhat unconvincing (or at the least no less speculative, and more implausible, than the opposite argument), his insistence that slave resistance in the Caribbean derived important influence from the international movement against slavery is highly plausible and in keeping with the argument I am making.

2　Louis-Joseph Janvier, *Les constitutions d'Haïti (1801–1885)*, 2 vols. (Paris: Flammarion, 1886).

3　The anonymously published *History of the Island of St. Domingo* (London, 1818), contains excerpted translations of the early constitutions. Interestingly, Dessalines's constitution of 1805, which deals explicitly with issues of skin color, is not reprinted. Instead we find the "Order of Ceremony" for the coronation of Dessalines as emperor. There are no documents at all from Pétion's republic, but both of Christophe's constitutions (1807 and 1811) are excerpted at some length. See the following chapter for possible explanations. Prince Saunders's *Haytian Papers* (Westport, Conn.: Negro Universities Press, 1969), also contains excerpts from some of Haiti's foundational texts.

4 Luis Mariñas Otero, ed., *Las constituciones de Haiti,* with a preface by Manuel Fraga Iribarne (Madrid: Ediciones Cultura Hispánica, 1968), 14. See Franklin J. Franco, *Los negros, los mulatos y la nación dominicana,* 8th ed. (Santo Domingo: Editora Nacional, 1989), esp. 89–96, for a discussion of the effects of the constitution on the Spanish territory.

5 Fédéric Marcelin, *Questions haïtiennes,* quoted in Claude Moïse, *Constitutions et luttes de pouvoir en Haïti (1804–1987),* vol. 1 (Montreal: CIDIHCA, 1988), 14. See also the play *Les îles de tempête,* by Bernard Didié from the Ivory Coast, which derives some of its humor from the Haitian constitutions.

6 W. W. Harvey, *Sketches of Hayti, from the Expulsion of the French, to the Death of Christophe* (London: Seeley, 1827), 31.

7 Compare also Article 3, "All Haitian citizens are brothers; the equality in the eyes of the law is incontestably recognized, and there can be no titles, advantages, or privileges except those which result necessarily from the consideration and compensation for services rendered to the cause of liberty and independence." This last provision is most likely meant to allow for special compensation for officers of the revolutionary wars.

8 This provision refers to women married to Haitian men, and the German and Polish mercenaries who deserted Leclerc's troops to join the insurgent armies.

9 Michel-Rolph Trouillot comments briefly on Dessalines's attempts to eliminate distinctions of color by law, calling it "sincere, but naive" (Trouillot, *Haiti: State against Nation. The Origins and Legacy of Duvalierism* [New York: Monthly Review Press, 1990], 46). In the same context, however, Trouillot makes a reference that suggests that the issue was not so much naïveté but a particular revolutionary understanding of the role of legislation. Talking about Boisrond Tonnerre, a light-skinned *ancien libre* with a French education who became Dessalines's "trusted private secretary and the probable architect of many imperial policies," Trouillot describes him as someone "who fanatically believed in the Jacobinist principle that legislation could transform the most cherished customs" (46).

10 Moïse, *Constitutions et luttes,* 33.

11 The ban on non-Haitian property survived countless constitutional changes, until in 1918 a new constitution was written under U.S. guid-

ance. Apparently Franklin D. Roosevelt liked to boast that it was he who wrote the new Haitian constitution. (Thanks to Matthew Baugh for this information.)

12 Translation by David Nicholls, in his *From Dessalines to Duvalier: Race, Colour, and National Independence in Haiti* (New Brunswick: Rutgers University Press, 1996), 79, where he quotes Thomas Madiou's *Histoire d'Haïti, 1843–46.*

13 Nicholls, *From Dessalines to Duvalier,* 5.

14 Compare the French constitution of 1793, which under the title "Acte Constitutionnel" devotes three articles to citizenship issues and contains a long list of criteria that allow someone to claim French citizenship. See Jacques Godechot, ed., *Les constitutions de la France* (Paris: Flammarion, 1995).

15 The phrasing in the 1805 and 1806 constitutions is identical, except for the subject of the sentence, which in 1805 is "the Emperor" rather than "the Republic."

16 While Art. 1 bans the institution of slavery from Haitian soil, Art. 2 implies that runaway slaves from other territories who take up residence in Haiti will not be returned to their owners.

17 A comparison with the French revolutionary constitutions is very interesting here. The conflict between the Jacobins and the Girondins evolved to some degree around the issue of whether or not one can export liberation. In 1790 the constituent Assembly had solemnly declared that the French nation renounced wars of conquest and that it would never use its military force against the liberty of any other people. But, of course, two years later France was at war, and the Girondin propagandist Anacharsis Cloots fervently advocated the cause of extending the benefits of "the most beautiful constitution of the universe" to the oppressed peoples of Europe.

Now, the French constitutions do contain noninterference clauses, although they too, are significantly different from those in the Haitian constitutions. Title VI of the 1791 constitution consists of a paragraph about the relationship between France and neighboring nations in which France "renounces undertaking any war with the aim of making conquests and will never use its forces against the liberty of any people." This provision is followed by provisions that regulate the rights of foreigners in France. This includes the explicit right to own property in France. In the debates preceding the adoption of the Jacobin constitution of 1793, Robespierre had proposed the inclusion of four articles with a clear internationalist intention: "Men of all countries are brothers and their different people must assist each other according to their abilities like the citizens of the same State. He who oppresses one nation declares himself the enemy of all. Those who make war against a people in order to stop the progress of liberty and to annihilate the rights of men must be prosecuted by all, not like ordinary enemies, but like assassins and rebellious bandits. The kings, the aristocrats, the tyrants, whoever they are, are slaves in revolt against the sovereign of the earth, which is the human race, and against the legislator of the universe, which is nature" (Godechot, *Les constitutions de la France*, 72). Much could be said about Robespierre's draft—including the odd choice of metaphor that likens tyrants to "rebellious slaves." Suffice it to say here that Robespierre's proposal was not accepted.

The compromise constitution of 1793 contains a noninterference clause, which is nevertheless framed in a very telling way: "Art. 118—The French people are the natural friends and allies of all free people. Art. 119—They will not interfere in the government of other nations; they will not tolerate that other nations interfere with theirs. Art. 120—They will give asylum to foreigners banned from their fatherland for the cause of liberty. They will deny it to tyrants." These provisions need to be read in the context of the political situation, when the fear of counter-revolutionaries invading from Koblenz and elsewhere was the crucial concern of French policy. By introducing a second clause according to which France will not tolerate interference from other countries, the first clause, which promises abstention from interference in other countries' affairs, is weakened considerably, as it could be interpreted as possibly justifying a preventive war.

18 Doris Sommer, *Foundational Fictions: The National Romances of Latin America* (Berkeley and Los Angeles: University of California Press, 1991), 256.

## 12. LIFE IN THE KINGDOM OF THE NORTH

1 See Hubert Cole, *Christophe, King of Haiti* (New York: Viking Press, 1967), 239. Cole also quotes Christophe's letter to Wilberforce in which he announces his intentions. The liberal *Edinburgh Review*, however, preferred Pétion's "virtuous constitutional rule" over Christophe's "cruel tyranny." Quoted in Susan Buck-Morss, "Hegel and Haiti," *Critical Inquiry* 26 (2000): 859 n. 121.

2 For a translation of the correspondence between Christophe and Clarkson, Christophe's letters to members of his family, and related materials, see Earl Leslie Griggs and Clifford H. Prator, eds., *Henry Christophe and Thomas Clarkson: A Correspondence* (Berkeley and Los Angeles: University of California Press, 1952).

3 Cole, *Christophe, King of Haiti*, 248.

4 For excerpts of the exchange of letters between Clarkson, Wilberforce, and Zachary Macaulay concerning the royal family in exile, see Griggs and Prator, *Henry Christophe and Thomas Clarkson*, 77–80. Neither Wilberforce nor Macaulay was prepared to have anything to do with them. Griggs and Prator quote a reassuring note from Macaulay to his wife in which Macaulay tells her that although the women were "perfectly mod-

est and virtuous," she need not worry about them: "Madame Christophe . . . is not likely to come near us" (78–79). See also Cole, *Christophe,
King of Haiti,* 276.

5  See David Nicholls, *From Dessalines to Duvalier: Race, Colour, and National Independence in Haiti* (New Brunswick: Rutgers University Press,
1996), 115–17, for what he calls the "black legend" of Christophe, according to which Christophe was an inventive genius, a new Peter the
Great. Nicholls quotes one of the *noiriste* historians as saying, "If our
men of state had continued the work of Christophe, Haiti would be one
of the richest countries on earth" (116). Mulatto historians had a rather
different view. Saint-Rémy (*Essai sur Henri-Christophe,* 1839), for instance, describes Christophe as "the tyrant of the North" and "a second
Caligula," whose dictatorial regime meant a return to the practices of
colonial times (quoted in Nicholls, *From Dessalines to Duvalier,* 99).
Genovese's assessment, quoted at the beginning of the following
chapter, is something of an exception as far as historians outside Haiti
are concerned. But even Genovese's praise for Christophe's economic
achievements is somewhat generic, as it applies equally to Toussaint
Louverture and Dessalines and does not offer an evaluation of Christophe's policy in particular.

6  Rémy Zamor, "Un administrateur génial pour son époque: Le Roi
Christophe," *Conjonction,* no. 107 (1968): 83.

7  The play, which was intended as a critical commentary on the Ethiopian
crisis, was quite badly received by the British audiences and was never
published. In 1967, C. L. R. James rewrote the play in light of the
anticolonial struggles that had taken place in the interim. A typescript
(titled "The Black Jacobins") can be found in the Schomburg Library in
New York City. Special thanks to André Elizee for his help in finding the
text. The reasons for the lack of success of the play are fairly obvious, as
it fails to translate the complexities of the historical study into theatrical
terms. For dramatic effect, James helps himself to some rather crude
melodramatic devices that hide neither the didacticism nor the fact that
he has not come up with a strong dramatic idea. The epilogue is set in a
contemporary "underdeveloped country" and features a conversation
between two heads of state in a hotel room after an international sum-
mit. The actor who had played Christophe represents a modern political
leader whose politics amount to an opportunistic exploitation of the
game of alliance and nonalliance during the Cold War.

8  O'Neill's play establishes the reference to the Haitian occupation at the
beginning: "The action of the play takes place on an island in the West
Indies as yet not self-determined by White Marines." See also Dudley
Murphy's low-budget film version of the play (1933), in which Jones is
played by Paul Robeson. Both the film and the play are most remarkable
(and unsettling) in that they remain ambiguous between a denunciation
of the American occupation and a denunciation of Third World authori-

tarianism (which of course served as the justification for the American occupation). The way they maintain this ambiguity is by leaving open the question whether Brutus Jones acts as an American usurper or as a black man who falls in with the unenlightened habits of the inhabitants of the island on account of some supposed racial memory.

9 Biographical information on Henri Christophe is often inflected by the ideological position of the authors. Many British sources assert, for instance, that he had been a slave—a claim more suitable for an antislavery ideology that never had much to say about free blacks and their political agency. See, e.g., Griggs and Prator, *Henry Christophe and Thomas Clarkson*, 38. Vergniaud Leconte argues that Christophe was born free, and that he was placed as a cabin boy at a young age by his father because of his "unsubmissive and disagreeable" character; see *Henri Christophe dans l'histoire d'Haïti* (Paris: Editions Berger-Levrault, 1931), 1–2.

10 Bound by a constitution designed to rein in Christophe, Pétion soon started to modify inconvenient provisions for his own purposes, and the need for constitutional reform in 1816 appears to have been felt in part at least because Pétion had in fact ruled outside the constitutional frame devised in 1806.

11 The translation is, with some modifications, that of Prince Saunders, in *Haytian Papers* (Westport, Conn.: Negro Universities Press, 1969), 126–27.

12 Louis Joseph Janvier, *Les constitutions d'Haïti (1801–1885)*, vol. 1 (Paris: Flammarion, 1886), 100.

13 See the French monarchical constitution of 1791, 3.2.1.1.

14 There is an interesting parallel to the problem raised by the Haitian situation in the history of English legal theory. In *The Concept of Law*, 2d ed. (Oxford: Clarendon Press, 1994), H. L. A. Hart quotes Bishop Hoadly's sermon before the English king (1717): "Nay whoever hath an absolute authority to interpret any written or spoken laws it is he who is the Law-giver to all intents and purposes and not the person who first wrote or spake them" (141). Hart—speaking as a twentieth-century legal scholar in a highly literate country—rejects this idea on the grounds that the official interpreters, the ones whose interpretation is given legal effect, are not the only people who *can* interpret the law, so that there is an external check on whether the official interpreters are getting it right or not. By negation, this view supports my reading in that the constraint is ineffective when there is only an extremely small group of potential interpreters. (Thanks to Liam Murphy for this reference.)

15 In a striking parallel to the illegitimate (*"fantaisiste"*) Masonic lodges (see chapter 1), the state-appointed church hierarchy would have lacked any legitimacy as far as the Catholic Church was concerned, since the Vatican did not recognize Haiti until 1860 and refused all dealings with the revolutionary state.

16  Cole, *Christophe, King of Haiti*, 191–92.

17  W. W. Harvey, *Sketches of Hayti, from the Expulsion of the French, to the Death of Christophe* (London: Seeley, 1827), 144.

18  Harvey, *Sketches of Hayti*, 185–86.

19  Léon-François Hoffmann, *Essays on Haitian Literature* (Washington: Three Continents Press, 1984), 55. While I tend to think that Egypto-centrism in its various forms predates Vastey (see chapter 1), it speaks to the political and ideological importance of Vastey to have developed this idea in writing and thus provided a basis for arguments we find throughout the nineteenth century in Haiti.

20  Baron de Vastey, *An Essay on the Causes of the Revolution and Civil Wars of Hayti, Being a Sequel to the Political Remarks upon Certain French Publications and Journals concerning Hayti*, trans. W. H. M. B. (1823; New York: Negro University Press, 1969), 117–18.

21  "Can any folly be carried to a greater height . . . than the attempt to confound rank, and establish a system of equality in society? Can the rich and the poor, the feeble and the strong, the brave and the coward, the learned and the illiterate, can they be regarded as equal? Do not the simple dictates of common sense proscribe this imaginary equality?" (quoted in Nicholls, *From Dessalines to Duvalier*, 58).

22  This account follows Cole, *Christophe, King of Haiti*, 209–12, whose pro-Christophe sympathies make it unlikely that the account would be exaggerated for polemical effect.

23  Zamor, "Un administrateur génial," 82.

24  Harvey, *Sketches of Hayti*, 128.

25  Cornevin, *Le theatre Haïtien des origines à nos jours* (Montréal: Leméac, 1973).

26  Leconte, *Henri Christophe dans l'histoire d'Haïti*, 326.

27  The existence of a painterly tradition prior to the creation of the Centre d'Art in Port-au-Prince in 1944 itself deserves commentary. DeWitt Peters, the American founder of the Centre, has always insisted that it was he who discovered Obin and a few other painters of the naive style, brought them to the Centre, and thereby created a style of painting that has by now become ubiquitous in the Caribbean. Lerebours's *Haiti et ses peintres* is a powerful attempt to show that there was a painterly tradition before the American intervention, and that there are stylistic elements shared by nineteenth-century paintings and twentieth-century popular styles. Unfortunately the combination of a humid climate, a lack of resources that could be devoted to conservation, and Haiti's tumultuous political history had the effect that most of the pictorial legacy is lost, and much of the argument has to be made on the basis of descriptions and archival research. Eva Pataki ("Haitian Painting: The Naives and the Moderns" [Ph.D. diss., Teachers College, Columbia University, 1987]) quotes letters that testify to the number of portraits even in modest

houses and mentions that in the South, Pétion passed a law in 1817 that required foreign artists to register and obtain licenses at a fee, in order to protect local artists. This too indicates, albeit *ex negativo,* that there was a considerable local pictorial tradition.

28  Emilio Rodríguez Demorizi, in *Pintura y escultura en Santo Domingo* (Santo Domingo: Librería Hispaniola, 1972), provides documentation according to which Velázquez, who had the reputation of being "a great physiognomist" who could do portraits after having had just one look at a person, was invited by Christophe to paint portraits of the king and his family and to decorate the palace. The anecdote Demorizi relates is that Velázquez asked that the paintings not be revealed until finished. When the curtains were lifted, Christophe saw to his great delight that they were scenes from Greek mythology with black protagonists. Cándido Geron's *Enciclopedia de las artes plásticas dominicanas (1844–2000),* 4th rev. ed. (Santo Domingo: Editora Corripio, 2000), mentions Velázquez's activities at Christophe's court but does not confirm that he decorated the walls.

29  Hénock Trouillot, *Les origines sociales de la littérature haitienne* (Port-au-Prince: N. A. Théodore, 1962), 29.

30  Trouillot, *Les origines sociales,* 31. Note the echoes of the Marseillaise.

31  Milscent is the author of many neoclassical pieces that were published in the republican newspaper *L'Abeille Haytienne:* there is, for instance, a fable inspired by La Fontaine, entitled "Le Rossignol et l'Hirondelle"; or a little prose text about two birds named Philomene and Procne, who sit in a cypress tree reminiscing about old adventures. A bird catcher approaches, offering the choice of cage or clutch; one bird says to the other, "Let's flee to where the kite *(milan)* is—he only wants our life, but the bird catcher wants our liberty" (Trouillot, *Les origines sociales,* 32–34). No doubt we are to read this as a rewriting of the revolutionary slogan "Liberty or Death" in light of Christophe's authoritarianism.

32  Trouillot, *Les origines sociales,* 35.

## 13. LIBERTY AND THE RHETORIC OF STATE

1  Eugene Genovese, *From Rebellion to Revolution: Afro-American Slave Revolt in the Making of the Modern World* (Baton Rouge: Louisiana State University Press, 1979), 89.

2  See David P. Geggus, "The French and Haitian Revolutions, and Resistance to Slavery in the Americas: An Overview," in *La révolution française et les colonies,* ed. Jean Tarrade (Paris: Société française d'histoire d'outre-mer, 1989), 122–23, for a more historical critique of Genovese's schematic account of revolutionary movements.

3  Genovese, *From Rebellion to Revolution,* 92.

4  Ibid.

5 Sidney Mintz, *Caribbean Transformations* (New York: Columbia University Press, 1989), 263.

6 In an article about Baron de Vastey, Christophe's chief adviser, Nicholls makes the revealing argument that "true liberationist thought" is often found in a country's more conservative faction and its concern for national cohesiveness. From a political perspective which I do not share, Nicholls thus offers evidence to the effect that the emancipatory agenda of the revolution was indeed put on hold through a nationalist ideology; see his "Pompée Valentin Vastey: Royalist and Revolutionary," *Jahrbuch für Geschichte von Staat, Wirtschaft und Gesellschaft Lateinamerikas* 28 (1991): 107–23.

7 It may be worth pointing out that the "equal protection clause" included in Article 5 has a precedent in the French revolutionary constitutions, but was, for obvious reasons, not included in the Constitution of the United States until the Reconstruction Amendments.

8 Jacques Godechot, ed., *Les constitutions de la France* (Paris: Flammarion, 1995), 96. Strangely, Godechot's commentary seems to suggest that the 1793 constitution contained a provision banning slavery, which it did not.

9 See, for instance, Etienne Balibar, "The 'Rights of Man' and the 'Rights of Citizen,'" in his *Masses, Classes, Ideas*, trans. James Swenson (New York: Routledge, 1994), 39–59.

10 Constitution du 22 Frimaire An VIII (December 13, 1799), Article 5: "The exercise of the rights of French citizens is suspended . . . through the state of being a hired domestic worker, attached through personal or household services."

11 See Franklin J. Franco, *Los negros, los mulatos y la nación dominicana*, 8th ed. (Santo Domingo: Editora Nacional, 1989), 89–97, for a critical discussion of this conflict and its effects on Spanish Santo Domingo.

12 See Janvier's passionate attack on the historian Ardouin, who had characterized the conflict between Pétion and Christophe as a conflict between democracy and liberty on the one hand and autocracy on the other. In practice, both ruled despotically, Janvier argues. Before 1807, Christophe had not shown himself to be less republican than Pétion. Pétion himself had already shown his autocratic tendencies by pushing through a constitution with two hundred articles in one session in the Senate, without any debate, and with heavy reliance on intimidation tactics, and by having fifteen people vote on the proposed constitution who were no deputies at all (Louis-Joseph Janvier, *Les constitutions d'Haïti*, vol. 1 [Paris: Flammarion, 1886], 80).

13 Michel-Rolph Trouillot, *Haiti: State against Nation. The Origins and Legacy of Duvalierism* (New York: Monthly Review Press, 1990), 40.

14 Nicholls's *From Dessalines to Duvalier: Race, Colour, and National Independence in Haiti* (New Brunswick: Rutgers University Press, 1996), in many ways an excellent book, frequently falls into that trap.

15  The monarchy and the republic—as early embodiments of the conflict-ing narratives—have been explained variously as reflections of the long-standing antagonism between old and new affranchis, between blacks and mulattoes, or as a result of regional divisions, which had existed before the revolution and simply reemerged after independence (see, e.g., Nicholls, *From Dessalines to Duvalier*). In the latter version, the conflict between the monarchy and the republic, as well as that between the mulattoes and the blacks, is seen as a mere smoke screen for eco-nomic interests and simple hunger for power—an ideological conflict only in the sense that it distorted and mystified real interests. There is, of course, some truth to this—the conflicts between North and South and blacks and mulattoes are at times used to disguise, or to give intellectual and political cachet to, a conflict that was, for the most part, a conflict between two oligarchies—the class of the old affranchis, which emerged during the colony, as a result of racial slavery, and the class that emerged during the war, as a result of colonial warfare. See Claude Moïse, *Con-stitutions et luttes de pouvoir en Haïti (1804–1987)*, 2 vols. (Montreal: CIDIHCA, 1988), for an account that explains political conflict in Haiti as the effect of a conflict between two oligarchies.

16  Trouillot, *Haiti: State against Nation*, 44.

# Index

abject, 84–94; Kristeva on, 89–90

abolition, 3, 11, 14, 17; in Cuba, 56, 111; in Dominican Republic, 132, 167, 170; in Haiti, 229–36; passage of law in Brazil, 19; passage of law in France, 217, 219–21, 264; passage of law in Spain, 42; political autonomy and, 2, 37, 56, 117, 120, 223, 304 n. 82, 322 n. 43; in Saint Domingue, 214–26, 227, 229, 262. *See also* abolitionism; antislavery; emancipation; slavery

abolitionism, 2, 10, 16, 17, 18, 20, 37, 48, 97, 124, 146, 170, 181, 257, 287 n. 1, 290 n. 6, 290 n. 7; black (United States), 2, 291 n. 9; British, 17–18, 81–82, 97, 107, 245–46, 256, 290 n. 7; competition of empires and, 290 n. 6; in Cuba, 107–28; in film, 17–18; French, 10, 52, 211, 216, 222–26, 246, 291 n. 7; in literature, 10, 17–19, 43, 107–28; melodrama and, 18; moderate, 17, 18, 37, 42, 108, 117, 137, 230; radical, 2, 9, 11, 16, 17, 18, 25, 36, 37, 43, 47, 51, 54, 83, 94, 110–12, 118, 178, 182, 190, 274, 287 n. 1, 289 n. 3, 290 n. 6, 304 n. 82, 321 n. 39; in Spain, 111; women and, 17, 298 n. 49. *See also* abolition; antislavery; emancipation; revolutions; slavery

Academy San Alejandro (Cuba), 57, 60, 73–75, 313 n. 4. *See also* painting: in Cuba

Adams, John Quincy, 4

Adorno, Theodor W., 34

aesthetics: Espada and, 72; of for-mer slaves, 254; "good taste" and, 61–66; hierarchies and, 60, 63; judgment, ix, 70, 91, 95; neo-classicism and, 91, 96; in Plácido criticism, 89–93; race and, 57–76; romanticism and, 96. *See also* literature; painting; poetry; taste

Africa, 10; Aponte and, 44, 49, 50; diasporic cultures and, 34–36, 50, 53; Haitian Revolution affected by, 13–16; in Saint Domingue theater, 212–13

Afrocentrism, 48–54

agency, 9, 42, 137, 146, 344 n. 12; of slaves, 110–11, 117, 145–46

Age of Revolution, ix, xi, 1, 7, 98, 274, 287 n. 1; in Caribbean, 20, 60

Alexis, Jacques Stephen, 206

Alix, Juan Antonio, 172. *See also* literature, Haitian

American Revolution, ix, 7–9, 304 n. 82

Amis des Noirs, 7, 52, 111, 215–16, 221, 222, 291 n. 7

Anderson, Benedict, 259

Angulo Guridi, Alejandro, 193

Angulo Guridi, Javier, 157–58, 193. *See also* literature, Dominican

antislavery: Aponte conspiracy, 41–56; Escalera Conspiracy, 77–83; slave insurgency and, 1, 4, 5, 260; transnational politics and, 1–2, 11, 19, 44, 50, 51, 77, 226, 236–44, 259, 304 n. 82. *See also* abolition; abolitionism; disavowal; emancipation; revolutions

Patterson, Orlando, 25, 110, 288
n. 2
Penson, César Nicolás, 174–79
Peña Batlle, Manuel Arturo, 146,
191, 228
Pérez, José Joaquín, 173, 183–84,
197; *Fantasías indígenas*, 158–61
Pétion, Alexandre, 202, 207, 227,
236, 239, 248, 257, 260, 268, 270
"Petrona y Rosalía" (Tanco y Bosmeniel), 122
Pierrot, Louis, 235
Plácido [pseud. of Gabriel de la Concepción Valdés], 18, 77–106, 210,
254; the abject and, 84–93; on
Carlist Wars, 101–4; Del Monte
on, 88, 93, 94, 96; Escalera Conspiracy and, 79–83; Hostos on,
97, 101, 105, 322 n. 42; on María
Cristina, 97, 102–3; Menéndez
Pelayo on, 92; on Poland, 97–
100; political poetry and, 87–106;
popular poetry and, 85–87; revolutionary thought in Haiti and
France and, 104–5; on slavery, 84,
96–106; on Spanish rule, 101–4;
Varona on, 93; Vitier on, 321 n.
39. *See also* aesthetics; emancipation: conflicting projects of; literature, Cuban
*Plácido* (Giral), 78
plantation economy, 1, 12, 17, 145,
149–50, 230, 235, 255–56, 261,
267, 269–70
poetry, 115; "Afro-Dominican," 181–
82; Haitian-Dominican, 182;
improvisation and, 85–86. *See
also* Plácido
Pontecorvo, Gillo, 17
pornography, in representations of
Haiti, 172, 177
postcoloniality, in Dominican
Republic, 132, 146; study of, 10
Price-Mars, Jean, 203, 205
"Profecía, La" (Bonilla y España),
173
progress, 94, 132, 154, 182–91, 195–
96, 261; ideologies of, xi, 10, 14,
18, 94, 146, 153–54, 196; regres-

sion and, 94; repetition in history
vs., 137, 165–66; slavery and, 112.
*See also* modernity;
modernization
Prospero complex, 338 n. 15
psychoanalysis, x, 38; historical
experience and, 135–37

*Queimada* (Pontecorvo), 17

racism, 146, 148, 191; scientific, 54,
227
Rainsford, Marcus, 229, *A Historical Account of the Black Empire of
Haiti*, 6–7, 240
Rama, Angel, x
Raymond, Julien, 205
Raynal, Abbé Guillaume Thomas
de, 210–11, 342 n. 23
*Reino de este mundo, El* (Carpentier),
247
republic, 8; in France, 215–22, 225;
in Haiti, 202, 227, 245, 252–53,
258, 268, 271, 312 n. 25, 353–54 n.
15. *See also* monarchy; state form
revolutions, 1–16, 142; American,
ix, 7–9, 304 n. 82; bourgeois-
democratic, 14–16, 260, 263,
246; economic determinism and,
260–61; French, ix, 7–9, 45, 214–
26; Haitian, *see* Haitian Revolution; Spanish American, 287 n. 1;
Žižek on, 142–43
Ribié, Louis-François, 210–12. *See
also* theater, in Saint Domingue
Rigaud, André, 202, 236
rights: bill of, 264, 266; natural,
225, 244; property, 82; social, 264
Robeson, Paul, 246, 349 n. 8
Robespierre, Maximilien de, 7, 8,
216, 220, 221, 222, 224, 226
Romain, Jacques, 204. *See also* literature, Haitian
romanticism, 182, 270
Rose, Jacqueline, 135–36, 164
Rousseau, Jean-Jacques, 24, 126,
306 n. 86
rumor, x, 4, 5, 110

*Sab* (Gómez de Avellaneda), 107,
115–16, 121

Saco, José Antonio, 73, 109, 111
Saint Just, Louis-Antoine de, 220
Saint-Rémy, Joseph, 205
Sánchez Valverde, Antonio, 193. See also literature, Dominican
Schoelcher, Victor, 52
scopophilia, 176–77; Mulvey on, 177, 338 n. 14
secularism, 152, 158, 165, 167, 173–74
Sharp, Granville, 221
silence, 11, 37; in Haitian historiography, 21–22; about Haitian Revolution, ix, x, 2, 3, 4, 16, 20, 21, 38, 110, 182; in Hegel, 27–32; about slavery, 35, 109–11, 120; about women's role in abolitionism, 16–17. See also denial; disavowal; memory
slavery: ancient 25, 26, 288 n. 2; capitalism and, 12, 19, 295 n. 36; concept of, 24–25; desire for political autonomy and, 117; in Enlightenment discourse, 24; as exploitation or as domination, 17, 18, 288 n. 2, 302 n. 71; genocide of American Indians and, 238, 240, 244, 266; Hegel on, 24–33, 302 nn. 72–73; memory of, 35–38, 197; modern, 11–13, 18; as political question, 7–9; in political theory, 7–9, 25; premodern, 10, 224; racial, 4, 24, 25, 27, 197, 201, 288 n. 2; as social question, 7–9. See also abolition; abolitionism; antislavery; emancipation
Smith, Adam, 10
Sofía (Morúa Delgado), 122
Solás, Humberto, 17
Sommer, Doris, 124, 229, 242
Sonthonax, Léger-Félicite, 204, 214, 215, 216, 222, 226, 227
Souulouque, Faustin, 202–3
sovereignty, 201; liberty and, 99; national 98, 100, 220, 224–25, 274, 304–6 n. 82; popular, 104–5, 258, 304–6 n. 82, 345 n. 19. See also liberation; liberty; nation; nationalism

state form, 48; in Haiti, 227
Suárez y Romero, Anselmo, 107, 121; Francisco, 122
Sublime Object of Ideology (Žižek), 142–44
subordination: political, 3; racial, 3, 34, 37, 100, 108, 111, 114, 118, 119, 263; sexual, 16, 37
syncretism: Afro-Caribbean, 14, 17, 213, 226; in Aponte, 46, 53; in Haitian Revolution, 14; in Plácido, 95–96; in revolutionary Atlantic, 213

Tanco y Bosmeniel, Félix, 107, 109, 112, 114–15, 118, 120, 121; "Petrona y Rosalía," 122
taste, 60–71; Africanization of Cuba and, 71; Domingo Del Monte and, 319–20 n. 21; good/bad, 61–65, 73, 75, 313 n. 4; moralization of, 58; perspectival painting and, 63, 66, 313 n. 4; standards of, 91; regression and, 89; violations of, 84–93, 210. See also aesthetics
theater, Haitian, 206–13; Creole language and, 207; Fouchard on, 207, 217; Laroche on, 206, 207; mixture of genres and, 208–10; Moreau de Saint-Méry on, 208; pantomime and, 210–13; Trouillot on, 207. See also cultural production; literature, Haitian
theater, in Saint-Domingue, 207–13, 214–26; L'Héroïne Américaine, 210–13; Héros Africain, 212–13; Héros Américain, 210–13; La Liberté Générale, 214–22, 225. See also theater, Haitian
Toussaint Louverture 3, 6, 14, 15, 25, 131, 138, 148, 170, 171, 180, 192, 201, 204, 211, 212, 216, 239, 247, 255, 269; constitution of, 227, 229–30, 263–67; Davis on, 304 n. 82; Genovese on, 260–61; representations of, 42, 49, 243
transculturation, 12, 213, 296 n. 37; of Egyptocentrism, 53–54
transference, 142, 330 n. 16

SIBYLLE FISCHER

is an associate professor in the Literature
Program at Duke University.